This is Cambridge University Press's second volume of studies based on the work of Heinrich Schenker, now recognized as this century's most influential figure in the areas of music theory and analysis. The first section of the book contains archival studies that derive from the contents of Schenker's *Nachlass*, recently made available to scholars. Schenker's unpublished papers also supplement several of the analytical studies in the second, larger, section of the book. These essays fall into four groups: studies in the Classic and Romantic repertory, studies in twentieth-century music, rhythmic studies, and studies in the theory of Schenker's fundamental analytical constructs, the *Urlinie* and the *Ursatz*.

Carl Schachter is Distinguished Professor Emeritus of Queens College of the City University of New York, and on the faculty of the Mannes College of Music, New York. He is co-author of *Counterpoint in Composition* and *Harmony and Voice Leading*.

Hedi Siegel is Adjunct Associate Professor at Hunter College of the City University of New York. She is editor of the first volume of *Schenker Studies*.

Schenker Studies 2

Schenker Studies 2

edited by
Carl Schachter and Hedi Siegel

CAMBRIDGE UNIVERSITY PRESS
Cambridge, New York, Melbourne, Madrid, Cape Town, Singapore, São Paulo

Cambridge University Press
The Edinburgh Building, Cambridge CB2 2RU, UK

Published in the United States of America by Cambridge University Press, New York

www.cambridge.org
Information on this title: www.cambridge.org/9780521470117

© Cambridge University Press 1999

This publication is in copyright. Subject to statutory exception
and to the provisions of relevant collective licensing agreements,
no reproduction of any part may take place without
the written permission of Cambridge University Press.

First published 1999
This digitally printed first paperback version 2006

A catalogue record for this publication is available from the British Library

ISBN-13 978-0-521-47011-7 hardback
ISBN-10 0-521-47011-0 hardback

ISBN-13 978-0-521-02832-5 paperback
ISBN-10 0-521-02832-9 paperback

CONTENTS

Abbreviated references to Schenker's writings	page ix
Preface	xi

ARCHIVAL STUDIES

Levels of understanding: an introduction to Schenker's *Nachlass* *Robert Kosovsky*	3
When "Freier Satz" was part of *Kontrapunkt*: a preliminary report *Hedi Siegel*	12
Schenker's unpublished work with the music of Johannes Brahms *Allen Cadwallader and William Pastille*	26

ANALYTICAL STUDIES

C. P. E. Bach and the fine art of transposition *Wayne Petty*	49
Comedy and structure in Haydn's symphonies *L. Poundie Burstein*	67
"Symphonic breadth": structural style in Mozart's symphonies *David Gagné*	82
"Structural momentum" and closure in Chopin's Nocturne Op. 9, No. 2 *John Rink*	109
On the first movement of Sibelius's Fourth Symphony: a Schenkerian view *Edward Laufer*	127
Voice leading as drama in *Wozzeck* *Arthur Maisel*	160
Sequential expansion and Handelian phrase rhythm *Channan Willner*	192
Strange dimensions: regularity and irregularity in deep levels of rhythmic reduction *Frank Samarotto*	222
Diachronic transformation in a Schenkerian context: Brahms's Haydn Variations *Timothy Jackson*	239

Bass-line articulations of the *Urlinie* 276
Eric Wen

Structure as foreground: "das Drama des Ursatzes" 298
Carl Schachter

Index 315

ABBREVIATED REFERENCES TO SCHENKER'S WRITINGS

The following works of Heinrich Schenker will often be cited by title alone. Complete bibliographic information is given below, with the abbreviated form appearing in bold type.

Harmonielehre, Volume I of *Neue musikalische Theorien und Phantasien* (Stuttgart: Cotta, 1906); reprint edition (Vienna: Universal Edition, 1978)
Harmony, translated by Elisabeth Mann Borgese, edited and annotated by Oswald Jonas (Chicago: University of Chicago Press, 1954, republished 1980); reprint edition (Cambridge, Mass.: M.I.T. Press, 1973)

Kontrapunkt, Volume II of *Neue musikalische Theorien und Phantasien*, Book 1 (Stuttgart: Cotta, 1910), Book 2 (Vienna: Universal Edition, 1922); reprint edition (Hildesheim: Olms, 1991)
Counterpoint, Books 1 and 2, translated by John Rothgeb and Jürgen Thym, edited by John Rothgeb (New York: Schirmer Books, 1987)

Beethovens neunte Sinfonie (Vienna: Universal Edition, 1912); reprint edition (Vienna: Universal Edition, 1969)
Beethoven's Ninth Symphony, translated and edited by John Rothgeb (New Haven: Yale University Press, 1992)

Erläuterungsausgabe. *Die letzten fünf Sonaten von Beethoven: Kritische Ausgabe mit Einführung und Erläuterung* (Vienna: Universal Edition, 1913–20); new edition, revised by Oswald Jonas (Vienna: Universal Edition, 1971–72)
    Sonate E dur, ***Op. 109***, published 1913; revised edition, 1971
    Sonate As dur, ***Op. 110***, published 1914; revised edition, 1972
    Sonate C moll, ***Op. 111***, published 1915; revised edition, 1971
    Sonate A dur, ***Op. 101***, published 1920; revised edition, 1972
    (Op. 106 was never published.)

Der ***Tonwille***, Issues 1–10 (Vienna: A. J. Gutmann, 1921–24, later republished in three volumes by Universal Edition); reprint edition (Hildesheim: Olms, 1990)

Das ***Meisterwerk*** *in der Musik*, Yearbooks I–III (Munich: Drei Masken Verlag, 1925, 1926, and 1930); reprint edition (Hildesheim: Olms, 1974)

Abbreviated references

***The Masterwork** in Music*, Volumes I–III, translated by Ian Bent, Alfred Clayton, William Drabkin, Richard Kramer, Derrick Puffett, John Rothgeb, and Hedi Siegel, edited by William Drabkin (Cambridge: Cambridge University Press, 1994, 1996, and 1997)

Fünf Urlinie-Tafeln (Vienna: Universal Edition, 1932; New York: David Mannes Music School, 1933)
Five Graphic Music Analyses, republication of *Fünf Urlinie-Tafeln* with a new introduction and glossary by Felix Salzer (New York: Dover, 1969)

Der freie Satz, Volume III of *Neue musikalische Theorien und Phantasien* (Vienna: Universal Edition, 1935); second edition, edited and revised by Oswald Jonas (Vienna: Universal Edition, 1956). Page references are to the second edition unless otherwise noted.
Free Composition (*Der freie Satz*), translated and edited by Ernst Oster (New York: Longman, 1979); reprint edition (New York: Schirmer Books)

PREFACE

Like its predecessor, Cambridge University Press's first volume of Schenker studies published in 1990, this book offers a broad and inclusive survey of the field of Schenkerian research. It gives an accurate, if necessarily partial, view of the field at the present time; a number of the essays could not have been written twenty, or even ten, years ago. Only twenty years have passed since Ernst Oster's translation of *Der freie Satz* appeared. This publication has been the catalyst for the ambitious scholarly enterprise of publishing the entire corpus of Schenker's work in English translation. A significant part of this enterprise has been achieved with the translation of the three volumes of *Das Meisterwerk in der Musik* as well as other important works by Schenker. Perhaps the most striking recent development, however, has not been a publication. Rather it has been the availability to scholars of Schenker's *Nachlass*, at both the Oster Collection of the New York Public Library and the Jonas Collection at the University of California, Riverside. In addition, Mrs. Felix Salzer has generously granted access to items in her husband's private collection. In so doing she has contributed to the realization of Felix Salzer's long-held goal of bringing Schenker's unpublished work to light. Thus an almost entirely new area of research has been opened up: the development of Schenker's theories as revealed by the study of his voluminous papers. The first section in *Schenker Studies 2* consists of three archival studies. Robert Kosovsky suggests guidelines for the scholarly study of the *Nachlass*. Hedi Siegel traces the origins of *Der freie Satz* to unpublished sections of *Kontrapunkt*. The contribution by Allen Cadwallader and William Pastille is devoted to the "Brahms folder" in the Oster Collection. The contents of Schenker's *Nachlass* have also begun to permeate analytical work within the Schenker community as is evidenced by several of the analytical studies in this book.

The larger part of the book is devoted to analytical studies. These eleven essays fall roughly into four groups: studies in the Classic and Romantic repertory, studies in twentieth-century music, rhythmic studies, and studies in the theory of the *Urlinie* and *Ursatz*. The first of these four groups contains music from the repertory that Schenker himself drew upon. For Schenker, C. P. E. Bach was one of the greatest composers, and Bach's *Versuch* had a profound influence on the development of his theories. Later Schenkerians have devoted relatively little attention to the music of this important master. The essay by Wayne Petty explores an unusual facet of Bach's compositional technique and reveals that what seem to be simple and literal transpositions are in fact highly imaginative recompositions. The article by L. Poundie Burstein uses analytical readings of Haydn symphonies as points of departure for the examination of humor in music. David Gagné integrates the analysis of harmony and voice leading with a close reading of texture and orchestration in Mozart's symphonic movements to show how performance medium and genre condition the tonal structure of a work. John Rink turns to a familiar composition, frequently analyzed by Schenker and his followers – Chopin's Nocturne Op. 9, No. 2 – and offers a new and compelling view of its form and structure.

The contributions by Edward Laufer and Arthur Maisel deal with music by Sibelius and Berg that Schenker himself would have violently rejected. The application of Schenker's theories to twentieth-century music has been and remains a controversial enterprise, but one that continues to engage excellent musicians and scholars. Of the two essays, Laufer's modifies Schenker's approach much less than Maisel's, but that is clearly because Sibelius's music is closer to the tonal tradition than Berg's. Laufer takes pains to show antecedents in eighteenth- and nineteenth-century music for Sibelius's highly original way of writing. Maisel draws interesting parallels between the tonal structure of *Wozzeck* and the dramatic structure of the libretto. At the same time he takes a somewhat polemical stance with respect to current posttonal theory.

The next three studies – by Channan Willner, Frank Samarotto, and Timothy Jackson – return to the Schenkerian repertory, with a focus on the topic of rhythm. Willner explores the very elusive and subtle phrase rhythm in the music of the high Baroque. In Samarotto's essay, durational reduction reveals deep rhythmic structures in two Beethoven pieces that are inherently asymmetric – a discovery that can have far-reaching implications for the study of rhythm in general. Jackson's comprehensive study of Brahms's Haydn Variations explicates this complex work from a perspective that takes in conflicts and contradictions between levels. Jackson draws upon study of Brahms's sketches and upon archival work with Schenker's published and unpublished material on the Variations; in doing this, he sets new directions for rhythmic studies as well as studies in the foundations of Schenker's theory.

Schenker's fundamental analytical constructs, the *Urlinie* and the *Ursatz*, form the topics of Eric Wen's and Carl Schachter's contributions. Wen concentrates on an unusual but by no means infrequent manipulation of the *Urlinie* – its transfer into the bass. This possibility has been acknowledged by earlier Schenkerian analysts (and by Schenker himself), but never studied in depth. Schachter studies situations where the *Ursatz* – far from remaining in the "background" – participates strikingly in the salient features of the foreground, including its contradictions and conflicts.

While most of the essays in this volume originated as papers read at the Second International Schenker Symposium held in 1992 at the Mannes College of Music in New York, several were presented at other conferences. Among these are Edward Laufer's essay: though related to the paper he read at the Schenker Symposium, it is derived from a presentation given at the Second International Sibelius Conference held in Helsinki in 1995. A shorter version of Channan Willner's essay was first delivered at the Sixth Biennial Conference on Baroque Music held in 1994 at the University of Edinburgh. Carl Schachter read an earlier version of his essay in London at the 1991 City University Music Analysis Conference. The paper he read at the 1992 Schenker Symposium has been published elsewhere, as have a number of other papers on the conference program (with several remaining unpublished). Thus, unlike the first *Schenker Studies*, this book does not owe its contents to a single conference.

In the studies that discuss Schenker's *Nachlass*, items held by the Oster Collection are reproduced by courtesy of the Music Division of the New York Public Library, Astor, Lenox, and Tilden Foundations. We are very grateful to Mrs. Felix Salzer for her permission to reproduce or transcribe items from the *Nachlass* in her possession. The Pierpont Morgan Library, Mary Flagler Cary Music Collection, kindly gave us permission to reproduce the facsimile included in David Gagné's essay. We thank Universal Edition and the estate of Ernst Oster for their permission to reprint two figures from *Free Composition* in Timothy Jackson's essay.

The illustrative examples in this book do not include extensive excerpts from the musical works discussed; therefore the reader is asked to consult the relevant scores. We extend our thanks to the music typesetters who contributed to the preparation of the examples: to Dejan Badnjar for the complex graphs of Edward Laufer's essay, to Frank Samarotto for the examples in his own essay, and to Timothy McCord and Paul Carter, who carefully laid the groundwork for the examples of several essays. We owe special thanks to Arthur Maisel who drew on his musicality, expertise, and experience in setting the majority of the examples in the book. The preparation of the musical examples was made possible by a generous grant from the Mannes Music Theory Fund.

We wish to thank Jonathan Finkelman, Joshua Gilinsky, Linnéa Johnson, and Suzanne Osborne for their watchful checking of manuscript and proof, and Stephen Slottow for his attentive preparation of the index. Finally, this book would not have become a reality without the support and sympathetic guidance of Penny Souster and the work of her colleagues at Cambridge University Press.

Carl Schachter
Hedi Siegel
New York City

ARCHIVAL STUDIES

Levels of understanding: an introduction to Schenker's *Nachlass*

Robert Kosovsky

One of the more unusual results of the first International Schenker Symposium, held at the Mannes College of Music in 1985, was the creation of a petition signed by over 300 people – attendees and their colleagues. Addressed to the New York Public Library, this petition was a request for making accessible to the public the Oster Collection – a major portion of Heinrich Schenker's papers. This impressive demonstration of academic support helped in the Library's efforts to obtain a preservation grant from the National Endowment for the Humanities. Since 1990 access to the collection has been provided not only for Library visitors, but also – by means of microfilm – for individuals and institutions throughout the world.

Heinrich Schenker's *Nachlass*, made available fifty-five years after the appearance of his last publication, has opened entirely new paths of access to the study of this unique individual and his theories. His archive, with its tens of thousands of documents, is a veritable treasure-trove of information. These papers will no doubt serve to inform, reshape, and redirect our thinking about Schenker and his theories; they may also influence the future course of the discipline, with Schenker source studies becoming a field in its own right. Even the most enthusiastic researcher, however, will encounter numerous problems. Not the least is Schenker's handwriting, which is often barely legible. The *Nachlass*'s peculiar arrangement also portends some difficulties. The plethora of documents – 18,000 in the Oster Collection alone – presents an immediate obstacle: there is quite literally an overabundance of data. In defining such problems and suggesting solutions, this article hopes to serve as a preliminary guide to source studies involving Schenker and his papers.

Essential to an understanding of the *Nachlass* is an awareness of its history. For several months after Schenker's death, on January 14, 1935, his widow Jeanette tried to continue her husband's activities. In a manner poignantly revealing of her devotion to his work, she continued to clip notices and paste them into their scrapbook, and managed to make a few more entries in Schenker's diary. No doubt to alleviate her new financial burden as well as to ease the emotional pain of her bereavement, she moved from their apartment at Keilgasse 8 to Cottagegasse 21, an address further from the center of Vienna. Moving may have a disorienting effect on people and often creates disorder in their belongings; this was true in Jeanette Schenker's case. Schenker's own arrangement of the papers was largely ignored, and the *Nachlass* was packed haphazardly. After moving, Jeanette Schenker was confronted with a disorganized mass of papers. Realizing the necessity of instituting some kind of arrangement, and unable to restore the original order, she renumbered the files and created an inventory. The resulting *Verzeichnis* lists eighty-three files (*Mappen*), whose contents reveal the confused state of the papers. For example, analyses of Chopin are found in two disparate locations, files 10 and 32; material for *Der freie Satz* is even more widely scattered. But the *Verzeichnis* did serve the purpose of identifying the material, even if it was not in an optimal arrangement.

It served another purpose as well. Just as the widow Constanze Mozart sought to keep her husband's work "alive" by publicizing her desire for people to complete his fragmentary works, so did Jeanette Schenker compile her list with the aim of having some of her husband's works published. She was careful to mention locations of analytical graphs, particularly those that were *Reinschriften* – "clean copies" – that would be suitable for publication. On occasion she added editorial comments. To her listing of the contents of file 12 (which contains writings on non-musical topics), she added the note, "Very worthwhile for the magazine!"[1] The reference is to the periodical *Der Dreiklang*, founded shortly after Schenker's death by two of his students, Oswald Jonas and Felix Salzer. In fact, the first issue of this periodical contained an article giving an overview of Schenker's papers,[2] and successive issues published several "worthwhile" fragments.

Like Constanze Mozart, Jeanette Schenker, too, needed to raise funds for her survival. Thus, the division and dispersal of Schenker's papers came about as a means of assisting his widow. Most of his books and scores, including many unusual editions, were sold to the dealer Heinrich Hinterberger. Papers were sold to students, including Wilhelm Furtwängler and Felix Salzer.

As a result of the Nazis' annexation of Austria in 1938, many of the students and other members of Schenker's circle left Vienna. One exception was Oswald Jonas's student Ernst Oster, who had made his way from Germany to Vienna shortly after Schenker's death, and who was unable to leave the city immediately. When it became possible for him to leave, Jeanette Schenker, apparently unwilling to emigrate herself, entrusted to Oster the majority of the remaining working papers while holding on to some of the musical scores, most of the correspondence, and items of a personal nature. After Oster had left the country, and when she finally realized her own danger, she gave the remaining items in her possession to another member of Schenker's circle, Erwin Ratz, for safekeeping. She was deported to the Theresienstadt concentration camp in 1942, where she died only a few months before the camp was liberated. The papers she had given to Ratz survived intact, and in the 1950s he passed them on to his friend Oswald Jonas, who had settled in the United States.

Today the bulk of the *Nachlass* is divided between two collections. The Oster Collection in the Music Division of the New York Public Library holds the items brought by Ernst Oster to New York City from Vienna: the majority of

---

1. "Sehr wertwoll für die Zeitschrift!"
2. "Der Nachlass Heinrich Schenkers," *Der Dreiklang* 1 (April 1937), pp. 17–22. This article is unsigned; it was probably written jointly by Jonas and Salzer, with the possible collaboration of other Schenker students.

Schenker's working papers in the form of numbered files, as well as a significant number of his musical scores. The Oswald Jonas Memorial Collection at the University of California, Riverside, holds the manuscripts for Schenker's published works, a larger portion of his scores, the bulk of the correspondence, and Schenker's diary, along with other personal papers and memorabilia.[3]

Archival materials relating to Schenker are also found in other collections. The papers of notable musicians such as Ferruccio Busoni, Wilhelm Furtwängler, August Halm, Rudolf Réti, and Arnold Schoenberg include correspondence to and from Schenker, as do the archives of the Gesellschaft der Musikfreunde in Vienna. Over 400 letters from Schenker to his publisher, Universal Edition, are owned by the Vienna Stadts- und Landesbibliothek. A few numbered files of working papers (completing the series in the Oster Collection) are in the possession of Mrs. Felix Salzer, who also owns graphs prepared by Salzer and annotated by Schenker. The papers of other Schenker students provide additional archival sources: this is by no means a complete list.

When the contents of the Oster Collection were transferred to the New York Public Library, the papers were found in a more jumbled and confused state than suggested by Jeanette Schenker's orderly list. They were virtually unusable, and a decision had to be made regarding their arrangement. There appeared to be three possible solutions: to attempt a reconstruction of the original ordering used by Heinrich Schenker, to set up an ordering based on Jeanette Schenker's list, or to devise a new arrangement sorting the papers according to type. Since any new arrangement would destroy intellectual evidence, the third solution was felt to be undesirable. Though tempting, the first solution was resisted as well. In certain cases it was clear that several files belonged together and actually constituted a single file, yet it was impossible to deduce how Schenker had ordered every existing file. Following the organization of Jeanette Schenker's list seemed the most logical choice, as that list clearly preserves a particular historical state of the *Nachlass*, and is the most detailed documentation concerning the collection.

Leaving aside the arrangement of the collection itself, it is useful to survey the contents by type. Most of the papers fall into one of five categories: clippings, published items, correspondence, writings, and analyses.

1. *Clippings*. There are several hundred clippings in the Oster Collection, dealing with both musical and non-musical topics. Articles on such subjects as literature (including poetry), literary criticism, painting, architecture, politics, government, religion, and philosophy reflect the wide range of Schenker's interests. An examination of such ephemera often allows us to view his ideas in a broader context; his annotations and glosses on what he read provide corroborative justification for many of these ideas. A case in point is his preoccupation with Albert Einstein: Schenker clipped articles by and about the famous physicist. In annotating these clippings, Schenker refined the thoughts

---

3. See Robert Lang and JoAn Kunselman, *Heinrich Schenker, Oswald Jonas, Moriz Violin: A Checklist of Manuscripts and Other Papers in the Oswald Jonas Memorial Collection* (Berkeley: University of California Press, 1994).

on the notion of "genius" that he was later to set down in *Free Composition*.[4]

A large group of clippings are collected in a scrapbook. Started by Schenker in 1902, this scrapbook later became one of Jeanette Schenker's pet projects. It sheds light on Schenker's little-known early activities: several notices that predate his theoretical publications refer to him as being well known in Viennese circles as a pianist specializing in the music of Bach. Schenker always clipped reviews of his published works, and in addition often saved articles which, though not containing any direct mention of him, revealed his growing influence upon the musical world. An amusing example is a review of the 1927 première of the opera *Jonny spielt auf*, in which a naïve critic misuses Schenker's new vocabulary and complains that Ernst Krenek's music lacks an *Urlinie*.[5]

2. Published items. Throughout his adult life, Schenker acquired a large library of publications – both musical and non-musical. Most are listed in the 1936 catalogue of the antiquarian Heinrich Hinterberger, to whom they were sold.[6] Of the many published books Schenker once owned, the Oster collection contains just a handful. One of the most interesting is an annotated copy of Gustav Jenner's book on Johannes Brahms.[7] One can trace the transformation of Schenker's glosses into the detailed notes that prepared the way for his article "Erinnerungen an Brahms."[8] Also important – especially for the preparation of new editions or translations – are the copies of Schenker's own publications that contain his corrections or emendations.

Fortunately, Schenker's collection of musical scores has survived, and is divided between the Oster and Jonas Collections. Recent articles have discussed the value of studying Schenker's annotated scores from the point of view of the performer.[9] In some cases, Schenker's markings bear directly on his analyses: one finds a correlation between Schenker's notes and analytical graphs and the markings in the scores.[10] A study of these scores is thus an essential component of further research on Schenker's analytic work.

---

4. See *Free Composition*, p. xxiv. Schenker's anti-democratic political views and pan-German nationalism have attracted a growing amount of scholarly attention in recent years. How important these views are for an understanding of his musical ideas remains a controversial topic. While study of the *Nachlass* will certainly not settle this controversy, it will at least provide a useful basis for discussion and argument.
5. Hans Liebstöckl, "Krenek spielt auf," *Die Stunde* (Jan. 1928), Oster Collection, file 2, p. 74. (Unless otherwise specified, all subsequent references to files from the *Nachlass* are to those in the Oster Collection.)
6. A copy of the catalogue is in the Oswald Jonas Memorial Collection, box 35, folder 2; see Lang and Kunselman, p. 96. A facsimile is printed as Anhang II of Martin Eybl, *Ideologie und Methode: Zum ideengeschichtlichen Kontext von Schenkers Musiktheorie* (Tutzing: Hans Schneider, 1995), pp. 161–92.
7. Gustav Jenner, *Johannes Brahms als Mensch, Lehrer und Künstler*. Schenker owned the second edition (Marburg an der Lahn: N.G. Elwert'sche Verlagsbuchhandlung G. Braun, 1930). It is preserved in file 30, together with Schenker's notes (items 42–51).
8. The article was published in the *Deutsche Zeitschrift* (a continuation of *Der Kunstwart*) 46/8 (May 1933), pp. 475–82.
9. One example, drawing on items in the Jonas Collection, is William Rothstein's "Heinrich Schenker as an Interpreter of Beethoven's Piano Sonatas," *19th-Century Music* 8/1 (1984), pp. 3–28.
10. Examples may be found in the scores of works by Chopin and Brahms, among many others.

3. *Correspondence.* The majority of Schenker's correspondence is located in the Oswald Jonas Memorial Collection. The letter files in the Oster Collection are mostly confined to specific topics. Several files include correspondence with his students and with other theorists, such as August Halm and Rudolf Réti. There is a file containing an exchange of letters between Schenker, Wilhelm Furtwängler, and Ludwig Karpath (a leading Viennese music critic) concerning an unsuccessful attempt to secure a teaching appointment for Schenker. Another contains the final correspondence received by Schenker before his death.

One of the most voluminous correspondence files in the Oster Collection (file 52) concerns Schenker's publisher, Universal Edition. Containing over 900 items, this file not only documents the history of Schenker's publications, but also traces the rise of one of the most important and influential music publishers of the twentieth century. The earliest letters in this file date from 1901, and are addressed to the men who founded that adventurous publishing firm. As a witness to the founding of Universal Edition, Schenker developed a close personal relationship with Emil Hertzka, the firm's director during its first two decades. At first Hertzka took a great interest in Schenker's work. When Schenker submitted the first issue of a publication he called "Kleine Bibliothek" ("Little Library"), there was some question about whether the title was appropriate. The correspondence shows that it was Hertzka who suggested that the title be changed to *Der Tonwille* (literally, "The Tone-Will").[11] In the course of time, however, Schenker fell out of favor with Hertzka, who promoted contemporary music as the centerpiece of his publishing house. Partly because of his concern for the negative attitude toward contemporary music that Schenker projected, Hertzka had *Der Tonwille* published under the imprint of an imaginary publisher, the "Tonwille-Flugblätterverlag," thereby disassociating Schenker from the imprint of Universal Edition – an association that Hertzka increasingly came to see as detrimental. By 1924, Schenker felt that Hertzka was not doing enough to promote his publications and, while looking for another publisher, brought legal action against Universal Edition to release him from his contract. Letters concerning this legal action show that it took up the greater part of an entire year. After Hertzka's death in 1932, Schenker was able to resume cordial relations with Universal Edition and with Hertzka's successor, Alfred Kalmus.

4. *Writings.* There are many writings on musical and non-musical topics in the Oster Collection. These range in size from a tiny scrap of paper, containing just one word, to substantial manuscripts. There are in fact several lengthy unpublished texts. One of these, entitled "Das Tonsystem," is identified by Jeanette Schenker as one of Schenker's earliest theoretical formulations.[12] Comprising

---

11. Although the title may have been Hertzka's, the idea behind it – that musical tones embody will – is Schenker's. In the preface to *Harmony*, for instance, he writes: "I should like to stress in particular the biological factor in the life of tones. We should get used to the idea that tones have lives of their own, more independent of the artist's pen in their vitality than one would dare to believe." See *Harmony*, p. xxv; *Harmonielehre*, p. vi.

12. Located in file 31, items 360–86.

eighty-nine typewritten pages and left unfinished, it probably dates from Schenker's years as a music critic before the turn of the century. Another unfinished work, "Niedergang der Kompositionskunst,"[13] dates from the time of World War I. In it, Schenker discusses the problems of modern music and its failure to synthesize musical resources. Also among Schenker's unpublished works is "Eine Lehre vom Vortrag," which includes an alphabetically arranged dictionary of topics relating to performance. The original manuscript notes for this work are in the Jonas Collection. The copy in the Oster Collection was made by Ernst Oster; it is supplemented by his own annotations and additional examples.[14]

The most extensive and perhaps the most important of the unpublished works is an early version, dating from between approximately 1915 and 1920, of Schenker's magnum opus, *Der freie Satz*. Like many of Schenker's unpublished writings, it consists of lengthy portions of text on long strips of paper (written down from dictation by Jeanette Schenker) interleaved with little scraps of paper containing Schenker's notes and emendations. Together with its musical examples, this document contains over 5,000 items. In Jeanette Schenker's arrangement, these items are divided among four separate files. This unfortunate dismemberment presents a challenge. How could accessibility be improved without disturbing the arrangement? I found a solution to this problem by making a detailed reconstruction of the table of contents, listing all paragraph headings, and identifying their location within the collection.[15]

5. *Analyses*. There are several files of analyses, which are organized by composer. The majority of these analyses are not of complete pieces, but of individual movements, particular sections, or even small passages. A substantial number of them appear to be related to Schenker's continuing work, over a period of more than twenty years, on *Der freie Satz*. Indeed, some of them exist in several versions. For example, there are numerous representations of the diminutions in Chopin's Nocturne in F♯ major, Op. 15, No. 2, the earliest dating from about 1909. Other analyses appear to have come about as the result of Schenker's teaching activities. Sometimes two nearly identical graphs are found side by side – one in Schenker's hand and one by a student – indicating that the copying of his graph by a student was part of his pedagogical method. The pedagogical purpose of many analytical graphs helps explain the limited scope of the analyses found in the Oster Collection. The overwhelming majority are from the literature of solo piano music, mainly of works by Bach, Beethoven, Brahms, and Chopin. There are, however, a few extensive analyses of works for orchestra, and it is intriguing to discover that Schenker left us analyses of music by composers such as Bruckner, Richard Strauss, Wagner, Wolf, and others not usually associated with his analytical repertory.

13. Located in file 31, items 28–153.
14. Schenker's writings on performance, edited by Heribert Esser and translated by Irene Schreier, will be published by Oxford University Press in the near future.
15. Robert Kosovsky, *The Oster Collection: Papers of Heinrich Schenker. A Finding List* (New York: New York Public Library, 1990), Appendix A.

How is a scholar to approach this collection? "Did Schenker make a graph of a particular work?" is the question most often asked, whether by performers, musicologists, music theorists, professors, students, or amateurs. All are usually seeking information about a specific work or group of works, and they view Schenker's archive as a means of acquiring this information. Although their question is certainly legitimate, it can lead to a limited and even distorted perspective on how Schenker's papers might best be used. Archival collections like this one are not really analogous to a large reference tool that one might consult in order to find instant answers to questions. Taking from the *Nachlass* only what is immediately needed – and ignoring the circumstances of its creation – makes it impossible for the researcher to gain a comprehensive understanding of either the musical work in question or the development of Schenker's ideas.

It must be remembered that the Oster Collection is an archive that contains documents in various stages of completion. To be sure, there are a good many graphs that Schenker might have published had he lived longer, but there are also graphs that he probably wished to leave unpublished. Like many others, he would try out ideas on paper as a kind of experiment, without necessarily committing himself to them. While the inexperienced researcher may be seeking specific bits of information (analogous to a "foreground" view), archivists are interested in entire collections of documents. Gathering information on the physical and intellectual contents of documents and on the context in which those documents were created is seen as integral to understanding. Once the large organizational picture (the "background" view) is obtained, the significance of each individual document will become clear. Thus, in order to do justice to the *Nachlass*, it is necessary first to determine how Schenker generated and used his papers.

One of the most striking impressions conveyed by the *Nachlass* is of Schenker's seemingly compulsive drive to commit a thought or idea to paper. At times he appears to have had an almost maniacal desire to use what was at hand, grabbing whatever he could, whenever the moment.[16] For instance, after an analysis had been published, he would often cut up the manuscripts and drafts (which he had little interest in retaining) and use the blank sides for making new notes. A beautiful, multicolored graph of the Preludio from Bach's E Major Partita for solo violin was reused, cut up, and placed in several different locations.

Once committed to paper, these voluminous notes were placed into files. What were Schenker's organizing principles? While many files deal with current or ongoing projects such as lessons with students, others have a more complex origin. Schenker's procedure seems to have been an almost unbelievably thoroughgoing application of the basic mental process first identified by the

16. There are notes written on nearly every imaginable type of paper: unused sides of letters he received, drafts of his own letters, proof sheets for his publications, unpublished compositions, unwanted graphs, bills from restaurants in Vienna or from hotels in the Austrian Alps, gas and electric bills, insurance bills, legal documents, solicitations from charitable organizations, blank portions of newspapers and magazines, appointment calendars, maps, streetcar tickets, lottery tickets, electioneering handbills – even the wrapping paper from his bathroom tissue.

philosopher John Locke as the association of ideas. Schenker gradually built up a structure of thought by developing and cultivating associations between a large number of ideas, some obviously related, and others seemingly unrelated.[17] For Schenker a single idea can give rise to innumerable associations.[18]

In some cases the archive reveals how Schenker brought together ideas scattered on several snippets of paper.[19] After his wife had copied these fragments into a longer text, he cut up and distributed the new pieces among other files, thereby creating new associations. It is not an exaggeration to say that virtually every item in the collection can be found to have some kind of association with several other disparate ones. Thus even the smallest detail could have multiple meanings for Schenker and would lead him to discover new connections and insights. Wilhelm Furtwängler describes Schenker's thought process and breadth of knowledge, characterizing him as "a person, who not only took an active interest in everything possible, but . . . [was] one who knew personal, productive answers to a thousand questions which on the surface had nothing to do with music theory. For the questions which Schenker addressed . . . were of universal relevance."[20]

In order for this kind of associative thinking to be effective, it must be continuously at work. Persistent examination, revision, and reshaping are necessary if the ideas are to be fully integrated.[21] Schenker's working system for controlling this process is manifested by two words frequently scribbled on many of the fragments: "Paralipomena" and "Wolle." Schenker had his own private meaning for the term "Wolle," which is not usually applied to the classification of ideas: he may possibly have used it in the sense of "raw material," denoting ideas in rough form.[22] He used "Paralipomena" as a kind of catch-all heading for supplementary material or ideas not fully put to use.[23] I am suggesting that many of Schenker's "Paralipomena" were items he wished to keep in "active" files so that he could continue to make additions or revisions and eventually integrate them in new ways. The items he regarded as rough ideas, probably unsuitable for development, he would place in the "Wolle"

---

17. Among modern philosophers these ideas are most prominently articulated by Michel Foucault, particularly in *The Archaeology of Knowledge and The Discourse on Language*, trans. A. M. Sheridan Smith (New York: Pantheon Books, 1972).
18. A similar thought process may be observed in *Free Composition*, where Schenker not only makes frequent references to his earlier works, but also supplies numerous cross-references to ensure comprehension.
19. Examples may be found in files 12 and 83.
20. Wilhelm Furtwängler, "Heinrich Schenker: A Contemporary Problem," trans. Jan Emerson, *Sonus* 6/1 (Fall 1985), p. 2. This is a translation of "Heinrich Schenker: Ein zeitgemässes Problem," in *Ton und Wort* (Wiesbaden: Brockhaus, 1954), pp. 198–204.
21. This is evident in the various files dealing with the early version of *Free Composition*. Schenker made copious revisions in the text – there are at least six versions of the heading for the opening paragraph in which Schenker defines the relationship between harmony and voice leading.
22. The phrase "in der Wolle gefärbt" comes to mind ("dyed in the wool," i.e., while in a raw state).
23. This usage is not unique to Schenker. Schopenhauer's collected writings, which Schenker knew well, include a volume entitled *Parerga und Paralipomena: kleine philosophische Schriften*. Schopenhauer describes this volume as a gathering of essays and ideas on a variety of subjects that either did not directly belong within the systematic plan of his works or were conceived too late to be included. See the preface (dated 1850) to Vol. 7/1 of Arthur Schopenhauer, *Werke* (Zurich: Diogenes, 1977).

files.[24] Most of Schenker's unpublished writings and graphs reflect this ongoing process; they are "Paralipomena" slated for further revision and new associations. In essence, this is the major challenge posed by Schenker's papers. One cannot isolate a graph or text and disregard its physical, chronological, and intellectual context. Each document should be regarded as a detail in a complex web of interrelated documents. Researchers who expect to work on only a portion of Schenker's papers must necessarily become familiar with most, if not all, of the related papers in an attempt to recreate Schenker's path of thought.

As part of my work at the New York Public Library I compiled a finding list of the Oster Collection. Funds were insufficient for a complete itemization, so my list does not always go into the detail that many scholars would find useful. But would a detailed finding list be enough? I believe it should be supplemented by other research tools. Better intellectual access could be provided by creating reference sources from the most significant works. An index to Schenker's 4,000-page diary would have a high priority. In addition, an index to Schenker's lesson books, which record in detail the lessons he gave to students over a period of twenty years, would provide information concerning the chronology and context of Schenker's studies of musical works.[25] An annotated index to Schenker's correspondence would provide more than just biographical information; there are many letters in which Schenker set down philosophical and musical insights not found in other sources. As stated over fifty years ago, "a collection of these letters would yield a compendium of theories on performance and composition."[26]

With the availability of the Oster Collection, and the accessibility of other archival sources, we are about to see a significant increase of new information and research concerning Heinrich Schenker. In recent times, journals in the field of music theory have published articles about Schenker or his theories in virtually every issue, and a good number of these articles include observations based on work with the Oster Collection. Schenker's *Nachlass* is indeed on its way to becoming a fundamental research tool. It is hoped that by learning more about the nature of the collection, students and scholars will reach a new level in their understanding of Heinrich Schenker's lifework.

24. Some files may have been discarded altogether. On the cover of file 76, one of the files containing "Wolle," there is an instruction to burn its contents after it has been checked. Though that file has survived, there are probably many others which did not.
25. I am currently in the process of preparing such an index.
26. "Der Nachlass Heinrich Schenkers," *Der Dreiklang* 1 (April 1937), p. 18.

When "Freier Satz" was part of *Kontrapunkt*: a preliminary report

Hedi Siegel

In January of 1920, Schenker wrote a letter to his friend August Halm. The letter includes the following passage:

> Most important for me is II² [the second book of *Kontrapunkt*]¹, in which the voice leading of free composition and its *complete identity* with that of so-called strict counterpoint is uncovered and demonstrated. "Semper idem, sed non eodem modo" penetrates into every section: the torchlight from this same motto emanates from strict counterpoint in three voices, shines upon counterpoint in four and more voices, upon combinations of the species, and then upon free composition. Here it continues to illuminate the sections on scale degrees, composing-out, voice leading, parallel fifths and octaves, the passing tone, the suspension, keyboard style and abbreviations, thorough bass, the chorale, etc., etc. Only for the sake of this demonstration have I withheld an entire volume of material that was ready for publication years ago; for no sort of argumentation could produce the result that I expect from the purely external effect of bringing strict and free composition together in the compass of a single volume.[2]

Obviously, Schenker was not referring to the relatively slim second book of *Kontrapunkt* as we know it. The book he had in mind may be reconstructed – in broad outline – as shown in Figure 1.[3]

We see what Schenker meant when he traced the contents of this projected volume for Halm. He proceeds from strict counterpoint in three voices (Part 3) through counterpoint in four and more voices (Parts 4 and 5). Combinations of the species in several voices begin Part 6, "Bridges to Free Composition," which is logically followed by Part 7, "Free Composition." Part 8 then discusses the voice leading of thorough bass. Much of the unpublished material that continues from Part 6 is preserved in the Oster Collection of the New York Public Library. The text of most of Part 7, "Freier Satz," and of the epilogue that was

---

1. Schenker's abbreviated references to his works will be familiar to most readers: Roman numerals are used for the volumes of the *Neue musikalische Theorien und Phantasien*, with superscript Arabic numbers designating the separate books of Vol. II (*Kontrapunkt*).
2. From Schenker's letter to August Halm, January 18, 1920; see Hellmut Federhofer, *Heinrich Schenker: Nach Tagebüchern und Briefen in der Oswald Jonas Memorial Collection* (Hildesheim: Olms, 1985), pp. 141–42. The translation (altered slightly) is by William Pastille; see his review of Federhofer's book, *Journal of the American Musicological Society* 39/3 (1986), p. 672. The letter and circumstances surrounding it are noted in Matthew Brown and Robert Wason's review of *Counterpoint*; see *Music Theory Spectrum* 11/2, (1989), p. 236. See also Nicolas Meeùs, *Heinrich Schenker: une introduction* (Liège: Mardaga, 1993), pp. 33ff.
3. Schenker's early plan for the second book of *Kontrapunkt* is mentioned in the prefaces to *Free Composition* written by Oswald Jonas (p. xvi) and Ernst Oster (p. xii). See also the highly informative typed pages prepared by Oster found at the beginning of file 79 in the Oster Collection of the New York Public Library. (All subsequent references to files are to those in the Oster Collection.)

Figure 1 The eight parts of *Kontrapunkt* (according to Schenker's early plan)

KONTRAPUNKT, erster Halbband (*COUNTERPOINT*, Book 1)

Vorrede (Preface)
Einleitung (Introduction)

    1. ABSCHNITT: Cantus firmus als Grundlage der Kontrapunktstudien
    (PART 1:   The Cantus Firmus as the Foundation of
                            Contrapuntal Studies)

    2. ABSCHNITT: Zweistimmiger Satz
    (PART 2:   Two-Voice Counterpoint)

KONTRAPUNKT, zweiter Halbband (*COUNTERPOINT*, Book 2)

Vorwort (Preface)

    3. ABSCHNITT: Dreistimmiger Satz
    (PART 3:   Three-Voice Counterpoint)

    4. ABSCHNITT: Vierstimmiger Satz
    (PART 4:   Four-Voice Counterpoint)

    5. ABSCHNITT: Vom fünf-, sechs-, sieben- und achtstimmigen Satz
    (PART 5:   Five-, Six-, Seven-, and Eight-Voice Counterpoint)

Einleitendes (Introductory Remarks)

    6. ABSCHNITT: Übergänge zum freien Satz
    (PART 6:   Bridges to Free Composition)

Einleitendes (Introductory Remarks)

    7. ABSCHNITT: Freier Satz
    (PART 7:   Free Composition)

    8. ABSCHNITT: Von der Stimmführung des Generalbasses
    (PART 8:   The Voice Leading of Thorough Bass)

Von der musikalischen Kausalität – Rückblick und Epilog
(Musical Causality – Summing-Up and Epilogue)

to serve as the conclusion to the entire *Kontrapunkt* is found on long strips of paper written in manuscript by Jeanette Schenker from her husband's dictation.[4] Also preserved in the Oster Collection is Part 8, "Von der Stimmführung des Generalbasses," in the form of a typescript prepared by Ernst Oster;[5] the manuscript of the thorough bass section is among the items from Schenker's *Nachlass* that came into the possession of Felix Salzer, as is a second, slightly different typescript.[6]

What of Schenker's assertion to Halm that the material for the volume had been "ready for publication years ago"? In fact, a manuscript draft of the entire second book of *Kontrapunkt* had been completed three years before Schenker wrote the letter. The "Freier Satz" section was finished by the summer of 1917; in June of that year Schenker wrote to his friend Moriz Violin, telling him that he was finally coming close to the end of his work on *Kontrapunkt*.[7] In July, he wrote to Otto Vrieslander, saying that he was now "facing the *Generalbassabschnitt*."[8] He completed it by the end of the following month; the date on which Schenker finished dictating the manuscript appears on the last page: "29.VIII.17." Two days later, on August 31, which was his wife's birthday,[9] the epilogue was completed; the final page is dated "Lie-Liechens Geburtstag 1917" (see Plate 1).[10]

It is clear from Schenker's letter to Halm that in 1920 he was still revising the manuscript that had been completed in 1917. (In March of 1918, he had written to Emil Hertzka of Universal Edition, telling him he was devoting his entire energies to Book 2 of *Kontrapunkt*.)[11] Material in the Oster Collection shows that he started to make major revisions of the "Freier Satz" section, mainly of the two opening chapters, which presented important material on the scale degree and on composing-out. He cut the manuscript of these chapters into pieces, which he either discarded or collated with new material. In some cases the headings of the individual small sections are all that remain. These revisions fostered the emergence of the ideas of *Urlinie* and *Ursatz*, and Schenker began to rethink and rewrite his entire presentation of free composition. He essentially abandoned the completed Parts 7 and 8 and decided to publish a truncated version of Book 2, ending with Part 6. It appeared in 1922, and Universal Edition announced that there would be a third book of *Kontrapunkt*, titled *Der freie Satz*.[12] The reference "II³" had already appeared in Schenker's published

---

4. Files 51, 74, and 79.
5. File 6.
6. Salzer acquired several folders of the *Nachlass* from Schenker's widow in 1936.
7. See Federhofer, *Heinrich Schenker*, p. 29; the letter is dated June 13, 1917.
8. See Federhofer, *Heinrich Schenker*, p. 25, n. 44; the letter, written in Seefeld (in Tirol, where Schenker was spending the summer), is dated July 3, 1917.
9. Federhofer, *Heinrich Schenker*, p. viii, gives Jeanette Schenker's date of birth as August 31, 1874. Federhofer also transcribes a diary entry concerning the celebration of her birthday (p. 37, n. 57); the date given – August 30, 1932 – is the eve of her birthday.
10. I am grateful to Mrs. Felix Salzer for her permission to reproduce the ending of Part 8 shown in Plate 1, and for granting me continuing access to the materials from Schenker's *Nachlass* in her possession.
11. See Federhofer, *Heinrich Schenker*, p. 29.
12. A possible reason for the subtle change in title from "Freier Satz" to "Der freie Satz" is discussed in William Drabkin's reviews of two translations: of *Counterpoint* in *Music Analysis* 8/1–2 (1989), pp. 198–200, and of Felix-Eberhard von Cube, *The Book of the Musical Artwork: An Interpretation of the Theories of Heinrich Schenker*, in *Indiana Theory Review* 9/2 (1988), pp. 142–43.

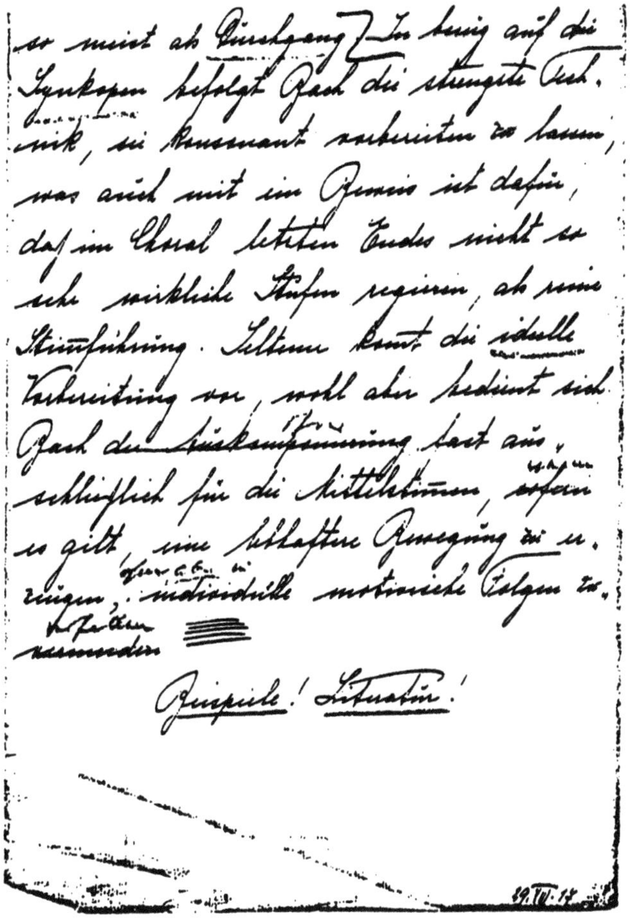

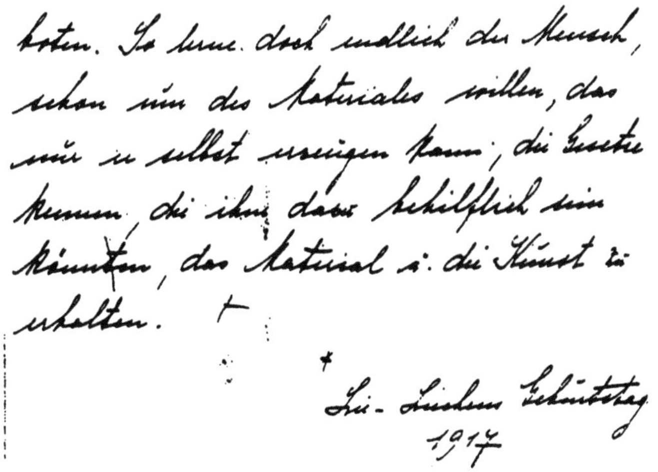

Plate 1 Closing text of Part 8, "Generalbass," completed on August 29, 1917 (from the collection of Felix Salzer), and of the epilogue, completed on August 31, 1917 (from file 51/item 1391, Oster Collection)

writings by 1920.[13] Around 1925 Schenker began thinking of *Der freie Satz* as a separate *volume* of the *Neue musikalische Theorien und Phantasien*. When published as Volume III in 1935 – containing only vestiges of what had been completed in 1917 – it was no longer part of *Kontrapunkt*.[14]

But if we go back to the time when the sections on free composition and thorough bass *were* part of *Kontrapunkt*, we may visualize their general contents as shown in Figure 2.[15]

Turning first to Part 7, the "Freier Satz" section, we see that the items Schenker had listed under free composition in his letter to Halm, "scale degrees, composing-out, voice leading, parallel fifths and octaves, the passing tone, the suspension," are in fact subsections or chapters. The organization familiar from the published *Der freie Satz* – under the headings of background, middleground, and foreground – is nowhere in evidence. Instead, in the first main section of Part 7,[16] free composition is discussed in relation to *Stufe* (scale degree) and *Stimmführung* (voice leading), the fundamental laws Schenker referred to as *Urgesetze*.[17]

These two fundamental laws are the focus of his introductory remarks to the "Freier Satz" section. One of several versions of the opening sentence reads as follows:

Two independent spheres begin to bear a relationship to each other for the first time in free composition: the scale degree and voice leading. Both, secure in their own laws, continue to retain these laws in interaction. Whatever form their intermingling takes, neither of the two need sacrifice anything essential to the other.[18]

---

13. See, for example, the well-known passage on the *Urlinie* in Schenker's *Erläuterungsausgabe, Op. 101*, p. 22 (rev. edn, p. 7). There are of course many references to II^3 in *Kontrapunkt* 2. (In *Counterpoint* 2 a citation to the relevant place in the published *Free Composition* has been substituted where possible; see Rothgeb's note 4 to Part 3, Chapter 1 on p. 274). Sometimes Schenker specifically names the seventh "Abschnitt"; e.g., in *Kontrapunkt* 2, pp. 177, 185, and 248 (the last of these references is retained in *Counterpoint* 2, p. 257). He even refers to specific subsections and chapters; e.g., in *Kontrapunkt* 2, pp. 4, 24, 36, 44, 59, 65, 75, 101, and 209.
14. Schenker had originally planned to reserve Vol. III of his series for a study of form; see Federhofer, *Heinrich Schenker*, p. 26. Some of his notes for this study are preserved in file 83.
15. Figure 2 is based on Schenker's detailed table of contents of Parts 7 and 8 found in file 51. Charles Burkhart, in his Society for Music Theory keynote address "Reflections on Schenker: From 'Free Composition' to *Free Composition*," given in New York in 1995, presented a valuable discussion of several aspects of Part 7.
16. The second "Hauptstück" – on abbreviation and keyboard writing – is not as extensive as the first, and its contents were perhaps not as central to Schenker's theory of free composition.
17. It is important to Schenker's ideology that the fundamental laws be very few in number. He writes in the unpublished epilogue to *Kontrapunkt* 2 (the following translation is mine, as are all subsequent translations unless otherwise indicated): "Music knows but few laws – ancestral mothers – from which everything derives." ("Die Musik kennt nur wenig Gesetze – Urmütter – aus denen alles kommt.") Oster Collection, item 51/1386 (the first number identifies the file, the second the individual item; subsequent references to manuscript sources, all from the Oster Collection, will use this abbreviated format).
18. "Zwei eigene Welten treten im freien Satz zum erstenmal zu einander in Beziehung: Stufe und Stimmführung. Beide in eigenen Gesetzen ruhend behalten diese Gesetze auch im Zusammenwirken. Welche Formen immer das Durchdringen beider annehmen mag, braucht die eine der andern keine Opfer am Wesen zu bringen" (item 79/101). A revision places voice leading at the head of the first sentence, reflecting the course of events in the volume: "Zur Stimmführung tritt nun im freien Satze zum erstenmal die Stufe in Beziehung" (item 51/145).

Schenker goes on to reveal that the explication of the two *Urgesetze* lay behind the overall plan for his *Neue musikalische Theorien und Phantasien*:

Now it is clear (cf. the preface to II¹ [*Kontrapunkt* 1]) why I had to begin by familiarizing the student with the fundamental laws of scale degree and voice leading (in Volume I [*Harmonielehre*] and in Volume II [*Kontrapunkt*], Parts 1–6) before I could finally undertake a systematic presentation of the prolongations that arise when the two spheres act together.[19]

And the promise he made in his letter to Halm, that he would demonstrate the "complete identity" of the voice leading of strict counterpoint and free composition, reflects the statement he makes as his introductory remarks continue:

... in my exposition of free composition (and of thorough bass), I adhere to the same fundamental concepts and even to the same order in which they appeared when we first became conscious of them in strict counterpoint.[20]

In the "Freier Satz" section this applies to the organization of the "Stimmführung" subsection (refer again to Figure 2): the chapters relate to the first four species of strict counterpoint. After an introductory Chapter 1 that links the outer voices of a free composition to two-voice counterpoint, Chapter 2 is derived from the treatment of consecutive perfect intervals in first species counterpoint. Chapter 3 takes the passing tone of second (or third) species as its point of departure, and includes a discussion of the accented passing tone and neighboring tone. The elements of second and third species carry over into Chapter 4, where Schenker discusses the seventh and seventh chords; both derive from passing motion. Chapter 5, on suspensions, syncopes, and rhythmic shifts, is of course based on fourth species counterpoint. The "same fundamental concepts" to which Schenker adheres are the concepts of strict counterpoint on which each chapter is founded. Schenker is in fact carrying out what he described in the last paragraph of his "Bridges to Free Composition" section: "... the doctrine developed in my work takes as its first point of departure the fundamental concepts of voice leading, and, ... after enumerating those fundamental concepts, I then proceed to teach how they are preserved even in free composition, always and everywhere...."[21] The *Urbegriffe* of voice

19. "Nun begreift man wohl auch (vgl. Vorrede zu II¹), weshalb ich den Kunstjünger zuvor mit den Urgesetzen der Stufe und Stimmführung bekannt machen musste (in Band I und Band II, 1.–6. Abschnitte) ehe ihm endlich die aus der Mischung beider Sphären gewonnenen Prolongationen des freien Satzes in systematischer Weise vorgeführt werden konnten" (items 51/145–46). The opening passages of the introductory remarks to Part 7 recall Schenker's preface to *Kontrapunkt* 1, to which he refers. See especially pp. xxiii ff. (*Counterpoint* 1, pp. xxv ff.), where he begins his presentation of the subject matter of the volume as follows: "All musical technique is derived from two basic ingredients: voice leading and the progression of scale degrees."
20. "... wie ich denn auch in der Darstellung des freien Satzes (sowie des Generalbasses) noch immer nur an denselben Urbegriffen, ja sogar auch an derselben Ordnung festhalte, in der sie im strengen Satze zum erstenmal an unser Bewusstsein traten" (items 51/146–47).
21. "... die in meinem Werke durchgeführte Lehre geht zunächst von den Urbegriffen der Stimmführung aus, und ... ich, erst aber nach Aufzeichnung der Urbegriffe, endlich dahin schreite zu lehren, wie dieselben Urbegriffen sich auch im freien Satze bewähren, immer und überall bewähren...." *Kontrapunkt* 2, p. 261 (*Counterpoint* 2, p. 271). See also §156 on p. 95 of the published *Der freie Satz* (*Free Composition*, p. 55), the beginning of the section entitled "Begriffe des Strengen Satzes" (The Concepts of Strict Counterpoint).

Figure 2 A comparison of Parts 7 and 8 of Kontrapunkt (according to Schenker's early plan)

Einleitendes
(Introductory Remarks)

7. ABSCHNITT: FREIER SATZ	8. ABSCHNITT: VON DER STIMMFÜHRUNG DES GENERALBASSES
(PART 7: FREE COMPOSITION)	(PART 8: THE VOICE LEADING OF THOROUGH BASS)
1. HAUPTSTÜCK: Von den inneren Gesetzen des freien Satzes: Von der Stufe und Stimmführung	
(SECTION 1: On the Intrinsic Laws of Free Composition: On the Scale Degree and Voice Leading)	
A: Von der Stufe und ihrer Auskomponierung	1. Kapitel: Allgemeines
(A: On the Scale Degree and its Composing-out)	(Chapter 1: General Aspects)
1. Kapitel: Von der Stufe	2. Kapitel: Von der Stufe
(Chapter 1: On the Scale Degree)	(Chapter 2: On the Scale Degree)
2. Kapitel: Von der Auskomponierung	
(Chapter 2: On Composing-out)	
B: Von der Stimmführung	3. Kapitel: Von der Stimmführung
(B: On Voice Leading)	(Chapter 3: On Voice Leading)
1. Kapitel: Von der Stimmführung der Aussenstimmen im Besonderen	
(Chapter 1: Specific Observations on the Voice Leading of the Outer Voices)	
2. Kapitel: Von Oktav- Prim- und Quintfolgen	4. Kapitel: Von den offenen Oktav- und Quintfolgen
(Chapter 2: On Successions of Octaves, Unisons, and Fifths)	(Chapter 4: On Successions of Open Octaves and Fifths)
3. Kapitel: Vom Durchgang, bezw. Wechselnote und Nebennote	5. Kapitel: Vom Durchgang usw.
(Chapter 3: On the Passing Tone, the Accented Passing Tone, and the Neighboring Tone, respectively)	(Chapter 5: On the Passing Tone, etc.)
4. Kapitel: Im Speziellen von der Sept als Durchgang und der Vierklangsbildung	6. Kapitel: Von der Sept
(Chapter 4: Specific Observations on the Seventh as a Passing Tone and the Formation of the Seventh Chord)	(Chapter 6: On the Seventh)
5. Kapitel: Von den Vorhalten, Synkopen und Rückungen	7. Kapitel: Von den Vorhalten
(Chapter 5: On Suspensions, Syncopes, and Rhythmic Shifts)	(Chapter 7: On Suspensions)

2. HAUPTSTÜCK: Von der Abbreviation und dem
　　　　　　　　Klaviersatz im Besonderen
　　(SECTION 2:　Specific Observations on Abbreviation
　　　　　　　　and Keyboard Style)

1. Kapitel:　Von der Abbreviation
　(Chapter 1:　On Abbreviation)

2. Kapitel:　Vom Klaviersatz im Besonderen
　(Chapter 2:　Specific Observations on Keyboard Style)

8. Kapitel:　Von der Abbreviation
　(Chapter 8:　On Abbreviation)

Nachtrag:　Ein Wort über den Choral
　(Afterword:　A Comment on the Chorale)

leading – the behavior of such elements as the passing tone or the suspension – provide an essential thread of continuity between strict counterpoint and free composition, the "semper idem" of Schenker's motto.[22]

To trace this thread of continuity succinctly through each of the *Urbegriffe*, I will present short extracts from the manuscript text, mainly from Schenker's own summaries in his introductory remarks to Part 7. I will begin, however, with a passage from the text of the *Stimmführung* subsection.[23] In Chapter 1, one of the headings characterizes "melodic fluency" (*fliessende Linie*) as the principle that governs both outer voices.[24] Under this heading, Schenker makes a specific reference to his discussion of this principle in *Kontrapunkt* 1.[25] There, in Part 1, on the cantus firmus, he had spoken of the interval of the second as the primary ingredient of melodic fluency. He had explained that melodies

---

22. It is important to note Schenker's terminology; he differentiates these *Urbegriffe* from the *Urgesetze*, the fundamental laws of scale degree and voice leading that govern them. The *Urgesetze* and the *Urbegriffe* were, in a very concrete sense, the organizing forces behind Schenker's preparatory work: he used them as keywords when making preliminary notes. The Oster Collection preserves these notes as he and his wife organized them. Though written hastily on pieces of paper of varying sizes, the notes for Parts 7 and 8 are carefully labeled: along with the heading "II²", Schenker wrote a keyword (usually in abbreviated form) for one of the laws or concepts: "Stufe," "Stimmführung," "Durchgang," "Sept," "Vorhalt," and so on. These snippets of paper, together with the long strips of completed manuscript text in his wife's hand, were gathered in makeshift file folders for each chapter. These "folders" were often made out of discarded issues of journals within which the material pertaining to the individual small sections was filed in "subfolders" created between the pages. Keywords, such as "8–8/5–5" for the chapter on consecutive octaves and fifths, or "Dg" (Durchgang) for the chapter on the passing tone, were written in colored pencil on the front of the journal issues.
23. Subsection B, "Von der Stimmführung" (refer to Figure 2). As mentioned above, most of the text of Subsection A, "Von der Stufe," exists only in fragmentary form.
24. §4: "Fliessende Linie nach wie vor Gesetz beider Aussenstimmen" (item 51/47).
25. The manuscript leaves a blank for the page reference, but the context makes it clear that Schenker is referring to *Kontrapunkt* 1, p. 136 (*Counterpoint* 1, pp. 94–95). Significantly, this is the same passage Schenker was to cite a few years later in the *Erläuterungsausgabe, Op. 101*, p. 22 (rev. edn, p. 7), as an antecedent of the *Urlinie* idea. See William Pastille, "The Development of the *Ursatz* in Schenker's Published Works," in *Trends in Schenkerian Research*, ed. Allen Cadwallader (New York: Schirmer Books, 1990), pp. 71–77.

which fulfill the conditions of melodic fluency exhibit an inherent beauty, manifest in their overall shape, though they lack the internal groupings found in free composition. Now he takes the idea of melodic fluency a step further, and writes:

> Of course one must imagine away all of the unessential traits of both bass and soprano if one wishes to gain the impression of a principal line.[26]

On the concept of prohibited parallel perfect intervals, discussed in Chapter 2, Schenker writes in his introductory remarks:

> The voice leading of free composition also retains the prohibition against parallel fifths. But the countless fifths one finds in the best compositions do not contradict this prohibition, because . . . these, arising by happenstance from composing-out, take on the illusory appearance of parallels; there is no question at all of their being true parallel fifths in the strict sense of this fundamental concept.[27]

He also touches on aspects of Chapters 3 and 5; Schenker speaks of the passing tone in conjunction with the suspension:

> In free composition, dissonance can again manifest itself only in the two main types: horizontally, as a passing tone surrounded by two consonant tones, or vertically – by means of a passing tone that is abbreviated – as a suspension with a consonant preparation and an equally consonant resolution.[28]

Here Schenker is reiterating an idea he had worked out in *Kontrapunkt* 1.[29] Now, speaking of free composition, he goes on to say that the cantus firmus, which in strict counterpoint facilitated the differentiation of these two types by creating an upbeat and a downbeat, is only seemingly absent. As long as one is not deterred by the surface rhythm, by the concealments or abbreviations, then the passing tones and suspensions of free composition behave just as if the cantus firmus were present. This is a direct continuation of the last topic discussed in Part 6, "On the elision of a voice as a bridge to free composition," where he says:

> . . . free composition, despite its extensively altered appearances, is mysteriously bound by this elision, as though by an umbilical cord, to strict counterpoint. . . .[30]

In Chapter 4, the fundamental concept of the seventh is derived from the passing tone. An idea that has its origins in *Harmonielehre* is now stated this way:

---

26. "Nur hat man freilich die unwesentlichen Züge sowohl beim Bass als beim Sopran wegzudenken, wenn man den Eindruck einer Hauptlinie gewinnen will" (item 51/47).
27. "Die Stimmführung [hält] auch im freien Satze am Verbot offener Quintfolgen fest. Diesem Verbot widerstreiten aber noch durchaus nicht die zahllosen Quintfolgen die wir auch in den besten Werken antreffen, da diese . . . durch verschiedene Zufälle der Auskomponierung bloss den Schein von Quintfolgen annehmen, ohne in Wahrheit gerade als solche Intervallfolgen in der strengen Bedeutung des Urbegriffes überhaupt schon in Frage zu kommen" (item 51/152).
28. "Die Dissonanz kann sich im freien Satze auch wieder nur in den beiden Haupttypen äussern und zwar in horizontaler Richtung als ein zwischen zwei konsonanten Tönen eingebetteter Durchgang oder auf dem Wege einer Durchgangsabbreviation in vertikaler Richtung als ein konsonant vorzubereitender und ebenso konsonant aufzulösender Vorhalt" (item 51/149).
29. See *Kontrapunkt* 1, Part 2, pp. 335–36 (*Counterpoint* 1, pp. 261–62).
30. *Kontrapunkt* 2, p. 261 (*Counterpoint* 2, pp. 270–71).

The triad of free composition often likes to borrow a passing tone from voice leading – specifically the seventh that comes from the octave.... The seventh still remains... what it always has been, simply a passing tone.... Thus the so-called seventh chord of free composition is no more than the sum of a consonant triad and the passing tone of a seventh.[31]

Schenker promises that all of these concepts and the laws that govern them will be fully worked out in the text of the free composition section – and in fact they are worked out in the most minute detail.[32] Though the difficult task of reconstructing the "Freier Satz" text is just at the very beginning stages, it is evident that Schenker's early theory of free composition recalls the excursions into free composition that are found in *Kontrapunkt* 1.[33] In a footnote pasted into the manuscript, Schenker speaks of removing his examples of free composition from Parts 1 and 2 if he were ever to prepare a revised edition of the first book of *Kontrapunkt*. Parts 1 through 5 would thus form a true "Strenger Satz" section – devoted to strict counterpoint alone – while all discussion of free composition would be contained within the "Freier Satz" section that would follow Part 6.[34]

When Schenker first conceived of his plan for *Kontrapunkt*, he had intended to trace the theory of voice leading from strict counterpoint to free composition by way of an intermediate step: the voice leading of thorough bass. His study of thorough bass would demonstrate how voice leading and scale degree worked together in figured-bass examples, which he regarded as a type of of free composition particularly suitable for didactic purposes.[35] He held the same to be true, though in a different sense, for chorale settings. Thus in the preface of *Kontrapunkt* 1, he had stated his intention to order the sections as follows: 1) strict counterpoint, 2) thorough bass, 3) the chorale, and 4) free composition.[36]

Schenker refers to this plan at the end of his introductory remarks to Part 7:

31. "Der Dreiklang des freien Satzes entlehnt von der Stimmführung gern und oft speziell den von der Oktav kommenden Durchgang der Sept.... die Sept bleibt... nach wie vor was sie von Haus aus ist, bloss ein Durchgang.... Der sogenannte Vierklang des freien Satzes löst sich somit in die Summe eines konsonanten Dreiklangs und eines Durchgangs der Sept auf"(item 51/151).
32. See Robert Kosovsky, *The Oster Collection: Papers of Heinrich Schenker. A Finding List* (New York: New York Public Library, 1990), Appendix 1, which includes a reconstruction of all the headings of the individual small sections in Parts 7 and 8, giving the location of the material found in files 6, 51, 74, and 79.
33. See, for example, *Kontrapunkt* 1, Part 2, pp. 248ff. (*Counterpoint* 1, pp. 184ff.).
34. Item 51/146.
35. I discuss Schenker's views on the relation of thorough bass to free composition in greater detail in "A Source for Schenker's Study of Thorough Bass: His Annotated Copy of J. S. Bach's *Generalbassbüchlein*," in *Schenker Studies* (Cambridge: Cambridge University Press, 1990), pp. 19–21. See also the highly informative chapter on thorough bass in Wayne Petty's dissertation, "Compositional Techniques in the Keyboard Sonatas of Carl Philipp Emanuel Bach: Reimagining the Foundations of a Musical Style" (Ph.D. diss., Yale University, 1995), pp. 1–48. Petty (p. 41, n. 73) provides evidence, found in Hans Wolf, "Schenkers Persönlichkeit im Unterricht," *Der Dreiklang* 7 (October 1937), p. 181, that Schenker spoke of thorough bass as an "Übergang zum freien Satz" (though, as we know, the "Bridges to Free Composition" in Part 6 of *Kontrapunkt* deal with quite different material).
36. *Kontrapunkt* 1, p. xxxii (*Counterpoint* 1, p. xxx, translation slightly altered: "The theory of voice leading is to be presented here as a discipline unified in itself; that is, I shall show how, after being worked out first of all on a purely vocal basis and then revealing its presence in the technique of thorough bass, in chorales, and finally in free composition, it everywhere maintains its inner unity.").

I was tempted to have the theory of thorough bass follow immediately after the theory of strict counterpoint. This would point up the contrast between the two disciplines (and would be in keeping with a historical approach), thus heightening the differences between two theories that are still mistakenly viewed as being based on allegedly corresponding voice-leading principles. Yet I was faced with the fact that the voice leading of thorough bass could never be correctly understood without a knowledge of free composition, an artistic and logical relationship that urgently begged to be considered. I permitted the latter to win, and thus gained the advantage of not having to burden my exposition of thorough bass with all kinds of preconditions.[37]

Therefore the "Generalbass" section succeeds the "Freier Satz" section,[38] and Schenker organizes his material along precisely the same lines (compare the contents of Parts 7 and 8, which are shown side by side in Figure 2). After an introductory Chapter 1, Chapters 2 and 3 of Part 8 discuss the fundamental laws of scale degree and voice leading. This relationship poses some particular problems in figured bass, for, as Schenker states:

The figure cannot, unfortunately, lead us to the inner meaning; thus there remains only one possible course: to derive the specific meaning of each given figure from a complete understanding of the context. Exactly the same is true for free composition in general, where the context alone can elucidate a particular sonority.[39]

In figured-bass examples, which of necessity focus on voice leading, the musical meaning – in Schenker's words – "sometimes depends entirely on the scale degrees one needs to supply."[40]

After discussing the special interaction of the fundamental laws, Schenker goes on to the fundamental concepts. Chapters 4 through 7 borrow their titles from the chapters of the "Stimmführung" subdivision of the "Freier Satz" section: parallel octaves and fifths, the passing tone, the seventh, and the

37. "War es zwar dann an sich verlockend, die Lehre vom Generalbass schon unmittelbar an die Lehre vom strengen Satze anzuschliessen, um, wofür übrigens auch die historische Betrachtung ein Wort einlegen möchte, den Kontrast beider Disziplinen die unverstandenerweise noch immer als angeblich koordinirte Stimmführungslehren gelten, nur desto anschaulicher zu machen, so hat anderseits der Umstand, dass die Stimmführungslehre des Generalbasses . . . ohne freien Satz überhaupt niemals recht verstanden werden kann, die Berücksichtigung eben dieses künstlerisch-logischen Zusammenhanges noch dringender gemacht. Ich liess nun den letzteren siegen und gewann damit eben den Vorteil, dass die Darstellung der Stimmführung im Generalbass und Choral nicht mit allerhand Voraussetzungen belastet werden musste" (items 51/155–56; compare the version in items 79/110–11).
38. The projected section on the chorale became a relatively short "afterword" in the thorough bass section. Schenker's extensive treatment of thorough bass did not find its way into the published *Der freie Satz*. In its introduction, however, Schenker stresses the importance of thorough bass instruction (pp. 15–16; *Free Composition*, pp. xxi–xxii), and he appears to have had other plans for his "Generalbass" (as mentioned in the diary entry of April 8, 1932, transcribed in Federhofer, *Heinrich Schenker*, p. 128). A translation of the complete thorough bass section will be published in *The Music Forum*, Vol. 6, Part 2.
39. "Ist nun die Ziffer leider kein Weg ins Innere, so gibt es nur eine Möglichkeit ihr zu entsprechen, den besonderen Sinn der Ziffer an der gegebenen Stelle aus der Situation selbst im vollen Umfange zu entnehmen, genau so, wie es im freien Satze überhaupt der Fall ist, wo nur die Situation allein Aufschluss über die betreffende klangliche Erscheinung gibt." From Chapter 1, §8: Von der Schwierigkeit in der Deutung der Ziffern, file 6, "Von der Stimmführung des Generalbasses," typescript, p. 13.
40. "Unter Umständen liegt ja gerade darauf, was an Stufen hinzugedacht werden muss, der eigentliche Nachdruck des Beispiels." From Chapter 2, §6: Vom Stufengang überhaupt, file 6, "Von der Stimmführung des Generalbasses," typescript, p. 19.

suspension are taken up in turn. Chapter 8 is a one-paragraph incomplete draft referring to the chapter on abbreviation in Part 7.

Schenker's presentation of figured bass in Part 8 often harks back to Part 7, and even to Part 6. To take only one example, from his discussion of the seventh chord in Chapter 7, Schenker cites C. P. E. Bach's description of a passage in which an A minor ⅗ chord is followed by a ⁴⁄₃ on D resolving to a ⁶⁄₃ on C. Bach states that both the third and the fourth of the ⁴⁄₃ enter freely over a passing tone whose initiating tone in the bass, E, has been elided.[41] Commenting on the example, Schenker writes:

If we also place a scale degree under the example . . . , what we see in the bass – which is to be regarded as if it were one of the upper voices – is a seventh passing from an octave.[42]

The "Freier Satz" section contains Schenker's explanation of this idea. Under the heading, "Der Satz der Aussenstimmen" ("The outer-voice setting"),[43] Schenker characterizes the actual bass as one of the upper voices (i.e., an inner voice) when viewed in relation to an "ideal" bass line consisting only of scale degrees. Again, this idea stems directly from the section on the elision of a voice at the end of Part 6:

Usually [such a tone] will be supplied . . . by our perception . . . in the low register, where it provides a substructure for the upper voices and, especially, confers altered meanings upon the dissonances. Our guess is that it is the scale degrees that complete the setting in this way.[44]

We have seen that the thorough bass section can be understood only in light of the free composition section that precedes it – the early version of Part 7 which has been the main focus of this preliminary report. Yet the revisions of the "Freier Satz" section that Schenker undertook later, after he had finished dictating the entire *Kontrapunkt* 2 in the summer of 1917, hold the key to the further development of his theory. The reconstruction of these later revisions is an extremely complex task; here I can only give a brief hint of their importance. As Schenker worked out the role of the *Urgesetze* and *Urbegriffe* in free composition, he came close to the ideas of *Urlinie* and *Ursatz*. As mentioned above, the revisions made on the first two chapters of the "Freier Satz" section may document the origins of the term *Urlinie* itself. When he was revising a

---

41. See C. P. E. Bach, *Essay on the True Art of Playing Keyboard Instruments*, trans. and ed. William J. Mitchell (New York: Norton, 1949), pp. 236–37.
42. "Und so setzte man denn auch hier . . . die Stufe nun auch unter das Beispiel . . . , so erhalten wir wieder das Bild einer von der Oktav durchgehenden Sept im Basse, als einer oberen Stimme betrachtet." From Chapter 6, §1: Vom Begriff der Sept, file 6, "Von der Stimmführung des Generalbasses," typescript, p. 57.
43. See John Rothgeb's clarification of Schenker's use of the term *Aussensatz* in *Music Theory Spectrum* 16/1 (1994), p. 148, part of his response to Joseph Lubben's article, "Schenker the Progressive: Analytic Practice in *Der Tonwille*," *Music Theory Spectrum* 15/1 (1993), pp. 57–75.
44. *Kontrapunkt* 2, p. 261 (*Counterpoint* 2, pp. 270–71). Schenker took up this idea again in "Noch ein Wort zur Urlinie," *Tonwille* 2 (1922), p. 4, and also in his "Fortsetzung der Urlinie-Betrachtungen," *Meisterwerk* I, p. 188 ("Further Considerations of the Urlinie: I," trans. John Rothgeb, *Masterwork* I, p. 105); see Pastille, "The Development of the *Ursatz*," pp. 81ff. See also the discussion of the quoted passage in Joseph Dubiel, "'When You Are a Beethoven': Kinds of Rules in Schenker's *Counterpoint*," *Journal of Music Theory* 34/2 (1990), pp. 326ff.

heading in the reorganized "Stufe" chapter, "Vom Kern der melodischen Linie als Mittler zwischen Stimmführung und Stufe" ("The essence of the melodic line as the liaison between voice leading and scale degree"), Schenker wrote the word "Urlinie" in red pencil just above the words "melodischen Linie" that his wife had copied down, and the heading became "Von der Urlinie als Mittler zwischen Stufe und Stimmführung."[45] A similar insertion was made in the first heading in the subsequent reorganized chapter on composing-out. "Von einfachen Formen der Auskomponierung" ("The simple forms of composing-out") was changed to read "Von der Urlinie und den einfachen Formen der Auskomponierung."[46]

The close relationship of the *Urlinie* to the two *Urgesetze* of Schenker's early theory of free composition is strikingly evident in the first published appearance of the word. In 1920, soon after he had abandoned the idea of including "Freier Satz" in *Kontrapunkt* 2, Schenker introduced the *Urlinie* in the *Erläuterungsausgabe* of Beethoven's Op. 101. As the following quotations show, his language harks back to the "Freier Satz" section in its early version:

A composition springs to life woven out of *Urlinie, Stufe*, and *Stimmführung*....[47]

It is the artist's task ... to elicit from [the *Urlinie*'s] rise and fall – as well as from the fundamental laws of *Stufe* and *Stimmführung* – ever new configurations of unique motives and melodies, thus transforming the general into the specific: semper idem sed non eodem modo – the artist can do no more than this![48]

And echoes are heard when Schenker explains the importance of the *Urlinie* to his idea of *Synthese* (synthesis) in *Der Tonwille*, to cite one passage out of many:

The liaison between the horizontal version of tonality through the *Urlinie* and the vertical through the scale degree (*Stufe*) is voice leading (*Stimmführung*).[49]

As the important manuscript material from the early version of *Kontrapunkt* 2 is studied further, it will undoubtedly shed light on many passages in the *Tonwille* and *Meisterwerk* essays, for much of what Schenker wrote in the 1920s builds upon the theory of free composition he formulated in the "Freier Satz" and "Generalbass" sections. They serve to record one of Schenker's most original and significant contributions – a fully worked out theory of the relation between scale degree and voice leading in free composition. They also set the stage for the appearance of the *Urlinie* and the *Ursatz*, but paradoxically it was *because* of the emergence of these important ideas that Schenker had to abandon his plan of "bringing strict and free composition together in the

---

45. See item 51/804.
46. Item 74/91. It seems likely that Schenker is making a specific reference to this projected chapter when speaking of the forthcoming II³ in the opening paragraph of "Die Urlinie: Eine Vorbemerkung," *Tonwille* 1 (1921), p. 22.
47. *Erläuterungsausgabe, Op. 101*, p. 22 (rev. edn, p. 8).
48. Ibid.
49. "Noch ein Wort zur Urlinie," *Tonwille* 2 (1922), pp. 4–6. The translation is based on that by John Rothgeb in Oswald Jonas, *Introduction to the Theory of Heinrich Schenker* (New York: Longman, 1982), p. 136. An excellent discussion of Schenker's synthesis of *Urlinie, Stufe*, and *Stimmführung* as seen in *Der Tonwille* is found in Wayne Petty's introduction to his translation of Schenker's essay on Haydn's Sonata in E♭ major from *Tonwille* 3 (1922), *Theoria* 3 (1988), pp. 106–10.

compass of a single volume." The abandoned sections were superseded by his later work, yet for us they could help bridge the wide conceptual and temporal gap between the published second book of *Kontrapunkt* and *Der freie Satz*. So if we join Schenker in his early journey – if we cross the bridge that spans Part 6 and step off directly into Parts 7 and 8 – we will then be better equipped to move on to the more distant land of *Der freie Satz*.

Schenker's unpublished work with the music of Johannes Brahms

Allen Cadwallader and William Pastille

It is not known how Heinrich Schenker first met Johannes Brahms. Certainly by 1894 the two men had established an acquaintance that afforded Schenker various opportunities to visit with Brahms.[1] Schenker once described the nature of this association:

Nothing is farther from my intent than to represent myself as a surviving friend of Brahms. The very significant age difference, my great reverence and love for the master, concern for his time [– these] allowed me to approach him only when I had a serious request, such as arose for a variety of reasons: sometimes it was my compositions, published or unpublished, that took me to him, sometimes [my] reviews of his newly published works or other essays of mine, [sometimes] conveying or commending the requests of others.[2]

These meetings made a profound and lasting impression on Schenker, whose admiration and respect for Brahms increased as he pursued his musical studies; in later years, Schenker often referred to him as "the last great master of German music." It has even been suggested that Brahms's influence on Schenker was, in a way, the inspiration for his theoretical achievements.[3]

Curiously, however, Schenker's publications do not contain many analyses of Brahms's music. Although Schenker frequently used brief excerpts as examples, he published only one analysis of a complete work – a substantial essay on the Handel Variations, Op. 24.[4] This apparent neglect of Brahms's music is somewhat inconsistent with the notion that the composer had been a formative influence on Schenker and his work.

1. During the centenary year of Brahms's birth, Schenker wrote an article entitled "Erinnerungen an Brahms," published in the *Deutsche Zeitschrift* (a continuation of *Der Kunstwart*) 46/8 (May 1933), pp. 475–82. In the article he recalls that, following the death of Hans von Bülow in February of 1894, Maximilian Harden, the editor of *Die Zukunft*, had asked Schenker to inquire of Brahms whether Harden's journal might publish some letters from Bülow that were in Brahms's possession. Schenker's acquaintance with Brahms must have been well established by the time, or Harden would not have expected Schenker to meet with a favorable response from Brahms. Schenker also reports (p. 476) that he showed his already published Op. 1 piano pieces to Brahms at their first meeting. According to Hellmut Federhofer, *Heinrich Schenker: Nach Tagebüchern und Briefen in der Oswald Jonas Memorial Collection* (Hildesheim: Olms, 1985), p. 15, Schenker's Op. 1 was published sometime in 1892. Thus the first meetings between Brahms and Schenker must have taken place late in 1892 or early in 1893.
2. Schenker, "Erinnerungen an Brahms," p. 475. The translation is by the authors, as are all subsequent translations unless otherwise noted.
3. William Pastille, "Schenker's Brahms," *The American Brahms Society Newsletter* 5/2 (1987), p. 2.
4. Heinrich Schenker, "Brahms: Variationen und Fuge über ein Thema von Handel, opus 24," *Tonwille* 8–9 (1924), pp. 3–46.

The publication record, as it turns out, does not accurately represent the extent to which Schenker analyzed Brahms's music over the years. A large body of unpublished material on Brahms survives in the portion of Schenker's *Nachlass* housed in the Oster Collection at the New York Public Library.[5] For several years this collection has been fully accessible to the public on carefully reproduced microfilm. In addition, it has been painstakingly indexed by Robert Kosovsky, whose guide is an indispensable aid to scholarly work with the materials.[6]

It was well known, even before the Oster Collection was opened to the public, that the greatest concentration of material on Brahms is found in a single file folder that Schenker labeled "Brahms." In Kosovsky's catalogue, this folder bears the designation "file 34," but it has long been known to Schenker scholars simply as the "Brahms folder."[7] Interesting items relating to Brahms appear elsewhere in the collection, such as an extended analysis by Anthony van Hoboken of Brahms's Intermezzo in E♭ major, Op. 117, No. 1, containing annotations by Schenker.[8] This item is particularly fascinating, because there is also a complete commentary on the same piece by Schenker in the Brahms folder.[9]

In our preliminary attempts to classify the material on Brahms, we found that the items in the file could be categorized as follows: (1) casual remarks about Brahms and brief incidental examples from his music, contained mostly in incomplete essays; (2) analytical commentaries in complete and incomplete form, covering a time span from approximately 1914 to the late 1920s, contemporaneous with the commentaries of the *Erläuterungsausgaben*, *Der Tonwille*, and the first two volumes of *Das Meisterwerk in der Musik*; (3) draft sketches, in various stages of completion, in a style similar to the late graphs published in the 1930s; and (4) completed analyses, in the late style of the *Fünf Urlinie-Tafeln*, of selected piano pieces. In this article, which is conceived as a brief introduction to Schenker's unpublished work on Brahms, we will concentrate on materials pertaining to our second and fourth categories and will limit ourselves to illustrating, through a few examples, some general characteristics of the early analytical commentaries and of the later graphic analyses.

While it would be desirable to isolate a few of the analytical subjects that received special attention from Schenker during the period of the early commentaries on Brahms's music, it is impossible to do so, because Schenker seems to have been interested in everything: form, phrase structure, motivic relations, rhythm, harmony, counterpoint – anything that attracted his notice. Perhaps the most general characteristic of these early commentaries, a characteristic

---

5. Schenker's surviving papers now reside primarily in three separate collections: (1) the Oster Collection; (2) the Oswald Jonas Memorial Collection at the University of California, Riverside; and (3) a private collection in the possession of Mrs. Felix Salzer.
6. Robert Kosovsky, *The Oster Collection: Papers of Heinrich Schenker. A Finding List* (New York: New York Public Library, 1990).
7. Items in the Oster Collection are identified first by the number of the file in which they occur, then by their numerical sequence in that file. Thus the designation "item 34/138" identifies the 138th item in the Brahms folder; subsequent references will use this format. A partial list of sketches in the Brahms folder is presented in Appendix A.
8. Item 14/2.
9. Items 34/81–105 and 34/115–23.

that indeed typifies all of Schenker's work, is their extreme attention to detail. Because we cannot, however, isolate special interests, we will convey the character of Schenker's early work by discussing briefly a commentary on the E minor Intermezzo, Op. 119, No. 2. To illustrate Schenker's late graphs, we shall examine a draft sketch of the same piece, and a graphic analysis of the B minor Intermezzo, Op. 119, No. 1.

Plate 1 shows the opening paragraphs of the commentary on Op. 119, No. 2. Prepared by Jeanette Schenker from her husband's dictation, the manuscript was completed on October 22, 1914.[10] Those who are acquainted with Schenker's 1912 monograph on Beethoven's Ninth Symphony, or with the *Erläuterungsausgaben* of Beethoven's late piano sonatas that were published during the same decade, will find the style of this commentary familiar.

Schenker begins his commentary on the Intermezzo, as was his custom in the published works that appeared between 1910 and 1920, by proceeding from the large-scale form toward consideration of smaller and smaller parts of the form. He describes the large-scale A_1 section as "a series of variations to which, in a manner of speaking, fugal form has been applied." By "fugal form" he means the broad harmonic plan: that is, the first subsidiary section (bars 1–12) "retains the principal key," the second (bars 13–28) "introduces the modulations," and the third (bars 28–35) "returns to the principal key."

Within each of these subsidiary sections, Schenker identifies one or two "statements" (*Aufstellungen*), a term that relates to the thematic structure of the entire A_1 section. Two statements appear in the first section (bars 1–5 and 9–12), two in the second (bars 13–17 and 18–21), and finally, one in the third (bars 29–33), for a total of five.[11]

Furthermore, within each statement, Schenker distinguishes two smaller units, antecedent and consequent, for which he uses the metaphor "two berries on one stem." Consider, for instance, the first statement: the two berries consist, respectively, of bars 1–2 and 3–5. He also refers to the first of these as the "theme" and to the second as its "repetition"; here the two are separated by what Schenker calls an "interjection" (the $d\sharp^2$ of bar 2, to be enlarged in bars 5–8 as an extension of the first statement). Going even further into detail, Schenker distinguishes within each "berry" two parts forming a small parallelism, as in bar 1 and bar 2. Each part is called the "motive," but Schenker refers to the first as the "original" and the second as the "copy"; he notes that the copy abbreviates the original. He further points to the circling of the melodic line around the tone b^1 as the most noteworthy characteristic of the motive.

Having reached the basic unit of construction, all that remains to complete the motivic analysis is to specify the difference between the original form of the

---

10. Items 34/8–12. A complete translation of this commentary is provided in Appendix B.
11. The phrase structure of the A_1 section is unclear in many respects and it is perhaps best not to refer to a succession of phrases in the usual sense. Instead, unequal groups of measures appear with subtle overlaps and extensions, which contribute to the agitated, restless character of the section. Schenker's *Aufstellung* refers to an initial five-bar thematic pattern that is repeated (sometimes in varied form). Because he is not considering the extensions to those groups, his term is roughly analogous to the main body of what might be considered a "phrase" (the identifying bar numbers cited in the text are Schenker's). For another view of the melodic structure of this Intermezzo, see Edward T. Cone, "Brahms: Songs With Words and Songs Without Words," in *Integral* 1 (1987), pp. 37–43.

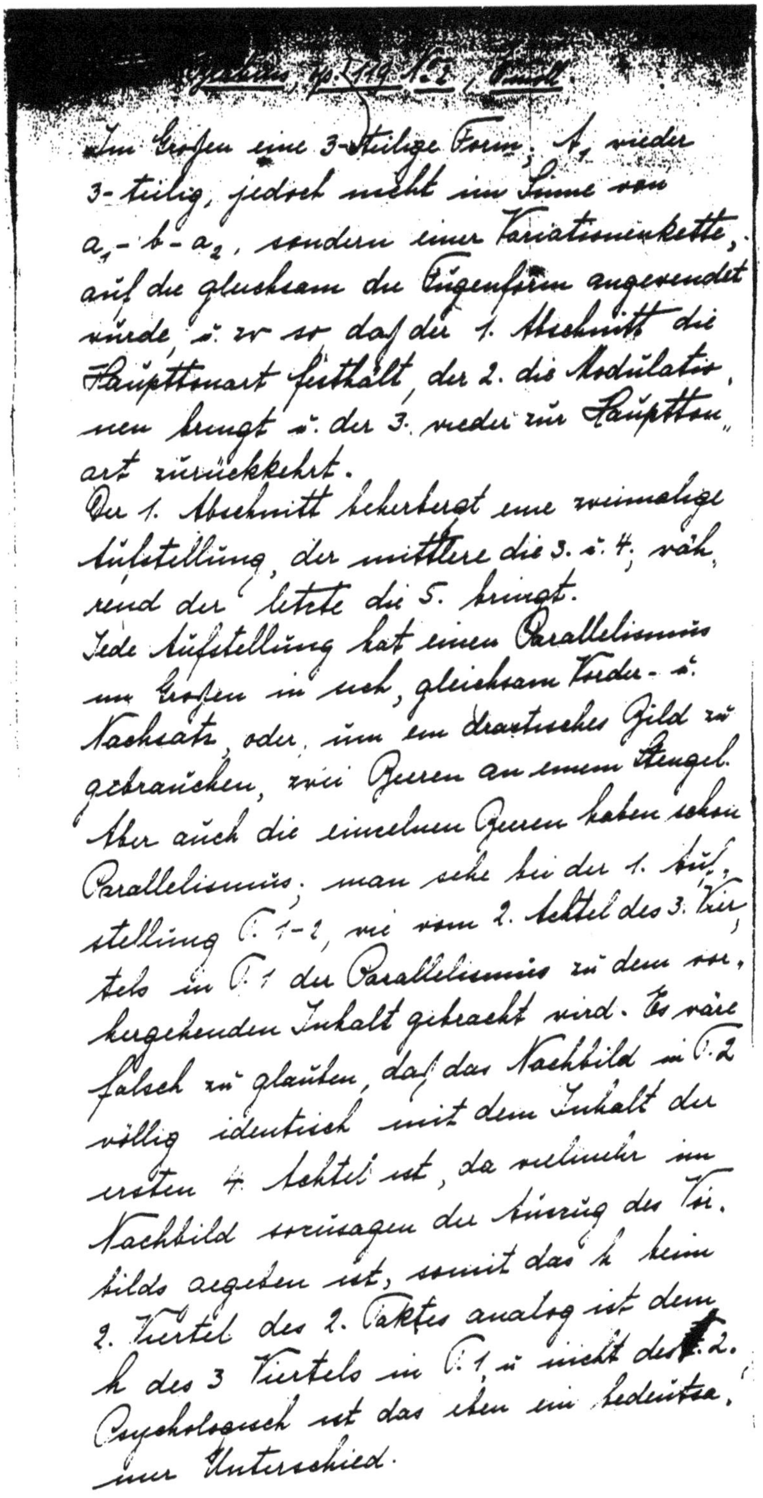

Brahms, Op. 119 No. 2, E moll

Im Großen eine 3-teilige Form; A_1 wieder
3-teilig, jedoch nicht im Sinne von
a_1-b-a_2, sondern einer Variationenkette,
auf die gleichsam die Fugenform angewendet
würde, u. zw. so daß der 1. Abschnitt die
Haupttonart festhält, der 2. die Modulatio-
nen bringt u. der 3. wieder zur Haupttonart zurückkehrt.
Der 1. Abschnitt beherbergt eine zweimalige
Aufstellung, der mittlere die 3. u. 4., wäh-
rend der letzte die 5. bringt.
Jede Aufstellung hat einen Parallelismus
im Großen in sich, gleichsam Vorder- u.
Nachsatz, oder, um ein drastisches Bild zu
gebrauchen, wie Beeren an einem Stengel.
Aber auch die einzelnen Beeren haben schon
Parallelismus; man sehe bei der 1. Aufstellung T. 1-2, wie vom 2. Achtel des 3. Viertels in T. 1 der Parallelismus zu dem vor-
hergehenden Inhalt gebracht wird. Es wäre
falsch zu glauben, daß das Nachbild in T. 2
völlig identisch mit dem Inhalt der
ersten 4 Achtel ist, da vielmehr im
Nachbild sozusagen die Kürzung des Vor-
bilds gegeben ist, somit das h beim
2. Viertel des 2. Taktes analog ist dem
h des 3 Viertels in T. 1, u. nicht dem 2.
Psychologisch ist das eben ein bedeutsa-
mer Unterschied.

Plate 1 The opening of Schenker's commentary (1914) on Brahms, Intermezzo Op. 119, No. 2 (from file 34/item 8, Oster Collection)

motive in bar 1 and its copy in bar 2. It would be a mistake, according to Schenker, to regard the copy as an imitation of the first four eighths of the original form, because the copy is a condensation of the original. Therefore, the b^1 that concludes the copy on the second beat of bar 2 (over the dominant) is analogous to the *last* b^1 in bar 1, and not to the first. Psychologically, Schenker says, there is a significant difference between the two interpretations.[12]

If Schenker is concerned with psychological motivic distinctions at such a detailed level, he is no less concerned with contrapuntal and harmonic characteristics. At the time he wrote this commentary, both *Harmonielehre* and the first book of *Kontrapunkt* were well behind him, and he had already made considerable progress in the task he had set for himself almost two decades earlier; namely, "to bring the so-called 'disciplines of harmony and counterpoint' into a desirable proximity with free composition."[13] So it is not surprising to find that Schenker's painstakingly precise analysis – in many cases descending even to the level of individual pitches – combines in equal measure both harmonic and contrapuntal factors.

For instance, Schenker concentrates his attention on the precise meaning of the very first c^1 in the upper voice. It is an accented embellishing tone (*Wechselnote*)[14] – in this case, an upper neighbor – revealed as such, he maintains, by the relation of the bass note E (the root of the tonic harmony) both to the b^1 on the upbeat to bar 1 and to the same tone that enters after a detour through the g^1 on the second eighth of the bar. For Schenker, the resolution of the accented neighbor (to b^1 on the second quarter of bar 1) above the subdominant A instead of the tonic E does nothing at all to alter the contrapuntal function of the c^1. But the change of harmony obviously has an effect on the b^1 of the resolution, which now acquires the character of an accented passing tone. For if the b^1 had entered earlier, on the second eighth of bar 1, then, according to Schenker, it would have appeared as a 9–8 suspension above IV on the second quarter of bar 1.

This situation is one in which Schenker's attention focuses on a contrapuntal phenomenon attended by harmonic considerations. There are also cases in

---

12. Schenker's description of the musical surface suggests that he already distinguishes the function of tones at different structural levels. As is discussed below, the b^1 on the second quarter of bar 1 can be considered a passing tone at the foreground level (between c^2 and a^1); consequently, it functions differently (and at a lower level) than the occurrences of b^1 on the anacrusis and the second eighth of the third quarter. From the perspective of his later ideas, this explains the "significant difference" Schenker mentions.
13. Schenker conceived this project in the 1895 essay "Der Geist der musikalischen Technik," repr. in *Heinrich Schenker als Essayist und Kritiker*, ed. Hellmut Federhofer (Hildesheim: Olms, 1990), pp. 135–54; trans. by William Pastille as "The Spirit of Musical Technique," *Theoria* 3 (1988), pp. 86–104; see p. 93.
14. Schenker used the term *Wechselnote* for passing and neighboring tones that fall on the beat. The term is sometimes translated literally as "changing note" – for example, in *Harmony* – but "changing note" has a number of usages in English, none of them equivalent to Schenker's. In *Counterpoint*, Rothgeb and Thym use "accented passing tone" throughout, with a note (*Counterpoint* 1, p. 354, n. 1 to Part 2, Chapter 2) stating that Schenker uses it only with that meaning. Here, however, Schenker is clearly referring to an accented neighbor, and even in *Kontrapunkt* 2, p. 75, he seems to mean *Wechselnote* as "accented neighbor" rather than the "accented passing tone" used in *Counterpoint* 2, p. 75, at Example 122. Schenker's discussion of Example 122 is pertinent to the Brahms analysis, because it deals with the sixth as consonant neighbor – the very situation we find in bar 1 of the Brahms.

which the focus of his attention is a harmonic phenomenon attended by contrapuntal considerations. For example, on the second beat of bar 23, we find "the characteristically Brahmsian combination of I and ♯IV," that is, of an E minor chord and an A♯ diminished seventh chord. Schenker continues, referring only to beat two: "the first [the E minor chord] is reinforced by its fifth; the second [the A♯ seventh chord] is completely represented; but in such a way that its fifth, which lies in the bass, makes the leap of a fifth upward [that is, from E to B], because it is simultaneously presenting itself as the root of I." Schenker indicates that he considers this harmonic event to be rooted in counterpoint: "compare," he notes, "C. P. E. Bach on the explanation of such a phenomenon as a passing motion."[15]

This concise look at one of Schenker's early commentaries on Brahms's music should be sufficient to convey some idea of the character of these analyses. We now turn our attention to Schenker's later work on Brahms's music.

Plates 2 and 3 show the first and second parts of the graph of the B minor Intermezzo, Op. 119, No. 1, one of a surprisingly large number of completed analyses in file 34.[16] These beautiful fair-copy graphs were carefully prepared by Angi Elias, who was one of Schenker's first and most devoted students. In the later years, she appears also to have acted as Schenker's assistant; she prepared the final copies of his completed analyses, perhaps for publication. Much of our knowledge about her comes from Schenker's lesson books, another part of the Oster Collection, which detail his teaching activities from 1912 to 1932.[17] We know, for example, that in October of 1926 Elias began to study the B minor Intermezzo; the sketch presented here may quite possibly be the result of Elias's work completed under Schenker's close supervision.[18]

In Plate 2, one can immediately recognize two aligned analytic levels, the typical format for the completed analyses of the late piano pieces. The character of the sketch and the specifics of its graphic notation are consistent with other late published analyses. For instance, the lower level is similar to the first foreground example in Schenker's 1925 analysis of Bach's Largo for unaccompanied violin: it is a chordal reduction, with the bar lines and surface rhythm of the 3/8 meter expressed throughout.[19] Also characteristic of Schenker's later analytical work are the broken slurs that highlight the retention of a single pitch over larger spans of the foreground and middleground. Below the bass in

---

15. Schenker is probably referring to Bach's description of the chord of the major seventh, $\frac{7}{4}$: "This chord appears as a passing relationship [*im Durchgange*] over a stationary bass." See C. P. E. Bach, *Essay on the True Art of Playing Keyboard Instruments*, trans. and ed. William J. Mitchell (New York: Norton, 1949), p. 294, paragraph 3, and Figure 370a.
16. The authors are planning a future publication that would present the completed graphic analyses and some of the incomplete working sketches with commentary.
17. The lesson books are contained in files 3 and 16.
18. Jeanette Schenker invariably assisted her husband in his work; most of the manuscript texts in the *Nachlass* are in her handwriting. The role played by Angi Elias is of a somewhat different nature. As the result of years of close tutelage, Schenker apparently considered Elias a skilled analyst and musician, one who could assist him in preparing his final and most advanced analyses. In addition to several of the Intermezzi, extensive analyses of the Waltzes Op. 39, and the *Studies on a Theme of Paganini*, Op. 35, are preserved in Elias's hand.
19. See Schenker, "The Largo of J. S. Bach's Sonata No. 3 for Unaccompanied Violin [BWV 1005]," trans. John Rothgeb, in *The Music Forum*, Vol. 4 (New York: Columbia University Press, 1976), pp. 142–43, 149. (For John Rothgeb's revised translation, see *Masterwork* I, pp. 31–38.)

Plate 2 Brahms, Intermezzo Op. 119, No. 1: graph of A_1 section by Schenker/Elias (from file 34/item 1, Oster Collection)

Example 1 Brahms, Intermezzo Op. 119, No. 1: reduction of bars 9–16

Schenker's hand, we see what appears to be the term "Quartzug" and a corresponding slur, both of which have been crossed out, indicating that Schenker changed his mind about his reading of this portion of the lower voice.

One of the matters that can be elucidated by these unpublished graphs is Schenker's attitude toward Brahms's allegedly "progressive" compositional tendencies. Consider the opening of this Intermezzo, which has been subjected to several different analytical approaches. Schenker finds a traditional descending-fifth progression, the root movement of which is camouflaged in the music by the overlapping, arpeggiated triads of the sequence. A virtually identical reading is given by Felix Salzer in his analysis in *Structural Hearing*.[20] By contrast, a more recent scholar, demonstrating progressive tendencies in Brahms's music, declared the opening ambiguous and a sequence of chords to be undemonstrable.[21] Another has made an even broader claim; that in his late piano music Brahms began to overturn a distinction of Classical and Baroque music – the distinction between principal and secondary voices.[22] But it is clear from his many unpublished analyses that Schenker found Brahms's music to be firmly grounded in the techniques of diatonic tonality. Brahms might have composed in ways that concealed or expanded upon earlier compositional procedures, but he nevertheless retained the techniques of his Classical heritage.

A few comments about Schenker's analysis can shed light on some aspects of Brahms's compositional style. In the higher level of Plates 2 and 3, Schenker shows that the primary tone $\hat{5}$ is literally, not just conceptually, prolonged through the A_1 and B sections, elaborated by repetitions of scale degree 6, a high-level neighbor note. At lower levels melodic activity is achieved through various diminutions that prolong the primary tone F♯ in the two-line octave, the obligatory register, or transfer it to the one-line octave and back again. The details of Schenker's foreground graph (the second level) reveal more precisely how Brahms achieves variety in an upper voice that is essentially static at a deep middleground level.

Consider bars 9–16 of Plate 2 in relation to the synoptic graph given in Example 1. If one examines the broader bass motion indicated by the slur that Schenker deleted, one would have to consider a slightly different organization of the upper voice than is indicated in Schenker's final interpretation: the line from f♯^{2} would outline a sixth plus a third, f♯^{2} down to a^1, then a^1 down to f♯^{1}.[23] (This reading corresponds closely to Felix Salzer's and can be offered as an alternative interpretation.) It reveals f♯^{2}–a^1–g♯^{1}–f♯^{1} as a related series of pitches in the foreground from bars 9–16. This tone succession, with G♮, first appears at the surface level in bars 1–2; it is subsequently expanded to delineate the upper

---

20. Felix Salzer, *Structural Hearing: Tonal Coherence in Music*, 2nd edn (New York: Dover, 1962), Vol. 2, pp. 248–51.
21. Jonathan Dunsby, "Structural Ambiguity in Brahms: Analytical Approaches to Four Works" (Ann Arbor: UMI Research Press, 1981), pp. 85–92.
22. Walter Frisch, "Brahms's Late Piano Works: Explorations in Musical Space," in *The American Brahms Society Newsletter* 9/2 (1991), pp. 1–2.
23. Schenker's final reading indicates that the octave from f♯^{2} to f♯^{1} is articulated at c♯^{2}, yielding a fourth plus a fifth (Schenker writes the word "Quintzug" above bars 12–16).

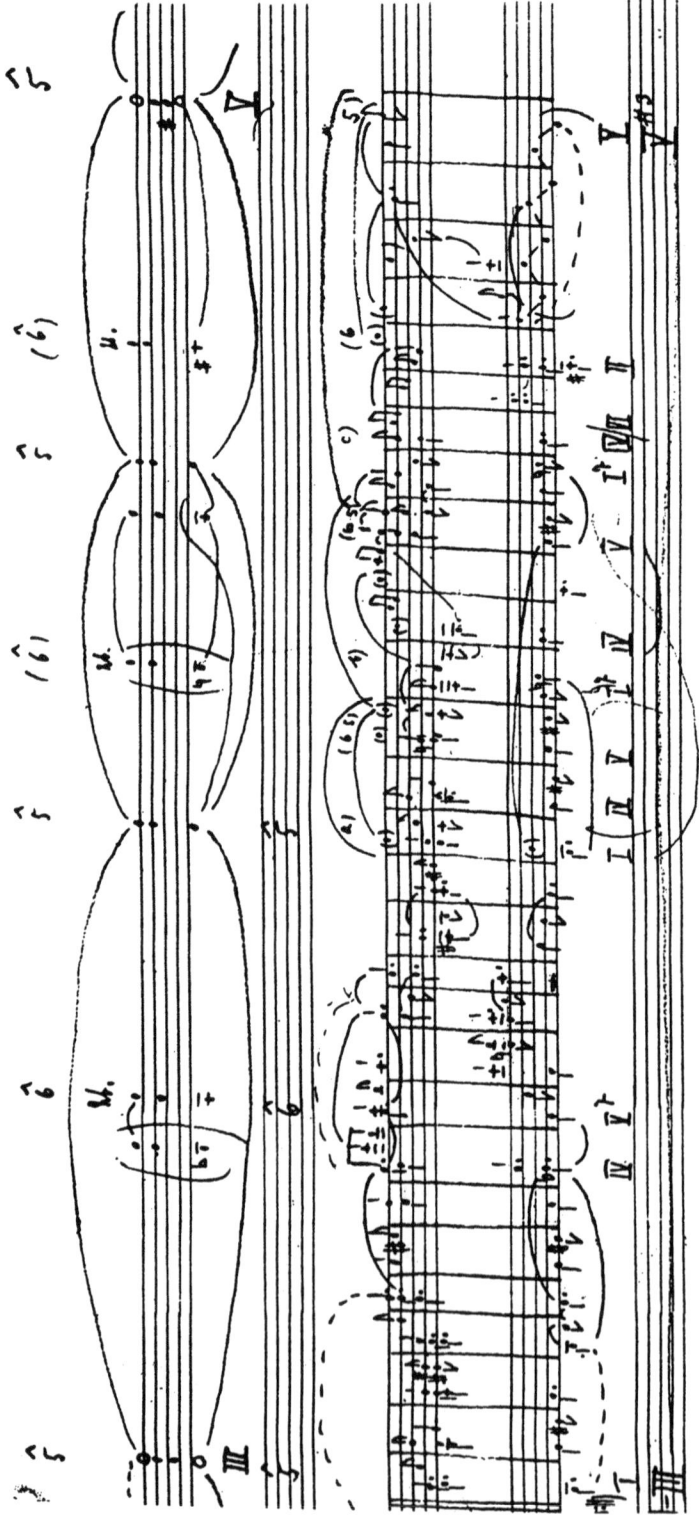

Plate 3 Brahms, Intermezzo Op. 119, No. 1: graph of B section by Schenker/Elias (from file 34/item 1, Oster Collection)

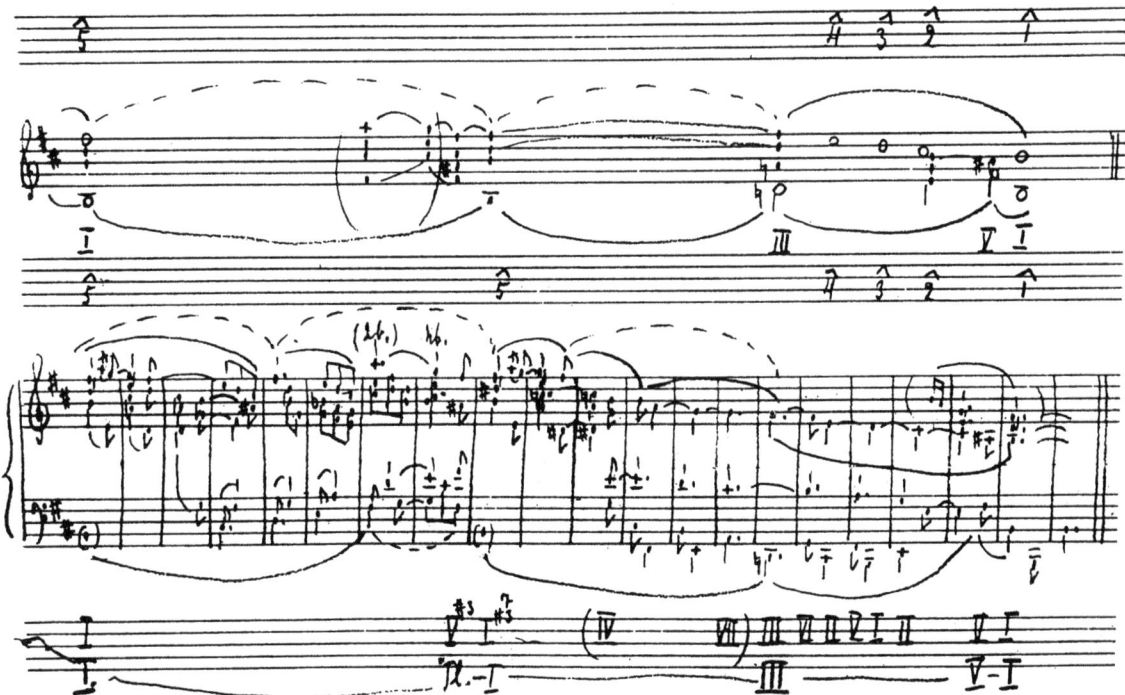

Plate 4 Brahms, Intermezzo Op. 119, No. 1: graph of A_2 section by Schenker/Elias (from file 34/item 1, Oster Collection)

voice of bars 5–9.[24] This reading reveals a hidden motivic relationship between the antecedent and consequent phrases: an enlarged repetition of the opening diminution becomes the structural framework of the upper voice in the second phrase, where, as part of a descending line, it transfers the primary tone to the one-line octave and marks the end of the A_1 section.[25]

The technique of sustaining scale degree 5 over large stretches of the middleground is one that might be considered a characteristic feature of Brahms's music. One ramification is that the completion of the structure is realized quickly, near the end of a section or piece. In Plate 4, which depicts the A_2 section, Schenker shows (in the foreground graph) the descent from $\hat{5}$ beginning six bars from the end; $\hat{5}$–$\hat{4}$–$\hat{3}$ is supported by parallel tenths at the fore-

---

24. Schenker's two "Nb" (*Nebennote*) designations (bars 7–8), the first of which he places in parentheses, constitute an interesting feature of this graph. In the tone succession f♯^{2}–a^2–g^2–f♯^{2}, the f♯^{2} in a sense "reaches over" to a^2, which is a neighbor (at a lower level) to the more fundamental neighbor-note g^2 that decorates the primary tone f♯^{2}. This identical figure appears (sometimes varied) in the Intermezzi in B♭ minor, Op. 117, No. 2 (f^2–a♭^{2}–g♭^{2}–f^2), A major, Op. 118, No. 2 (B section, c♯^{2}–f♯^{2}–e^2–d^2–c♯^{2}), and A minor, Op. 76, No. 7 (e^2–a^2–g^2–f^2–e^2). This figure, sometimes greatly expanded, maintains the presence of the primary tone while providing for melodic activity at lower levels.
25. This motivic process, in a reading that corresponds closely to Felix Salzer's, has been described by Allen Cadwallader in "Motivic Unity and the Integration of Structural Levels in Brahms's B Minor Intermezzo, Op. 119, No. 1," *Theory and Practice* 8/2 (1983), pp. 5–24.

Plate 5 Brahms, Intermezzo Op. 119, No. 1: Schenker's middleground sketch (file 34/item 2, Oster Collection)

ground, which are embedded in another descending fifth progression that expands the motion from the mediant to the dominant.

All of the details illustrated in Elias's fair-copy sketch are put into perspective in a graph in Schenker's hand (Plate 5), which is representative of a type of sketch that appears throughout the Brahms folder and occasionally in *Der Tonwille* – a middleground synopsis that summarizes the formal, harmonic, and contrapuntal properties of an entire piece. Schenker reads a $\hat{5}$-line over two bass arpeggiations, the first of which (I–III–V) articulates the A_1 and B sections of the form. At a lower level (shown on the lower staff), dividing dominants expand the tonic and mediant areas. These sketches and others like them leave us with little doubt that Schenker believed Brahms's music to be expressions of the Classical tonal principles he described and codified in *Der freie Satz*.

We now return to the E minor Intermezzo, Op. 119, No. 2. Besides the early commentary discussed above, the Brahms folder also contains an incomplete analytical sketch in Schenker's hand, dating probably from the first half of the 1920s. The incomplete sketches found in the folder range from short excerpts drawn on small pieces of note paper to extensively developed graphs on wide-format music paper. These are Schenker's everyday working sketches and are often very difficult to read, sometimes because the notes are unclear, and sometimes because Schenker scribbles comments on or above the staves.[26]

Example 2 shows Schenker's reading of the opening twelve bars; in the early

26. Because of the difficulties involved in reading Schenker's handwritten graphs, the Examples 2–4 (taken from items 34/13–15) are presented as "diplomatic transcriptions," which will preserve some of the appearance and character of his working sketches. We have also omitted some extraneous symbols that are indecipherable (to our eyes).

Example 2 Brahms, Intermezzo Op. 119, No. 2: Schenker's draft sketch of bars 1–12 (transcription)

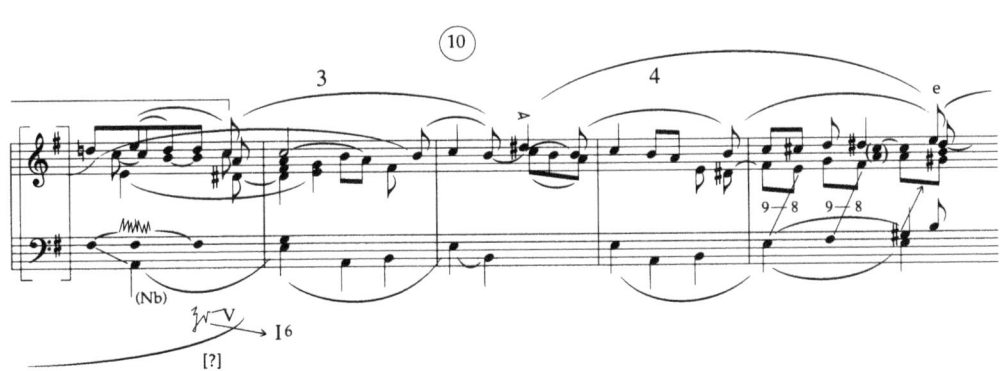

commentary, he designated these bars as the first section because the principal key is retained. Recall also that in 1914 he described the thematic structure in terms of "statements," each of which contains antecedent and consequent parts or, to use his metaphorical language, "two berries on one stem." Schenker did not abandon his early ways of thinking about this piece when he returned to it in later years. He remains very much concerned with surface and foreground detail, and he graphically recapitulates his colorful allusion. The large slurs with numbers in the sketch identify the berries on the stem, the antecedent/consequent units within the statements.

In the early commentary Schenker writes that the "motive" circles around the tone b^1. In the later sketch, he returns to this point. Most of his graph of the A_1 section traces the path of b^1 at the surface and foreground. In the opening bars, one can see some elaborations of scale degree 5: in bar 2 he writes "b c b"; above bar 5, "b a b"; and above bar 6, "b a♯ b". Over a longer span, in the modulatory second section, which is not shown in Example 2, b^1 moves out to e^2 and then to c^2 (bars 13–23); b^1 then returns over the prolonged dominant (bars 23–28), just before the return of tonic harmony signals the beginning of Schenker's

Example 3 Brahms, Intermezzo Op. 119, No. 2: Schenker's draft sketch of bars 27–35 (transcription)

third section (bar 29). It would seem, therefore, that scale degree 5 would be the logical first choice for the primary tone of the fundamental line.[27]

It is also evident in the graph that Schenker was considering the characteristics of deeper levels in relation to the features of the surface and foreground. Example 3, which shows the third section, suggests that Schenker probably did read the fundamental line initially from scale degree 5 and then changed his mind. The $\hat{5}$ at the beginning of the section, the first capped Arabic numeral to appear in the body of the sketch, is crossed out, and a small numeral $\hat{4}$ precedes a larger $\natural\hat{3}$. From the way the $\hat{3}$ appears on the page – it stands out from the surrounding graphics – we believe it must have been added after Schenker changed his mind about the structural status of the $\hat{5}$. Furthermore, Schenker highlights the designation "g^2" with an arrow, as if to underscore the meaning of his reevaluation. Schenker apparently decided upon scale degree 3 as the primary tone of the *Urlinie*, which appears late in the section in the two-line octave. It is subsequently transferred to the one-line octave (the obligatory register), over #4 in the bass, before the structural $\hat{2}$ appears.[28]

27. Schenker's reference in his early commentary to the "motive" of the piece requires some further clarification. A six-note tone succession is repeated throughout all sections of the Intermezzo: B–C–G–B–A–F#. The constant repetition of this tone succession is probably why Schenker refers to the A_1 section as a series of variations; in fact, this piece provides an excellent example of Schoenberg's notion of the *Grundgestalt* and the principle of "developing variation," because this motive appears in ever-changing rhythmic and tonal guises. Schenker's "motive," however, probably refers to the deeper contrapuntal elaborations of scale degree 5, which are naturally associated with the surface configuration. In an earlier study, Allen Cadwallader has referred to b^1–c^2–b^1 as the "basic motive," because it influences the path of the upper voice at deeper levels of structure. See his "Foreground Motivic Ambiguity: Its Clarification at Middleground Levels in Selected Piano Pieces by Johannes Brahms," *Music Analysis* 7/1 (1988), pp. 59–91.
28. Schenker's concern with the issue of the primary tone can perhaps be considered additional evidence that this is a relatively mature sketch. As late as 1924, Schenker (in his published works) was identifying multiple *Urlinien*, melodically fluent stepwise foreground or middleground lines that might ascend or descend. The logical next step in the development of Schenker's ideas was, of course, what we today understand as the descending *Urlinie*, the deepest upper voice and linear manifestation of tonic harmony. In a sketch such as the one being considered here, Schenker is clearly thinking along these later lines. See William Pastille, "The Development of the *Ursatz* in Schenker's Published Works," in *Trends in Schenkerian Research*, ed. Allen Cadwallader (New York: Schirmer Books, 1990), pp. 71–85.

Example 4 Brahms, Intermezzo Op. 119, No. 2: Schenker's draft sketch of bars 36–43 (transcription)

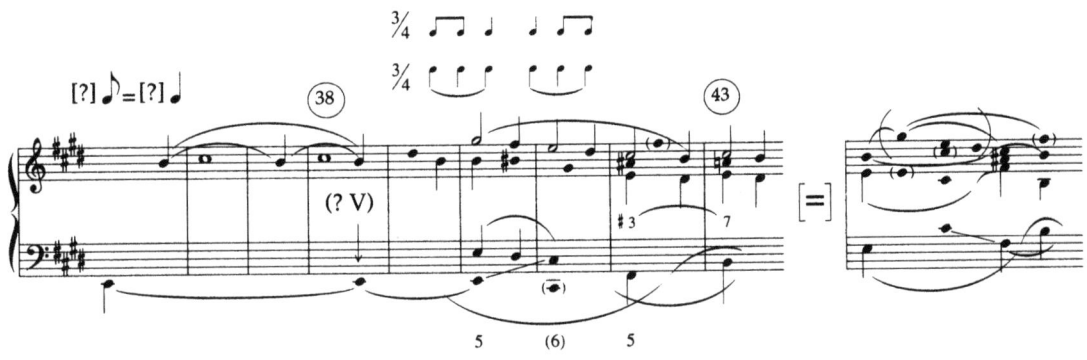

Example 4 shows the first phrase of the B section (Andantino grazioso), and may provide a clue as to why Schenker eventually decided on scale degree 3 as the primary tone of the entire piece. This section derives its contrast from a change of character and reworking of the original motive in the major mode, not through a shift in tonal center. Thus the series of motivic variations continues, and initially, so does the "circling effect" around the tone b^1: in the opening four bars of this section, b^1 is elaborated twice by its upper neighbor $c\sharp^2$. But in the fifth bar, $g\sharp^2$ marks the climax of this eight-bar phrase; because 3 appears so quickly at the beginning of the section, its structural relationship to 5 is more conspicuous than in the A_1 section. As Schenker shows in his synoptic sketch at the end of the line, b^1 is an inner-voice tone that leads out to $g\sharp^2$, which moves back into the inner voice under an implied $f\sharp^2$ at the end of the phrase. The shape of the upper voice in the first phrase of the B section is strikingly similar to that in the last phrase of the A_1 section, where 3 appears prominently in the same register. Considering the relatively weak support for 4 throughout this piece, this reading from $\hat{3}$ is compelling and deserves consideration.[29]

We are now in a better position to evaluate the designation that appears at the very beginning of the sketch (Example 2). It stands out from the surrounding context and was probably added after the sketch was finished, perhaps at the same time Schenker reevaluated his reading of the primary tone. The designation reads as follows: ♮$\hat{3}$ $\hat{2}$ $\hat{1}$ | ♯$\hat{3}$ $\hat{2}$ $\hat{1}$ | ♮$\hat{3}$ $\hat{2}$ $\hat{1}$. This is an indication, in shorthand form,

---

29. Two further points about Schenker's sketch of the E minor Intermezzo should be mentioned, even though the complete sketch has not been reproduced here. First, the only passage where the six-note surface motive is not present, where the motivic variations and circling effect apparently cease, is in bars 52–60, the b part of the large B section (a rounded binary form). Nevertheless, Schenker's graph clearly shows that the upper voice traverses an octave from b^2 to b^1 at the foreground and, at a deeper level, that b^2–$c\sharp^2$–b^1 is a figure embedded within the octave descent. Hence, one of the elaborations of scale degree 5 (5–6–5) does in fact shape the apparently contrasting b section, but it is expanded into the middleground (motivic repetition at a higher level produces contrast at a lower level). Second, in bar 60, at the end of the octave descent, the surface motive recurs, signalling the beginning of the *melodic* reprise. Because the bass motion occurs in the midst of the prolongation of V (bars 52–63), the *harmonic* reprise is out of phase with the upper voice (bar 64). The interesting point here is that the return of tonic harmony coincides not with the beginning of the initial theme but with G♯ in the upper voice, another compelling reason to consider Schenker's reading of this piece from $\hat{3}$.

of what would have been represented in a published *Urlinie-Tafel* in a separate middleground graph aligned above the surface and foreground: the interruption and repetition of the fundamental line that delineate the form, and the alteration of the primary tone that produces the modal contrast of the B section. The foregoing considerations illustrate that it is sometimes possible to reconstruct something of the development of Schenker's thinking about a particular piece from the wealth of material in the archives.

We have, of course, only begun to explore the vast body of material in the Oster Collection. As this part of Schenker's *Nachlass* becomes better known, it will become apparent that Schenker's study of Brahms's music is rivaled in scope only by his work with the music of Beethoven: there are analyses of dozens of pieces from virtually every genre in which Brahms composed – piano pieces, chamber works, songs, symphonies. These unpublished analyses are eloquent testimony to Schenker's love and admiration for the music of Brahms, with which he was deeply involved throughout his entire life.

APPENDIX A

Selected list of items from the "Brahms folder"
(Oster Collection, file 34)

Completed sketches by Schenker (with Angi Elias)

Op. 119, No. 1, Intermezzo in B minor. Clean copy of a graph by Elias; working sketches by Schenker

Op. 76, No. 2, Capriccio in B minor. Clean copy of a graph by Elias; working sketches by Schenker

Op. 76, No. 4, Intermezzo in B♭ major. Clean copy of a graph by Elias; working sketches by Schenker; photocopy of a synoptic graph by Ernst Oster

Op. 76, No. 7, Intermezzo in A minor. Clean fair copy of a graph by Elias; fair copy also by Schenker

Op. 39, Waltzes, Nos. 1–16. Extensive graphs in final, completed form. Multilevel *Urlinie-Tafeln*

Op. 35, Studies (Variations) on a Theme of Paganini. Extensive graphs in final, completed form

Incomplete (working) sketches by Schenker

Op. 119, No. 2, Intermezzo in E minor. Sketches for a graph, notes, and musical examples; complete written commentary in Jeanette Schenker's hand with emendations by Schenker, dated October 22, 1914

Op. 119, No. 3, Intermezzo in C major. Sketches for a graph; complete written commentary in Jeanette Schenker's hand, dated October 23, 1914

Op. 118, No. 2, Intermezzo in A major. Notes and musical examples; sketches for a graph; complete written commentary in Jeanette Schenker's hand, dated October 21, 1914

Op. 76, No. 1, Capriccio in F♯ minor. Sketch for a graph

Op. 79, No. 1, Rhapsodie in B minor. Notes and musical examples; sketches for a graph; incomplete commentary concerning the piece

Op. 79, No. 2, Rhapsodie in G minor. Notes and musical examples; sketches for a graph

Op. 117, No. 1, Intermezzo in E♭ major. Sketches for a graph; complete written commentary in Jeanette Schenker's hand, dated February 26, 1920

Op. 117, No. 2, Intermezzo in B♭ minor. Sketches for a graph; notes concerning the autograph

Op. 117, No. 3, Intermezzo in C♯ minor. Sketches for a graph; notes and observations about the autograph manuscript

Op. 10, No. 4, Ballade in B major. Text in Jeanette Schenker's hand; sketches for a graph

Op. 10, No. 1, Ballade in D minor. Musical examples and sketches for a graph

Op. 8, Trio in B major for piano, violin, and cello. Notes, musical examples, and sketches for a graph. Both versions of Op. 8 are represented, as are all movements

Op. 114, Trio in A minor for piano, cello, and clarinet (or viola). Notes, text, and musical examples; all movements are represented

Symphony No. 1. Sketches for a graph and notes. All movements are represented

Symphony No. 3. Complete commentary of first movement (mid-1920s?) and sketches

Symphony No. 4. Sketches; all movements are represented

APPENDIX B

A commentary on Brahms's Intermezzo Op. 119, No. 2, in E minor

Heinrich Schenker

On the whole, a three-part form; A_1 also three-part, but not in the sense of a_1 b a_2, rather, a series of variations to which, in a manner of speaking, fugal form has been applied in such a way that the first section retains the principal key, the second introduces the modulations, and the third returns to the principal key.

The first of these sections accommodates a double statement [*Aufstellung*],[1] the middle section introduces the third and fourth, and the last section the fifth.

Each statement has within itself a large-scale parallelism – antecedent and consequent, as it were; or, to use a vivid image, two berries on one stem.[2] But the individual berries have a parallelism too: in bars 1–2 of the first statement, note how, beginning on the second eighth of the third quarter in bar 1, the parallel is drawn with the preceding content. It would be incorrect to think that the copy in bar 2 is completely identical with the content of the first four eighths, because in the copy an abbreviation, so to speak, of the original is presented, so that the B of the second quarter of bar 2 is analogous to the B of the third quarter of bar 1, and not to the B of the second quarter. Psychologically, this particular feature is a significant difference.

One noteworthy characteristic of the motive is its circling around the tone B, which is expressed most succinctly in the copy and somewhat more extensively in the original. The parallelism in bars 3–5 promotes an expansion: see the first and second quarters [of bar 3] and the third and first quarters [of bars 4 and 5]. The goal here, however, just as in bar 2, is the dominant of E minor. The syncopated D♯, a kind of interjection [bar 2], is driven like a wedge between the theme and its repetition. In conformity with the broadening in bars 4–5, the interjection between the first complete statement and the subsequent second one is now also enlarged by means of the triple repetition of the tone D♯ and the detour over F♯ to B.

1. The word *Aufstellung* means "setting up," as one sets up an easel or a tent. It means "statement" in the sense of "something set up or set forth for consideration." It is also used in connection with the deployment of military forces. The closest English approximation to Schenker's intent would probably be "disposition," but because this term has other musical meanings, the more prosaic rendering "statement" is employed here.
2. Schenker's wording, "zwei Beeren an einem Stengel," may reflect his recollection of a line in Shakespeare's *A Midsummer Night's Dream* (which he would have known in the Schlegel translation): "Zwei holde Beeren, einem Stiel entwachsen." The line comes from a passage in act III, scene 2, where Helena speaks of herself and Hermia: "So we grew together, / Like to a double cherry, seeming parted, / But yet an union in partition – / *Two lovely berries moulded on one stem*" (emphasis added).

In bar 7 the second statement is ushered in by bringing back the initial interval of a second, B–C, in the manner of an introduction, as it were. This happens twice; the second time, across bars 7–8, it is greatly expanded. The second statement follows in bars 9–12; instead of an expansion or repetition, there is a modulation from E minor to A minor in bar 12, based on the simple chromaticization of the third – G♯ instead of G. Immediately, without an intervening interjection (which was in any case made superfluous by the syncopes in bar 12),[3] the third statement follows, in A minor [bars 13ff.]. It introduces a triplet motion that represents an increase in motion over the earlier rhythmic activity, which only appears to move in sixteenths, but actually moves in eighths. In the third statement one best discerns the organic character of the parallelism I described above as the "two-berry system"; for we see here in the third statement how Brahms maintains the five-bar count as the sum of the bars which the theme and its repetition (bars 1–5) had comprised during their first statement. This constraint on the number of bars allows Brahms to overthrow the reigning thematic material – thus the third through fifth bars of the third statement (bars 15–17), instead of essentially repeating the main motive, as do bars 3–5, introduce a sequential continuation of bar 14. Moreover, in the three bars just mentioned (bars 15–17) an additional modulation to C major takes place. And then, once again without the mediation of an interjection, the fourth statement follows with its two berries. Here the motion in eighths returns; the original – that is, the first berry – appears over the tone C, above which passes a minor dominant.[4] This C is reinterpreted as VI in E minor, so that the ensuing repetition takes place in E minor above a B pedal:

$$\begin{array}{cc} C_{4-3}^{6-5} & B_{4-3}^{6-5} \\ \nearrow & \nearrow \\ I/VI & V \end{array}$$

Only now, in bar 21, there is an interjection [of D♯] derived from bars 5ff., with a new and contrasting broadening in bars 23–24 to underscore the content of the succeeding bars 25–26.

The motive of a second in bars 27–28 heralds the eighth-note counterpoint to the main motive in bar 29, which, in comparison with the counterpoint from bar 1, shows a slight modification – to be precise, in the form of an accented embellishing tone [*Wechselnote*].[5]

The fifth statement differs from the preceding fourth one in that it adopts an upward path in its repetitions. The half cadence in bars 33–35 [serves] as the transition to the middle section of the entire piece; the quarter notes use the tones of the eighth-note counterpoint.

---

3. The syncopes make an interjection superfluous because they recall the interjections which also had syncopated rhythms. It is also possible that Schenker's reference to fugal form at the beginning of this commentary relates not only to the key structure but also to the alternation of *Aufstellungen* and *Interjektionen*, which might be regarded as analogous to the alternation of entrances and episodes in fugues.
4. The term *Molldominante* occurs here in the original. Schenker may have been thinking of the E♭¹ on the second quarter, which gives C the color of a minor dominant in F minor. Or, this may simply be a mistake in dictation or transcription for *Mollunterdominante* – the F minor chord passing above the bass C.
5. See note 14 to the text proper.

Concerning harmonic particulars

In bar 1, the first eighth C [is] an accented embellishing tone [*Wechselnote*]; this is revealed by the relation of the root E both to the preceding eighth B and to the B that enters after a detour through the second eighth G. The accented embellishing tone resolves on this last B; the fact that it does not coincide with the root E, but rather with a new one, namely the root of IV, alters nothing at all in regard to the character of the accented embellishment. Over IV, however, the B, now descending from C, again takes on the character of an accented embellishment; whereas, if it had been brought in earlier, it would have appeared as an actual ⌒9–8 suspension [over the root A].

In bars 4–5: I–IV–VII–V$^{\sharp3}$. In bar 4 on the first quarter: copy of the accented embellishing tone as it appears on the third quarter of bar 3. In accordance with free composition, however, it can also legitimately be considered a prepared suspension.[6]

Bar 8: (no) parallel fifths (F$\sharp^{7-6}$) – Bar 12: a series of ⌒9–8 ⌒9–8 attracts attention. The harmony of the second quarter [is] merely passing motion.[7]

Bars 15–16: inventive use of a progression by a third and a second instead of the customary progression by fifth.[8]

Bar 18: suspension $^{6-5}_{4-3}$ Bar 23: the characteristically Brahmsian combination of I and $\sharp$IV. The first is reinforced by its fifth; the second is completely represented, but in such a way that its fifth, which lies in the bass, makes the leap of a fifth upward, because it is simultaneously presenting itself as the root of I. (Compare C. P. E. Bach on the explanation of such a phenomenon as a passing motion.)[9]

Bars 29ff.: I–IV–V–VI–VII–III–II–V–I

Middle section in E major, likewise three-part

a_1 takes up the main theme in the first four bars by changing the first two beats into triple meter and transposing them to major. The continuation is freely invented. a_1 has an antecedent and a consequent; the antecedent [ends in] a half cadence, the consequent [goes] to B major. The $^6_4$ position on the third quarter [of bar 42] is merely a neighboring-tone harmony. The consequent modulates to B major.

b establishes itself in the territory of B minor and employs the motive of bar 36 as the leading motive – see bars 52 and 54 and the variants in bars 56 and 58. Bars 53, 55, and 57 are freely invented. Bar 59 can be explained as a line proceeding uninterruptedly out of the motive, in which each attained goal is at the same time the starting point of the next repetition. The harmonic degrees [in

---

6. Schenker is referring to the f$\sharp^1$ in the inner voice: f$\sharp^1$–e^1 is a copy of the preceding e^1–d$\sharp^1$.
7. This line is heavily annotated in Schenker's own hand. (His additions are given in parentheses.) It is a fairly certain conjecture that the first word of his comments on bar 8 is "keine." The "F$\sharp^{7-6}$" is clear. (Schenker is referring to the succession perfect fifth/diminished fifth, E–B/D$\sharp$–A, on beat 3, which is where the 7–6 over F$\sharp$ takes place.) There is a long annotation over his comments on bar 12 that is very difficult to make out and has therefore not been included in the present translation.
8. Schenker means that the roots in bars 15 and 16 move down a third then up a second: A–F–G–E–F; they would normally move entirely by descending fifths: A–D–G–C–F.
9. See note 15 to the text proper.

bars 52–58]: ♮VII–♮VI–II–I. In bar 59 I persists; above it sixth chords move in passing motion. This passing motion would have been clearer if, in the bass of bar 58, the tones B and A had preceded. – VI [of B minor] in bar 54 appears in $^6_4$ position instead of in $^6_3$ position, and does so for the sake of a better connection to the $^6_3$ position of the chord on II in bar 56. The succession II–I in bars 56–57[10] can be understood through the mediation of V or VII. In this [root-] progression by a second [C♯–B] it becomes evident that the space of two fifths cannot be composed out in its entirety, but only in its parts. Such partial segments function as follows: (a) the space between the root and the seventh in the case of the dominant (the dominant seventh chord); (b) the space between the third and the ninth (the seventh chord on VII); and finally (c) the space between the fifth and the ninth (II). Brahms likes to use the succession II–I in the sense of II–V–I; the progression is dangerous, because it can easily cause parallel fifths if the harmonic degrees rest on their actual root tones. Here, in the Intermezzo, he uses the $^6_3$ position – and not even in the best disposition, but rather in open position, which gives rise to parallel fifths in the upper voices.[11]

a_2 begins in bar 60, but the first two bars, 60–61, are still bathed in the hue of the modulation, since I [of B minor] from bar 59 is reinterpreted as IV in the direction of F♯ minor, which is then raised [chromatically] and leads to V precisely at bar 60, and in turn to I at bar 61. The I [of F♯ minor] in bar 61 is then reinterpreted as II of E major, whereupon the theme continues in that same key. It is therefore necessary to assume a modulation to F♯ minor as a bridge, because no direct path leads from B minor to E major. Bars 68ff. present an inspired retransition to A_2; it consists of a threefold[12] repetition of the first four tones of the theme (as already mentioned, the fourth tone is the same as the first). Through skillful placement, Brahms manages to put the second tone, C♯, on a different part of the measure every time. Thus, in bar 69 it occurs on the second quarter; in bar 70, on the third quarter; until in bar 72 the tone C instead of C♯ at last attains the position of the first quarter.

A_2 is somewhat abbreviated and even altered a bit at bars [75–76].[13]

Performance:
Literature: Kalbeck?

22.X.1914

---

10. The original reads erroneously "the succession I–II."
11. The parallel fifths cited by Schenker here are a diminished fifth and a perfect fifth, C♯–G/B–F♯, rather than two perfect fifths. According to Schenker's later reading, the B minor chord over the D in bar 57 is not heard as a tonic but as a neighbor to E, which moves to E♯ in bar 60.
12. The original reads erroneously "fourfold."
13. A space for the bar numbers was left blank in the original.

ANALYTICAL STUDIES

C. P. E. Bach and the fine art of transposition

Wayne Petty

In the short autobiography that he wrote in his sixtieth year, Carl Philipp Emanuel Bach mentions a feature of his musical style that has long been admired:

> Since I have never liked excessive uniformity in composition and taste, since I have heard so many and so many different kinds of good things, and since I have always been of the opinion that, no matter where it might be hidden, and even if we come across it only in the slightest degree, something good can be got from a piece – these, along with my God-given talent, are presumably how the diversity *(Verschiedenheit)* arose that people have noticed in my music.[1]

This diversity pervades the music of C. P. E. Bach. Not only was Bach the great eclectic, willing to embrace whatever he found good; but also he brought to the art of variation a degree of refinement few composers have matched. An elegant and distinctive variation technique is the cornerstone of his style, both in his celebrated use of the varied reprise and within sections of a work. Rare is the phrase that receives a literal repetition in C. P. E. Bach's music.

Given Bach's inventiveness and his dislike of "excessive uniformity," one feature of his keyboard sonatas seems curiously out of place: he insists on repetition when it involves transposition in the latter part of a sonata movement. Whether he is writing a binary sonata movement without recapitulation or a rounded binary with recapitulation, once Bach begins transposing music originally heard in the secondary key of the exposition, he almost always writes a bar-for-bar correspondence with the exposition. He steadfastly refuses to introduce changes into the transposed music beyond the minimum needed to invert the interval of transposition – say, from a fourth above to a fifth below – relative to the original statement in the exposition.

Why this curious mix of variation on the one hand and strict transposition on the other? First we might recall that the solo keyboard sonata was not only

---

1. "Da ich niemahls die allzugrosse Einförmigkeit in der Komposition und im Geschmack geliebt habe, da ich so viel und so verschieden Gutes gehört habe, da ich jederzeit der Meinung gewesen bin, man möge das Gute, es stecke wo es wolle, wenn es auch nur in geringer Dosi in einem Stücke anzutreffen ist, annehmen: so ist vermuthlich dadurch und mit Beyhülfe meiner mir von Gott verliehenen natürlichen Fähigkeit, die Verschiedenheit in meinen Arbeiten entstanden, welche man an mir bemerkt haben will." C. P. E. Bach, "Selbstbiographie" in *Carl Burney's Tagebuch seiner musikalischen Reisen*, trans. C. D. Ebeling (Hamburg, 1773), Vol. 3, p. 208; reprinted in *Selbstbiographien deutscher Musiker des XVIII. Jahrhunderts*, ed. Willi Kahl (Köln: Staufen-Verlag, 1948), pp. 34–44. The translation of this passage is mine; for a translation of the entire autobiography, see William S. Newman, "Emanuel Bach's Autobiography," *The Musical Quarterly* 51/2 (1965), pp. 363–72.

in a certain form; it was also a *genre*. Like any genre, the keyboard sonata carried conventions to which composers felt bound. Conventions, of course, become standard procedures because they make a good effect. In the case of strict transposition, the convention lent the sonata movement a clear formal design, which helped articulate the resolution of the large-scale dissonance created by the modulation in the exposition – what, in Schenkerian terms, would be the resolution of the interrupted $\hat{2}$ of the fundamental line. In addition to observing conventions of genre, C. P. E. Bach may also have regarded the sonata as a *style* distinct from that of the symphony, much as several eighteenth-century authors did.[2] By adhering to a bar-for-bar correspondence between recapitulation and exposition, he was able to preserve the small dimensions of his keyboard sonata movements. Rarely do these works assume symphonic proportions.

But even if genre and style can account for Bach's method, close correspondences between parallel passages in a style otherwise so heavily dependent on variation can easily seem rigid. Indeed, some recent critics have detected a stiffness in Bach's handling of the form, not only in his use of transposition, but also in other recurring features of his sonatas.[3] For instance, he tends to open the development section with the head motive that begins the other sections, and he normally writes a single strong cadence in a closely related key as the goal of the development section. These recurring patterns hold throughout his composing career. Meanwhile, Bach's sonatas become increasingly standardized in a different respect. Beginning with the *Probestücke* of 1753, the lengths of the individual phrases in the exposition and recapitulation become much more regular; the phrases unfold in lengths that are normatively some multiple of four bars. In the later works, irregular phrase lengths can usually be understood as modifications of a four-bar norm. Thus C. P. E. Bach, so often admired for the improvisatory freedom of his works, wrote dozens of sonatas that appear quite conventional. No one to my knowledge has gone so far as to say that he wrote the same sonata a hundred and fifty times (like the old saw about Vivaldi's concertos), but something along those lines has been suggested, and analysts seriously engaged with C. P. E. Bach's music need to come to terms with the apparent rigidity in Bach's approach to sonata form.

What have rarely been appreciated in C. P. E. Bach's keyboard sonatas, however, are the subtle ways in which the recapitulation uses the transposed music to recreate progressions heard in the earlier sections. One result of this procedure is often to make new connections between earlier passages, to make concealed relationships explicit. Another is to use the transposed music to con-

---

2. For a discussion of the differences between sonata and symphony styles with relevant citations, see Michael Broyles, "The Two Instrumental Styles of Classicism," *Journal of the American Musicological Society* 36/2 (1983), pp. 210–42.
3. The first author to describe Bach's keyboard sonatas in this way appears to have been Darrell Berg in her influential dissertation, "The Keyboard Sonatas of C. P. E. Bach: An Expression of the Mannerist Principle" (Ph.D. diss., State University of New York at Buffalo, 1975); see especially Chapters 4 and 5. Other writers who adopt a similar position include Pamela Fox, "Melodic Nonconstancy in the Keyboard Sonatas of C. P. E. Bach" (Ph.D. diss., University of Cincinnati, 1983) and David Schulenberg, *The Instrumental Music of Carl Philipp Emanuel Bach* (Ann Arbor: UMI Research Press, 1984).

tinue developing the tonal issues around which the other sections evolve, thereby recalling, summarizing, and resolving the tonal tensions at the end. The challenge, which Bach often met brilliantly, was to achieve this effect of summary and resolution within the generic and stylistic constraints noted earlier – that is, without using the kind of recomposition that other composers often used to create a similar effect. It is these techniques that this paper will address. What I hope to suggest is a variety of tonal procedures in Bach's recapitulations not altogether foreign to the other kinds of variety that pervade his style.[4]

C. P. E. Bach's imaginative use of close transposition emerges clearly from his G minor *Probestück* H.71 (W.63/2), third movement, the sixth of the eighteen practice pieces that he appended to the first volume of his *Versuch über die wahre Art das Clavier zu spielen* (1753).[5] As I noted earlier, the eighteen *Probestücke* are significant for Bach's composing career, since they mark the point at which the composer began adopting more regular phrase rhythm. In addition, these works are significant because they form a kind of compendium, not only of keyboard styles and techniques, but also of compositional designs. (In this sense, the works are to C. P. E. Bach much as the two books of the *Well-Tempered Clavier* had been to his father.) As a performance study, the G minor *Probestück* illustrates the brilliant and fiery Presto, which Bach says to play as briskly as possible, yet clearly.[6] As a compositional study, the piece illustrates a condensed sonata form, in which the exposition has no transition, and the development section and recapitulation each unfold as a single phrase. More subtly, though, the piece also shows how to use transposition to make connections between earlier passages. That is the issue on which I will focus here.

Example 1 compares the openings of the exposition and recapitulation of the G minor *Probestück*, including the point at which transposition begins. Example 1a shows a contrapuntal model for the opening phrase of the exposition, bars 1–6, aligned with sketches of two passages from the Sonata: bars 1–6

---

4. This aspect of C. P. E. Bach's compositional technique has not gone unnoticed. John Rothgeb remarks on a transposed passage from Bach's A minor *Probestück* H.70, second movement, "The ability to recapitulate a section and to make it appear logical and convincing in a different way in its new environment shows a thorough compositional mastery." See Rothgeb, "Design as a Key to Structure in Tonal Music," in *Readings in Schenker Analysis and Other Approaches*, ed. Maury Yeston (New Haven: Yale University Press, 1977), p. 91. On recapitulations generally, see also Ernst Oster, "Analysis Symposium on Mozart, Menuetto K.V.355: A Schenkerian View," in *Readings in Schenker Analysis*, p. 137, and Edward Laufer's review of *Free Composition* in *Music Theory Spectrum* 3 (1981), p. 173.
5. C. P. E. Bach's keyboard pieces are identified according to the numbering systems of Helm (H.) and Wotquenne (W.); see Eugene Helm, *Thematic Catalogue of the Works of Carl Philipp Emanuel Bach* (New Haven: Yale University Press, 1989), and Alfred Wotquenne, *Thematisches Verzeichnis der Werke von Carl Philipp Emanuel Bach (1714–1788)* (Leipzig: Breitkopf & Härtel, 1905). A facsimile of the first edition of the eighteen *Probestücke* may be found in *The Collected Works for Solo Keyboard by Carl Philipp Emanuel Bach 1714–1788*, 6 vols., ed. Darrell Berg (New York: Garland, 1985), Vol. 1, pp. 39–59; the G minor *Probestück* appears on p. 45. A reliable modern edition is *C. Ph. E. Bach, Sechs Sonaten: Achtzehn Probestücke zu dem "Versuch über die wahre Art das Clavier zu spielen" (1753)*, 2 vols., ed. Erich Doflein (Schott Werk-Reihe für Klavier, ED 2353 and 2354); the G minor *Probestück* appears in Vol. 1 on pp. 11–12.
6. Bach writes, "... ich verlange, daß die Probestücke aus dem G und F moll ... auf hurtigste wiewohl deutlich gespielt werden müssen." *Versuch*, Part I (Berlin, 1753), Chapter 3, §1, p. 116. See also the translation by William J. Mitchell, *Essay on the True Art of Playing Keyboard Instruments* (New York: Norton, 1949), p. 148.

Example 1 C. P. E. Bach, G minor *Probestück*, Sonata H.71 (W.63/2), third movement: comparison of bars 1–6 and 27–32

a) Model for bars 1–6

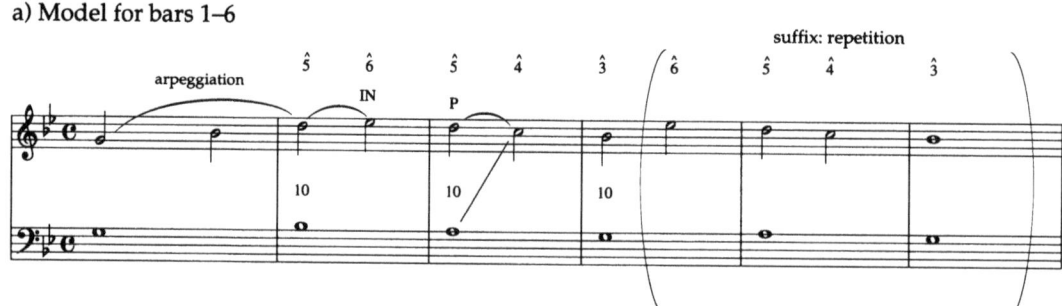

b) Exposition, bars 1–6

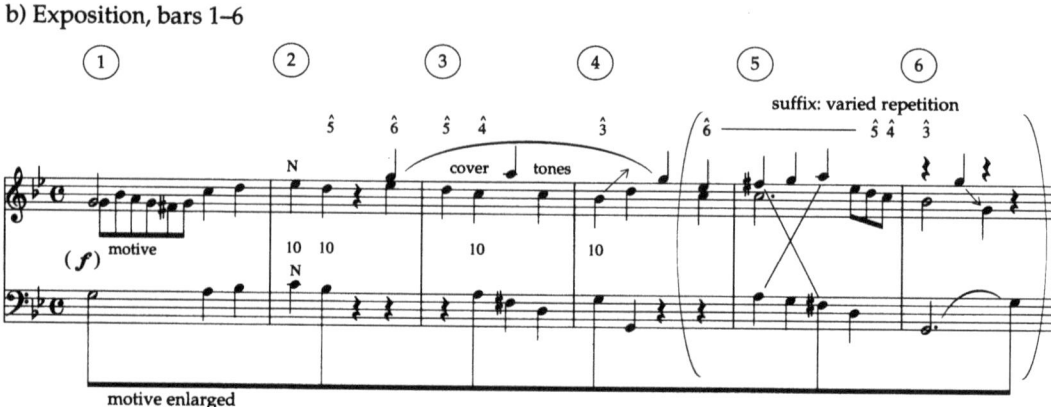

c) Recapitulation, bars 27–32

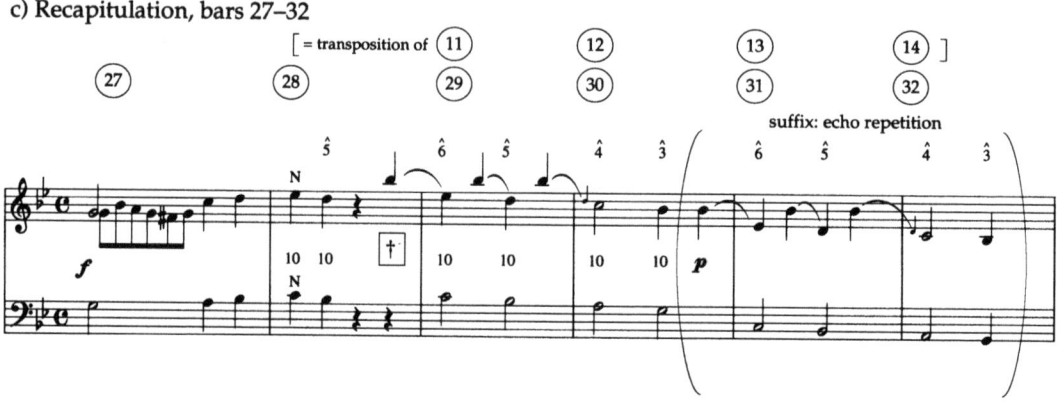

(Example 1b), and the first six bars of the recapitulation, bars 27–32 (Example 1c). In this example and those following, the symbol "†" (meaning "crux") indicates the point at which transposition to the tonic begins.[7] The crux in this piece occurs on the upbeat to bar 29, which corresponds to the upbeat to bar 11 (not shown in the example).

In the contrapuntal model shown in Example 1a, an initial arpeggiation establishes the primary melodic tone $\hat{5}$ (d^2), and a third-progression $\hat{5}$–$\hat{4}$–$\hat{3}$ follows in parallel tenths with the bass. Diminution in the upper voice transforms the melodic progression into $\hat{5}$–$\hat{6}$–$\hat{5}$–$\hat{4}$–$\hat{3}$; a two-bar suffix then repeats the $\hat{6}$–$\hat{5}$–$\hat{4}$–$\hat{3}$ ending.[8] In the exposition sketched in Example 1b, Bach approaches the primary melodic tone $\hat{5}$ with a set of outer-voice tenths culminating in the simultaneous accented upper neighbors e♭^{2} and c^1 on the downbeat of bar 2, preparing the tenths that will accompany the upper part in the next two bars; he also adds a covering voice to bars 3–4. In the suffix of bars 5–6, Bach extends the upper neighbor $\hat{6}$ until the final beat of bar 5 and intensifies the covering voice as the outer voices exchange between A and F♯. The immediate impetus for the suffix is the rising diminution at the phrase ending in bar 4, which calls forth a repetition that ends with a falling diminution. (See the rising and falling arrows in Example 1.) But there may be another reason for the suffix. The intensification of the covering voice in bars 5–6 not only emphasizes the upper-voice a^2, it also emphasizes the bass note f♯ by voice exchange. As the annotations "motive" and "motive enlarged" in Example 1b suggest, the bass of bars 1–6 enlarges the opening six-note motive in the right-hand part, an enlargement made possible only by the addition of the two extra bars in the suffix. Thus, to some extent, the two-bar suffix, conventional though it is, arises from a development of the opening flourish in bar 1.

Bach's recapitulation, sketched in Example 1c, restates only the first two bars of the exposition, at which point the crux occurs on the upbeat to bar 29. Something remarkable happens in the next four bars. Although Bach ends the repetition of the opening phrase on the upbeat to bar 29, the first six bars of the recapitulation (bars 27–32) nonetheless recreate the main phrase-rhythmic features of the first six bars of the exposition: the melodic pattern $\hat{5}$–$\hat{6}$–$\hat{5}$–$\hat{4}$–$\hat{3}$ of the upper voice, in tenths with the bass, plus the two-bar suffix, now heard as a transposition of the echo repetition in bars 13–14 of the exposition. The melodic groupings in the first six bars of the recapitulation differ from those in the exposition, but the main tonal and phrase-rhythmic features remain. As a result, the listener who follows the stepwise lines of Bach's piece enjoys a double recognition in bars 29–32. As these bars recreate both bars 11–14 and bars 3–6 of the exposition, Bach makes explicit what was initially a concealed relationship between those two earlier passages: the connection between bars 11–14

---

7. The term "crux" originates in Ralph Kirkpatrick's work on the keyboard sonatas of Domenico Scarlatti, although Kirkpatrick uses the term in a slightly different way, to describe "the meeting point in each half of the thematic material which is stated in parallel fashion at the ends of both halves with the establishment of the closing tonality." See his *Domenico Scarlatti* (Princeton: Princeton University Press, 1953), p. 255.
8. The term "suffix" refers to subordinate music added to the end of a phrase, the *Anhang* of eighteenth-century theory. See William Rothstein, *Phrase Rhythm in Tonal Music* (New York: Schirmer Books, 1989), pp. 70–73.

and 3–6 becomes audible to the listener. As Bach makes this connection, one begins to sense that the different sections have arisen from a development of the opening phrase.

Many of C. P. E. Bach's sonata movements use similar techniques in the recapitulation, although most have transitional music in the exposition that the composer must negotiate in the recapitulation. Bach's handling of the recapitulation is no less ingenious in these longer works. For the remainder of this paper, I have chosen two sonata movements that illustrate how transposed music recreates earlier progressions in such a way that all the sections can be heard as evolving from the same tonal issues. Before turning to these examples, however, it might be well to consider how Bach designs his exposition and recapitulation in these works.

Figure 1 shows two designs that Bach adopts for his expositions and recapitulations. I will term these designs Plan A and Plan B. Shaded regions in Figure 1 indicate music in the secondary key of the exposition; as in Example 1, the symbol "†" indicates the position of the crux. These plans do not exhaust the possibilities for the exposition and recapitulation, of course; but they do represent two of the most common strategies. I have chosen them for their especially straightforward use of transposition.

C. P. E. Bach's expositions normally consist of three basic phrases, which I will call the *opening phrase, transitional phrase,* and *closing phrase*. The opening phrase typically leads from I to I, as in the G minor *Probestück* just discussed, or from I to V, as in Plans A and B; the transitional phrase aims for V of a new key; and the closing phrase confirms the modulation by ending with a perfect cadence in the new key. In the two plans given in Figure 1, the closing phrase consists of two subphrases: a lead-in approaching the tonic of the new key, and a cadential progression approaching the confirming cadence. Thus C. P. E. Bach's closing phrases are not quite like the "second themes" of the Classic-period sonata form, which usually begin on a root-position tonic of the new key and consist of more than one phrase. Instead, the closing phrase more closely resembles the ending segment of a Baroque *Fortspinnung* type: a single phrase with a large cadential function.[9] If music follows the cadence in the new key, I will term that music the *postcadential phrase*. The postcadential phrase, which counts as a large suffix to the exposition, may refer back to the opening phrase, as in Plan A, whereas in other cases it introduces a new subject not explicitly based on the opening.

Plan A shows the simplest way of handling the recapitulation. Here Bach repeats the opening phrase (with little or no variation), omits the modulating transitional phrase, and transposes the entire closing phrase. The V chord that ends the opening phrase in the recapitulation corresponds to the V in a new key that ended the transitional phrase in the exposition. Plan B is probably Bach's most common strategy for the recapitulation. It follows Plan A in all respects

---

9. In other movements the closing phrase more closely resembles the "second theme" of the Classic period sonata by beginning on a root-position tonic of the new key; see, for example, the D minor Sonata H.208 (W.57/4), first movement. David Schulenberg gives a valuable account of C. P. E. Bach's expositions and their relation to Baroque and Classic procedures in *The Instrumental Music of Carl Philipp Emanuel Bach*, pp. 100–106.

Figure 1 Two plans for C. P. E. Bach's expositions and recapitulations

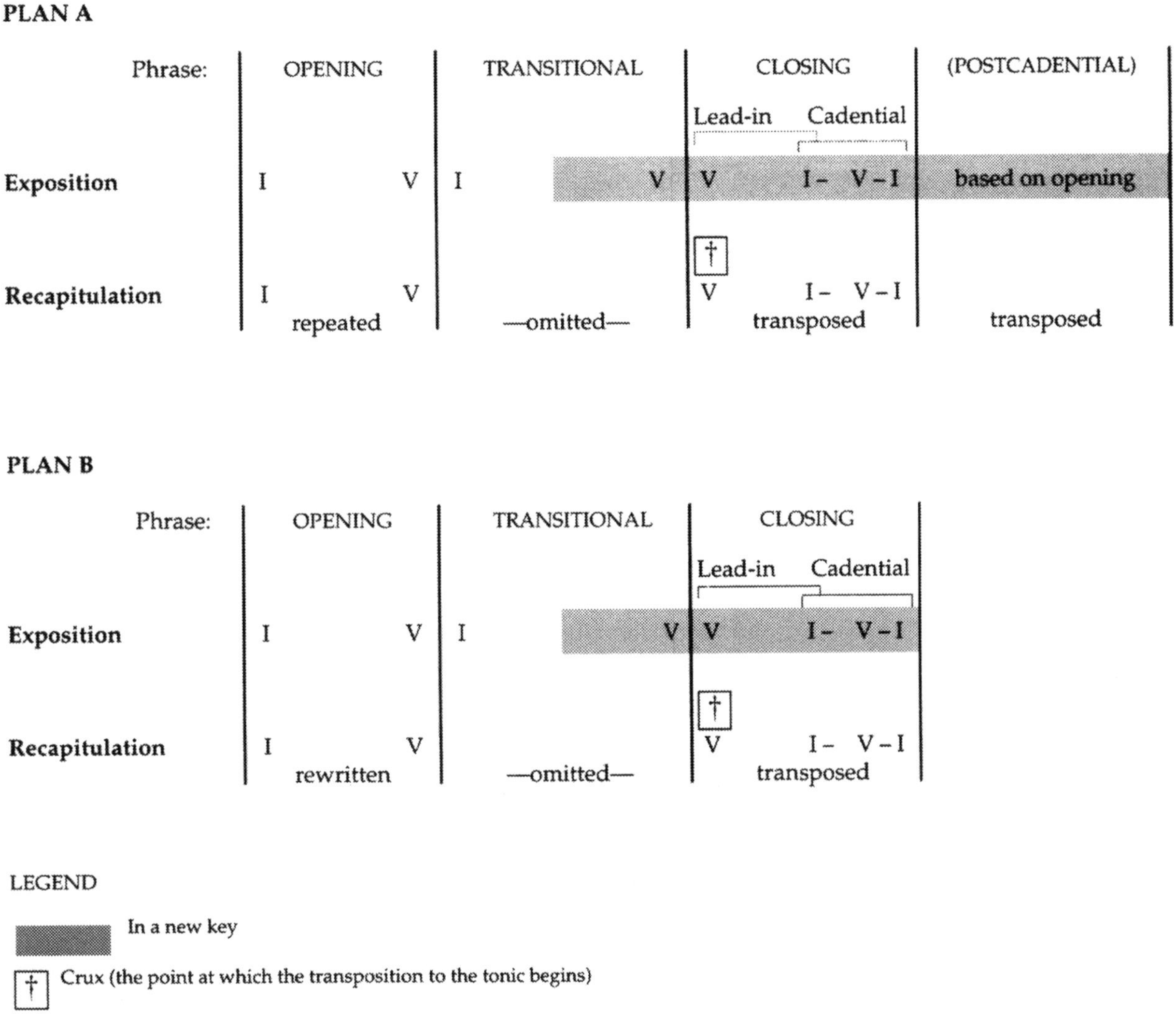

PLAN A

Phrase:	OPENING	TRANSITIONAL	CLOSING	(POSTCADENTIAL)
			Lead-in Cadential	
Exposition	I V	I	V V I– V–I	based on opening
Recapitulation	I V	—omitted—	† V I– V–I	transposed
	repeated		transposed	transposed

PLAN B

Phrase:	OPENING	TRANSITIONAL	CLOSING
			Lead-in Cadential
Exposition	I V	I	V V I– V–I
Recapitulation	I V	—omitted—	† V I– V–I
	rewritten		transposed

LEGEND

▬ In a new key

† Crux (the point at which the transposition to the tonic begins)

but one: rather than simply repeating the opening phrase in the recapitulation, he rewrites it. If the opening phrase leads to I in the exposition, Bach will almost always rewrite it in the recapitulation; he will often do so when the opening phrase leads to V as well. In both plans, he transposes the entire closing phrase with only such adjustments as are needed to invert the level of transposition.

With these observations in place, we now turn to sonata movements based on these two plans. In each movement, the straightforward transposition scheme of the recapitulation gives the work an unusually clear formal design. At the same time, the listener enjoys the kind of double recognition that I noted earlier in the G minor *Probestück*. The transposed music will recreate progressions heard in the earlier sections, restating, summarizing, and resolving the tonal tensions of the entire movement. These relations between the transposed music and the earlier sections enable the composer to transcend the mechanical effect that such literal transposition might have produced.

The simple design of Plan A underlies what is perhaps Bach's best known sonata movement, the opening of the F minor Sonata H.173 (W.57/6).[10] This work, made famous in part by Forkel's celebrated review, in part by its probable influence on Beethoven's first published piano sonata, must be counted among Bach's finest, not least because of the innovative tonal structure of its development section.[11] But even more impressive in this piece is the way in which the three main sections work together.

Example 2 presents a middleground reading of the first movement of H.173, with exposition and recapitulation aligned for comparison. Headings across the top of the example show the main phrases of the movement, along with their subphrases. In this example I use the terms *presentation phrase* and *continuation phrase* that William Caplin has devised for the two subphrases of an eight-bar sentence.[12]

Bach designed the exposition of H.173 as four main phrases, each of which has a basic length of eight bars. The opening and transitional phrases are sentences; the closing phrase consists of a lead-in and cadential subphrase; and the postcadential phrase is an eight-bar period. Bach modifies the eight-bar lengths by adding a suffix to the transitional phrase (the dominant pedal point in bars 16–19) and by overlapping the lead-in and cadential subphrases of the closing phrase at bar 23, transforming the closing phrase into a seven-bar length. A slightly different transformation lengthens the postcadential phrase by two bars, as Bach elongates the after-phrase of this eight-bar period.[13]

As the exposition of H.173 unfolds, Bach gradually introduces chromatic elements that will become the central issue around which the movement evolves.

---

10. For a facsimile of the first edition of H.173, see *The Collected Works for Solo Keyboard*, ed. Darrell Berg, Vol. 2, pp. 360–68. Reliable modern editions include those edited by Schenker (Universal Edition No. 548b, pp. 66–75) and Carl Krebs (Kalmus Piano Library 3092, pp. 108–15), but with the following emendations: in bars 53–54 read B♭♭ for all the B♭s; in bars 57–58 read E♭♭ for all the E♭s. The double flats that Schenker puts in parentheses in bars 53–54 and bar 58 of his edition are indeed in Bach's original edition, written as single flats slightly larger than normal. David Schulenberg discusses this passage in *The Instrumental Music of Carl Philipp Emanuel Bach*, pp. 114–15.

11. Johann Nikolaus Forkel, "Ueber eine Sonate aus Carl Philipp Emanuel Bachs dritter Sonatensammlung für Kenner und Liebhaber, in F moll, S. 30. Ein Sendschreiben an Hrn. von * *," in *Musikalischer Almanach für Deutschland auf das Jahr 1784* (Leipzig, 1784), pp. 22–38. Relations between this movement and the first movement of Beethoven's Op. 2, No. 1, have been noted by scholars at least as far back as Dino Sincero, "La 'Sonata' di Filippo Emanuele Bach," *Rivista Musicale Italiana* 5 (1898), pp. 682–83. To my knowledge, the first to find evidence for such a relation in Beethoven's sketch work on Op. 2, No. 1, was Oswald Jonas. See Jonas's "Bemerkungen zur Komposition" in his edition of C. P. E. Bach's *Kurze und leichte Klavierstücke mit veränderten Reprisen* (Universal Edition No. 13311), p. 5.

12. Caplin's account of the sentence appears in his *Classical Form: A Theory of Formal Functions for the Instrumental Music of Haydn, Mozart and Beethoven* (New York: Oxford University Press, 1998); see especially Chapter 3. In the present essay I have adopted some of Caplin's terms without employing his entire system; readers interested in his approach should consult his work directly. A valuable discussion of the eight-bar sentence may also be found in Janet Schmalfeldt, "Towards a Reconciliation of Schenkerian Concepts with Traditional and Recent Theories of Form," *Music Analysis* 10/3 (1991), pp. 233–87; see especially pp. 239ff.

13. Bars 31–34 elongate bars 28–29. The term "after-phrase" for the second phrase of a period follows Rothstein, *Phrase Rhythm*, pp. 18–19.

As the top staff of Example 2 shows, this process begins when he adds two chromatic neighboring progressions near the beginning of his modulating transitional phrase: f♯^{2}–g^2 in bar 10, and b^2–c^3 in bar 12. The continuation in bars 13–16 then modulates in a conventional way, reinterpreting I as IV of V then passing through I of V in bar 15 on the way to V of V in bar 16. Bach varies this conventional modulatory progression, however, in a way that highlights the chromatic note B and points toward future events. His usual way of moving from I to the passing I of V is to lead the outer voices in tenths, with a stepwise falling bass. Here, however, tenths appear only at the beginning and end of the progression (bars 13 and 15); a voice-exchange pair in the outer voices substitutes for the intermediate tenths. This voice-exchange pair develops the B–C idea of bar 12, while also introducing a melodic augmented second in the upper part from bar 13 to bar 14. Bach's modulation thus goes beyond his usual skillful introduction of the leading tone: chromatic elements assume increasing emphasis as the movement unfolds.[14]

These chromatic elements introduced in the transitional phrase assume even greater prominence as the exposition continues. First, the obsessively repeated F♯–G idea above the dominant pedal point in bars 16–20 develops the chromatic neighboring progression of bar 10 (note the triplets in both cases), then the chromaticism erupts into the titanic diminished seventh chords that begin the closing phrase in bar 20. These diminished seventh chords develop the augmented second idea of bars 13–14 in two ways, first by setting the outer voices with the interval B-over-A♭, then by using melodic augmented seconds to exchange the outer voices in the flourish that announces the beginning of the cadential progression leading into bar 23. Thus the chromatic elements introduced in bars 9–12 gain ever-increasing prominence and guide the modulation to the minor dominant.

Bach's development section continues reworking these chromatic elements in a bold and ingenious manner. He works out a progression in descending major thirds connecting the minor dominant that ends the exposition to the dominant seventh chord that ends the development section; the bass moves C–A♭–F♭(/E♮)–C. Against this pattern of falling major thirds, he writes an upper line that descends chromatically from C through C♭ to B♭, the B♭ preparing the return of the A♭ that begins the recapitulation. At two points in the development section, he provides enharmonically equivalent consonant settings of dissonances heard in the exposition: a minor third A♭–C♭ beginning in bar 49 reinterprets the striking augmented second A♭–B of bar 20, and the major third A♭–F♭ in bars 53–54 reworks the diminished fourth A♭–E of the phrase ending in bars 7–8. (Example 2 illustrates the diminished fourth/major third with a curly bracket.) Indeed, the stunning F♭ triad in bars 54–57, which forms the focal point of the development section, sets both leading tones of the exposi-

---

14. On the skillful introduction of the leading tone, see Bach, *Essay*, p. 434; *Versuch*, Part II (Berlin, 1762), Chapter 41, §8, p. 330. A point of clarification on the reading of bars 13–16: the C minor triad in bar 15 is a chord produced by bass arpeggiation against a prolonged F root; it also provides an initial consonant setting of a passing e♭^{2} between f^2 and d^2. When the root F returns at the end of bar 15, the e♭^{2} does not simply hold to become a dissonant seventh; instead, it gives way to a d^2 which anticipates the fifth of the G major triad that arrives in bar 16.

Example 2 C. P. E. Bach, Sonata in F minor, H.173 (W.57/6), first movement: middleground analysis

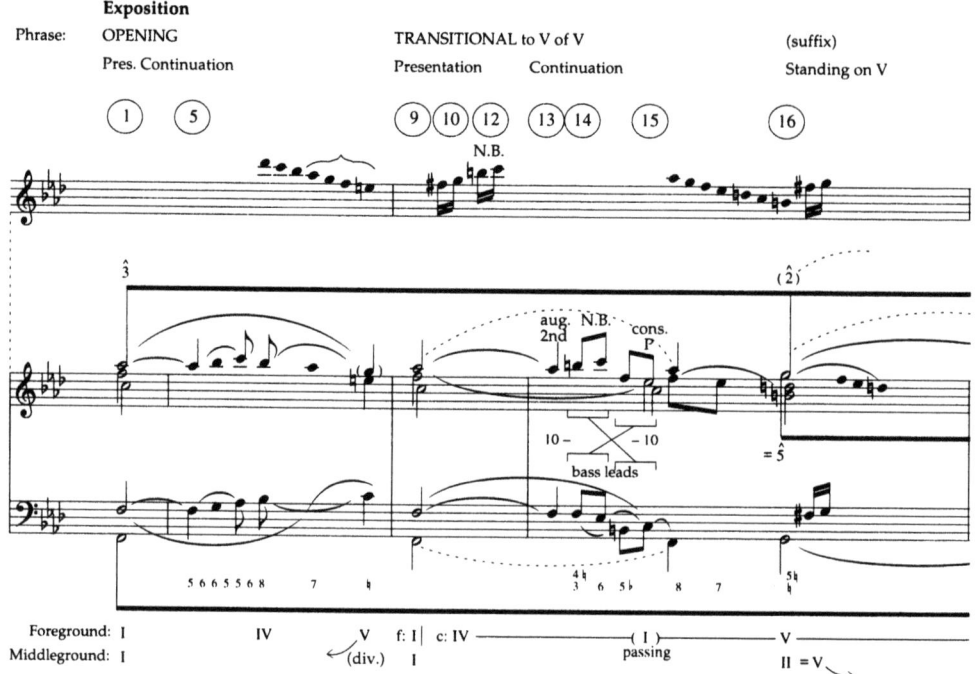

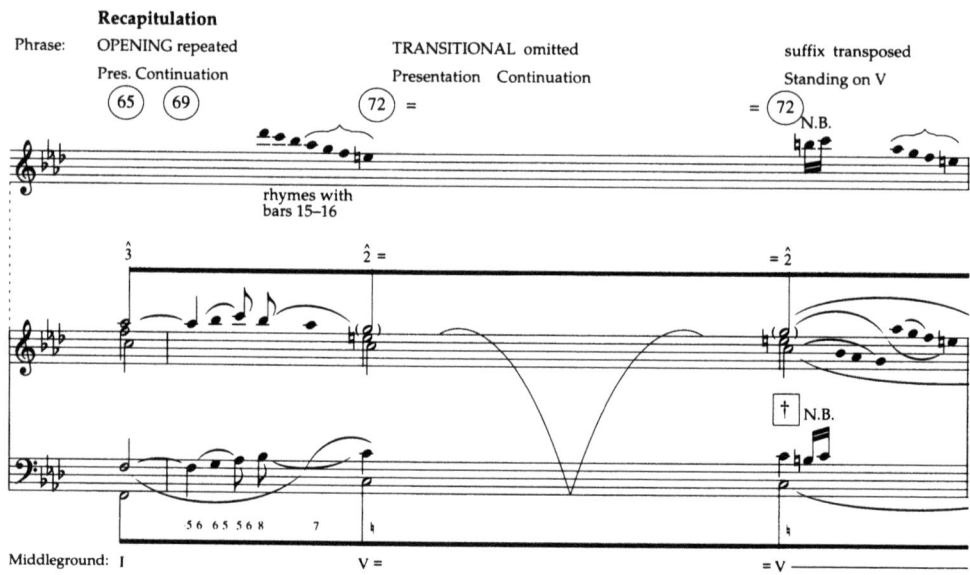

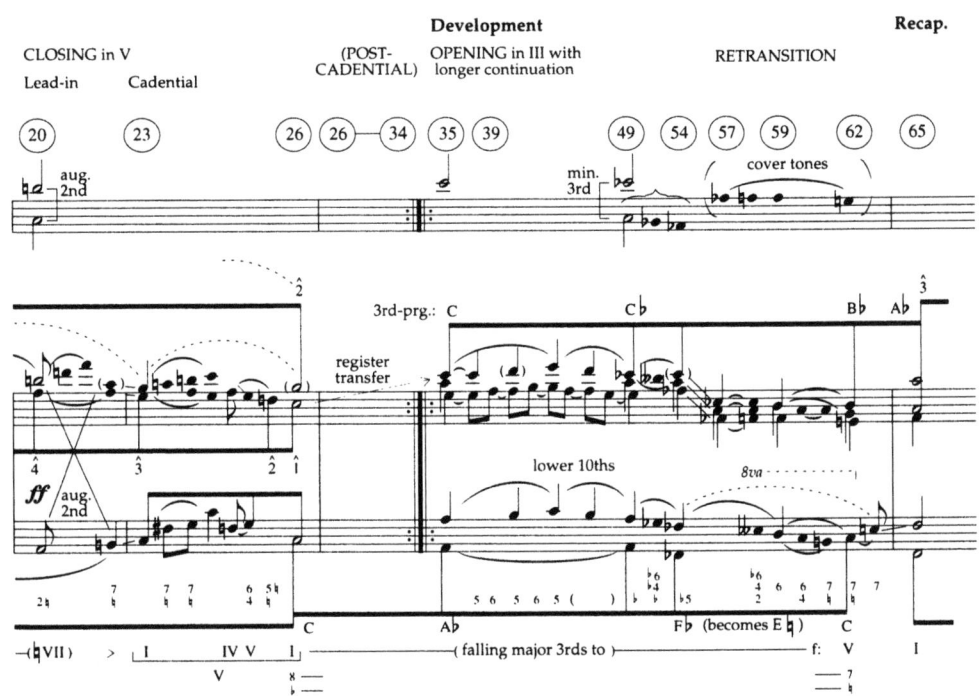

tion, E and B, to be consonant with each other. Thus some of the prominent chromatic notes in the exposition finally become temporarily stabilized in the development section when they assume an enharmonically equivalent guise.

The recapitulation will take up these chromatic notes and restore their original tendencies in the key of F minor. As the lower system of Example 2 illustrates, what was originally the obsessive F♯–G idea above the dominant pedal point in bars 16–20 of the exposition now becomes B–C in the transposed closing phrase of bars 72–76, as if to revoke the chromatic progression C♭–B♭ of the development section. In addition, Bach revisits the diminished fourth A♭–E at the end of the opening and transitional phrases in the recapitulation, now highlighting the return of the leading tone E to the domain of F minor. Thus transposition in this case serves not only the formal requirement of resolving the large-scale dissonance created by the modulation in the exposition. It also serves to restore, and emphasize through surface repetition, the tonal tendencies that the enharmonic progressions in the development section had overthrown.

In this F minor Sonata, Bach shows a mastery of chromatic harmony for which he was justly famous in his time. Chromatic elements grow in prominence as the work unfolds, they finally assume provisional stability in the development section, then they return with comparable emphasis in the recapitulation as their original tendencies in F minor are restored. Bach was no less a master of diatonic writing, however, and some of his more modest works show an equally uncanny ability to use simple transposition in his sonata recapitulations. Our next work, the A major *Probestück* H.72 (W.63/3), first movement, is of this type.[15]

Bach based the A major *Probestück* on Plan B, which is to rewrite the opening phrase, omit the transitional phrase, and transpose the closing phrase. In the exposition, he writes the opening phrase (bars 1–8) and transitional phrase (bars 9–16) as eight-bar periods; the closing phrase consists of a four-bar lead-in (bars 17–20) overlapping with a four-bar cadential phrase aiming for a perfect cadence in bar 23. A parenthesis delays the cadence, however, until bar 28. In the recapitulation, after rewriting the opening phrase, he departs from literal transposition at two points in the closing phrase. First, he changes the transposition level from a fourth above to a fifth below at the end of bar 59; second, he rewrites the parenthesis beginning in bar 63, in part to regain the high register for the final cadence in bar 68. (Why he might have made these changes in the recapitulation will become clear when we consider the middleground structure.) In this piece, as in the F minor Sonata just discussed, all the sections develop around issues of tonal tendencies, except that now those tendencies involve diatonic elements.

In the opening phrase of the A major *Probestück*, Bach establishes a compositional idea that he will develop throughout the piece (Example 3). He treats the stable scale degrees $\hat{1}$ and $\hat{5}$ as though they tend to move toward the active scale degrees that serve as their upper neighbors. When the time comes for these

---

15. For editions of the *Probestücke*, see note 5 above. For the A major *Probestück*, see *The Collected Works for Solo Keyboard*, ed. Darrell Berg, Vol. 1, p. 46; and the *Sechs Sonaten*, ed. Erich Doflein, Vol. 1, pp. 12–13.

Example 3 C. P. E. Bach, A major *Probestück*, Sonata H.72 (W.63/3), first movement, bars 1–4

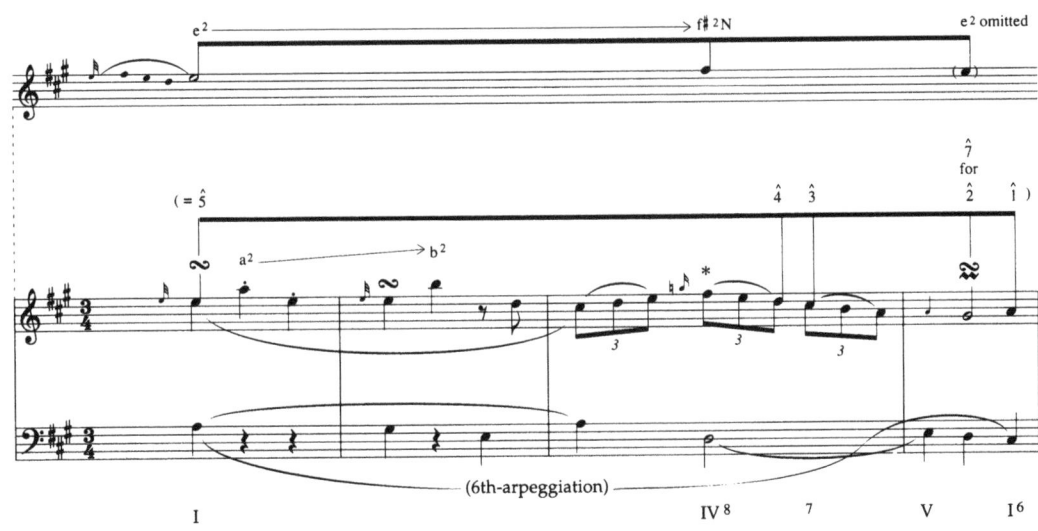

active elements to return to their stable points of origin, however, they are left hanging, resolved only implicitly. As Example 3 illustrates, Bach activates the dominant pitch e² from the start, with the snapped turn ornament (*geschnellter Doppelschlag*), then he leads the e² to its upper neighbor f♯² over subdominant harmony in bar 3, marking the f♯² for special emphasis with the short appoggiatura g². A return to e², however, occurs only implicitly. A similar progression ornaments the tonic pitch a² in this opening. Bach leads the a² to b² in bars 1–2, but he leaves the b² hanging, not literally resolved in the foreground. What begins to emerge is a reversal of tonal tendencies. The stable scale degrees move directly to their upper neighbors, but the return occurs only indirectly or implicitly.

Having set up these tendencies in his opening phrase, Bach works them out in both the exposition and recapitulation. Example 4 aligns middleground readings of the outer sections of the A major *Probestück* to illustrate how he accomplishes this impressive compositional feat. As Bach begins the modulation in the transitional phrase of the exposition, a 5–6 exchange in bar 9 introduces f♯² as upper neighbor to the primary melodic tone e². Bach will prolong this upper neighbor f♯² through the arrival on V of V in bar 16. (The descent from 3̂ to 2̂ and fifth-progression from 2̂ thus occur in an inner voice.) The primary tone returns at the beginning of the cadential part of the closing phrase in bar 20, graced by its upper neighbor again, as a kind of summary, concealed in the triplets of bars 20–22. Thus the middleground of the exposition develops the idea of leading E to F♯ but returning only indirectly to E.

Bach's foreground also expresses this idea. As the upper staff of Example 4 illustrates, he highlights an F♯ at several points (see the asterisks at bars 5, 9, 13, 21), but, except for the lead-in to bar 9, each time the F♯ appears, he undermines a direct connection back to E. (These frustrated returns to E are marked "x" in Example 4.) The F♯ rises (bar 5), it leads to E♯ rather than to E (bar 10), the

Example 4 C. P. E. Bach, A major *Probestück*, Sonata H.72 (W.63/3), first movement, exposition and recapitulation: middleground analysis

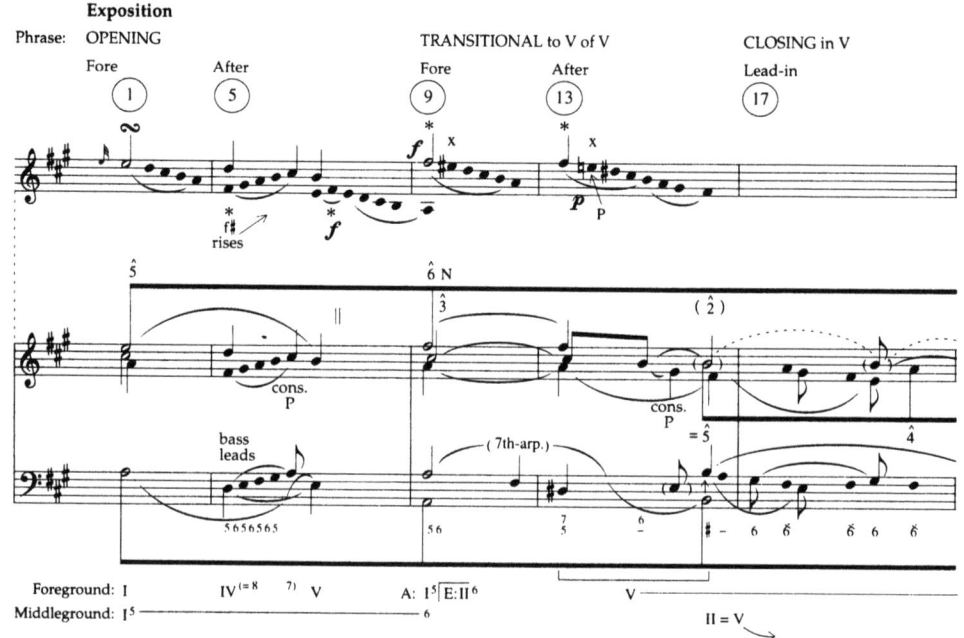

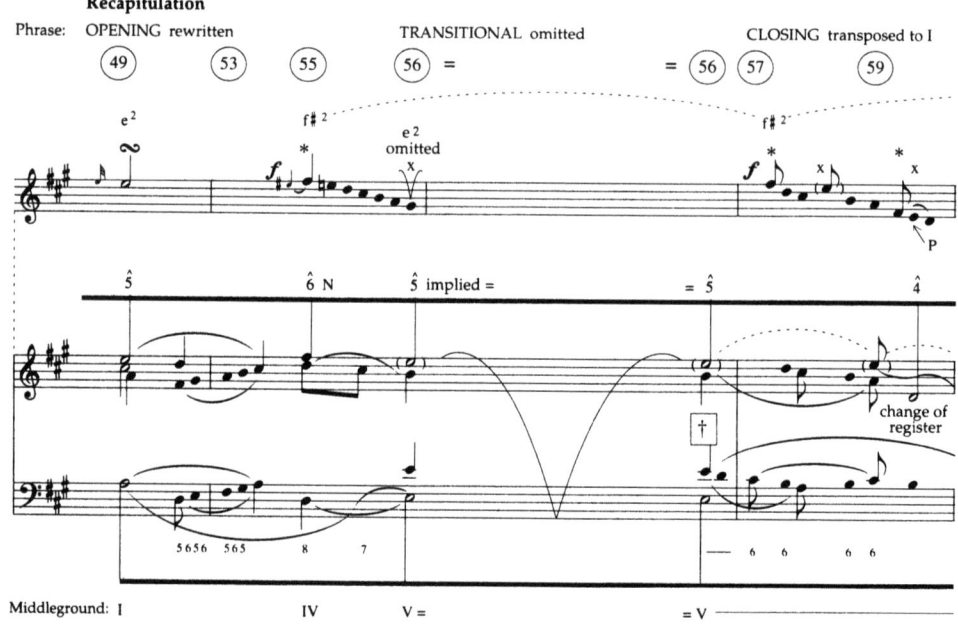

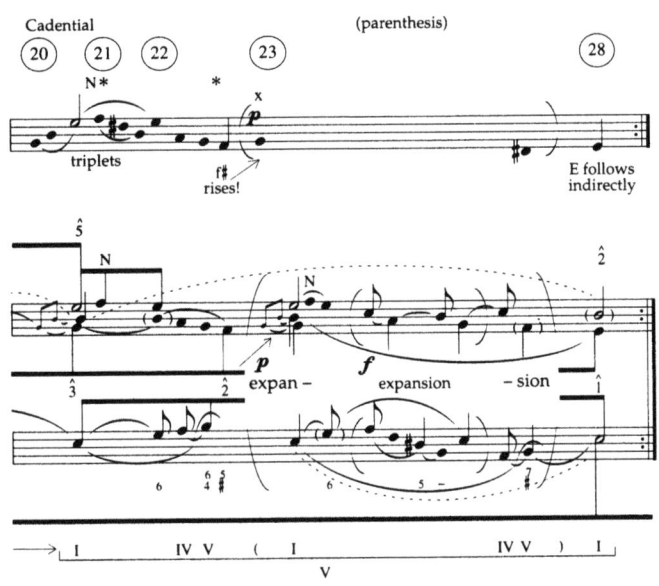

Example 5 C. P. E. Bach, A major *Probestück*, Sonata H.72 (W.63/3), first movement, bars 55–56

would-be resolution E turns out to be a passing tone (bar 14, at the sudden *piano* dynamic), and so forth. Even the conventional imperfect cadence that initiates the parenthesis in bar 23 speaks of this idea: F♯ (now heard as $\hat{2}$ of E major) can lead only indirectly to E, after the parenthesis intervenes. And even in those cases where the F♯ leads more directly to E, as in bars 21–22, Bach conceals the progression in the diminution.

Bach now faces a compositional problem in the recapitulation: how to recreate the effect of the prolonged neighboring tone $f\sharp^2$ in a section that will not modulate or prolong a harmony that might support the $f\sharp^2$. His solution is brilliant. He achieves such an effect by keeping $f\sharp^2$ melodically active without technically prolonging it. First, as Example 5 shows, he rewrites the opening phrase to introduce $f\sharp^2$ in bar 55, as part of the approach to the half cadence at the end of the opening phrase. The half-cadential diminution in bar 55 is based on the progression IV^{8-7}–V, in which the $f\sharp^2$ would normally return to e^2. As he did in the exposition, however, Bach omits the e^2 resolution. In bar 56 he leaves the $f\sharp^2$ hanging, only to pick it up a moment later in the transposed closing phrase (bar 57). As the "x" markings in Example 4 indicate, he continues to avoid a direct return to e^2 in the transposed closing phrase. (The e^2 in bar 58 and the e^1 in bar 59 cannot be considered resolutions of the $f\sharp^2$ of bar 57.) Having left the $f\sharp^2$ hanging, Bach then changes the transposition level to a fourth below the exposition in bar 59, as a way of leaving the high register open. Only after having regained the high register in the rewritten parenthesis (bar 65) does he return to the $f\sharp^2$ and provide the resolution to e^2. Thus he has recreated the effect of a composed-out neighboring tone $f\sharp^2$ in the recapitulation to answer that of the exposition, but he does so by leaving the $f\sharp^2$ melodically active, a hanging note that hovers over much of the recapitulation.

At the same time, Bach's transposed music and rewritten parenthesis develop the other issue present from the start: the tendency of B to return to A only indi-

Example 6 C. P. E. Bach, A major *Probestück*, Sonata H.72 (W.63/3), first movement, development section: middleground analysis

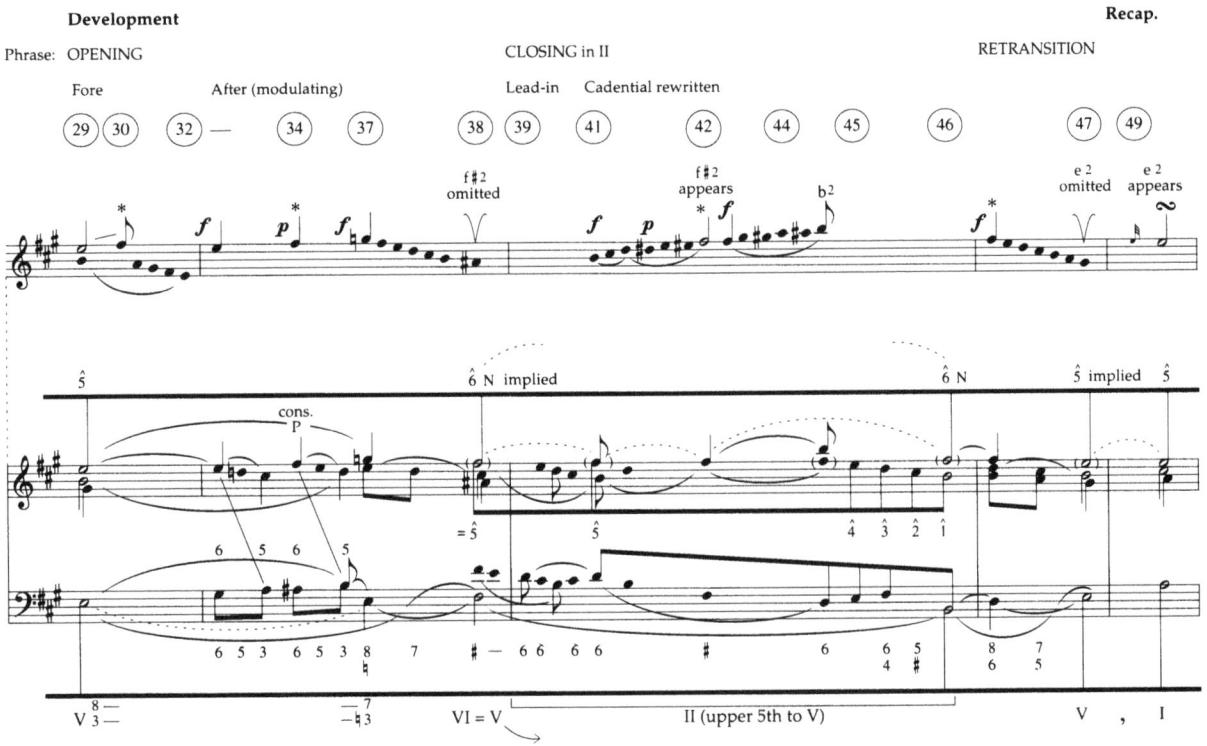

rectly. The imperfect cadence that prevented a direct progression from F♯ to E in bars 22–23 of the exposition now becomes transposed to the indirect progression B–A in the recapitulation. Thus Bach has found a way to restate the indirect progression from B to A that was also present in the opening. The rewritten parenthesis beginning in bar 63 finally provides a clear statement of the b^2–a^2 progression as well, in bars 65–66.

The relations just described in the exposition and recapitulation also help account for Bach's choice of B minor for the modulation in his development section. The middleground analysis of Example 6 illustrates that the development, like the other sections in this piece, composes out the upper neighbor $f\sharp^2$, now as the local primary tone $\hat{5}$ in B minor. As before, e^2 leads directly to $f\sharp^2$ (bars 32–34), but now it passes through the $f\sharp^2$ to approach the half cadence in B minor in bar 38, where $f\sharp^2$ is implied. The $f\sharp^2$ appears in the middle of the closing phrase in bars 42–43, leading chromatically up to b^2 in bar 44 just before the cadence. Thus by modulating to B minor in the development section Bach has not only recreated the composed-out upper neighbor F♯ of the exposition; he also provides a stable setting of its tonic image B. The quick retransition then restates the $f\sharp^2$, only to leave it hanging, precisely as the recapitulation will then do.

In the A major *Probestück*, then, all the sections develop around the central idea for the composition, which is to treat the stable tone E as though it has a tendency to move to its upper neighbor F♯, then to return from F♯ to E only indirectly or implicitly. The tonic pitch A and its upper neighbor B receive similar treatment. We have seen that Bach's recomposing of the opening phrase and his modified transposition of the closing phrase in the recapitulation served this idea by recreating structures like those heard earlier. This manner of composing testifies to Bach's sensitivity to diatonic tonal relationships and the creativity with which he used close transposition.

I began by noting that C. P. E. Bach's keyboard sonatas present a curious mix of free diminution and strict transposition, a combination which has led some scholars to sense a rigidity in his handling of the sonata form. While it may be true that some of Bach's sonatas fail to transcend the rigid effect of close transposition, in his best sonatas, like those discussed here, he found imaginative ways to use strict transposition without such an effect. In the G minor *Probestück,* he used transposition to make explicit a concealed connection between two passages in the exposition. In the F minor Sonata and the A major *Probestück,* the transposed music developed the same tonal issues that organize the other sections. Through such creative techniques, C. P. E. Bach raised the device of transposition to a fine art, with an inventiveness not so far removed from that which informed other features of his style.

Comedy and structure in Haydn's symphonies

L. Poundie Burstein

That then which seems generally the cause of laughter is the bringing together of images which have contrary additional ideas, as well as some resemblance in the principal idea: this contrast between ideas of grandeur, dignity, sanctity, perfection and ideas of meanness, baseness, profanity, seems to be the very spirit of burlesque; and the greatest part of our raillery and jest are founded upon it.

Francis Hutcheson, Thoughts on Laughter (1758)

The foundations of humor

"Lowliness" and humor

As the second movement of Haydn's Symphony No. 93 draws to its conclusion, the exquisite opening subject is stated for the first time by the full orchestra in a resounding *forte* (bar 71). But the expected peroration is soon cut short. After two bars the music becomes increasingly quiet, increasingly broken up into shorter and shorter fragments. Eventually it becomes immobilized on the third C–E, sounded by flutes and violins, whose entrances are separated by delicate pauses, much as if the incomplete theme is nodding off to sleep. In bar 80, however, it is rudely awakened by the two bassoons, who interrupt the reverie with a unison low C, played *fortissimo*. The sound is reminiscent of someone attacked by a bout of flatulence – a striking contrast with the refinement of the rest of the movement.

This well-known passage exemplifies the humor for which Haydn has long been celebrated. Yet one might well wonder how such coarseness can find a place within a serious work of art. And, putting this question within the larger framework of humor in general, one might ask: why do people delight in the crassness, silliness, and degradations of comedy?

The humor equation

The answer lies largely in the ability of comedy to provide a counterweight to life's disappointments and failures. The joys of striving toward ideals are often accompanied by a sense of shame and frustration as we fall short of our goals. By deriding our attempts to achieve a higher, more serious, better, and "lofty" place in life, humor helps relieve the tension between such attempts and our failure to achieve them. The higher the goal, the greater the relief comedy can provide. In a way, humor celebrates excellence by recognizing the struggles that are faced in striving toward greater dignity.[1]

In humor, "lowly" aspects are always linked and thus contrasted with higher elements. By such means the derisive elements of humor differ from pure derision. The linking and contrasting of things that are somehow serious, sensible, logical, or "lofty" with things that are trivial, silly, illogical, or base creates what I shall refer to as the *humor equation*. The degree of humor directly relates to the degree of contrast between high and low elements, as well as to the persuasiveness with which the two are related.

Audiences tend to recognize only the lower side of the humor equation by focusing on the ridiculous. Skilled comedians, on the other hand, realize that the "setup" is as important to a joke as the punch line, and that the person assuming the role of the "straight man" is as vital to a comedy skit as the jokester. For a full understanding of the sources of comedy, it is important to realize that humor is not derived merely from low elements; both high and low elements must be present for comedy to exist.

For example, in Aristophanes's *Lysistrata*, the lustful intentions of the Greek women are contrasted with their grand designs to stop a war by controlling their passions (designs which are ultimately unsuccessful owing to their lack of willpower). Without this contrast between low and high, their erotic desires would not be funny, but merely pornographic. Similarly, Charlie Chaplin's tramp tickles us not simply because of his destitute state, but also because of the airs of gentility and power he adopts despite his ragged condition. And in Symphony No. 93, the crass sound of bar 80 is funny precisely because the sounds of the previous seventy-nine measures are so refined.

Appreciation of the impact of the high elements of the humor equation is particularly crucial in approaching musical humor. Within a serious piece of music, there is a limit to the emphasis a composer can place on the low end of the humor equation. Other arts allow for a clearer distinction between a "persona" projected by the work (for instance, a character in a novel or play) and the work's creator. (For example, it is obvious that Mrs. Malaprop's absurdly mangled English results from Sheridan's mastery of the language.) But it is relatively difficult to make such distinctions in music. As a result, an excess of silliness might tend to mar the integrity of a composition.

This problem can be avoided if the composer emphasizes the high end of the humor equation. The advantages of stressing the serious side of a joke are well known to all good comedians. This explains why characters who intimidate us or whom we regard as powerful or exalted (such as politicians or clergymen) are prime material for humor. With such people, the serious aspect of the humor equation is so accentuated that comic contrast can easily be established. Likewise, a composer can readily create comedy in music by stressing the serious side of the humor equation, so that only a small degree of silliness is

---

1. See James K. Feibleman, *In Praise of Comedy* (1938; reprinted New York: Horizon Press, 1970), pp. 178ff.; Elder Olson, *The Theory of Comedy* (Bloomington: Indiana University Press, 1968), pp. 13–14; Arthur Asa Berger, *An Anatomy of Humor* (New Brunswick: Transaction Publishers, 1993), p. 11; and Marcel Gutwirth, *Laughing Matter: An Essay on the Comic* (Ithaca: Cornell University Press, 1993), pp. 59ff., among others.

required to create humor. By such means, musical humor can be created without having to resort to truly ludicrous effects.

Of course, the musical idiom of the Classical period incorporates a panoply of styles and topics ranging from learned contrapuntal writing, stately marches, and eerie *ombra* passages on the "lofty" side to *opera buffa* elements and raucous peasant dances on the "lowly" side.[2] In the hands of a master composer who is also a master humorist, this musical language is an unsurpassed means for the creation of the most varied kinds of compositional comedy.

Incongruity and humor

Though incongruity is vital to humor, humor cannot derive from incongruity alone. I find untenable the notion that humor results merely from the reconciliation of incongruities.[3] This theory arises partly out of a confusion between humor and wit. Although humor and wit are frequently treated as equivalent in everyday language, they are not quite the same. Wit is a kind of cleverness that uncovers and expresses paradoxical relationships between unlike things. Though witty statements can be quite funny, they are not necessarily so. The resolution of incongruities may indeed form the main source of wit, but one should avoid concluding that such resolution by itself constitutes the essence of humor, for incongruously linked things are by no means always funny.[4]

Consider the following passages:

> But ere the crown he looks for live in peace,
> Ten thousand bloody crowns of mothers' sons
> Shall ill become the flower of England's face.
> (Shakespeare, *Richard the Second*, III.iii.94–96)

> Now is the winter of our discontent
> Made glorious summer by this sun [son] of York,
> (Shakespeare, *Richard the Third*, I.i.1–2)

These two ingenious puns of Shakespeare each set up incongruities, yet these incongruities do not involve a conflict between high and low interpretations. The puns actually ennoble both their subjects; nothing is trivialized. As a result, these quotations display much wit, but no humor.

If a pun is to be funny, it must link a sensible interpretation of a word to a trivial or absurd interpretation. Such a linkage occurs in the following joke:

2. See Leonard Ratner, *Classic Music: Expression, Form, and Style* (New York: Schirmer Books, 1980), pp. 9–26 and 386ff.
3. See, for instance, Stephen Leacock, *Humor and Humanity* (New York: Henry Holt, 1938); Mary K. Rothbart and Diana Pien, "Elephants and Marshmallows: A Theoretical Synthesis of Incongruity-Resolution and Arousal Theories of Humor," in *It's a Funny Thing, Humour*, ed. Anthony Chapman and Hugh Foot (Oxford: Pergamon Press, 1977), pp. 37–40; Jerry M. Suls, "Cognitive Processes in Humor Appreciation," in *Handbook of Humor Research*, ed. Jeffrey Goldstein and Paul McGhee (Berlin: Springer-Verlag, 1983), pp. 81–99; various essays in *The Philosophy of Laughter and Humor*, ed. John Morreall (Albany: State University of New York Press, 1987); and John Morreall, "Enjoying Incongruity," *Humor: International Journal of Humor Research* 2/1 (1989), pp. 1–18.
4. For more on the distinction between wit and humor, see C. S. Lewis, *Studies in Words* (Cambridge: Cambridge University Press, 1960), pp. 86ff.; Charles Gruner, *Understanding Laughter* (Chicago: Nelson-Hall, 1978), pp. 91ff.; and Thomas MacArthur, ed., *The Oxford Companion to the English Language* (Oxford: Oxford University Press, 1992), p. 1116.

> Why don't people become hungry in the desert?
> Because of all the sandwiches [sand which is] there!

To be sure, the difference between the logical and silly interpretations here involves little shift in status. Accordingly, this pun (like most puns involving simple word play) is not very funny.[5]

In truly funny jokes, the high and low elements must be starkly contrasted:

> Groucho Marx (as Captain Spaulding): One morning I shot an elephant in my pajamas. How he got into my pajamas, I'll never know.
>
> (*Animal Crackers*)

Despite its simple structure, this statement manages to deflate an imposing show of bravado by means of an utterly ludicrous statement. Thus, though it is less clever or incongruous than the sandwich riddle, Groucho Marx's joke is far funnier.[6]

Humor stems from the degree of incongruity only insofar as the incongruity delineates a shift in status between high and low interpretations. This notion becomes crucial when approaching humor in music. In compositions, incongruous elements are frequently associated by means of motivic parallelisms, enharmonic associations, and other musical analogies to puns. Of course, one cannot say that all such musical devices are comedic. As in literature or speech, a musical pun becomes funny only when it links passages or elements that are serious with those that are less serious.

Parody

"Clown humor"

It may appear that certain comic forms, such as burlesque or clown humor, stress only silly or foolish aspects. Such an emphasis does not negate the presence of contrast, however, for seemingly pure silliness will almost inevitably be contrasted with an unnamed, general standard.

For example, it might appear that Bottom's transformation to half man, half ass in Shakespeare's *A Midsummer Night's Dream* is an instance of pure silliness. After all, Bottom is clearly a fool from the moment he steps on the stage, and thus there seems to be no contrast with a higher element. Nevertheless, foolish as he is, Bottom has at least some dignity, and his ass's ears are funny insofar as they represent an insult to whatever little dignity he has. (Even so, the contrast becomes greater, and the situation more humorous, through Bottom's pre-

---

5. For an excellent discussion of puns, see Ralph Piddington, *The Psychology of Laughter* (New York: Gamut Press, 1963), pp. 98–104. Also, a number of incongruity-resolution humor theorists (such as those cited in note 3 above) have made insightful observations on the mechanics of puns and similar jokes, though I feel they often wrongly credit the working-out of these incongruity resolutions as the main source of humor.

6. The mechanism of humor in this joke can be further demonstrated by trying to reshape it as follows:
   > One morning I shot an elephant in my ballet tutu. How he got
   > into my ballet tutu, I'll never know.

   Though the above statement is more ludicrous than and just as incongruous as Groucho Marx's joke, it lacks a serious side – there is nothing that provides a contrast to the silliness. As a result, it is not funny.

tentious bragging as well as Titania's infatuation with him.) If Bottom had been truly deformed (so that his appearance could not be fairly compared to that of a normal person), he would inspire pity, not laughter. Here again, the degree of humor directly relates to the degree of contrast between high and low elements, regardless of whether the context explicates the opposing aspects.

Music, too, can establish humor merely by emphasizing the ridiculous. Yet such an emphasis does not deny the presence of contrast with loftier elements. After all, a certain amount of grandeur normally accompanies a performance of a symphony or other serious piece of music. Thus broad extra-musical mimicry and other obvious jests, such as may be found in Symphonies No. 60 ("Der Zerstreute") or No. 94 ("The Surprise"), are readily recognized as humorous, for they glaringly conflict with the atmosphere one expects from a symphony.[7]

Playing with musical convention

Not all of Haydn's parodies are so blatant, however. To appreciate the passages in which Haydn plays with conventions in a gentler fashion, one needs familiarity with eighteenth-century style and genres. A person totally unfamiliar with other works from Haydn's time would find nothing peculiar or humorous in the closing movements of Symphonies No. 45 ("The Farewell") and No. 46 (where the minuet returns in the midst of the finale). Those acquainted with the historical situation, however, will quickly see the mockery in these works.

The most extensive published investigation of Haydn's manipulation of convention in the service of humor may be found in Gretchen Wheelock's book, *Haydn's Ingenious Jesting With Art*. Wheelock declares that "Haydn's gambit in a musical jest is to make the simplest stock-in-trade convention opaque, its expected function indecisive, and to subvert the most familiar topic, rendering it ambiguous."[8] In her study, Wheelock examines the stylistic norms of Haydn's time and describes the various ways by which Haydn subverts them to create humor. This strategy has been used by many other analysts of Haydn. Indeed, Haydn's parody of convention – along with his use of broad mimicry – are central to most discussions of Haydn's humor in the recent literature.[9]

---

7. The most notorious example of parody in the repertoire is Mozart's "Ein musikalischer Spass." This composition can hardly be considered a true musical artwork; the antics here are so wild that they do not merely parody convention, but rather they parody the futile pretensions of lesser musicians (with Mozart temporarily adopting the persona of a mediocre composer). Even so, the humor in this piece does not come from pure silliness, for it maintains enough of a normal compositional framework to allow ready comparison with a work created with high artistic aspirations. Significantly, the writing in "Ein musikalischer Spass" is most clumsy at those moments where the musicians are traditionally expected to flaunt their skill, such as at the cadenza or the fugato section. Without such a frame of reference, this piece would not be funny, but merely bad.
8. Gretchen Wheelock, *Haydn's Ingenious Jesting With Art* (New York: Schirmer Books, 1992), p. 205.
9. See James C. Kidd, "Wit and Humor in Tonal Syntax," *Current Musicology* 21 (1976), pp. 70–82; Jane Perry-Camp, "A Laugh a Minuet: Humor in the Late Eighteenth Century," *College Music Symposium* 19 (1979), pp. 19–29; Steven E. Paul, "Comedy, Wit, and Haydn's Instrumental Music," in *Haydn Studies: Proceedings of the International Conference, Washington, D.C., 1975*, ed. Jens Peter Larsen, Howard Serwer, and James Webster (New York: Norton, 1981), pp. 450–56 (as well as Paul's Ph.D. dissertation, "Wit, Comedy, and Humour in the Instrumental Music of Franz Joseph Haydn," Cambridge University, 1980); Howard Irving, "Haydn and Laurence Sterne: Similarities in

Humor through musical contrast

The humor equation and harmonic structure

It is not necessary, however, that one side of the humor equation draw on references or material outside the composition itself. Many of Haydn's humorous works do not parody convention; rather they set up a contrast within the composition itself. The "lowly" parts in such works need not be funny in themselves. If the contrast between high and low elements is strong enough, and these elements are linked convincingly through harmonic, motivic, or other structural means, then humor will result. Humor arising from such means is responsible for some of the most brilliant and subtle examples of Haydn's comic craft.

An example of such humor may be found in the first movement of Symphony No. 78 in C minor. Nothing is overtly crude or ridiculous in this movement. Yet humor arises in the exposition as Haydn juxtaposes the earnest and the mirthful through harmonic means.

This movement begins in a *Sturm und Drang* fashion, but quickly establishes a more cheerful mood by the second theme group. The second theme group becomes increasingly boisterous until bar 48, where there is a sudden shift back to a serious mood. At this point, a somber theme appears that starkly contrasts with its jovial surroundings. This dark, *ombra* theme is more reminiscent of the first theme group, with its C–B♮–C neighbor motion, F–F♯–G passing motion, and emphasis on D♭.

That this somber section would more readily fit into a section in minor can be seen in the recapitulation, for it returns precisely within such a setting in bars 162ff. The second theme group is transposed from E♭ major to C minor here, but the measures analogous to bars 47ff. return untransposed. This untransposed passage is thoroughly compatible with the mood of the recapitulation, where the contrast set up in the exposition no longer obtains.

Example 1 shows how the somber passage (set off in this example by brackets) is tightly woven into the larger harmonic framework of the exposition, much as the analogous passage is woven into the recapitulation. Yet the passage is not reconciled to its cheerful surroundings, but rather seems shoved aside as it is swallowed by the larger E♭ major context. (Note in particular the ungainly parallel $^6_4$ chords of bars 52–53, which lead back to the key of E♭ major; the D major $^6_4$ chord here substitutes for a diminished $^6_5$ over a bass A♮.) This integrated harmonic structure helps make light of the severity of bars 47ff. by embracing them within a playful harmonic framework.

Footnote 9 (*cont.*)

Eighteenth-Century Literary and Musical Wit," *Current Musicology* 40 (1985), pp. 34–39; Hubert Daschner, *Humor in der Musik* (Wiesbaden: Breitkopf & Härtel, 1986), pp. 98–174 (*passim*); Mark Evan Bonds, "Haydn, Laurence Sterne, and the Origins of Musical Irony," *Journal of the American Musicological Society* 44/1 (1991), pp. 57–91; and Janet M. Levy, "A Source for Musical Wit and Humor," in *Convention in Eighteenth- and Nineteenth-Century Music: Essays in Honor of Leonard G. Ratner*, ed. Wye J. Allanbrook, Janet M. Levy, and William P. Mahrt (Stuyvesant, N.Y.: Pendragon Press, 1992), pp. 225–56. Most other discussions of humor and music tend to focus on the impact of surprise: see below.

Example 1 Haydn, Symphony No. 78 in C minor, first movement

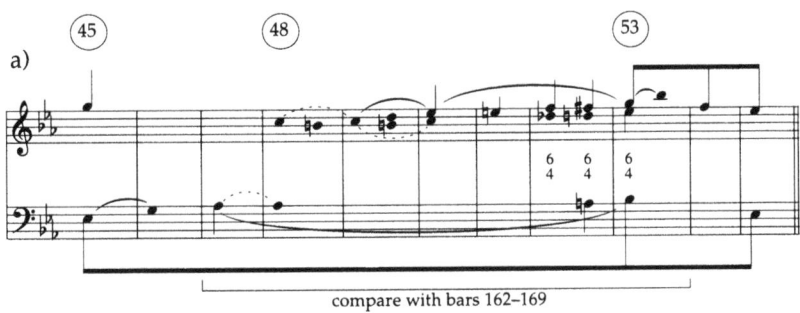

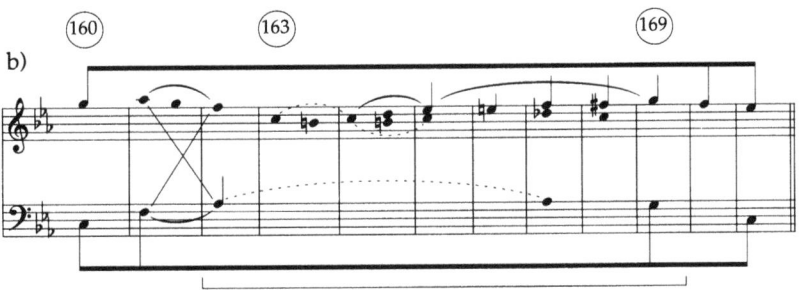

The humor equation and motivic structure

Sometimes the contrasting elements of the humor equation are linked through motivic parallelism rather than through harmonic connections. Such is the case in the first movement of Symphony No. 83 ("La Poule"), which opens with a powerfully angry theme (shown in Example 2a). This theme features a chromatic motion from $\sharp\hat{4}$ to $\hat{5}$, followed by dotted rhythms. The second theme section mimics these motives (Example 2b). Here, the once threatening $\sharp\hat{4}$ is demoted to the rank of a harmless grace note, as a wind instrument travesties the formerly ominous dotted rhythms.

Even without the motivic connections, the second theme would be funny. As suggested by this symphony's nickname, the theme reminds us of barnyard noises, and these sounds do conflict with the dignity normally associated with a symphonic work. Still, by motivically joining this giddy theme to the undeniably grim theme of the opening, Haydn increases the contrast and, correspondingly, the humor.

The fourth movement of Symphony No. 93 provides another example of contrasting elements linked motivically in the service of humor. The jocund opening theme of this finale features a neighbor-note motive (Example 3a). This motive reappears at the stormy climax of the development section, over a V of the apparent local key of F♯ minor. Here, however, the positions of the chord tones and neighbor tones are reversed (Example 3b). But the musical situation quickly restabilizes itself: the bass C♯ at the end of the development is

Example 2 Haydn, Symphony No. 83 in G minor ("La Poule"), first movement

Example 3 Haydn, Symphony No. 93 in D major, fourth movement

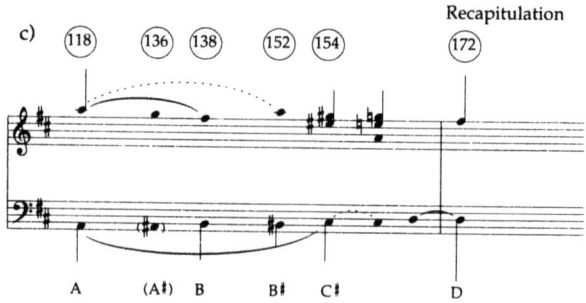

Example 4 Haydn, Symphony No. 58 in F major, fourth movement

a) First theme group of Exposition and Recapitulation

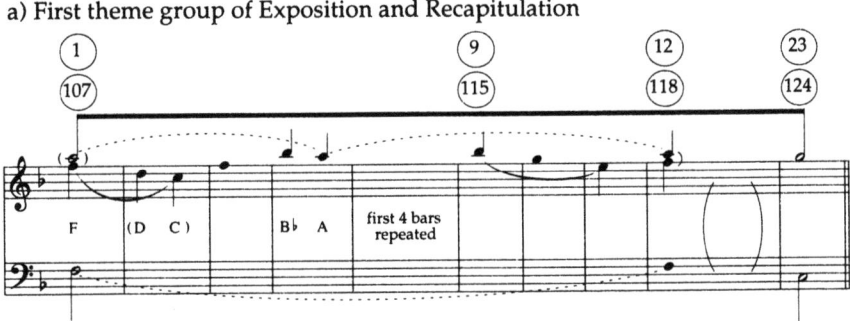

b) Second theme group of Recapitulation

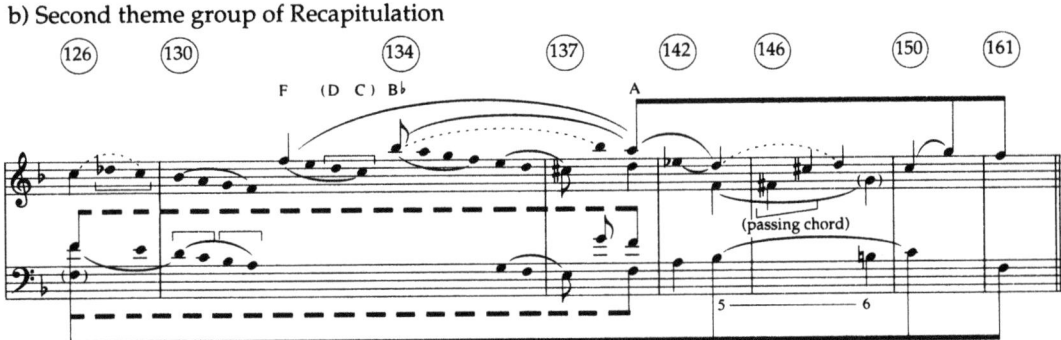

reinterpreted as a leading tone, heralding the return of the main theme in the background tonic key of D. The restoration of the neighbor-note motive in its original format and context mocks the dark pretensions of these very same notes only a few bars earlier.

The harmonic and formal structure amplify the humor here. The motion from the C♯ chord to D at the end of the development is not illogical, forming as it does a part of a large-scale ascent (see Example 3c). Yet after such a strong and lengthy emphasis on C♯ as an apparent dominant, the sudden resolution of this chord as a VII♯ of D is utterly flippant. The premature arrival of the tonic in bar 170 in particular seems to debase the rhythmic figure that in the previous measures seemed so dire and forbidding.

In the fourth movement of Symphony No. 58 (see Example 4), high and low elements are likewise linked both harmonically and motivically. The tight harmonic framework embraces even bars 146–47, with their menacing effect, incorporating them within a passing chord that elaborates a 5–6 contrapuntal motion. The motivic parallelisms occur in the middleground, as the F–(D–C)–B♭–A motive from the first theme returns in expanded form during the second theme. (This motivic connection between the first theme and second theme arises both in the exposition and the recapitulation, though it is more obvious in the recapitulation, where a registral shift in bar 134 highlights the motive; compare bar 134 with bar 33 in the score.) The various connections humorously disarm the more serious parts by embedding them within a lighthearted context.

The humor equation and surprise

The connection between surprise and humor is often emphasized, especially in writings on humor in music.[10] Yet one should be careful not to exaggerate this connection. Many things are surprising but not funny. To a certain extent, all but the most mediocre artworks contain some aspect of the unexpected. If humor were simply the product of surprise, then almost every work would be funny. The reverse is also true: elements of a work can be funny without being surprising. For example, consider the scene in Molière's *Scapin* where Scapin continually fools his master into being beaten (III.ii), or Abbott and Costello's famed "Who's on First" skit, with its hilarious repetitions. In these cases, the humor actually increases as the actions become less surprising. An example of musical humor that is not dependent on surprise may be found in Variation IV of the finale to Haydn's Symphony No. 72. Here the jovial and the serious are mixed without the benefit of surprise as a dark, lugubrious contrabass plays an inappropriately dainty melody in *stile cantante*.[11]

Nevertheless, surprise frequently does play an important auxiliary role in creating humor. A surprising event can on the surface appear quite illogical. That is, a seemingly irrational, surprising event can form one part of the humor equation if contrasted with a logically constructed underlying framework. (The *Paukenschlag* of the "Surprise" Symphony is incongruously funny not so much because it contrasts soft music with a loud sound, but rather because it contrasts a logically constructed passage with an illogically brusque event.) Also, low and high elements can be tightly conjoined and thus contrasted when something lighthearted surprisingly replaces the expected arrival of something serious. In many of Haydn's rondo finales, for example, a development section seems to lead to the arrival of a thunderous theme in a minor key. If, instead, an arrival of a lighthearted melody in a major key replaces the anticipated tragic theme, our darker expectations are mocked.

For instance, in Symphony No. 88, the development of the rondo finale seems to lead to the parallel minor; in Symphony No. 93, to the minor mediant (see Example 3 above); and in Symphony No. 64 ("Tempora mutantur") to the minor submediant. In each of these movements, however, the recapitulation in the tonic major key appears unexpectedly. The thematic return in Symphony

---

10. See Henry F. Gilbert, "Humor in Music," *The Musical Quarterly* 12/1 (1926), pp. 40–55; James C. Kidd, "Wit and Humor in Tonal Syntax," *Current Musicology* 21 (1976), pp. 70–82; Gretchen Wheelock, "Wit, Humor, and the Instrumental Music of Joseph Haydn" (Ph.D. diss., Yale University, 1979), pp. 1–6; and Susan Wollenberg, "A New Look at C. P. E. Bach's Musical Jokes," in *C. P. E. Bach Studies*, ed. Stephen L. Clark (Oxford: Clarendon Press, 1988), pp. 295–314, among many others.

11. See the discussion in Daschner, *Humor in der Musik*, pp. 155–56, regarding the comic use of low instruments.

Example 5 Haydn, Symphony No. 55 in E♭ major ("Der Schulmeister"), first movement

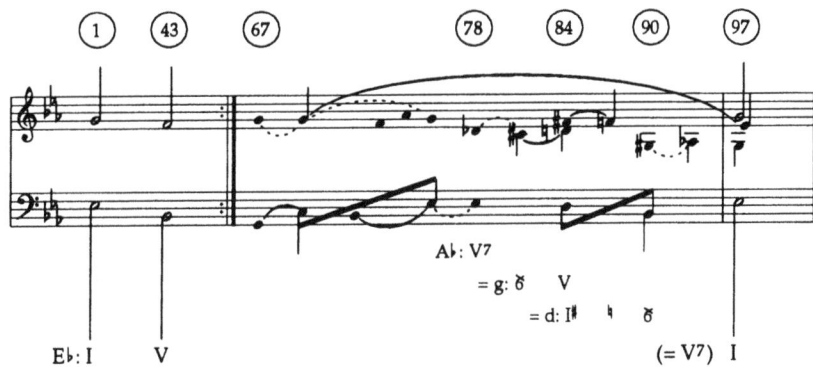

No. 64 contains a particularly brilliant twist. The development section of this work seems to end on a V^9 chord of F♯ minor (bars 109ff.). Yet the upper notes of this portentous chord are reinterpreted retrospectively as forming part of a V^7 of A major. This quickly defuses the anticipated tragic outcome by reintroducing the main theme.[12]

Another ingenious instance of a surprising harmonic reinterpretation in the service of humor occurs in the opening movement of Symphony No. 55 ("Der Schulmeister"; see Example 5). Toward the beginning of the development section, a V^7 is reinterpreted as an augmented sixth chord and unexpectedly moves toward G minor (bars 78–83). The harmonies get increasingly darker, appearing to foreshadow a bitter theme in a minor key. At its darkest point, however, there is another harmonic reinterpretation, the reverse of the earlier one: in bars 92–96, an augmented sixth chord is recast as a V^7. The entrance of the first theme in bar 97 makes sport of the more somber outcome suggested by the previous harmonies.

A further source of humor in this passage from Symphony No. 55 involves a conflict of levels. As shown in the graph of Example 5, the V^7 chord of bars 90–96 represents a background dominant. Initially, however, one expects it to function on a much lower level as an augmented sixth of primarily local significance. The contrast in purpose between these prospective and retrospective interpretations adds to the comic feeling. It is as though the lowly local chord (like Chaplin's tramp in *City Lights*) is suddenly thrust into a position of power on the largest scale. Such contrast of levels in the service of humor no doubt influenced Beethoven, who often exploited this comic technique in his compositions.

Incidentally, the succeeding section of Symphony No. 55 "corrects" the pranks of bars 67–96. The E♭ dominant seventh of bars 103–104 resolves as

---

12. Many writers have commented on Haydn's comic use of surprising thematic returns in his rondo finales; see, for instance, Wheelock, *Haydn's Ingenious Jesting*, pp. 117ff., and Charles Rosen, *The Classical Style* (New York: Norton, 1972), pp. 337ff.

expected to A♭ (compare with the E♭ chord of bars 78–83), and the augmented sixth chord of bars 111–12 resolves as expected to a dominant chord (compare with the apparent augmented sixth chord of bars 92–96).[13]

A combination of techniques: Symphony No. 90

As I have argued, humor arises not merely through an emphasis on low elements, nor merely through incongruity, but through the incongruous contrast of low and high elements. In most cases musical humor does not depend on the degree to which a situation is ridiculous; rather, it relies on the daring and conviction with which serious and playful events are combined and contrasted. Haydn achieves this through harmonic connections, motivic parallelisms, reversals of expectation, and conflicts between levels.

In the first movement of Symphony No. 90, Haydn combines all of these techniques in the service of humor. This movement opens with a stately Adagio introduction, whose opening phrase ends with the expressive cadential idea of bars 5–8. The mood suddenly brightens as the first theme of the exposition arrives in bar 17. The theme is none other than the earlier cadential idea (bars 5ff.) whose cantabile portato notes are now replaced by sprightly staccatos in *buffo* style. Yet in spite of the drastic mood change, the first phrase of the exposition is so tightly connected to the previous material that it indeed seems to parody the introduction. As Example 6a shows, a single harmonic progression spans both the regal introduction and the animated first theme. Bars 17–20 are not simply a variation of bars 5–8; they conclude the consequent phrase of the introduction, and thus form a direct structural parallel to the earlier passage. (Incidentally, in no other Haydn symphony are the introduction and first theme of the exposition so firmly bound together.)

This opening strategy produces a number of conflicts that enhance the humor. For instance, bar 17 is a moment of great consequence from the standpoint of the formal design. The harmonic structure, on the other hand, belittles the importance of this formal juncture by treating it merely as a component of a larger progression. Also, there is syntactic conflict here: bars 17–20 are uncomfortably forced to operate as an opening, though (as has already been seen in bars 5–8) this material is more suited to be the conclusion to a phrase. (Compare this with the well-known syntactic conflict in the first movement of Haydn's String Quartet in G Major, Op. 33, No. 5.) The opening theme even manifests an implied rhythmic conflict. Taken by itself, the beginning

---

13. In my view, the appearance of the so-called "false recapitulation" of bars 97–102 should not be regarded as an example of humor. Haydn used this device frequently in his symphonies written around this time. As a result, listeners sensitive to his style would not be surprised by the "false recapitulation," but would recognize it as a standard feature of Haydn's symphonic sonata form. (Accordingly, I feel that the strong reappearance of the first theme in bar 97 announces a structural return to the tonic, and is not merely an apparent tonic within the larger modulation scheme of a development section.) For more regarding the historical context and aesthetic implications of the false recapitulation, see Peter A. Hoyt, "The False Recapitulation and the Conventions of Sonata Form" (Ph.D. diss., University of Pennsylvania, 1996).

There are examples in other works where the composer seems deliberately to trick us with a false return (see, for instance, bars 158ff. of Beethoven's Sonata for cello and piano, Op. 5, No. 2, third movement). But no such tomfoolery arises in Symphony No. 55.

Comedy and structure in Haydn's symphonies

Example 6 Haydn, Symphony No. 90 in C major, first movement

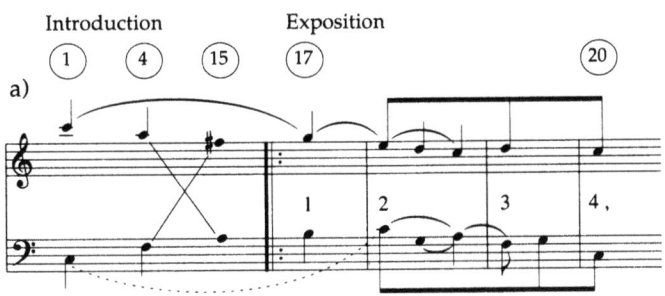

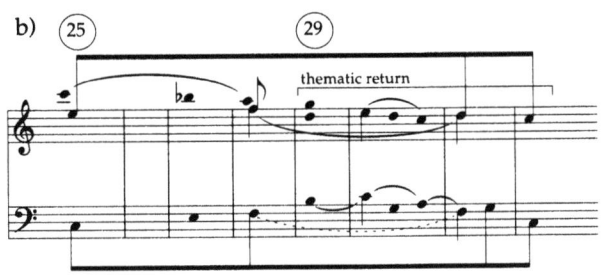

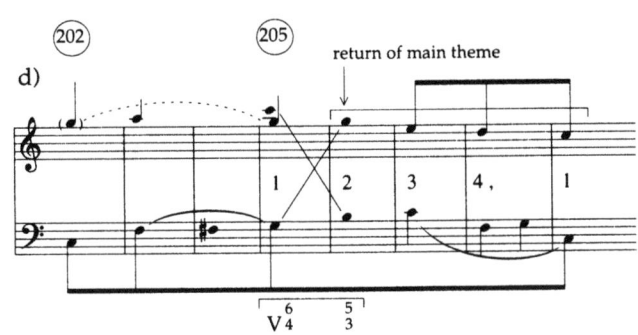

of the theme would have the character of an upbeat. Yet because of the emphasis created by the formal design, its initial bar is perceived as strong, thus expressing a kind of rhythmic conflict between the trivial and the consequential.

The task of composing a return to a theme such as this one (which seemingly begins in the middle of something) poses a problem. In surmounting this difficulty Haydn exploits the theme's comic possibilities: he introduces the thematic returns by preceding them with forceful gestures that are in turn harmonically linked to the playful theme.[14] For instance, consider the approach to the thematic return toward the end of the first theme group. Following the burlesque of the introductory material in bars 17–20, the bassoons and violas waddle in broken octaves as the flutes play a variation of material from bars 9–10. Matters soon appear to become more serious with a strong motion leading to a subdominant chord in bar 28. The resulting tension is instantly defused, however, when the first theme returns in its original lighthearted form in bars 29–32. As a result of the emphasis on F in the preceding measures, however, the harmonic structure of the theme is reinterpreted here (see Example 6b). In this context, the first tonic chord of the theme is demoted to an apparent tonic, offering consonant support to a passing tone within a deeper prolongation of the IV chord.

A sudden decrease in tension also occurs at the repeat of the exposition. The vehement, reiterated drum strokes on G in the timpani and low strings at the end of the exposition are quickly transformed into the *buffo* repeated notes of the opening theme. A similar but even greater contrast occurs at the beginning of the recapitulation. During the development, material derived from the first theme is treated with the utmost seriousness, undergoing intricate contrapuntal treatment. As shown in Example 6c, the development section is structured by a large expansion of a third-motion from G to E, a motive which relates to the initial notes of the first theme. This motivic structure is realized through a chain of intense modulations which lead to an apparent V of A minor. Yet once again, the tension is defused as the first theme is recapitulated in its original, much less serious form in bar 153, as if mocking the ardent aspirations of the thematic material in the development section.

After the introductory section, the main theme is treated in a serious manner only at the end of the second theme group (bars 84–87 and 206–209). Here, the theme no longer apes the beginning of a phrase, but arises firmly and comfortably as a phrase close. Furthermore, Haydn precedes the theme at these points with a cadential $^6_4$ (Example 6d). This cadential $^6_4$ chord forces a rhythmic reinterpretation of the theme, causing the first bar of the theme to be heard in its more "natural" state as an upbeat bar. As a result, for the first time in the piece the theme arises in its "appropriate" syntactic and rhythmic setting. It is as though the theme matured from its prankish youth to become an upstanding member of its musical environment. Haydn seems to celebrate this final, staid presentation of the theme by following it with a flourish and – in the

---

14. This is a frequent comic strategy of Haydn's; compare the first movements of Symphonies No. 92 and 94.

recapitulation – a triumphal phrase that swiftly unites material from various parts of the movement (bars 209–17).

Yet Haydn seems unwilling to end the movement on a serious note. Immediately following the powerful cadence of bar 217, the playful main theme pokes its head in one more time. For the first time in the movement, the theme here (bars 218–21) appears by itself, and not contained within a larger harmonic progression. After a short diminuendo passage, the repeated eighth-note motive brusquely appears a final time in the two closing bars of the movement. In a sense, the quick transformation of the opening motive in the coda from impish to bombastic swiftly sums up the "maturation" of the motive seen throughout the course of the entire movement, hilariously ridiculing it in the process.

In closing, I would like to mention one other apparent incongruity: the incongruity of discussing humor in a book devoted to Schenker. After all, Schenker is not widely regarded as a notably funny fellow. His concern for compositional unity might seem to de-emphasize the importance of oddities and quirks which are often cited as the hallmarks of humor. If one argues that musical humor should be regarded solely in terms of extramusical or stylistic concerns, Schenker's organically oriented approach would appear irrelevant. Indeed, it has been implied by some that Schenker's structuralist approach is antithetical to any discussion of musical drama or emotion.

Admittedly, aspects of the rhetoric of Schenker and his followers may well have inspired such impressions. The insights Schenker's theories give for understanding the unifying elements of a composition are so powerful that many essays relying on his theories might seem to seek unity as an end unto itself, as the sole function of analysis.

The presence of unity by no means contradicts the presence of emotion or drama. On the contrary, unifying musical relationships are often the catalyst for some of the most powerful expressions of emotions in music. This is certainly true of musical humor, where an understanding of the ability of structure to combine and contrast often proves vital.

Structural analysis does not counteract appreciation of oddities or quirks, but rather highlights them by contextualizing them. It is the ability of the context to convince, rather than the extent of the ridiculous, that in most instances has the greatest impact on the comic in music. As Schenker himself noted in *Free Composition*, "We hear in the middleground and foreground an almost dramatic course of events. . . . [Music] may pursue its course by means of associations, references, and connectives; it may use repetitions of the same tonal succession to express different meanings; it may simulate expectation, preparation, surprise, disappointment, patience, impatience, and humor."[15]

15. *Free Composition*, p. 5.

"Symphonic breadth": structural style in Mozart's symphonies

David Gagné

Most music theorists and historians would surely agree that the style and structure of a composition are conditioned in various ways by its performance medium. Nevertheless, in dealing both with individual works and with general categories – sonata-allegro form, for example – analysts tend to focus primarily on thematic, harmonic, and (more recently) voice-leading factors with the medium regarded only as a means of realization. Analytical essays seldom consider how the structure of a sonata-allegro or other movement of a symphony, quartet, or sonata might have been shaped and, to some extent, even determined by the nature of the medium. On the other hand, historical studies of a given style – studies that may include a consideration of performance media and genres – typically discuss the music in primarily descriptive terms.[1]

In no genre are medium and structure more inseparable than in the symphony, where the variety and grouping of instruments within the ensemble can influence virtually every facet of the compositional process. In a sense one cannot speak of the symphony as a single genre, since the makeup and character of the orchestra changed so radically from the era of mid- and late-eighteenth century ensembles to the larger orchestras of the nineteenth and twentieth centuries. Nevertheless many aspects of symphonic style that were well established in Mozart's era, often initiated by Mozart himself, continued to have profound implications for the structural character of later symphonic works.

In the eighteenth century, the size and composition of orchestras varied considerably; moreover, at the time when Mozart wrote his first symphonies there was not yet a firm distinction between orchestral and chamber music. Nevertheless the symphony was generally understood to be "a piece of instrumental music for many voices."[2] Augustus Kollman, in *An Essay on Practical Musical Composition* published in London in 1799, states that the symphony is specifically conceived as "a piece calculated to be performed by *more than one*

---

1. One notable exception is James Webster's recent book, *Haydn's Farewell Symphony and the Idea of Classical Style: Through-Composition and Cyclic Integration in His Instrumental Music* (Cambridge: Cambridge University Press, 1991). I am making a distinction here between the type of *description* that characterizes many discussions of style, and *analysis*, which penetrates more deeply into a work's structure.
2. J. A. P. Schulz, "Symphonie," from J. G. Sulzer's dictionary of the arts, *Allgemeine Theorie der schönen Künste* (Berlin and Leipzig, 1771 and 1774), trans. by Bathia Churgin as "The Symphony as Described by J. A. P. Schulz (1774): A Commentary and Translation," *Current Musicology* 29 (1980), pp. 7–16.

Performer to each part."³ Thus it is not only the multiple instrumental groupings, but also the assumption that parts may be performed by many players that is fundamental to the symphony as a genre, as J. A. P. Schulz pointed out in 1774:

> In the symphony, where each part is more than singly performed, the melody must contain its greatest emphasis in the written notes themselves and cannot tolerate the slightest embellishment or coloration. Also, because the symphony is not a practice piece like the sonata but must be played immediately at sight, no difficulties should occur therein that could not be grasped at once by a large group and performed distinctly.⁴

As for the reading at sight, Mozart probably made fewer concessions to such performance conditions than did many of his contemporaries; see for instance the Finale of the "Haffner" Symphony, with its difficult string parts. In addition, the Viennese orchestra players are reported to have been extremely accomplished players and quick studies.⁵

I shall explore the ramifications of such factors for what might be termed *structural style*: the characteristics of a work's harmonic and voice-leading structure, in conjunction with rhythm and with design features (such as texture, orchestration, and dynamics) that constitute the totality of a musical composition. Passages from the opening sonata-allegro movements of three of Mozart's symphonies will be considered: Symphony No. 34 in C major (K.338), the "Haffner" Symphony (K.385), and the "Prague" Symphony (K.504). The opening of Mozart's String Quartet in G major (K.387) will also be examined.

In contrast to a solo performer or a chamber ensemble, the massed forces of any orchestra, regardless of its size, constitute a primary aesthetic factor in a number of respects. One is a fundamental duality between the proclivity of the orchestra to form a unified whole and the opposing tendency for each section, and for individual instruments within sections, to function with varying degrees of independence. A similar spectrum between unanimity and diversity also exists in chamber music conceived for one player on a part – but in orchestral music the size of the ensemble becomes an almost gravitational factor that may be expressed, for example, in extended tutti sections, and in broader sweeps of a single type of texture than are generally characteristic of music for a chamber group such as the string quartet. These considerations are inherent in the medium, and necessarily influence the creative imagination of a composer writing a work for orchestra in both obvious and subtle ways. Moreover, as this study will show, the dynamic interrelationships of the instruments and sections of the ensemble may condition not only the way the structure is articulated but also the nature of the structure itself.

Symphony No. 34 in C major, K.338

Example 1 presents the opening of the exposition of Symphony No. 34 in two levels of analytical reduction. The gesture of the single tonic chord, performed

---

3. Augustus Frederic Christopher Kollmann, *An Essay on Practical Musical Composition* (London, 1799), repr. with an introduction by Imogene Horsley (New York: Da Capo Press, 1973), p. 15.
4. Schulz, "Symphonie," trans. Churgin, p. 11.
5. See the introductory essay by Paul Badura-Skoda to his edition of Mozart's D minor Concerto (London: Ernst Eulenburg, 1981), p. 1.

Example 1 Mozart, Symphony No. 34 in C major, K.338

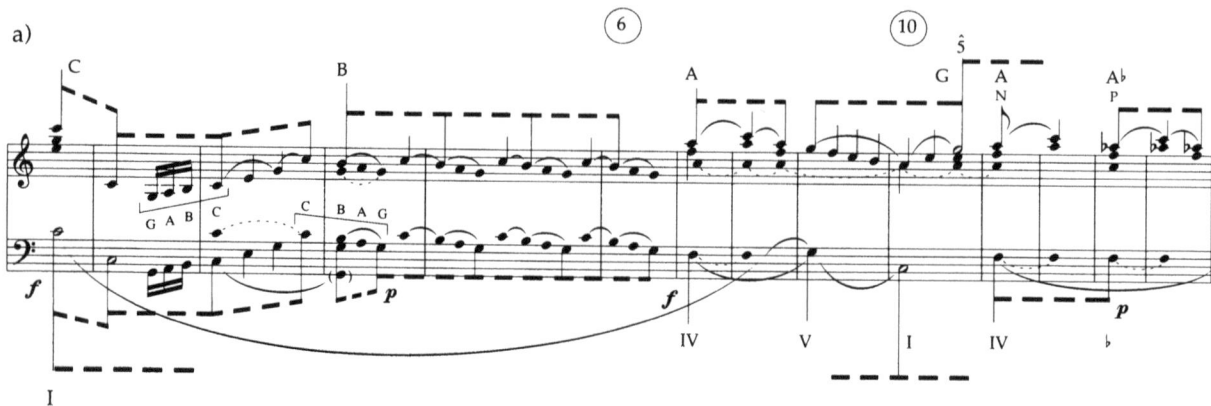

forte by the full orchestra and isolated by rests, and the following unison that begin the work constitute an expression of the unity of the ensemble representing one of the poles of symphonic texture that have been described. The very word "symphony" is synonymous with the words "concord" or "accord" that may be used to characterize such a beginning.[6] Psychologically, the impact of the ensemble and the volume of sound produced create an entirely different effect than a similar opening would produce in a chamber or solo work. This type of massed beginning was typical of many eighteenth-century symphonies, though with notable exceptions such as Mozart's Symphony No. 40 in G minor. It also conveys a heroic or ceremonial quality that was often associated with the allegro movements of symphonies at this time, as stated by J. A. P. Schulz: "The symphony is excellently suited to the expression of the good, the festive, and the noble."[7]

The unison writing that maintains this unanimity of ensemble through bar 6, and its sharply delineated rhythmic and melodic contour, are also characteristic of symphonic style as described by Schulz: "The allegros of the best chamber symphonies contain great and bold ideas, . . . strongly marked rhythms of different kinds, [and] powerful bass melodies *and unisons*."[8] In bars 3 and 4, a quasi-independent brass figure basically supports the unity of ensemble rather than disturbing it.

6. According to *Webster's Unabridged Dictionary* (2nd edn, 1979), the word "symphony" originates in the Greek word *symphōnia* (music), which itself is derived from the words *symphōnos* (agreeing in sound, harmonious), *syn* (together), and *phōnein* (to sound). Thus the word connotes not only the act of playing together, but also harmony and agreement – or concord – in sound.
  The New Grove Dictionary of Music and Musicians, ed. Stanley Sadie (London: Macmillan, 1980), Vol. 18, p. 438, points out that the Greek meaning of the word was transmitted "through the Latin *symphonia*, a term used during the Middle Ages and the Renaissance. It is essentially in this derivation that the term was used by Giovanni Gabrieli (*Sacrae symphoniae*, 1597), Schütz (*Symphoniae sacrae*, 1629) and others for concerted motets, usually for voices and instruments." In the seventeenth century the term was often applied to introductory movements of operas, oratorios and cantatas; the opera *sinfonia* was an immediate predecessor of the eighteenth-century symphony.
7. Schulz, "Symphonie," trans. Churgin, p. 11.
8. *Ibid*., p. 12 (emphasis added). In addition to the chamber symphony, "which constitutes a whole in and for itself and has no following music in view," Schulz describes the opera symphony (or overture), the French symphony (or operetta overture), and church symphony, which "consists often of only a single movement."

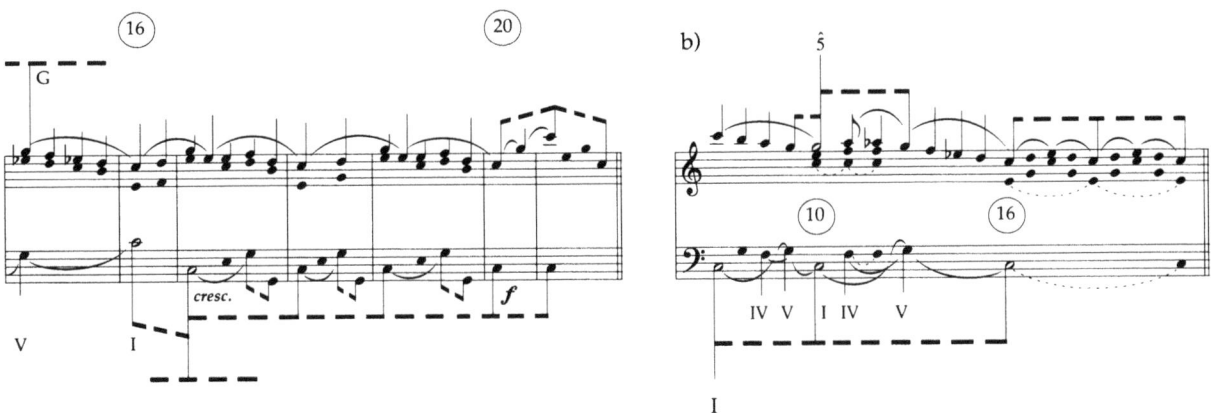

The dynamic quality of the unison writing is reinforced by the participation of the full string section, and the concise thematic ideas and repetitions. Such consistency of texture and ensemble for relatively extended passages occurs frequently in symphonic writing, reflecting the considerations of ensemble and performance discussed above.

The descending motion from C to G in bars 3–4 is echoed by the strings and bassoons, extending the opening phrase through bar 6. (This falling figure echoes in inversion the tones in the rising fourth G–C in bars 2–3, as indicated by the brackets in Example 1a. However, because of the dominant harmony that is prolonged by implication in bars 4–6, its meaning is different: the falling figure is subdivided, with the accented tone B initiating a descending third to G.) In solo and chamber works such a phrase extension would typically be created by variations in melodic and harmonic structure; here the extension is created entirely through the repetition of the figure, modified only by the contrasting *piano* dynamic level and the reduction in instrumentation. While such use of unvaried multiple repetitions could certainly occur in any genre, it is especially characteristic of symphonic writing, and often contributes to the type of "force and energy" described by Heinrich Christoph Koch in the following comparison of (solo) sonatas and symphonies:

Because it depicts the feelings of single people, the melody of the sonata must be extremely developed and must present the finest nuances of feelings, whereas the melody of the symphony must distinguish itself not through such refinements of expression, but through force and energy."[9]

If we now examine the entire passage analyzed in Example 1, it also becomes clear that the harmonic rhythm is slower than is typical in chamber music genres such as the string quartets of Haydn and Mozart. A common characteristic of symphonies in this period, such a relatively slow rate of chord change results in part from the kind of repetitions and broad thematic gestures that we

---

9. Heinrich Christoph Koch, *Versuch einer Anleitung zur Composition* (Leipzig: Adam F. Böhme, 1782, 1787, 1793); Sections 3 and 4 trans. by Nancy Kovaleff Baker as *Introductory Essay on Composition* (New Haven: Yale University Press, 1983), p. 203.

have seen, and partly from the fact that the bass and inner parts are often less melodically active than in contemporaneous solo and chamber genres.[10] I shall return to this point shortly.

The writing itself is also primarily diatonic. The only element of chromaticism in the first group (bars 1–20) is the sudden change to minor in bars 13–15, enhanced by the drop in dynamic level from *forte* to *piano*. While a work for any medium may of course be more or less chromatic, the prevalence of diatonicism in many symphonies of this period is at least partly related to the nature of brass instruments and timpani at the time. Since valves were not yet in use on brass instruments, and retuning timpani was a slow and laborious process, the number of notes available for these instruments was limited. Consequently, as Kollman observed:

> If a Symphony for an Orchestra shall not be imperfect, its principal *Subjects* ought to be of such a nature, that all Instruments can *execute* them, or at least *join* in them in the principal Key. If this rule is not attended to, a Symphony cannot answer the purpose of employing the whole Orchestra to advantage; and *Haydn* will be found very particular in attending to this rule, for the subjects of most of his best Symphonies are not only calculated for the Horn and Trumpet, but even for the Kettle Drums..."[11]

Because of the participation of the brass and timpani, this consideration is undoubtedly a factor in the prevalence of tonic and dominant tones in the opening of Symphony No. 34; these tones in turn create a strong conditioning factor for the harmonic structure, which consists essentially of primary triads (tonic, dominant, subdominant). In particular, scale degree 1 as a top-voice tone is emphasized in ways that would not normally characterize a solo or chamber piece. This is perhaps not only because of the practical limitations imposed by the brass and timpani, but also because of the size and weight of the initial sonoric fabric, which seems to demand the most stable and deeply-rooted location in tonal space. Many symphonies (and not so many quartets and solo sonatas) give this kind of prominence to scale degree 1 at the beginning.

The voice-leading structure is similarly influenced by such instrumental and ensemble characteristics as well as by expressive elements. In the eighteenth century, for example, the specific associations of trumpets with the military and horns with the hunt were vivid in the minds of musicians and the public alike. Accordingly the exposed "horn fifths" in bars 16–20 represent a distinct and characteristic figure of the type that Leonard G. Ratner calls a musical *topic*; yet they are fully integrated into the structural context.[12] The rising third C–E in bars 16–17 (which recalls the repeated third B–G in bars 4–6) invokes a response in falling thirds in the oboes in bars 17–18. The oboe entrance is accompanied by unison arpeggiation of the tonic chord in the strings and bassoons, which continues as both figures are repeated in bars 18–20. Though more elaborated, the rising and falling thirds in the structural top voice,

---

10. In this study the term "bass" will sometimes specify the composite cello/bass part as notated in the score (as here), and sometimes the string bass as an instrument, depending on context.
11. Kollmann, *An Essay on Practical Musical Composition*, p. 17.
12. Leonard G. Ratner, *Classic Music: Expression, Form, and Style* (New York: Schirmer Books, 1980). Ratner calls this topic "military and hunt music" (see pp. 18ff.).

moving between the root and the third of the tonic triad, echo the falling motions from the third to the root of the dominant triad in bars 4–6.

It is difficult to imagine this passage composed for any other medium, not only because of the interchange of different instrumental colors, but also because of the character – and in particular the relative simplicity – of the structure itself. In this final passage of the first group the repeated third motions, in conjunction with the harmonic tonic prolongation consisting solely of tonic and dominant chords, create a pattern that both results from the nature of the orchestra (especially the brass instruments and their associations, as described above), and depends upon the varied sonoric resources of the orchestral medium for a realization of this elemental tonal fabric that is not dull or overly repetitive.

The fundamentally symphonic character of the opening of K.338 will become even more apparent through a comparison with a chamber work. Example 2 presents, in two stages of reduction, the opening ten bars of Mozart's String Quartet in G major, K.387, composed in 1782 (two years later than K.338, and the same year as the "Haffner" Symphony, K.385). This initial phrase, like bars 1–20 of K.338, is an opening period that constitutes the first group in the sonata-allegro form. The basic harmonic motions of the respective passages are also comparable in the two works: I–IV–V–I (with a varied repetition) in K.338 (Example 1b), and I–II^6–V–I in K.387 (Example 2b).

However the particular ways in which these essential progressions are elaborated – many specifically related to the respective genres – result in marked differences in the later structural levels. In the Symphony, the opening tonic prolongation is achieved with two chords (I and V), which are expanded with considerable repetition. The Quartet's opening bars involve more complexity: the essential progression I–II–V^6–I is expanded with a large number of other sonorities in conjunction with animated and independent voice leading. It is notable that the cello participates as actively as the other parts, establishing fluid chordal motion as well as rapid harmonic rhythm in comparison with the opening of K.338 where, as noted above, the bass moves more slowly.

Consequently one can speak of more structural levels in K.387 than in K.338. In bars 1–2 of this Quartet, for example, it is possible to distinguish at least five structural levels, as shown in Example 3: (a) the essential motion I–II; (b) the use of the V^6 of II as a passing chord between I and II, in conjunction with an incomplete neighbor in the top voice; (c) the expansion of this motion with the intervening chord V^6 on the downbeat of bar 2 (with its bass note, F♯, serving as a neighbor to the initial G); (d) the expansion of the initial tonic chord with the rise to G and descent to D in the top voice, and with the bass following in parallel sixths; (e) the addition of figuration tones such as the first violin suspensions in bars 1 and 2 and the passing D♯ in bar 2.[13] In the C major Symphony, on the other hand, the sustained C major chord in bars 1–3 is embellished only by figuration, creating fewer levels of structure. Of course

---

13. Note that the top-voice descending second D–C shown in Example 3 occurs within the larger descending third D–B of bars 1–4 (Examples 2a and 2b).

Example 2 Mozart, String Quartet in G major, K.387

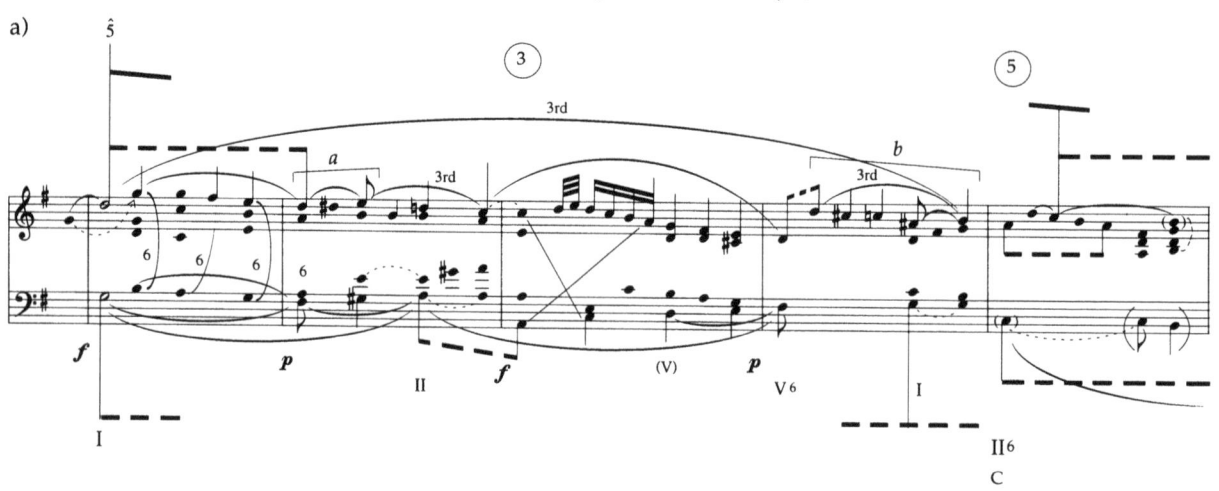

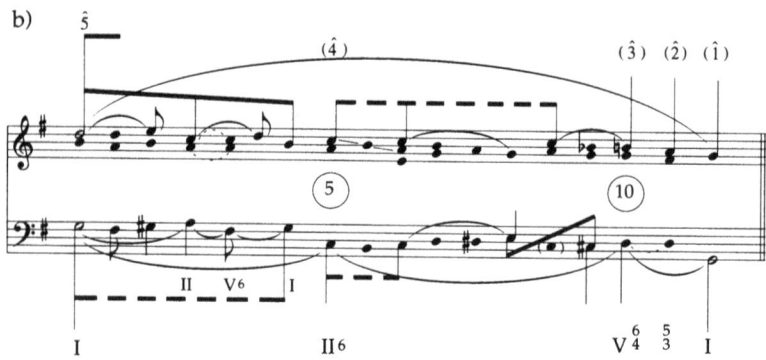

many symphonies begin with more complexity – and many quartets with less – than in these examples. Nevertheless the present comparison reveals differences that are broadly characteristic of works composed during the Classical period, and that strongly influenced the evolution of these genres.

Returning to Example 2a, we observe the supple polyphonic and motivic character of the opening of this Quartet. The rising chromatic figure D–D♯–E in bar 2, first violin (marked "a"), is answered by a falling chromatic figure (marked "b") in bar 4. The last two tones of figure a are echoed an octave higher in bar 7 (in the figure marked "a¹"), followed in the next bar by a rhythmically extended statement of figure a in the bass. Other chromatic figures such as the rising semitones A♯–B (bar 4) and G♯–A (bar 9) enhance the richness of this opening passage. Such motivic complexity occurs more freely and characteristically in an ensemble of individual instruments than in the orchestra of Mozart's period for reasons noted above;[14] that such factors are not limited to

14. However the late symphonies of Mozart (and a number of Haydn's symphonies) introduced considerably more complexity into symphonic style.

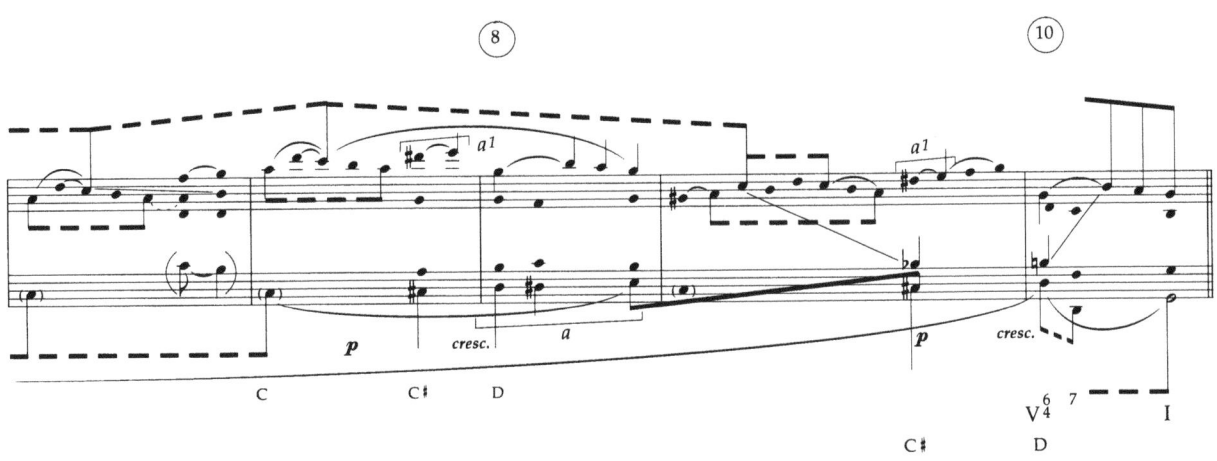

the Classical period is demonstrated by the well-known fact that many later composers have written some of their most refined and complex music for the string quartet.

The melodic freedom and independence accorded to all four instruments results in a relative lack of metrical reinforcement in comparison with the beginning of K.338; however Mozart articulates the beginning of each of the first four bars by changes in dynamic level, with the common rests at the end of bars 2 and 4 further reinforcing the metrical groupings at the outset of the work. The use of dynamics, accents, changes in texture, and other aspects of design to articulate meter and form can of course occur in any genre, but is especially common in the quartet because of the complex and independent voice leading that so frequently occurs.

A thinner and more differentiated texture begins in bar 5, articulating the beginning of a new phrase. The imitation of the viola by the second and the first violins employs contrasts of register and tone color in ways that commonly

Example 3 Mozart, String Quartet, K.387, bars 1–2

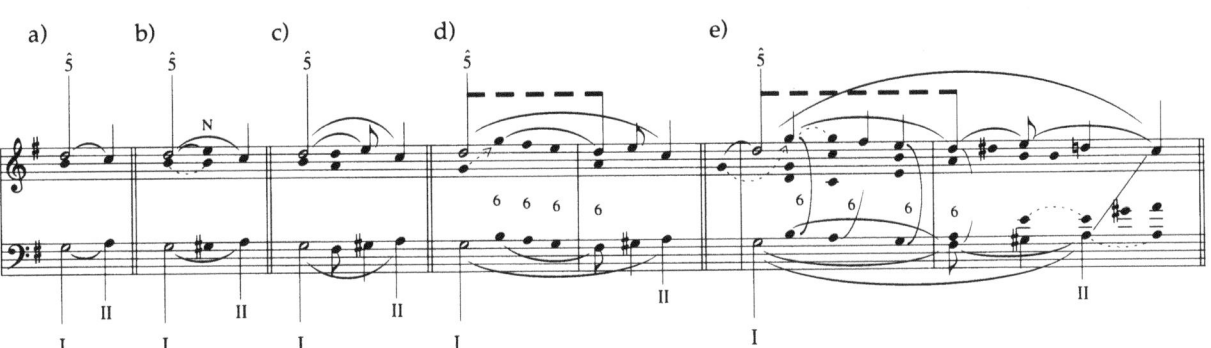

occur in orchestral music. We should also consider, however, another general characteristic of the quartet that is relevant both to the audience's outlook and to the composer's creative imagination: the combination of four individual players establishes an entirely different kind of visual and artistic impression than an orchestral ensemble where the players are perceived less as individuals than as parts of a ensemble. Furthermore, uniting several players in a single section imposes limitations on composer and performer that do not exist in the performance of a single part: in the eighteenth-century ensemble (as noted by J. A. P. Schulz in the passage quoted at the beginning of this essay) this involved such factors as complexity of line and improvisatory freedom. And yet, while each part in a string quartet may unfold more or less freely, ensemble playing also requires that such autonomy be partly relinquished, as poetically described in the following passage written by the French violinist and composer Pierre Baillot:

In the quartet, [the performer] sacrifices all the riches of this instrument to the general effect; he enters into the spirit of this other type of composition, whose charming dialogue seems to be a conversation among friends, who convey to each other their feelings, their sentiments, their mutual affections; their sometimes different opinions give rise to an animated discussion to which each gives his own development....[15]

Thus, despite any "sacrifices" of individuality that might occur, the flexibility that is possible in an ensemble of individual players fosters great freedom and spontaneity in structure and design. This results in a tendency toward more complex harmonic and voice-leading structure, as noted above, and a consequent richness of expression in the ensemble as a whole. (The artistic impression created by such a dialogue among the members of a string quartet is quite different from an exchange among players in the sections of an orchestra, where the visual and psychological impact of the complete ensemble – as expressed in tutti passages – is always present in the consciousness of the players and the audience alike; even solo passages are perceived within this larger context.) In an ensemble of four solo players rapid changes in texture may readily occur, facilitated by the relatively homogeneous sonoric character of the string quartet; this allows for great freedom in the interrelationships among parts.

In most orchestral writing of the mid- to late eighteenth century, the approach to texture typically forms a marked contrast to that of the string quartet excerpt just examined. Because the orchestra comprises distinct sections, composers frequently juxtapose or combine different sections in passages that maintain relative consistency of texture. This block-like approach to texture in turn invites greater length and more literal repetition than in solo or chamber music, conditions that are directly related to structure.[16]

15. Pierre Marie François de Sales Baillot, *L'art du violon: nouvelle méthode* (Paris, 1834), p. 268. The translation is from *Violin Technique and Performance Practice in the Late Eighteenth and Early Nineteenth Centuries*, trans. Robin Stowell (Cambridge: Cambridge University Press, 1985), pp. 276–77.
16. This continued to be generally true of later symphonies as well, as noted by Neal Zaslaw in his excellent book, *Mozart's Symphonies: Context, Performance Practice, Reception* (Oxford: Clarendon Press, 1989), p. 518: "In the 1760s, 1770s, and into the 1780s symphonies were generally viewed as a

Later in the exposition of K.338, following the initial antecedent and consequent phrases of the second group, a passage occurs that wonderfully illustrates what Schenker termed "symphonic breadth"[17] – that is, the large gestures that frequently occur in symphonic writing (see Example 4, a two-level graph of bars 64–82). The beginning of the passage (bar 64) is set off by a marked reduction of texture as the first violins begin alone in a relatively low register, *pianissimo*. When the second violins enter canonically in bar 66, the first violins have moved a third higher than their starting note in bar 64 and now stand apart from the imitating second violins because of staccato articulation, more active figuration, and a trill. As the canon continues in bars 68 and 69 the horns enter with a G pedal tone in octaves that binds the passage harmonically and texturally through bar 74. While the first violins continue to climb in register, the entrance of the cellos, basses, and woodwinds in bar 70 further intensifies this composed crescendo. The dynamic level of the newly entering instruments is *piano*, and the notated crescendo in bar 70 leads to the *forte* in bar 72. With the entrance of the violas, trumpets and timpani all instruments participate in the final phrase in the passage as the first violin line rises from g^2 (bar 70) to d^3 (bar 74), reinforced by the oboes at the lower octave and, as the ascent concludes (in bars 72–74), by the second violins a third below.

This precisely scored crescendo, employing so many aspects of design, is so fundamentally orchestral that it would be difficult to imagine in another medium.[18] Harmonically the entire passage – bars 64 to 74 – prolongs the G major triad as the local tonic of the second group, reinforced by the sustained tones in the horns referred to above, and the repeated bass tones that begin in bar 70. (The figuration and implied local chords elaborate but do not diminish the sense of a single harmony being sustained, as shown in Example 4.) In conjunction with this prolongation, the stepwise rising motion of the upper voice articulates the tones of the G major triad, covering the span of an octave and a fifth from g^1 to d^3, followed by repeated descents of a fifth through the G triad (Examples 4a and 4b).

Thus, despite the harmonic stability of this extended prolongation, Mozart creates intense energy and excitement through his skillful use of the orchestral medium. He does so not only through the gradual addition of instruments in conjunction with the large-scale crescendo, but also with the broad, steady ascent that underlies the figuration of the first violin part (as shown in Example 4) in contrapuntal play with the second violins. These elements, in conjunction with

---

'formality.' And even after the symphony's 'liberation,' its position relative to genres intended for connoisseurs – piano sonatas, Lieder, and string quartets, for instance – remained the same; Beethoven's and Schubert's symphonies too were for a larger public and, whatever their seriousness, they tended to avoid the more difficult and sometimes esoteric ideas of the 'private' genres, striving instead for large-scale gestures."

17. See Schenker's commentary on Fig. 124/5b (the slow movement of the "Haffner" Symphony) in *Free Composition*, p. 104.
18. J. A. P. Schulz takes note of this aspect of symphonic style: "The allegros of the best chamber symphonies contain . . . strong shadings of the forte and piano, and chiefly of the crescendo, which, if it is employed at the same time as a rising and increasingly expressive melody, can be of the greatest effect." Schulz, "Symphonie," trans. Churgin, p. 12.

Example 4 Mozart, Symphony No. 34

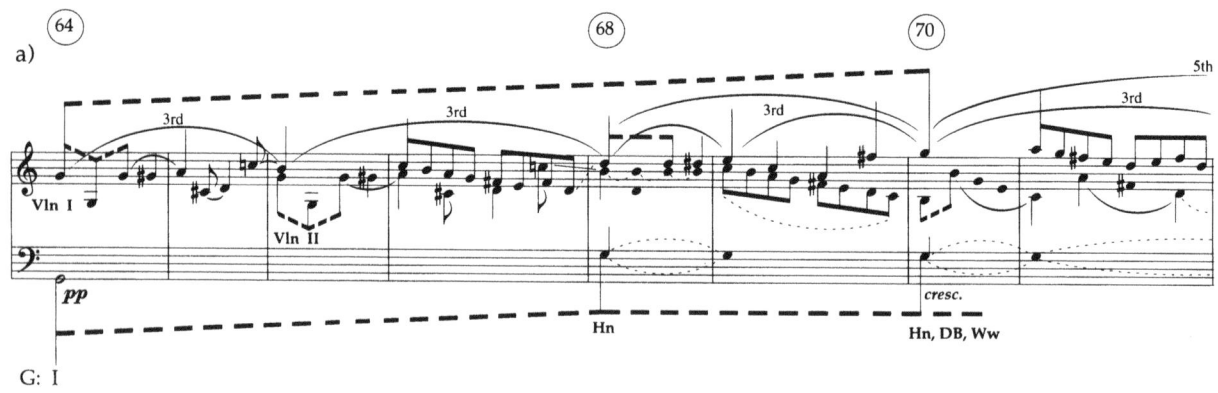

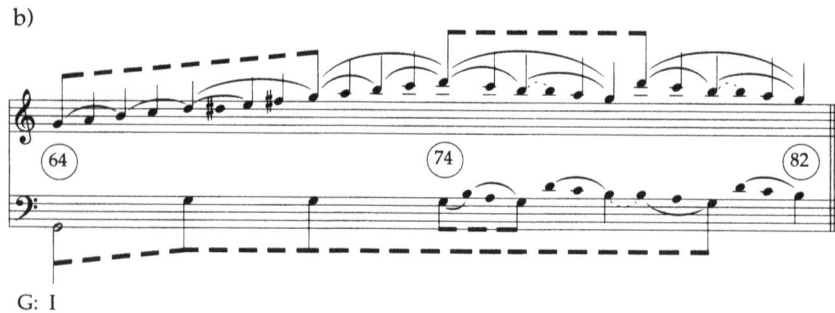

the prolonged G major harmony, create the characteristically symphonic breadth of this passage, which would scarcely be possible without them.

Symphony No. 35 in D major, K.385 ("Haffner")

It is well known that the "Haffner" Symphony originated as a Serenade composed in 1782. The Serenade was scored for two oboes, two bassoons, two horns, two trumpets, timpani, and strings, and included an introductory march and a second minuet in addition to the four movements of the symphony. Six months later Mozart decided to rework the Serenade as a symphony for his first public concert or "academy" to be given in Vienna in March of 1783. A facsimile of the first page of the autograph score is given in Plate 1.[19] On the autograph, it is possible to see the changes in scoring that were made: flutes and clarinets have been added to the existing manuscript, with the flutes on the top

---

19. Mozart, *Symphony No. 35 in D, K.385: "Haffner" Symphony*, facsimile edition with an introduction by Sydney Beck (New York: Oxford University Press, 1968). The autograph is found in the Pierpont Morgan Library, Mary Flagler Cary Music Collection.

(previously empty) staff of the autograph and the clarinets on the bottom staff (also previously empty).

The autograph provides further insights into Mozart's process of composition of this work, which is known from his letters to have been written in considerable haste at a time when he was in the midst of a number of projects. As a first stage of composition of the Allegro, virtually the entire exposition was written out in the violin and bass parts. The different shades of ink and the character of the handwriting show that the other instruments were added later;[20] moreover Mozart makes frequent use of abbreviations to indicate various types of doublings. The uses of these signs are enlightening in that they indicate how Mozart conceived the scoring: in the first bar the violas and the bassoons are marked "Col B" (with the bass), a recurring marking in the autograph. The second violins are frequently linked with the first violins in unison passages, as in bars 1–5. Such an approach to composition is consistent with the large gestures and broad, relatively consistent approach to scoring and texture that may be observed in the work itself. Thus there is a direct relationship between this kind of compositional procedure – especially the fact that Mozart began with just the violin and bass parts – and the voice-leading structure of the finished work, which itself often tends to reduce to two essential parts.[21] This is in marked contrast to other Mozart compositions such as chamber music works, where there are often four or more independent parts. The approach to the scoring of the work probably resulted, at least in part, from the haste with which it was written, but its style is also generally consistent with that of other Mozart symphonies composed before 1785.

A graph of bars 1–7 of the work is presented in Example 5. As in K.338, the opening is marked by unison texture, and, in this case, a unison doubling of the tonic note. It is also noteworthy that the melodic descending fourth from tonic to dominant plays a prominent role in the beginning of both symphonies,

---

20. The different shades of ink and the markings are most clearly visible on the original autograph.
21. See, for example, bars 19–35 (which are not reproduced here): one or two parts form the principal voice leading throughout this passage, sometimes with variations in figuration in different parts, while the remaining instruments complete the harmonic framework with sustained or repeated notes. Such writing occurs throughout much of the movement, alternating with more complex counterpoint in some sections.

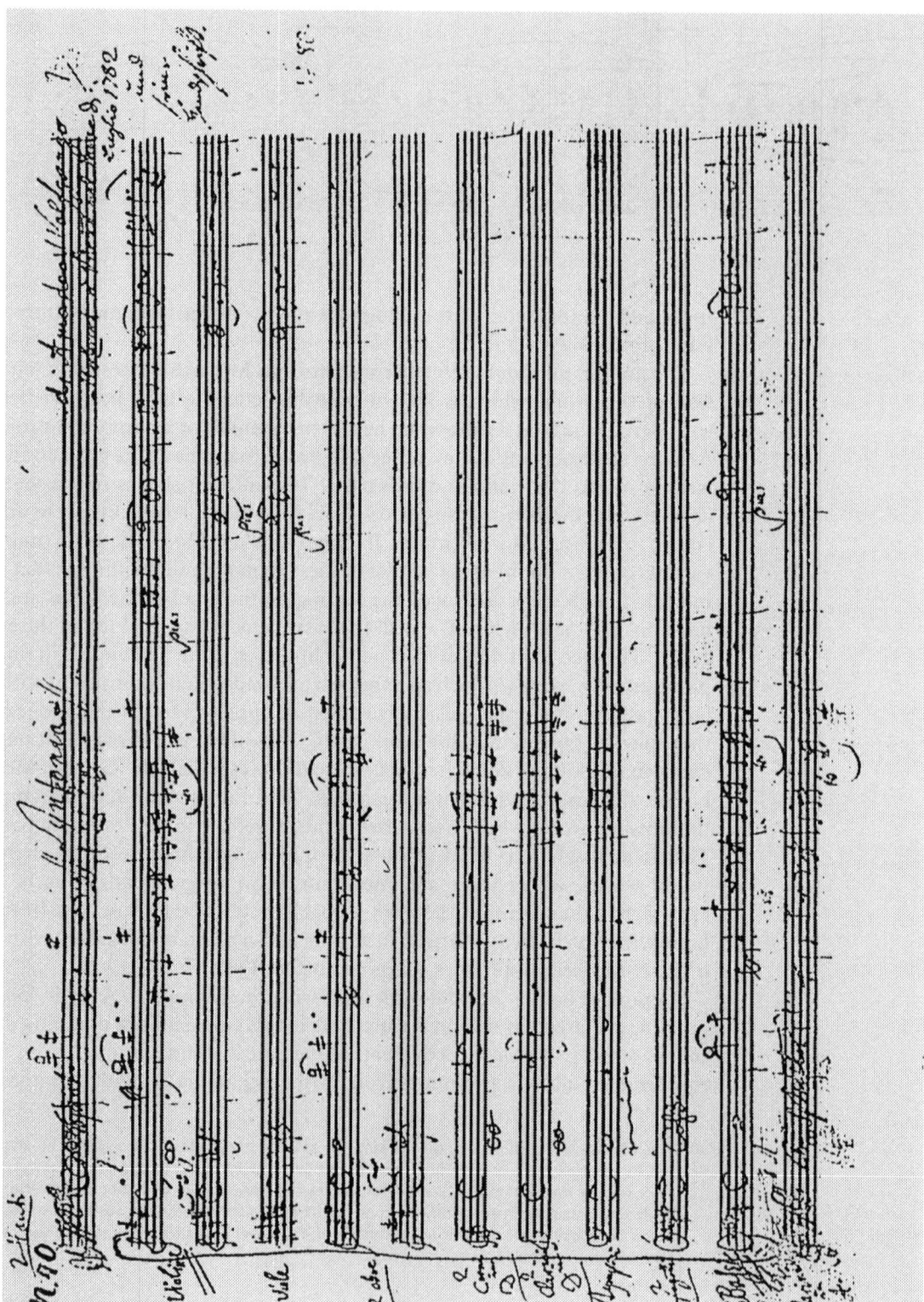

Plate 1 Mozart, Symphony No. 35 in D major, K.385 ("Haffner"): first page of the autograph

Example 5 Mozart, Symphony No. 35 in D major, K.385 ("Haffner")

though in contrast to the repeated C–G figure in the earlier work, the elaborated D–A motion forms the structural basis of the entire opening thematic statement (bars 1–5). This opening, with its striking leaps, illustrates Koch's comment that "the melody of the symphony must distinguish itself... through force and energy."[22] Michael Broyles elaborates on this point with an observation that is not applicable to all symphonies, but which perhaps has validity as a generalization about eighteenth-century style: "A symphony melody should be relatively simple, strongly directional, and rhythmically dynamic."[23] Both the rhythmic figures and the descending fourth itself serve as mottos for the movement.

As in K.338, scale degree 1 as a melodic tone receives a great deal of emphasis. Here the tonic pitch does not repeat as insistently as in the C major Symphony, but it is embodied in an idiomatically symphonic gesture – a two-octave leap in both violin parts, connected by grace notes that produce an arpeggiated triple stop on D – that draws the listener's attention irresistibly to this focal sound. It is a gesture that becomes a characteristic feature of the movement, both in exact quotation and in various transformations, some of them shown in Example 6. At the end of the movement, the rising two-octave flourish of bars 200–201 surely derives from the initial gesture, as do the triple stops, played no fewer than six times in the closing tonic chord (Example 6a). The tripled D is also the origin of the movement's many two-octave passages in sixteenth notes (for instance, bar 19, Example 6b). In association with a subdominant chord, it occurs prominently in the recapitulation's second theme (Example 6c). And, with an F♯ replacing the middle D, it even finds its way to a different harmonic context in the second theme in the exposition (bars 59 and 61, Example 6d), as part of the prolongation of A major. Perhaps the curious differences between the second themes in the exposition and

22. See page 85 above.
23. Michael Broyles, "The Two Instrumental Styles of Classicism," *Journal of the American Musicological Society* 36/2 (1983), p. 220. Broyles points out that while this represents a prototype for symphonic style in this period, individual works can be very different in character.

Example 6 Mozart, Symphony No. 35

recapitulation result, at least in part, from Mozart's wish to introduce this striking and characteristic sound at critical junctures throughout the movement.

The development section is characterized by broad swaths of uniform textures, highlighted through dynamic contrast, that are associated with broad voice-leading gestures. The first such passage, bars 95–104 (see Example 7), involves contrapuntal interplay between the two violin parts. In contrast to the *forte* ending of the exposition, the beginning of the development is set off by its *piano* dynamic level and low tessitura, as the second violins begin a statement of the opening theme on A. The first violins enter two bars later with an independent statement of the theme on G♯ (heard as a motion from the preceding A in the second violins), which proceeds through F♯ to F♮ and E. The first violin line thus traces a chromatically expanded form of the falling fourth motive that began the movement, now transposed to the dominant. Against this falling fourth the second violins rise a fourth from A, reaching D in bar 99, then resolving to C♯ in parallel thirds below the first violin in bars 100–101. The violin parts thus employ simultaneously rising and falling forms of the initial theme in a kind of inverted canon, a contrapuntal device that is facilitated by the elemental nature of the theme itself.

The accelerated echo of the first violin's descending fourth in bars 101–103, accompanied at the lower third by the second violin, is reminiscent of the phrase extension at the beginning of the C major Symphony; it is then reduced still further to a neighbor figure. Hence a progressive concentration of the motive occurs, from seven measures (bars 95–101) to a four-note figure (bars 101–102, repeated in bars 102–103), then to the neighbor motive (bars 103–104), a dynamic voice-leading gesture that is directed toward a single point – the A major chord of bar 104.

This extended voice-leading gesture is associated with a harmonic prolongation of A that begins with the unison in bar 95, and is reinforced by the pedal in the cello, bass, bassoon, and horns that sounds in three octaves. Used as both a harmonic and a textural element, the pedal contrasts with the active violin lines, unifying the passage in a manner that is characteristically symphonic.

Following a momentary silence in all parts, the next section begins in bar 105 with an unexpected and striking F♯ major chord, played *forte* by the full ensemble. The force and unity of the ensemble not only articulate the new phrase, but also highlight the unexpected arrival on – and modulation to – F♯ major. Similar effects may occur in solo or in chamber music, but the result is less intense than a sudden entrance by a full orchestra. Consequently such dramatic tutti passages occur with particular frequency in orchestral music, dynamically illustrating the principle of unity of ensemble, one of the poles of orchestral writing discussed above.

Despite the marked contrast as this phrase begins, its thematic elements remain consistent: the introductory theme recurs in imitation, beginning with the first violins in bar 105, with the cellos and basses entering a step lower in bar 107. Motion through a descending fourth is again primary, now in the bass (bars 105–11). In bars 109–10, the dramatic two-octave run from b to b^2 in the first violins highlights an important inner-voice tone (as indicated in Example 7a) and intensifies the motion to the C♯ dominant seventh chord, the goal of the descending fourth. It also creates an extraordinary scalar echo of the two-octave violin leaps at the opening of the movement.

As the C♯ chord is reached in bar 111, an orchestrated decrescendo begins, in an extension of the dominant chord that is comparable in function to the phrase extension of bars 101–104. In conjunction with a gradual reduction in instrumentation and a drop in dynamic level, the neighbor motion in bars 111–12 is followed by descending motion in the upper strings, then woodwinds, resulting in a falling off of tension. This descending motion (which concludes with the beginning of the new phrase in bar 117) and the *piano* dynamic level that continues into the next phrase link the two phrases, introducing the new phrase as subtly as the sudden tutti and *forte* in bar 105 dramatically announced the previous phrase. As an expressive device, this carefully shaped decrease in instrumentation concludes the phrase in a manner that is characteristically orchestral.

The third and last phrase of the development begins with the resolution to F♯ minor in bar 117. While similar to the first phrase in overall texture and dynamic level, it is harmonically more active and serves as a retransition section that culminates in the dominant chord of bars 127–28. Added to the contrapuntal dialogue in the violins is a new element, neighbor figures in the woodwinds. Up to this point in the development the primary role of the winds was to sustain tones to support and reinforce the more active string writing. Adam Carse, in his landmark study of the history of orchestration, speaks of an "instinct that wind instruments are constitutionally less active than strings," a feature of orchestration that was particularly prevalent in the eighteenth century when wind instruments had more limited technical possibilities than later types.[24]

In each of the three sections of the development, an extended voice-leading gesture or motion is associated with consistent texture and dynamics. As in the C major Symphony – and in contrast to Mozart's string quartets, where changes of texture and other facets of design tend to occur more frequently – Mozart treats each section of the orchestra rather in the manner of blocks or layers of texture which remain consistent for a time, and then take on a new aspect. An additional consequence of this compositional approach is the frequent tendency for phrases to be elided, as in bars 116–17 of this development, creating greater breadth of gesture. Koch remarks on this aspect of the symphony as follows:

---

24. Adam Carse, *The History of Orchestration* (London: Kegan Paul, Trench, Trubner and Co., 1925; repr. New York: Dover, 1964), p. 126.

Example 7 Mozart, Symphony No. 35

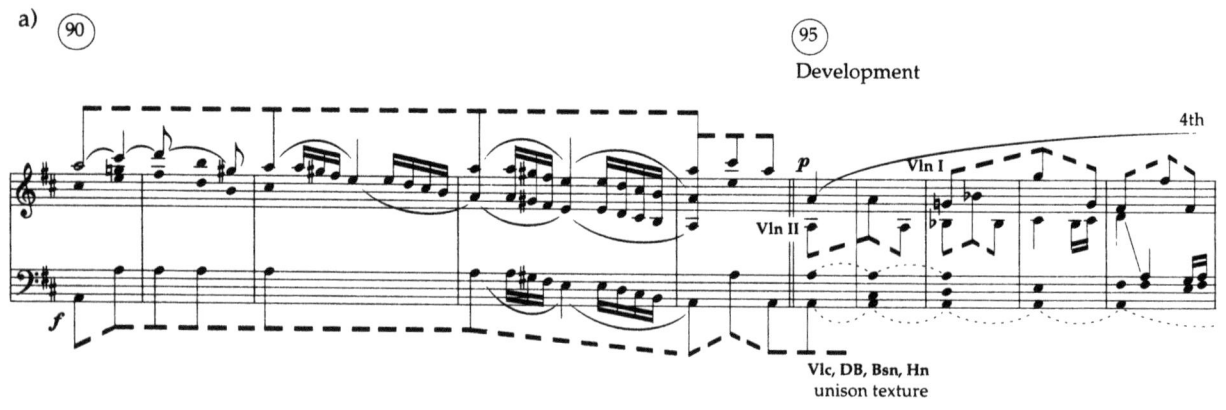

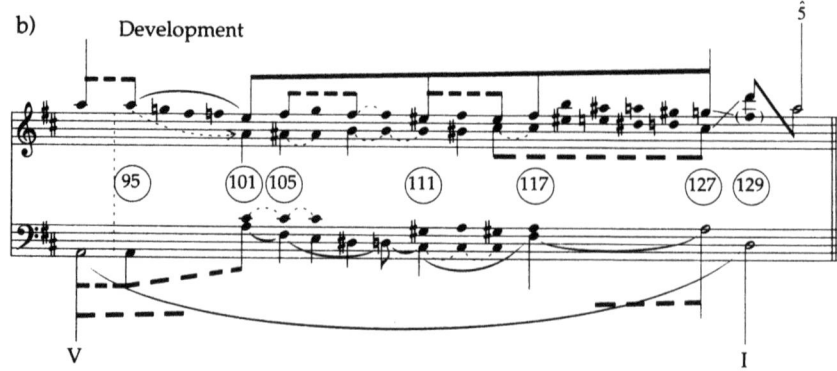

The structure . . . of the symphony differs from that of the sonata and the concerto . . . in that (1) melodic sections tend to be more extended already with their first presentation than in other compositions, and especially (2) these melodic sections usually are more attached to each other and flow more forcefully than in the periods of other pieces, that is, they are linked so that their phrase-endings are less perceptible.[25]

25. Koch, *Versuch*, trans. Baker, p. 199.

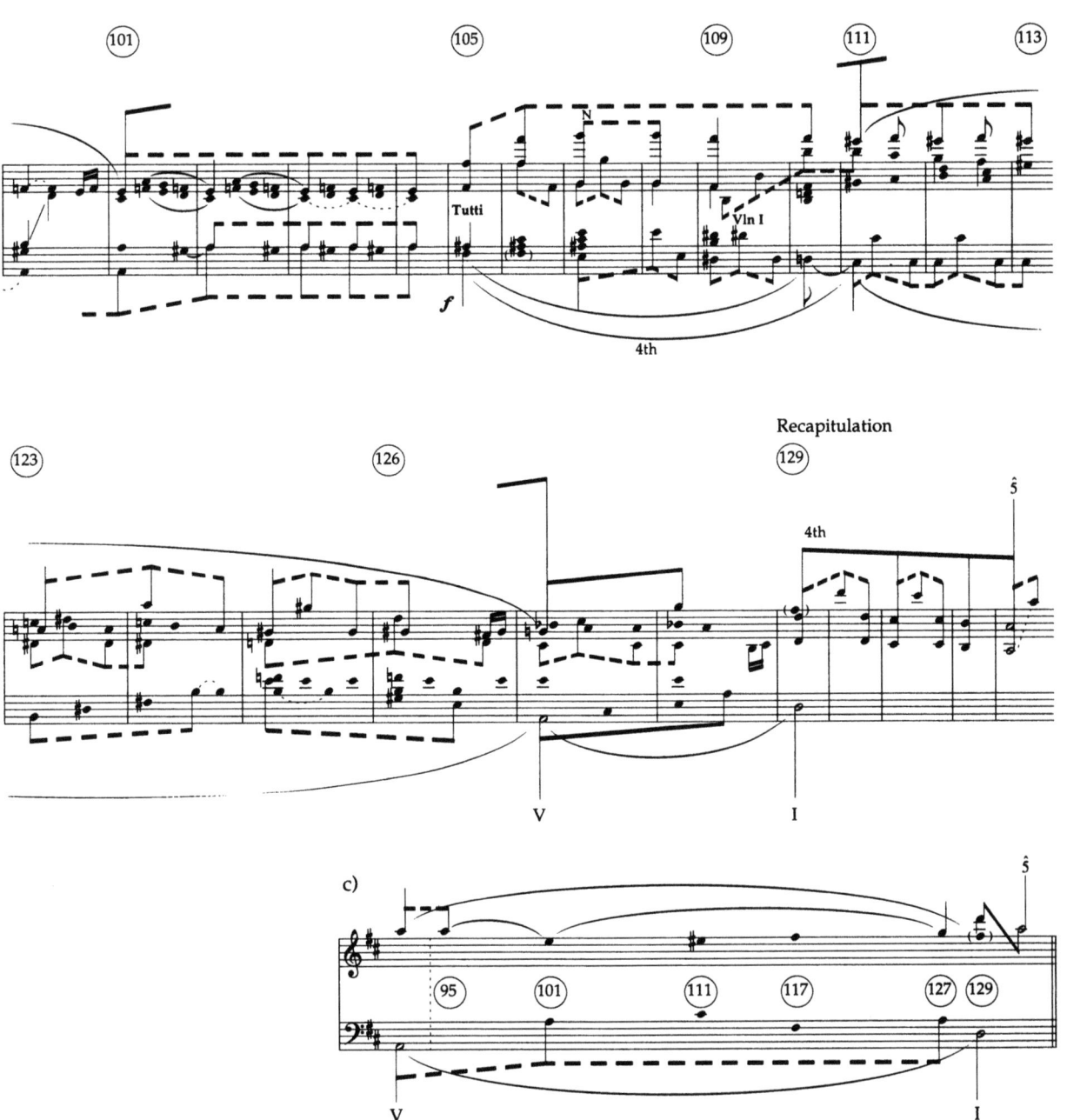

Because of these general characteristics of the symphony, a sudden break in continuity such as that created by the tutti chord in bar 105 becomes an intensely dramatic effect.

Symphony No. 38 in D major, K.504 ("Prague")

If the two symphonies that have been considered so far exemplify aspects of traditional eighteenth-century symphonic style, in the Symphony No. 38 in D major Mozart forged a new style entirely his own. The profusion of motives and themes, the richer textures and more intricate orchestration, and the contrapuntal majesty of the "Prague" Symphony make it a companion to the celebrated last three symphonies that follow it. Yet, despite the greater length and complexity of this work, it continues to reflect those aspects of style that arise from the symphonic medium and set Mozart's works for this genre apart from his other compositions.

In the first movement there is an extraordinary number of thematic ideas: undoubtedly few of Mozart's contemporaries could have incorporated them all into a unified framework. Mozart was able to harness the resources of the orchestra, and the sweeping gestures that the ensemble makes possible, to embrace the diverse (but related) motives in a veritable torrent of rhythmic and harmonic motion.

This is especially true of the development. To illustrate the diversity of its themes and motives, Example 8 excerpts some of them (labeled as figures a–h) and indicates where they first occurred in the exposition. We shall examine these figures in conjunction with Example 9, to show how they are combined and juxtaposed in a series of remarkable contrapuntal passages so as to form voice-leading motions and prolongations that are uniquely symphonic in conception. The nearly constant eighth- and sixteenth-note motion of the figures becomes a consistent rhythmic element that helps to integrate their diverse features into the contrapuntal fabric.

One further consequence of the interweaving of motives and the intense rhythmic momentum in the development is the almost completely seamless integration of phrases, as described by Koch (in the passage just quoted). This integration is enhanced by the more active participation of the winds, which frequently take part in the contrapuntal interplay. They also continue to express elements of harmony in sustained textures, as in the earlier symphonies, thereby establishing a consistent framework and support for the active string parts.

Example 9 represents the structure of the development in two levels of reduction. In bars 143–50 (see the score), a canon at the lower seventh (as the inversion of a second) occurs between the first and second violins in invertible counterpoint. A succession of canonic entries of the thematic figure a (see Example 8) progressively outlines the fifth A–E of the dominant chord that is prolonged from the end of the exposition. In bars 148–50 two contrapuntal lines emerge (Example 9): one continues the ascent to A in the two-line register, thereby completing the octave, while the other makes a cadential upper-voice descent from E to A.

Overall the canonic imitation traces a rising octave in a large-scale expansion of the initial rising octave in figure a. Both the octave and the articulated fourths that are linked in the descending portion of figure a are prominent throughout the development in voice-leading motions and melodic gestures.[26] An accompanying figure in the first violins (figure b, shown in Example 8) incorporates a descending octave, enhancing both the prominence of the octave as a motivic interval and the pronounced juxtaposition of ascending and descending motion in motivic figures throughout the development. Together with the rhythmic vitality and contrapuntal interplay, these elements create extraordinary vitality in performance.

Though only the strings participate in this initial phrase of the development, the juxtaposition of the rising and falling canonic lines in the violin parts and the accompanying motivic figures in the lower string parts creates a dense contrapuntal fabric. While such writing would not be unusual in a string quartet, the orchestras of Mozart's time must have found accuracy of ensemble difficult to achieve in this work, and in the final three symphonies that followed it (especially the great "Jupiter" Symphony). By making such demands he changed the character of symphonic composition, expanding its possibilities.

The prolongation of the dominant in the first phrase extends for eight measures (bars 143–50). Beginning in bar 151 a second canon occurs, now prolonging D major. Figure a is once again the subject of the canon, which occurs between the viola and the bass/bassoon parts with imitation at the second. An embellished form of the last part of figure b (see figure b¹ in Example 8) occurs in the violins. As the bass and the top voice ascend in parallel tenths (see Example 9) an eight-bar phrase comparable to the first is suggested.

Instead, a sudden cadential motion in bars 155–56 ends the prolongation of D after four bars. The cadence seems at first to resolve deceptively to G; however a new entry of the canonic subject on B in the bassoons, joined by the second violins, is introduced in the same measure (bar 156). The simultaneous resolution to G over B may be understood as a sixth replacing a fifth over B (in the manner of an implied 5–6); B is subsequently prolonged.

In the third canonic passage, where the imitation is again at the second, figure a enters alternately between the bassoon/second violin and the viola/bass parts. The growing intensity of the development is augmented by the rhythmic momentum of figure c (see Example 8), which is introduced in the first violins (bar 156), and by the entrance of the brass instruments. The successive canonic entries rise a sixth from B to G♯, which supports a VII⁶ of F♯ minor.

With the resolution to F♯ minor in bar 162 the first marked change in design occurs. The extended rising canonic motions and associated harmonic prolongations give way to more rapid descending sequential motion and to further

---

26. The descending portion of figure a is supported by an E chord as dominant of A (bar 144). Therefore the second fourth is a "structural" descent from one chord tone to another (E–B). However the first fourth begins with a suspension; the structural motion is from the third to the root of the E chord (G♯–E). In the context of the phrase the repetition of E and the rhythmic grouping articulate the figure into two groups of tones. Despite the fact that the initial tone is a tied suspension, a parallelism is created in which each group of four tones is perceived to traverse a fourth. These groupings are heard as such in melodic terms, independently of their relationship to the chordal structure. Both structural and non-structural melodic fourths occur frequently throughout the movement.

Example 8 Mozart, Symphony No. 38 in D major, K.504 ("Prague"): motivic figures in the development section

Figure a (cf. bars 43–45)

Figure b

Figure b¹

Figure c (cf. bars 41–43; bars 75ff.)

Figure d (cf. bars 55ff.; bars 21ff.)

motivic fragmentation. A descending-fifths pattern incorporates figure d (see Example 8) in a dialogue between first and second violins, figure c in the lower strings and bassoons, and figure a in the flutes and clarinet. The first statement of figure d spans two chords, F♯ and B, initiating a regular sequential pattern that continues until the arrival on G in bar 172. With its faster chordal motion, series of tonicizations, and associated chromaticism, the sequence creates a growing sense of agitation. This intensity is enhanced by more fragmented motivic interchange in the violins, and by an increasing concentration of motivic figures.

The G major chord in bar 172 is both the conclusion of the descending-fifths sequence and the beginning of a new sequence: a rising, chromaticized 5–6 motion. At this point the fragmentation of figure d and the interweaving of neighbor figures produce a texture that is saturated with motivic interplay throughout the orchestra, in conjunction with chromaticism and numerous layers of rising and falling contrapuntal motion as the gradual ascent occurs.

The subsequent four measures (bars 177–80) initiate the climactic passage of the development. Multiple layers of texture, concentrated interchange of motives, and rapid chordal motion are again employed. Interplay between the

Figure e (cf. bars 63ff.)

Figure f (cf. bars 63ff.)

Figure g (cf. bars 37ff.)

Figure h (cf. Figure a)

lower strings/bassoons and the upper strings gains increasing momentum at the cadence as the upper strings move entirely in sixteenth notes. In the higher woodwinds and brass, sustained tones occur in rhythmic alternation, with motions by the flutes into upper registers heightening the intensity. As in the preceding passages this dense textural and contrapuntal fabric is achieved with characteristically orchestral means, building tension through the accumulation of different elements that are expressed by the diverse parts of the ensemble.

The arrival at D major in bar 181 initiates a sharply contrasting texture in which the forces of the orchestra join together for a common thematic statement. While components of this statement are variously distributed among different instruments, the composite effect of this triumphant passage is one of unity.

Together, bars 177–80 and 181–89 form the focal passage toward which the sweep and momentum of the development have been directed. Example 9b clarifies the large-scale role of D as a support for F♯, neighbor to the prolonged $\hat{2}$ (E). These climactic bars have particular importance in the form: they restate bars 59–71 of the exposition, which do not subsequently appear in the recapitulation. Indeed, one might think that this strong arrival on the tonic is

Example 9 Mozart, Symphony No. 38

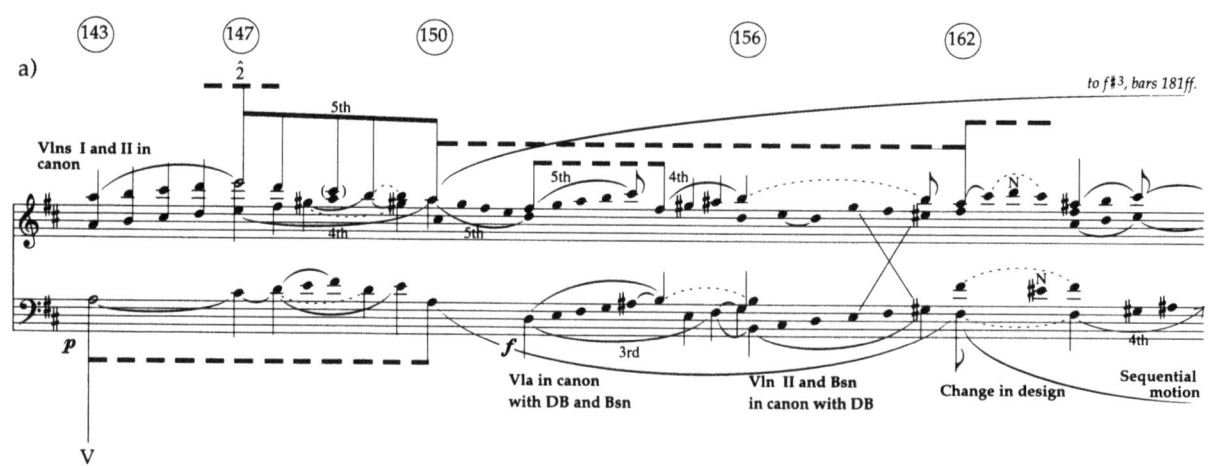

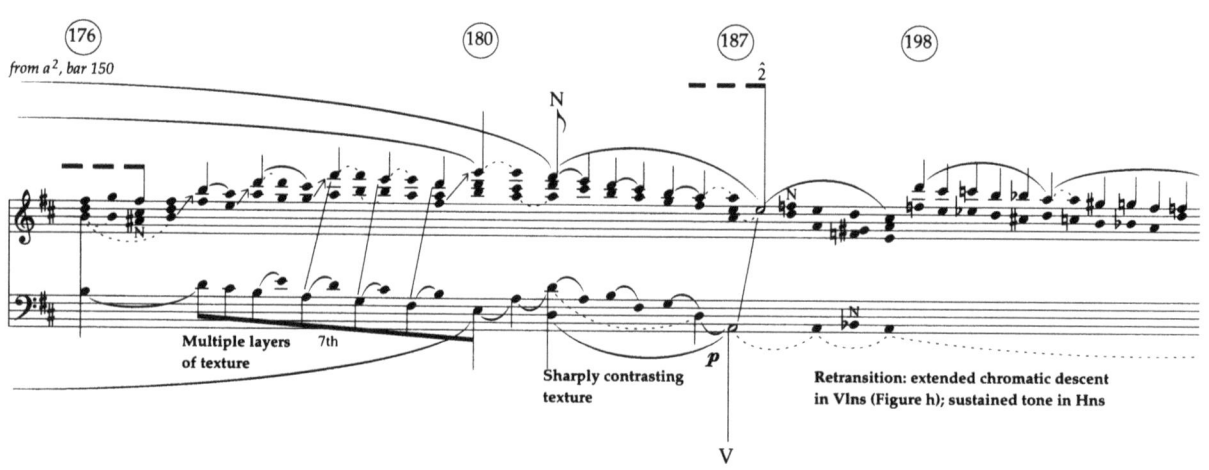

in fact the recapitulation, especially since it uses material from the first thematic group. However, this arrival is almost immediately followed by motion to the dominant, which is reached in bar 187. This D major passage might be compared to one of the so-called false recapitulations that are sometimes to be found in Haydn's sonata-allegro movements – but here the artistic purpose is different. Rather than a humorous, sleight-of-hand gesture, the passage seems to look ahead to the recapitulation, as if lost in a dream for a moment.

A comparison of the two occurrences of this passage reveals an intriguing difference in function. When first heard in the exposition (bars 59ff.) the passage forms part of the initial tonic prolongation, where D is functioning as a stable tonic harmony. It then moves from tonic harmony to the dominant that marks the beginning of the extended bridge section. In the development, on the other hand, the overall context is prolonged dominant harmony (Example 9b).

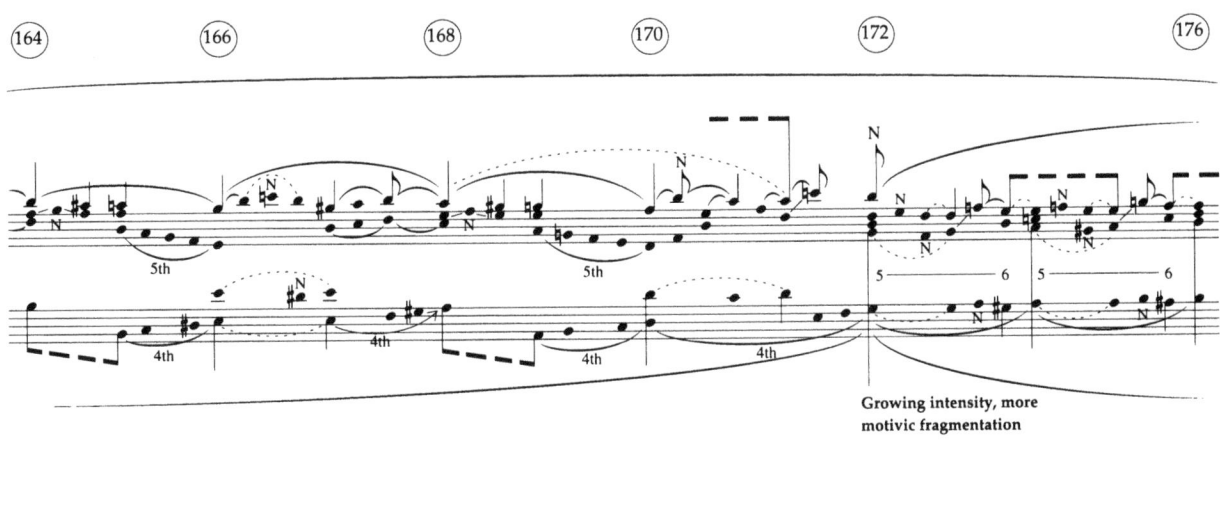

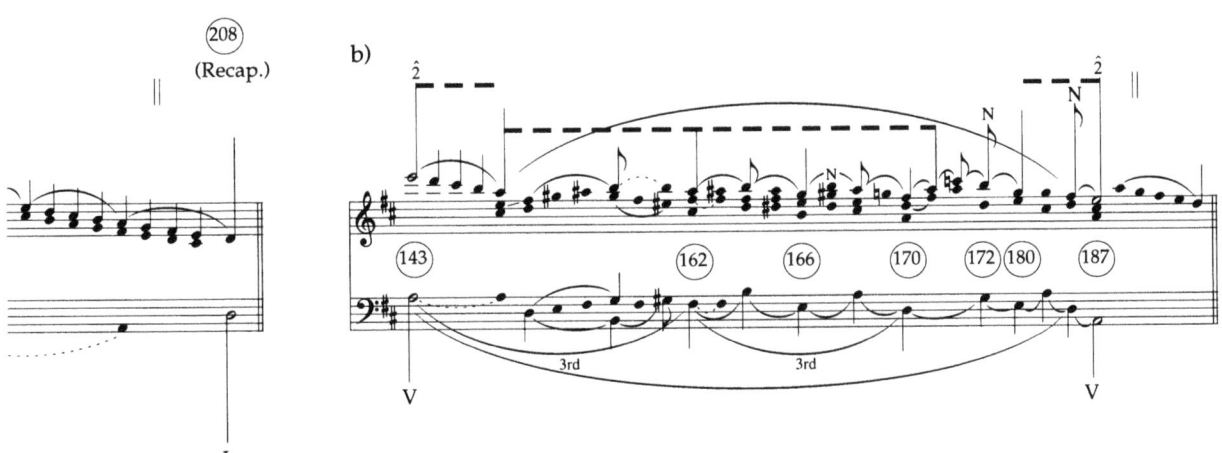

Beginning on a "local" D chord, the passage concludes on the dominant as the beginning of the retransition section (bars 187–89).

Hence the motion in the exposition is from a stable tonic to a less stable (and more local) dominant chord. Here, on the other hand, the passage represents a motion from D (functioning as a local and therefore less stable chord) to the return of V, the primary harmony of the development section.

Mozart's Piano Concerto in C major, K.503, was composed in the same year as the "Prague" Symphony. Two passages in the first movement of this concerto are related in a way that makes a remarkable comparison with those that we have just considered. The first passage, bars 26–50, begins in the tonic and modulates to the dominant. However the dominant is not yet stable, and is followed by a return to the tonic (minor) in bar 51.

Part of this passage recurs at the close of the exposition (bars 214–28), now entirely in the dominant key area. The last ten bars of both passages occur in the dominant and are identical. However, as in the "Prague" Symphony, the meaning of these passages is completely different. Donald Francis Tovey comments on this difference as follows:

> [The first passage] led to G and closed emphatically in that key, but yet under circumstances that made us feel that we were all the time only on the dominant of C. But now [in the second passage] . . . it begins in G, and Mozart so contrives that it remains there, instead of going on to the present dominant, D, as it would if transposed exactly; and it ends with the *very same notes* for no less than ten bars, *as in its original occurrence*, but now, of course, with the strongest possible feeling of being *in* G, not merely *on* the dominant. Thus Mozart cannot even do a mere repetition without shedding a new light that could not possibly be given by any variation. There is no describing the peculiar and subtle pleasure this device gives.[27]

Despite the differences in structural position and local details, the parallel between these two passages is striking. Both involve a structural reinterpretation of passages that are otherwise identical. Moreover, both were conceived for orchestral performance, and occur in movements of substantial length and scope. This kind of reinterpretation of blocks of material, while possible in any medium, is particularly characteristic of orchestral works in which such passages are often sharply defined by orchestration, texture, and rhythm in conjunction with thematic structure.

As the retransition section of the "Prague" Symphony begins, the parallel with the exposition continues: the opening measures (bars 189–99; see figure g in Example 8) echo the beginning of the transition section (bars 71–76). In the remainder of the transition figure c reappears, with its ascending fourth answered by the descending fourth of figure h (shown in Example 8). This figure then becomes the basis for an extended chromatic descent in the violins, joined by the flutes and bassoons. Overall the first violins descend two octaves, from d^3 in bar 198 to d^1 in bar 208 (the same tones that form the dramatic leap at the beginning of the "Haffner" Symphony). Here the many repetitions of the two motivic figures (unvaried, like the motivic repetitions we considered in K.338), together with the unbroken length and melodic span of the descent, create magnificent sweep and breadth in a way that would be difficult or impossible to achieve in another genre. (In this sense the passage may be compared to the stepwise ascent from g^1 to d^3 in bars 64–74 of K.338.)

The horns sustain the dominant tone throughout all but one bar of the retransition: this consistent element in the orchestral fabric again illustrates the layered approach to texture that we observed in earlier symphonies. It also serves as a referential element of structure that clearly and steadily defines the prolonged dominant, thereby allowing the other instruments to move freely.

Of all the symphonic passages we have examined, this development section illustrates Schenker's concept of symphonic breadth most dramatically. As in the earlier symphonies, the interplay of instruments and sections creates broad swaths of consistent texture in conjunction with extended motions and pro-

---

27. Donald Francis Tovey, "The Classical Concerto" (1903), reprinted in *Mozart: Piano Concerto in C major, K.503*, Norton Critical Score, ed. Joseph Kerman (New York: Norton, 1970), p. 157.

longations. Variations in orchestral setting are frequently associated with phrase elisions, so that the varieties of instrumental color make possible, and even foster, the scope and momentum that we have observed.

Perhaps the most remarkable aspect of this expansive development is Mozart's integration of so many thematic elements in a magnificently crafted contrapuntal web. Such a compositional plan would be almost impossible in another genre. The canons are associated with progressively denser texture and more thematic complexity; by carefully shaping the orchestration, he articulates all elements of the luxuriant texture with perfect clarity. The orchestral setting strengthens referential thematic relationships, such as the literal restatement of bars 59–71 in the different context of bars 177–89.

In larger terms, the structural plan also reflects the medium. Each of the quasi-independent structural gestures is characterized by its own contrapuntal processes and orchestral setting. Yet they are woven together through the constant repetition of motivic figures in association with instrumental timbres, and by the rhythmic momentum that these figures create. While the orchestral setting provides variety and color that articulate the diverse contrapuntal and thematic strands, it also integrates the complex structure through the essential unity of the symphonic ensemble.

Like Bach some decades earlier, Mozart was often criticized in his own time for writing works that were considered too complicated. Certainly the "Prague" Symphony represented a marked departure from his earlier orchestral style, and from the prevalent eighteenth-century symphonic tradition. In this sense Mozart may perhaps be seen as a link between eighteenth- and nineteenth-century symphonic styles. Many of the characteristics of the "Prague" Symphony, such as the contrapuntal framework created through varied combinations of themes, foreshadowed not only the Finale of the "Jupiter" Symphony but also many symphonic works by later composers.

Fétis stated in 1829:

It is [Mozart] who has introduced almost all the instrumental effects which are adopted in our time, and which the skill of instrumentalists and the perfection of instruments have farther developed. It is he, above all, who first gave to wind instruments their present importance in the orchestra. The effects which he drew from them are magical. . . . They are so multiform, so varied, that they defy all analysis.[28]

Despite their differences in style, the three symphonies discussed in this essay have many elements in common. The tendency toward extended phrases and broad compositional gestures, phrase elisions, and propulsive rhythms, all traits that were noted by commentators in Mozart's era, may be seen as an almost inevitable consequence of the makeup and character of the ensemble. Some stylistic traits in the earlier symphonies, such as the generally slower harmonic rhythm and more diatonic writing than was characteristic of Mozart's contemporaneous string quartets, may have resulted in part from the sym-

---

28. F. J. Fétis, *Traité de l'accompagnement de la partition sur le piano ou l'orgue*... (Paris: I. Pleyel et Cie., 1829), translated by Alfred Whittingham as *Treatise on Accompaniment from Score on the Organ or Pianoforte* (London: William Reeves, 1888), p. 52.

phonic tradition as it existed in Mozart's day, itself partly a result of the technical limitations of some instruments and perhaps the limited abilities of some orchestral players. Nevertheless Mozart clearly had his own vision of what the symphony could be, influenced no doubt by his experience as a composer of operas, and he eventually found ways to transcend some of these limitations while at the same time creating a distinctly symphonic style. The particular types of themes he chose for his symphonies, frequently in bold, elemental strokes that were ideally suited for development in the symphonic medium, and the large-scale structural gestures made the symphony not merely a grand, ceremonial genre, but one that was capable of the highest levels of artistic expression and refinement.

"Structural momentum" and closure in Chopin's Nocturne Op. 9, No. 2

John Rink

For all its grace, charm, and apparent simplicity, Chopin's Nocturne in E♭ major, Op. 9, No. 2, poses fundamental problems on close inspection. The fact that so many analyses of the piece – including those of Heinrich Schenker and Felix Salzer – fail to explain certain idiosyncratic aspects, in particular an unusual distribution of structural weight, gives some indication of the Nocturne's complexities at a profound level. Another thorny issue concerns John Field's influence on the work, which could extend beyond foreground features such as figuration to formal and structural characteristics, and which is implicit in Wilhelm von Lenz's comment that "the Nocturne is simply a refined Field, grafted onto a more interesting bass..."[1] A more detailed description of the piece by Lenz[2] – possibly derived from Chopin himself – also casts doubt on the nature of Op. 9, No. 2's construction.

This essay will review the studies of several authors and on the basis of these define a consensus view of the Nocturne's structure. I will then offer an analytical alternative and will consider how the work relates to other early compositions by Chopin, noting similarities which explain its more unusual characteristics, and differences which can perhaps be understood only by comparison with Field's Nocturnes Nos. 1 and 9, both in E♭ major.[3]

The first author to be considered, Lennox Berkeley, summarizes the Nocturne's form as "A1 A2 B1 A3 B2 A4 coda,"[4] while William Rothstein identifies a more succinct ternary plan: "The form of Chopin's piece is a simple ABA′ plus coda; the A and BA′ sections are each repeated with their figuration slightly altered. Each letter of this scheme stands for a four-bar phrase (also a

---

1. "Das Notturno ist nur ein veredelter, auf interessantere Bässe gepfropfter Field..." Wilhelm von Lenz, *Die grossen Pianoforte-Virtuosen unserer Zeit aus persönlicher Bekanntschaft* (Berlin: Behr, 1872), p. 41. (Published translations are used where available; all other translations are mine.) An earlier version of this essay appeared in *Chopin Studies* 5 (Warsaw: Towarzystwo imienia Fryderyka Chopina, 1995), pp. 82–104.
2. See note 10 below.
3. The publication history of Field's Nocturnes is long and complicated, in part the result of the composer's ambivalence about title (e.g., some were originally called "Romance") and his flexible approach to revision. The numbering in the Peters and Breitkopf & Härtel editions is used throughout this essay; note however that No. 9 in these editions appears elsewhere as No. 8 (as in Liszt's 1852 edition) or No. 10. For further discussion see Jeffrey Kallberg, "Understanding Genre: A Reinterpretation of the Early Piano Nocturne," in *Atti del XIV Congresso della Società Internazionale di Musicologia* (Torino: Edizioni di Torino, 1990), Vol. 3, pp. 775–79.
4. Lennox Berkeley, "Nocturnes, Berceuse, Barcarolle," in *Frédéric Chopin: Profiles of the Man and the Musician*, ed. Alan Walker (London: Barrie & Rockliff, 1966), p. 173.

Example 1 Chopin, Nocturne Op. 9, No. 2: middleground graph (from *Masterwork* II, p. 5)

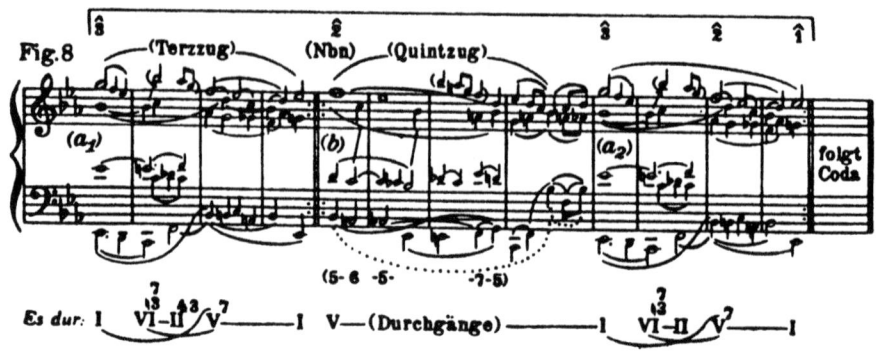

four-bar hypermeasure)."[5] This description indirectly derives from Schenker's analysis in the second *Meisterwerk* yearbook, which depicts the form as a_1–b–a_2 plus coda.[6] Schenker's graph is reproduced in Example 1; note that the coda is blank, the words "folgt Coda" and the empty staves indicating that this final section has no structural function.[7] Salzer likewise regards the Nocturne as a "three-part prolongation-form." More or less dismissing the ornamental variants of the principal sections, he suggests that "undue significance" should not be attached "to the figurated repetitions of each form section; they are not form making. A coda starts in meas[ure] 25 which has not been included in the graphs because it too does not affect the form construction. . . After the end of the third form section [A']. . . , nothing structural follows."[8]

A consensus can be proposed on the basis of these analyses (see Figure 1), in which the work is divided into three essential sections – A, B, and A' – linked by an interrupted descent in the fundamental line and an underlying progression of tonic and dominant harmonies. According to this scenario, the series of four-bar sections ends with a structurally insignificant ten-bar coda.

This consensus clashes with Hugo Leichtentritt's 1921 analysis, which outlines a "rondolike construction – A B A B A C C – consisting of nothing but four-bar phrases; only the final six-bar group extends the pattern":

> The sophisticated elegance of this salon piece reaches a peak near the end, where phrase C rises from a yearning *dolcissimo* to the opposite [extreme]: *con forza, stretto* to *fortissimo*. During a long pause, the cadenza's graceful ornamentation, in the highest register, dissipates the power of the *fortissimo* (which should not be taken altogether

---

5. He adds: "While the form may seem rigid stated thus, it is remarkable how much rhythmic variety Chopin manages to create within a very conventional framework." William Rothstein, "Phrase Rhythm in Chopin's Nocturnes and Mazurkas," in *Chopin Studies*, ed. Jim Samson (Cambridge: Cambridge University Press, 1988), p. 118.
6. Schenker, "Further Consideration of the Urlinie: II," trans. John Rothgeb, *Masterwork* II, p. 5. Schenker's other graphs of Op. 9, No. 2, appear in Figures 84, 88b, and 122/2 in *Free Composition*.
7. Compare the empty space (marked "u.s.w.") following bar 435 in Schenker's graph of the Finale from Beethoven's "Eroica," *Masterwork* III, p. 115.
8. Felix Salzer, *Structural Hearing: Tonal Coherence in Music*, 2nd edn (New York: Dover, 1962), Vol. 1, pp. 245–46. See also Examples 324 and 500 (Vol. 2, pp. 117–18 and 290–92).

Figure 1 Chopin, Nocturne Op. 9, No. 2: analytical consensus

Fundamental line:	$\hat{3}$		$\hat{2}$	‖	$\hat{3}$	$\hat{2}$	$\hat{1}$
Harmony:	I		V		I	V	I
Section:	‖: A	:‖:	B		A'	:‖	Coda
Bars:	1–4 5–8		9–12 17–20		13–16 21–24		25–34
Phrase structure:	‖: 4	:‖:	4	+	4	:‖	10 (subdivisions unspecified)

literally), until we return to *pianissimo* with the delicate, melodious E♭ major chord at the end.[9]

For Leichtentritt, the piece thus concludes not with a coda but with two sections (both labeled C) respectively four and six bars long.

Leichtentritt's analysis echoes the detailed description published by Lenz in 1872. (Whether these are Lenz's or Chopin's comments is ambiguous, as suggested above.) "The first four [bars] along with the upbeat are the theme; bars 5–8, the first variation; bars 9–12, ritornello, with a transition to the second variation in bars 13–16; bars 17–20, ritornello; bars 21–24, the third variation; and bars 25–34, ritornello and cadenza."[10] Once again there is no mention of a coda: in Lenz's analysis, the Nocturne ends with a ritornello (to be discussed later) and a cadenza.

The most troubling discrepancy between the first set of analyses and the latter two concerns the final ten bars, the so-called coda. To some extent, this can be attributed to the disparate meanings attached to "coda" in the literature: depending on context, the term can have numerous connotations. For instance, "coda" can generally describe formal units in songs, fugues, minuets, scherzos, and sonata-form movements, where, in the words of the *New Grove Dictionary*, "it refers to anything occurring after the end of the recapitulation."[11] In con-

---

9. "Konstruktion rondoartig, aus lauter Viertakten bestehend, nur die Schlußgruppe auf 6 Takte erweitert: A B A B A C C... Die mondäne Eleganz dieses Salonstücks kommt zur vollen Entfaltung gegen den Schluß hin, wo die Phrase C aus dem schmachtenden *dolcissimo* sich ins Gegenteil, *con forza, stretto* zum *ff* erhebt, um dann auf dem langen Halt in eine graziösverschnörkelte *cadenza* in der höchsten Oktave auszulaufen, in der sich die Kraft des nicht so ernst gemeinten *ff* wieder bricht, bis zur völligen Rückkehr auf den *pp* schmelzend hingehauchten Es-dur Schlußakkord." Hugo Leichtentritt, *Analyse der Chopin'schen Klavierwerke* (Berlin: Max Hesse, 1921–22), Vol. 1, pp. 5–6.
10. "[D]ie 4 ersten [Tacte] nebst Auftact sind Thema, der 5te bis inclusive 8te die 1ste Variation, der 9te bis inclusive 12te Ritornell, bezüglich Uebergang zur 2ten Variation: 13ten–16ten Tact, der 17te–20ste Ritornell, der 21ste–24ste die 3te Variation, der 25ste–34ste Ritornell und Cadenza." Wilhelm von Lenz, "Uebersichtliche Beurtheilung der Pianoforte-Compositionen von Chopin," *Neue Berliner Musikzeitung* 27/38 (1872), p. 297.
11. "Coda," in *The New Grove Dictionary of Music and Musicians*, ed. Stanley Sadie (London: Macmillan, 1980), Vol. 4, p. 515.

trast to these form-related definitions, which refer to its position rather than its function,[12] "coda" has a specific structural meaning in Schenkerian theory, which is more in keeping with both a literal interpretation of the word – "tail" – and its definition during the early to mid-nineteenth century (for instance in Koch's 1802 *Musikalisches Lexikon*[13] and the 1835 *Universal-Lexicon*[14]). In essence, Schenker maintained that when the fundamental line descends in a work, the main body reaches a structural conclusion: anything thereafter amounts to a coda. He writes in *Free Composition*: "The middleground and background . . . determine the definitive close of a composition. With the arrival of $\hat{1}$ the work is at an end. Whatever follows this can only be a reinforcement of the close – a coda – no matter what its extent or purpose may be. . ."[15] Thus, in Schenkerian theory the coda is essentially a foreground phenomenon, a view echoed by the definition of "coda" in the *New Harvard Dictionary*: "In instrumental music following regular musical forms, a concluding section *extraneous to the form* as usually defined; any concluding passage that can be understood as occurring *after the structural conclusion* of a work and that serves as a formal closing gesture."[16]

Generalization about Chopin's codas – whether structural or formal in nature – is not entirely straightforward: as Jeffrey Kallberg observes, "codas do not serve the same function for Chopin in all genres. . . [I]deally a separate model should be derived" for each.[17] Furthermore, inconsistent use of the term in the Chopin literature makes it difficult to draw conclusions: some authors allude to structural codas, others to formal ones, but in most cases the label is applied without distinction (as in the quotations above). Despite these problems, a few broad observations about Chopin's codas can be hazarded. Schenker's definition of the "structural coda," notwithstanding certain obvious shortcomings,[18] is of particular relevance to Chopin's music, a sizable proportion of which ends with a concluding section after the fundamental line's

---

12. This distinction is elaborated in Joseph Kerman, "Notes on Beethoven's Codas," in *Beethoven Studies 3*, ed. Alan Tyson (Cambridge: Cambridge University Press, 1982), p. 141.
13. "Coda, Anhang, Zusatz. Die Benennung desjenigen Satzes, der in einem Tonstücke, in welchem die Hauptperioden wiederholt werden, als völliger Schlußsatz hinzugefügt wird. Wenn z.B. in einem Allegro, welches aus zwey Reprisen bestehet, nach der Wiederholung des zweyten Theils oder der zweyten Reprise, noch eine besondere kurze Schlußperiode vorhanden ist, so wird sie Coda genannt." "Coda," in Heinrich Christoph Koch, *Musikalisches Lexikon* (Offenbach am Main: Johann André, 1802), col. 345.
14. "*Coda*, Schwanz, Anhang, Schlußsatz, heißt derjenige Satz oder Theil eines, aus mehreren Reprisen, d.h. zu wiederholenden Theilen, bestehenden Musikstücks, das durch sich selbst nicht zu einem völligen Schlusse abgerundet ist, der diesem als vollkommen beruhigender Schlußsatz hinzugefügt oder angehängt wird. . ." "Coda," in *Encyclopädie der gesammten musikalischen Wissenschaften, oder Universal-Lexicon der Tonkunst*, ed. Gustav Schilling (Stuttgart: Franz Heinrich Köhler, 1835), Vol. 2, p. 270.
15. *Free Composition*, p. 129. See also §§ 24, 267, 304 (in which the quoted excerpt appears), and §315. See Esther Cavett-Dunsby's discussion of "structural" and "formal" codas in "Mozart's Codas," *Music Analysis* 7/1 (1988), pp. 31–51; see also Kerman, "Notes on Beethoven's Codas."
16. "Coda," in *The New Harvard Dictionary of Music*, ed. Don Randel (Cambridge, Mass.: Belknap, 1986), p. 178 (my emphases).
17. Jeffrey Kallberg, "Compatibility in Chopin's Multipartite Publications," *The Journal of Musicology* 2/4 (1983), p. 404.
18. These are outlined in Cavett-Dunsby, "Mozart's Codas." My use of the terms "structural" and "formal" codas derives from her article.

descent – in other words, a structural coda. These conclusions vary from just one or two bars to passages of considerable length, which either restate material used earlier in the work (thereby effecting large-scale synthesis) or present new melodic or harmonic ideas. What they all have in common is their position outside the fundamental structure, that is, after the structural cadence. As for "formal codas" in Chopin's music, it would surely be more enlightening to describe new material after the recapitulation but before the structural $\hat{1}$ not as a "coda" (i.e., "formal coda"), but according to its specific contextual function:[19] for instance, expansion, extension, generation of momentum, peroration, and so forth.[20] These several techniques of preparing and highlighting the structural cadence are typical of Chopin, having become standard procedure in the nocturnes and etudes of the early 1830s (for instance, in bars 54–57 of the Nocturne in F♯ major, Op. 15, No. 2), and deriving from certain large-scale virtuosic works of the Warsaw period – the *Polonaise brillante*, Op. 3; *Rondo à la mazur*, Op. 5; Fantasy, Op. 13; Rondo, Op. 73; Waltz in E minor; and the two concertos – in which Chopin extends and embellishes the phrase immediately preceding the structural $\hat{1}$'s arrival, thus clearly separating the main body of the piece from the bravura finale that follows.[21] When codas – that is, structural codas – appear in Chopin's music from the Vienna and early Paris periods (and indeed in later works as well), they tend therefore to follow final surges of momentum preparing the close of the fundamental structure, generally reinforcing the structural cadence by means of a tonic pedal[22] or by close adherence to the principal diatonic harmonies: I, IV, and V.

With these points in mind, we must now question whether the section from bar 25 onward in Op. 9, No. 2, is a structural coda – that is, a coda in the Schenkerian sense. Precisely what function do the last ten bars of the piece serve? If the consensus defined earlier is correct – in other words, if the fundamental line descends to $\hat{1}$ in bar 24, followed by a ten-bar structural coda (leaving a "blank space" in the middleground and background from bar 25 to the end) – then the overall structure is oddly static, lacking what I term "structural momentum," that is, forward impulse or dynamic shape at a fundamental level. As this scenario would have it, closure is attained without any real convic-

---

19. I would almost suggest using the term "coda" only in the sense of "structural coda" when describing Chopin's music, except perhaps for those few genres (such as the sonatas) where its meaning is more precise.
20. Robert G. Hopkins catalogues some of the functions served by codas in "When a Coda is More than a Coda: Reflections on Beethoven," in *Explorations in Music, the Arts, and Ideas*, ed. Eugene Narmour and Ruth A. Solie (Stuyvesant, New York: Pendragon, 1988), pp. 398ff. See also Cavett-Dunsby, "Mozart's Codas," pp. 46–47 for a "summary of eight characteristics of Mozart's sonata-form codas."
21. I investigate this feature of Chopin's compositions in the *stile brillante* and its later use in his nocturnes and etudes from 1830 to 1832 in Part II of "The Evolution of Chopin's 'Structural Style' and its Relation to Improvisation" (Ph.D. diss., University of Cambridge, 1989). See also John Rink, *Chopin: The Piano Concertos* (Cambridge: Cambridge University Press, 1997).

    Other models impinging on Op. 9, No. 2, include the paired *cantabile–cabaletta* of Italian opera (of which Chopin was a devoted follower in both Warsaw and Paris) and variation form, in which a longer, more energetic section often rounds off a series of "standard" variations.
22. The use of a tonic pedal in Chopin's structural codas can result in overwhelming dissonance. See for instance bars 103–10 (the first of two structural codas) in the Barcarolle, Op. 60, which I discuss in "The *Barcarolle*: *Auskomponierung* and Apotheosis," in *Chopin Studies*, ed. Samson, pp. 203–4 and 210–12.

tion, as in many earlier works by Chopin.[23] Despite the broad three-part form underlying the first twenty-four bars, there is no compelling reason to regard the "third variation," A4, as a definitive conclusion to the chain of sections, which might even have been extended (albeit tediously) with additional alternating A and B sections containing ever more elaborate ornamentation. The metrically unaccented cadences within the A sections further undermine the sense of closure. Other problems with this scenario include the fundamental line's twofold descent in A3 and A4, and a formal disequilibrium implicit in the consensus view: the putative coda is ten bars long, as against only twenty-four bars for the "main body" of the work.[24] Although it could be argued that Chopin needed a lengthy coda such as this to compensate for the final A section's lack of definitive closure, this view is decidedly negative with regard to the function of the last ten bars, whereas the music's "narrative" process suggests both a positive function and an altogether different structural interpretation.

If one follows the music from bar 25 onward as it unfolds in time, without the preconceptions that synchronic formal and structural paradigms can impose on the listener, it becomes clear that although the section *starts* like a coda, it by no means *finishes* in the way one is initially led to expect. Chopin as it were "deceives" us into hearing the beginning of a structural coda, but then thwarts the anticipation of imminent closure when the music suddenly takes a new direction, in what retrospectively is perceived as no more – and no less – than a *formal* coda (to repeat, a final passage within the main body of a work, before the structural descent). Following in Leichtentritt's footsteps, I identify two principal sections after A4 which together constitute this formal coda: C1 (bars 25–28) and C2 (bars 29–32). A two-bar structural coda then follows in bars 33–34.

In the first two bars of C1, the tonic pedal, second inversion minor subdominant harmony, reflected motive E♭–F–G, restatement of the primary tone $\hat{3}$, and dynamic contraction from *piano* to *pianissimo* appear to function as standard codes or devices announcing the start of a structural coda, which promises at first to be brief, possibly only three bars in length, that is, bars 25–26 plus an additional bar, perhaps as in Example 2's hypothetical recomposed ending. Chopin however deftly extends this implied conclusion into yet another four-bar group. The voice leading of C1 as a whole is therefore similar to that of the A sections, in other words, a third-progression ($\hat{3}$–$\hat{2}$–$\hat{1}$), as the graph in Example 3 indicates.

The sudden profusion of performance markings in these bars – *poco rubato*, *sempre pp*, and *dolcissimo* – indicates the significance Chopin attached to the

---

23. See Part II, Chapter 1, in Rink, "The Evolution of Chopin's 'Structural Style.'"
24. See Hopkins, "When a Coda is More than a Coda," p. 394, on the proportion of codas within whole movements. Note that the consensus view is not wholly unjustified, even if it proves inadequate. First of all, bars 1–24 (in 12/8, played Andante) are substantial enough for the piece to end after section A4 had that been the composer's wish; moreover, the addition of further variations on the A and B sections to extend beyond bar 24 would, as I suggest above, be stultifying. So there are legitimate grounds for inferring the completion of the "main body" at bar 24, especially since weak closure is far from atypical in Chopin's music. That does not of course eliminate the possibility (or even necessity) of revising the implication of closure in the light of subsequent developments – and this is where the "blank space" in Schenker's and Salzer's analyses misses the point.

Example 2 Chopin, Nocturne Op. 9, No. 2: hypothetical recomposed "coda," bars 25–[27]

passage. The *poco rubato* is particularly telling. Rubato can assume different functions in Chopin's music according to context, but the general principle is one of borrowing or give-and-take, as in the Baroque era. In this passage the marking could be interpreted in at least two different ways. Jean-Jacques Eigeldinger observes that in Op. 9, No. 2, which is "a perfect example of *bel canto* adapted to the piano, it arises out of the Italian tradition: even if the rubato here is applicable to various other points in the same piece, it belongs essentially to one particular phrase of a more *pathéthique* character – to use [Pier Francesco] Tosi's own words."[25] Eigeldinger notes specifically that *poco rubato* falls "at the beginning of a new motive which is to direct the piece towards the final cadence," suggesting that the right hand should stretch the tempo while the left hand maintains a steady eighth-note pulse. Alternatively, Chopin might have specified *poco rubato* at this point and nowhere else in the work to achieve a more profound fluctuation in tempo, affecting "the musical structure from top to bottom, not merely the melodic line"[26] but the bass part as well. Whether it applies only to the treble or to both hands, the marking has a powerful effect: the result in either case is to slow the music quasi-ritardando as if approaching a final cadence – at the end of a short structural coda like that in Example 2 – and then, compensating for this slackening in tempo, to cause a slight acceleration carrying the music beyond the expected closural point to bar 28's metrically weak cadence. This breathtaking reversal of expectations is reinforced by the *sempre pp* and *dolcissimo* markings, which sustain the *pathéthique* quality, the sense of "yearning" (Leichtentritt's term)[27] created by the fluctuation in tempo, and which heighten the listener's uncertainty as to what will follow next.

At the beginning of section C2, the root-position minor subdominant in bar 29 foreshadows and indeed initiates the greater activity that ensues. *Con forza* and *stretto* markings replace the *poco rubato*, *sempre pp*, and *dolcissimo* of section C1, and, although melodic and harmonic patterns from C1 are restated (in yet another variation of the underlying structure), the bass motion is greatly

---

25. Jean-Jacques Eigeldinger, *Chopin: Pianist and Teacher as Seen by His Pupils*, trans. Naomi Shohet with Krysia Ososotowicz and Roy Howat, ed. Roy Howat (Cambridge: Cambridge University Press, 1986), p. 121, n. 99.
26. *Ibid.*, p. 120, n. 98.
27. See note 9 above.

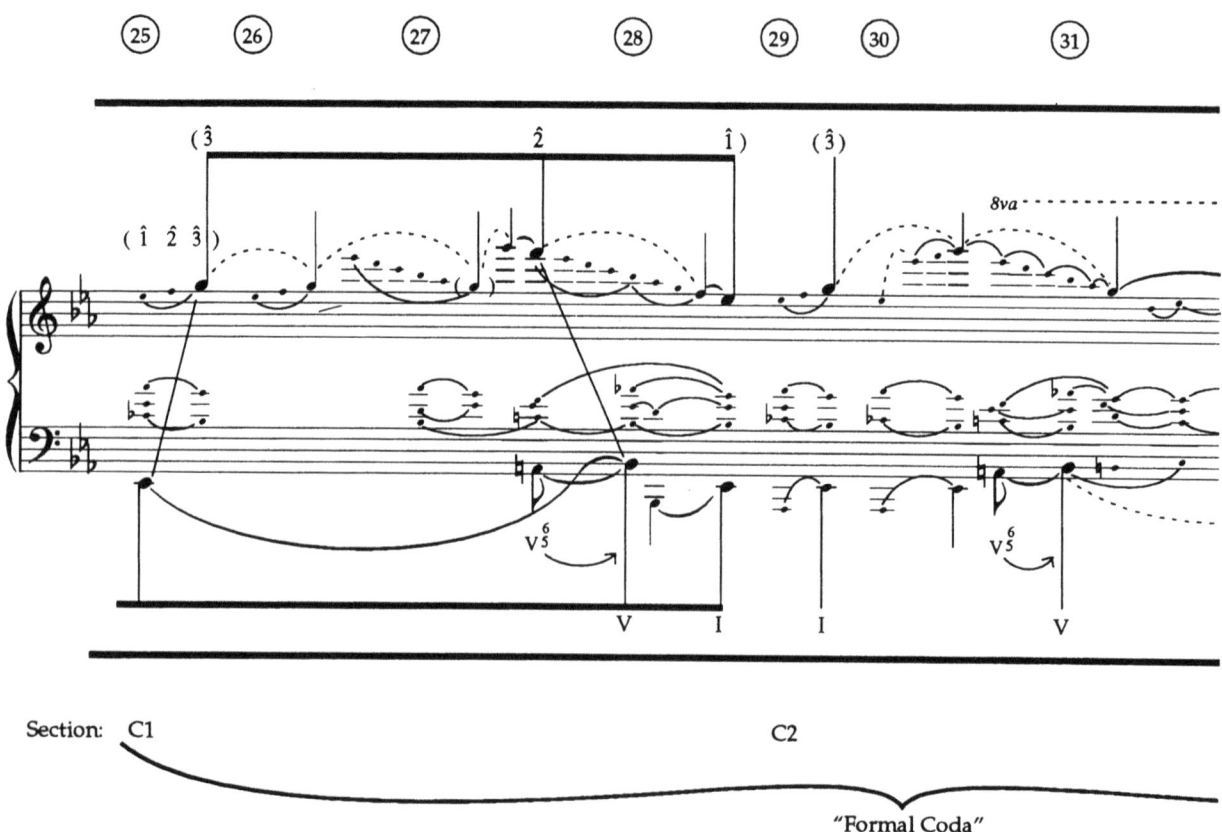

Example 3 Chopin, Nocturne Op. 9, No. 2: foreground graph, bars 25–34

accelerated: as Example 4 shows, an important cadential motive from the A sections returns in the bass, outlining a turning figure from B♭ through B♮, C, and A♮ back to B♭. The passage contains the Nocturne's most exciting music and dramatic climax, driving forward to what I regard as the structural $\hat{2}$, f^2, in bar 31, and the B♭ major harmony in bar 32 that acts as the structural dominant (see Example 3). This important point of arrival is emphasized by the Nocturne's loudest dynamic, *fortissimo*, and by the left-hand arpeggio figuration, which breaks the chordal accompaniment pattern for the first time in the piece.

The lengthy fermata in the cadenza, which, played *senza tempo*, sounds the Nocturne's registral peak (d^4) and also rearticulates in a slightly different order the pervasive bass motive (see Example 4), brings the first significant agogic deviation in the four-bar phrase patterns that hitherto have prevailed, greatly delaying and thereby stressing the fundamental line's imminent resolution to E♭, which occurs on the downbeat of bar 33 with the first metrically accented cadence in the work (versus the weaker cadences ending each A section). This concluding gesture – by far the most definitive moment of closure in the piece – leads to the two-bar structural coda, which cements the arrival on I.[28]

28. It is instructive to compare the ending of Op. 9, No. 2, with that of other works in the genre. In the contemporaneous Nocturne in B major, Op. 9, No. 3, Chopin similarly prolongs the structural $\hat{2}$ in a cadenza, followed by a two-bar structural coda after the descent to $\hat{1}$. Note too the recitative cum

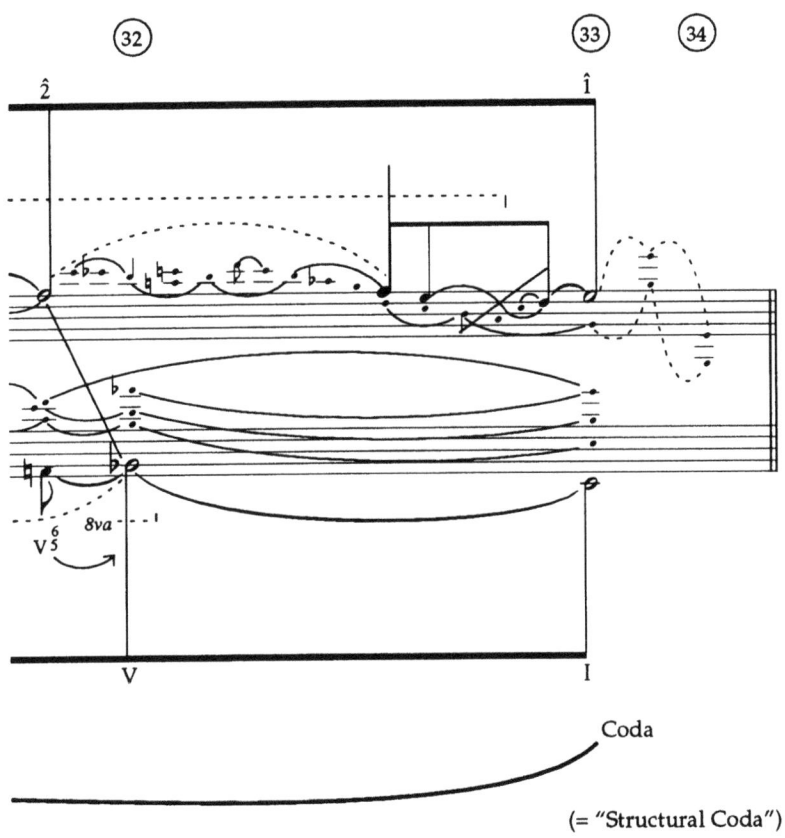

(= "Structural Coda")

My analysis of Op. 9, No. 2, thus reveals a considerably broader compositional conception than that discerned by Schenker and Salzer, highlighting in particular Chopin's exploitation of "structural momentum" to imbue the Nocturne with a sense of process, an underlying dynamic impulse propelling the music beyond the ostensible close in bar 24 to the double bar at the end. This comprehensiveness is implicit in Example 5's middleground graph, which adapts Schenker's Figure 84 from *Free Composition* to reflect my reading of the work's structure, whereby the original "blank space" now participates in the all-embracing structural sweep. The "ornamental melody" in sections A and B is thus given a long-range goal in a manner foreshadowing the apotheosis-like conclusions in Chopin's later music and consistent with the end-weighted structures typical of nineteenth-century music in general.[29]

As already implied, Chopin's sensitivity to "structural momentum" and

cadenza of the Nocturne in B major, Op. 32, No. 1, which likewise delays the fundamental structure's descent, although here there is no reinforcing structural coda afterward. In each piece, the cadenza prepares for rather than follows the principal close, creating "the sense of a prolonged dominant resolving with special solidity after the improvisatory digression" (Joseph Kerman's comment on Beethoven's cadenzas; Kerman, "Notes on Beethoven's Codas," p. 155). This is also true of the E♭ Nocturne.

29. See Hopkins, "When a Coda is More than a Coda," p. 410.

Example 4 Chopin, Nocturne Op. 9, No. 2: turning-figure motive

Section A1 (bars 3–4)

Section A2 (bars 7–8)

Section A3 (bars 15–16)

Section A4 (bars 23–24)

Section C1—fragment (bars 27–28)

Section C2 (bars 30–32)

Cadenza (bar 32)

Example 5 Chopin, Nocturne Op. 9, No. 2: middleground graph (adaptation of *Free Composition*, Figure 84)

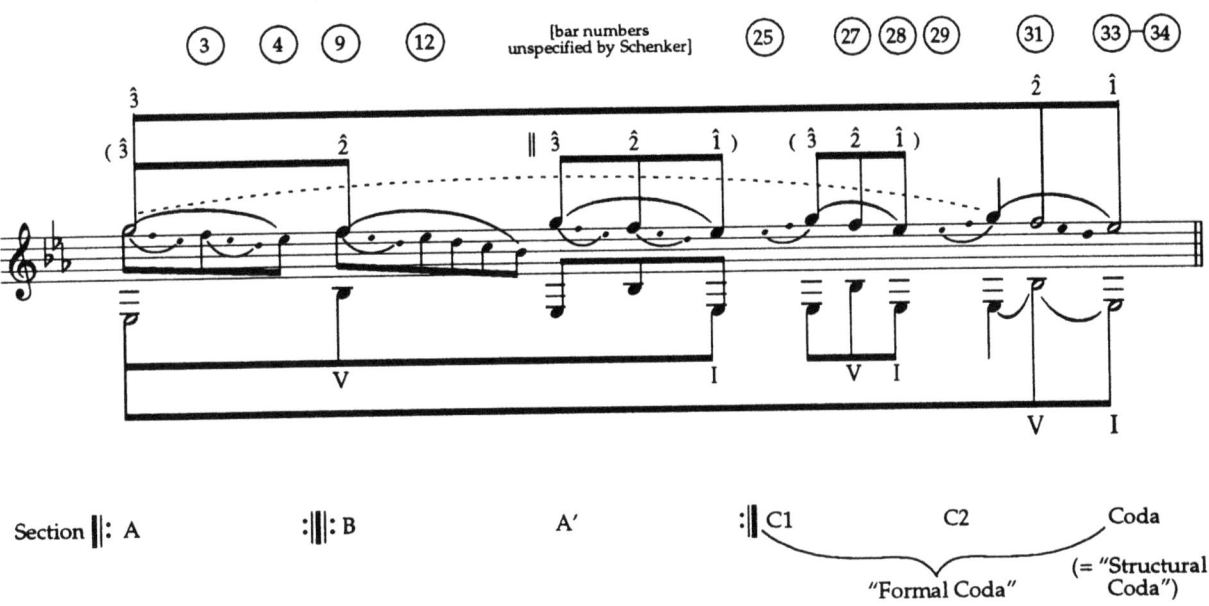

closure in Op. 9, No. 2, is by no means unique in his music of the early 1830s. Numerous compositional strategies are employed in this period to avoid what Kallberg calls the "paratactic" construction of earlier music,[30] among them the phrase extensions and energetic surges referred to above; also the use of rests, fermatas, reversed dynamics, and performance indications such as rubato and *smorzando* to differentiate the last section in an ABA form from earlier statements of the same section;[31] and finally, long-range resolution of dissonance or tonal tensions. The latter occurs for instance in the middle section of the Nocturne in B♭ minor, Op. 9, No. 1, where in a lengthy coda-like passage following the principal thematic statement in the relative major, Chopin adds C♭ to the *fortissimo* D♭ major harmony in bars 51–58 to create a dominant seventh. The expected resolution to G♭ major – the tonicized IV of D♭ major – never materializes, however: the second half of this "internal coda" (as I regard it) is based on D♭ major without the added C♭, accompanied by a dynamic contraction to *ppp* in bar 61 which stresses the implied elision. It is not until the fundamental line's descent via C♭ (♭2̂) in bars 79–80, and then the six-bar structural coda (bars 80–85), which highlights the motion between C♭ and B♭ by stating the Neapolitan harmony over a tonic pedal, that Chopin fully redresses the tensions created by C♭ within the "internal coda." Similar long-range resolution from an "internal coda" to a "final" structural coda can be observed in the Nocturne in F♯ major, Op. 15, No. 2, in which the emphatically repeated D♮–C♯ motive at the end of the middle section (bars 43–48 – earlier in bars 39–41 as

---

30. Jeffrey Kallberg, "The Problem of Repetition and Return in Chopin's Mazurkas," in *Chopin Studies*, ed. Samson, pp. 1–23 *passim*.
31. This can be observed in some of the sources for Op. 6 and Op. 7. For discussion see *ibid*.

Example 6 John Field, Nocturne No. 1 in E♭ major: ritornello passages and coda (bars 16–19, 35–42, and 58–66)

well), where it appears in the context of the dominant, returns in bars 58–61, diatonically "rectified" (Schenker's term)[32] to D♯–C♯ in the context of I.

Long-range resolutions such as these characterize other contemporaneous compositions by Chopin (including most of the Etudes, Op. 10), and it is therefore not surprising that a similar strategy should be employed in Op. 9, No. 2, namely, the redressing of tensions established in a coda-like passage (section C1, the first part of the formal coda) by means of a broad final gesture manifested in the cadenza, the structural descent in bars 31–33, and ultimately the "real" (i.e., structural) coda in bars 33–34. What distinguishes the E♭ Nocturne's generation of "structural momentum" from that in other contemporary pieces concerns the work's formal design: whereas typically momentum is used to join sections *within* an ABA form (as in the two Nocturnes just discussed), here "structural momentum" is generated only *after* the three-part plan has been completed. Op. 9, No. 2, is unique among the compositions of this period in that its structural descent, surge of energy, and long-range resolution of tonal and formal tensions lie entirely outside the ABA formal model. Of the various

32. *Free Composition*, p. 71.

factors that might explain this anomaly, perhaps the most compelling is the influence that John Field's first and ninth Nocturnes, also in E♭ major, had on Chopin when composing the work in 1830–31. The many obvious similarities between the three pieces have been exhaustively catalogued by various authors,[33] ranging from analogous left-hand accompaniment patterns and "almost identical"[34] opening gestures in the B sections to comparable melodic figuration toward the end of all three works. I would propose however that Field's Nocturnes inspired Chopin in a more profound way than just these foreground features: specifically, in the unusual formal design and unique means of generating "structural momentum" that we have observed in Op. 9, No. 2.

A brief look at Field's first Nocturne (published in 1812) reveals three principal sections – A, B, and A′, each fifteen bars long – separated by a ritornello which initially lasts four bars (bars 16–19; see Example 6) but is later extended

---

33. See for instance David Branson, *John Field and Chopin* (London: Barrie & Jenkins, 1972); Barbara Chmara, "Das Problem der Agogik der Nocturni von Field und Chopin," in *The Book of the First International Musicological Congress Devoted to the Works of Frederick Chopin*, ed. Zofia Lissa (Warsaw: Państwowe Wydawnictwo Naukowe, 1963), pp. 275–80; Eigeldinger, *Chopin: Pianist and Teacher*, p. 116, n. 84, and p. 152, n. 184; and Jim Samson, *The Music of Chopin* (London: Routledge and Kegan Paul, 1985), pp. 81–85.
34. Samson, *The Music of Chopin*, p. 83.

in bars 35–42 and bars 58–64, where it leads into a two-bar structural coda like Op. 9, No. 2's. Field's exploitation of the ritornello is noteworthy: the recurrent passage not only participates in the variation process linking A and A′, but also provides the definitive sense of closure lacking after all three principal thematic sections. In A and A′, continual return to the tonic harmony and tonic pitch E♭, with a perfect authentic cadence every few bars, prevents the melody from attaining either a satisfactory close or (in Jim Samson's words) "that built-in flexibility of rhythmic discourse and suppleness of melodic line which are so characteristic of the Chopin nocturne."[35] Block-like rigidity is partly mitigated by section B's more ambitious harmonies, but it is left to the three ritornellos to provide the melodic and harmonic impetus necessary to achieve closure once and for all. The final ritornello is particularly effective in this regard: not only does the harmony grow more complex, thus enhancing the listener's expectation of resolution, but Field reserves the Nocturne's registral peak, b♭^{3}, for the ritornello's last bar, from which a mostly linear descent falls through nearly two octaves to the structural cadence launching the short coda.

Similar sensitivity to large-scale closure can be observed in Field's 1816 Nocturne in E♭ major (originally, "Romance"; see Example 7). The composer's repeated attempts to conclude this equally episodic piece, following the strong perfect authentic cadence in bars 42–43 and the start of a quasi-coda in bar 44 (which, as in the Chopin, turns out not to be the *structural* coda), include a pause on I^6 in bar 49, a contraction in dynamics in the same bar (the *fioritura* ending with a double-neighbor pattern like that in Chopin's cadenza), and a final increase in momentum in bars 54ff. leading to the most definitive cadence of all, the structural close in bars 56–57, which is echoed and reinforced in a brief coda.

It is no coincidence that the superficial similarities between Field's and Chopin's E♭ Nocturnes are most abundant near the end of the three works, for here we also see the most profound resemblance: in each Nocturne, the composer generates "structural momentum" precisely at this point, imbuing the music with an urgency that helps overcome less definitive moments of closure earlier on. Whether Chopin was consciously emulating Field is a moot point without relevance to larger, more important issues: in fact, little more need be made of Field's influence than to note the greater subtlety with which Chopin shapes Op. 9, No. 2, masterfully generating "structural momentum" to overcome formal divisions such as those marring the 1812 and 1816 Nocturnes. This is not to deny the charm of Field's music: Liszt for one praised the "radiant happiness" and "overflowing felicity" in the earlier of the two works.[36] But any discussion of Field's influence on Chopin must inevitably end with acknowledgment of the younger composer's greater expertise.

It is possible, incidentally, that the unusually copious autograph variants[37] for Op. 9, No. 2, reflect Chopin's later attempt to disguise an apparently embarrassing debt to Field which both he and his contemporaries recognized. As

---

35. *Ibid.*
36. Franz Liszt, "On John Field's Nocturnes," trans. T. Baker, in *John Field: Eighteen Nocturnes for the Piano* (New York: Schirmer, 1902), p. vi.
37. See Eigeldinger, *Chopin: Pianist and Teacher*, pp. 150–52, nn. 183–84, for discussion of these.

Example 7 John Field, Nocturne No. 9 in E♭ major, bars 40–61

Example 8 Chopin, Nocturne Op. 9, No. 2: select variants

a) Bar 31, beat 4, right-hand part, and bars 34–35/36
variants in the Wiener Urtext edition, ed. Jan Ekier

Eigeldinger observes, Chopin might "have wished to impart a more personal stamp to this work, by means of these ornamental clusters which form part of a pianism and an *improvisando* conception transcending some of Field's somewhat fixed stereotypes."[38] For our purposes, it suffices to examine alternative versions near the end of the Nocturne, for in principle these could either corroborate or negate the structural interpretation proposed above. As Example 8a shows, variants 16a and 16b in Jan Ekier's Wiener Urtext edition preserve and indeed stress the structural $\hat{2}$ as defined earlier, just as the alternative cadenza reproduced in Example 8b highlights a prolonged F in readiness for the fundamental line's descent to E♭ in bar 33. The structural $\hat{2}$ is even more prominent

---

38. *Ibid.*, p. 152, n. 184.

b) Cadenza
as reproduced in the Peters edition (No. 8522), ed. H. Scholtz;
see Eigeldinger, *Chopin: Pianist and Teacher*, p. 151

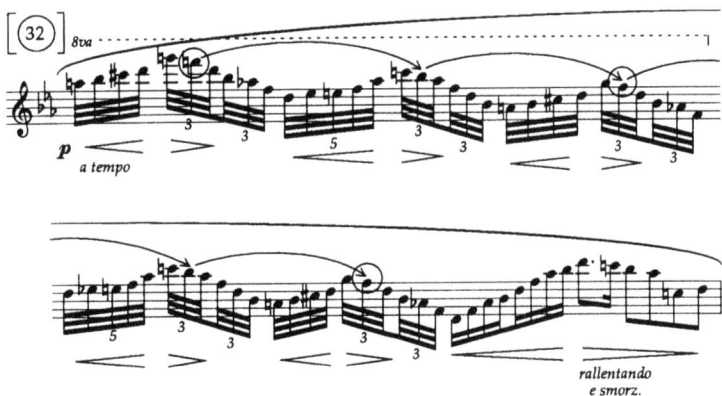

c) End of cadenza (following b♭³ in the thirteenth turning figure)
in the Zaleska-Rosengardt score,
as transcribed in Eigeldinger, *Chopin: Pianist and Teacher*, p. 238

in the cadenza variant shown in Example 8c.[39] Finally, the variant endings designated 17a and 17b by Ekier not only deviate from the original model – the first of Field's Nocturnes – but also reinforce this final section's function as a true coda, clearly distinguishing it from the more active and structurally integral sections C1 and C2 (the formal coda).

What then of Lenz's peculiar description of Op. 9, No. 2, in his 1872 article? The two B sections could conceivably be called a ritornello, but it would be ludicrous to regard C1 and C2 as yet another statement of the same ritornello, as the 1872 comments imply. Possibly Lenz – or Chopin – meant that the work

---

39. Of course, even if the structural F were less (rather than more) prominent in Chopin's variants, this would not deny my structural interpretation, as substitutions for the structural $\hat{2}$ frequently occur in tonal music.

In the variant shown in Example 8b, the circles and arrows have been added. See *ibid.*, pp. 237–38 for discussion of the variant shown in Example 8c (found in a score of the Nocturnes Op. 9 which Chopin presented to Zofia Zaleska-Rosengardt); see also Virginia Fortescue, "The Unknown Chopin, An Alternative to the Cadenza of the Nocturne Op. 9 No. 2," *South African Journal of Musicology* 1 (1981), pp. 45–51. Another autograph variant similar to Example 8c is reproduced as Plate 19 in Jean-Jacques Eigeldinger, *Chopin vu par ses élèves*, 3rd edn (Neuchâtel: Editions de la Baconnière, 1988); in this case, the cadenza appears to end with a c♭⁴–b♭³ anacrusis in sixteenths (probably to replace the thirteenth turning figure in the published version) preparing a "syncopated" quarter note f⁴ (= $\hat{2}$), which is tied to the first note in a descending chromatic zigzag like the one in Example 8c.

contains two different ritornellos: section B (which is played twice), and the opening bars of C1, which return in bars 29–30 as the point of departure for C2's surge of momentum, and which thus constitute a ritornello in the general sense of a "short recurring passage."[40] A more plausible explanation, however, concerns the aptness with which this description fits not Chopin's but Field's first Nocturne in E♭, which can of course be summarized as a succession of sections (including variations) separated by ritornellos. The 1872 description of Op. 9, No. 2, should probably be regarded as yet another indication of the close relationship between Field's and Chopin's Nocturnes: the terminology that so accurately sums up the former was simply appropriated by either Lenz or Chopin to describe, however imprecisely, the latter.

Before concluding, it is important to assess if only briefly what this piece represents in terms of Chopin's stylistic growth. Op. 9, No. 2, is often cited as an early example of the composer's "ornamental melody" and his assimilation of the *bel canto* tradition into a pianistic idiom. But at the same time the Nocturne reveals a new and significant stage in Chopin's handling of long-range formal and structural processes. The remarkable breadth of conception apparent here, whereby Chopin transcends a sense of concatenation in the successive sections, directing "structural momentum" toward the end of the piece to attain definitive closure, is also prophetic of the composer's fully mature works, in both extended and smaller genres. It is striking that Chopin's manipulation of form and structure – his "structural style"[41] – should have reached a level of such sophistication even at this early stage in his career.

40. "Ritornello," in *The New Grove*, Vol. 16, p. 57.
41. See Rink, "The Evolution of Chopin's 'Structural Style'," for definition and elaboration of this term.

On the first movement of Sibelius's Fourth Symphony: a Schenkerian view

Edward Laufer

Except for one reason, it should be unnecessary at this time to have to break a lance for Sibelius. The one reason, however, is that the North American academic music community, by and large, has appeared to be reluctant to take Sibelius seriously. Perhaps the basis of this reluctance is suspicion: there must be "something wrong" with a composer whose music enjoys a considerable popular following and yet does not seem to belong to any mainstream twentieth-century modernism. The assumption lurking here, perhaps, is that its underlying compositional ideas must be naive. We may disregard this careless kind of polemic, however, and merely note that as critical attitudes change, a number of musicians have begun to study Sibelius's music in light of Schenker's approach which, of course, provides a means of studying the music and of considering the underlying compositional ideas very carefully indeed.[1] To the extent that any analytical approach can presume to make judgments as to artistic value, surely a Schenkerian study can suggest how Sibelius, as a great composer, came from the tradition of the great masters and has become part of that tradition, having enriched it with his own individual voice.

Let us first consider some aspects of that individual voice, in terms of certain traditional compositional techniques which we recognize as adapted and modified by Sibelius. Among these typically "Sibelian" techniques would be, in the melodic sphere, motivic transformation and developing transition and, in the harmonic sphere, elision (as omission of notes that are due), oblique relationship (in which certain notes are to be understood as belonging together but are not aligned rhythmically with each other), and anticipation (in the sense of overlapping, whereby one or more notes are stated before the sonority to which they belong). I shall begin by citing a few precedents from the traditional literature that involve elision, oblique relationship, and anticipation, in order to point up the bold manner in which Sibelius expanded these harmonic techniques and made them a hallmark of his language.

An instance of elision may be seen in Schumann's song, "Ich grolle nicht" (Example 1). In bars 28–29, Schumann does not write the notes shown in parentheses in Example 1c; they may nonetheless be understood. The basic form of the progression is to be read as in Example 1a; it is elaborated in Example 1b. The reason for the elisions is to be sought in the text of the song.

1. See Veijo Murtomäki, *Symphonic Unity: The Development of Formal Thinking in the Symphonies of Sibelius*, Studia Musicologica Universitatis Helsingiensis 5 (Helsinki: University of Helsinki, 1993). See also the review by David Loeb in *Music Theory Spectrum* 17/1 (1995), pp. 124–28.

128 Edward Laufer

Example 1 Schumann, "Ich grolle nicht"

Example 2 Brahms, Ballade Op. 118, No. 3

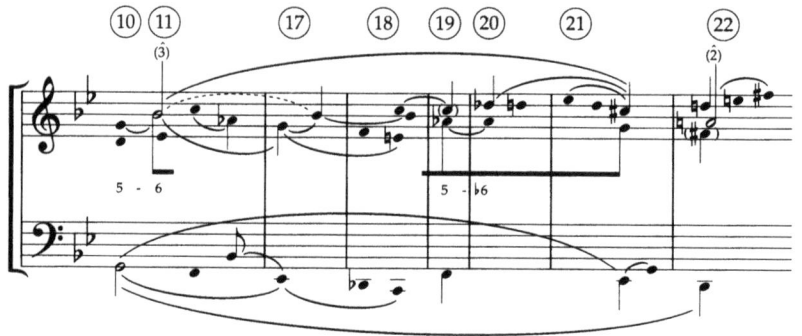

Example 3 Brahms, Waltz Op. 39, No. 14

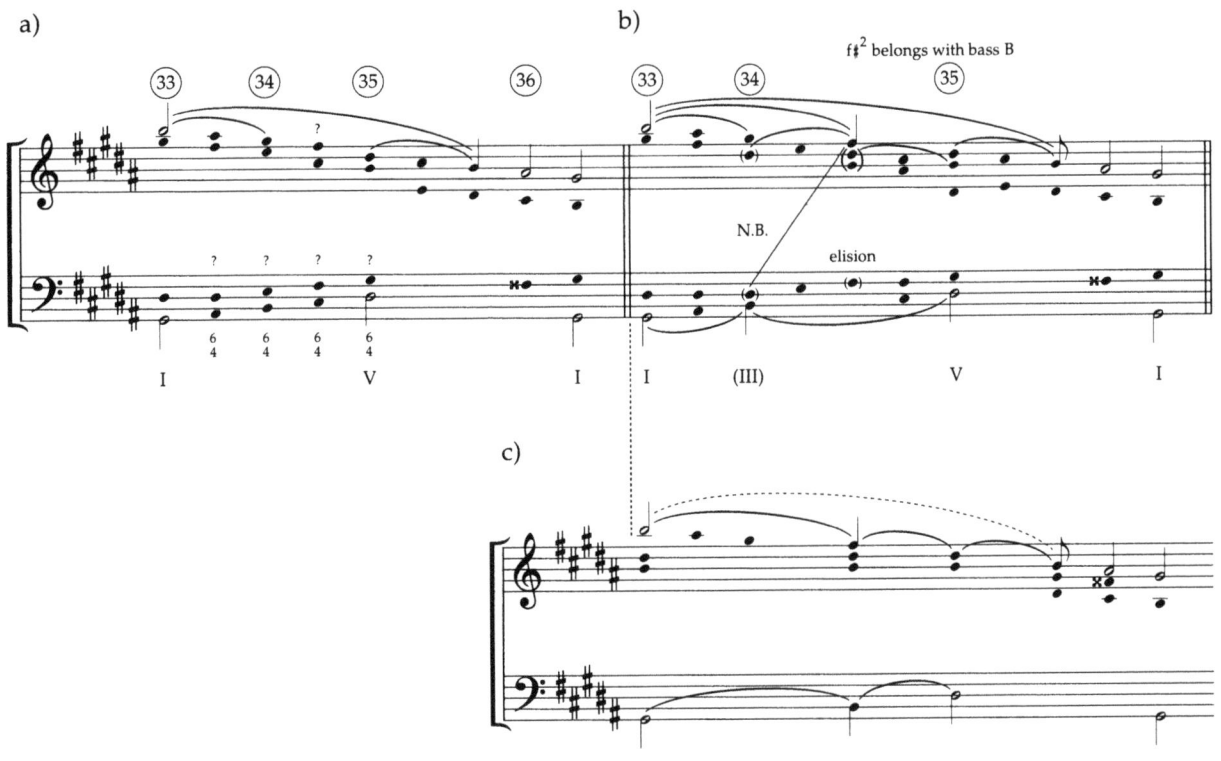

The neighbor-note figure e^1–f^1–e^1 is an underlying motivic idea; this figure, standing for yearning, pervades the song in many guises (a few are hinted at in Example 1b; see the asterisks). The figure is thrown into relief and intensified by the elisions (marked "N.B." in Example 1c). These also "expose" the $c\#^2$ and $a\flat^1$ (cf. bar 3 of the song), chromatic alterations suggesting the anguish of failed love. Another example of elision may be seen in Brahms's Ballade Op. 118, No. 3 (Example 2). In bar 19 a 5–6 motion must be understood, with the 5 (c^2) elided.

Brahms's Waltz Op. 39, No. 14, bar 34, illustrates oblique relationship as well as elision (Example 3). What is one to make of the series of $^6_4$ chords in Example 3a? As shown in Example 3b, the $f\#^2$ in bar 34 belongs with the bass B but is rhythmically shifted. The $d\#^2$ due with the $f\#^2$ is elided, so that the pattern of $^6_4$ chord sonorities can continue until the harmonic goal V is reached. Example 3c shows the underlying progression.

In the opening of Beethoven's Sonata Op. 109 (Example 4), we may note both oblique relationship and anticipation. Example 4a asks the question: where does the $^6_4$ chord in bar 14 resolve? In my view, only at the $c\#$ in bar 15, at the point where the scale figure changes direction. The progression is summarized in Example 4c. Thus the low B_1 bass enters before its time, as an anticipation of the real bass B to come; this is shown in Example 4b. The $^5_3$ that resolves the $^6_4$

Example 4 Beethoven, Sonata Op. 109

belongs, through a rhythmic shift (oblique relationship), with the bass f♯ in bar 15. The resultant harmonic overlapping creates a most unusual sense of intensity, which is resolved only with the clear arrival of the dominant (bar 15). At the same time, there is also some sense of a parenthetical insertion (as indicated in Example 4a) which is also "resolved" or clarified at the same moment!

A passage from Schubert's "Gretchen am Spinnrade" (Example 5) also shows an anticipation combined with oblique relationship. The basic progression (Example 5a), indicates the f^2 occurring with its bass note d. In Example 5b the f^2 which belongs with the bass d has been rhythmically shifted: by the time the

Example 5 Schubert, "Gretchen am Spinnrade"

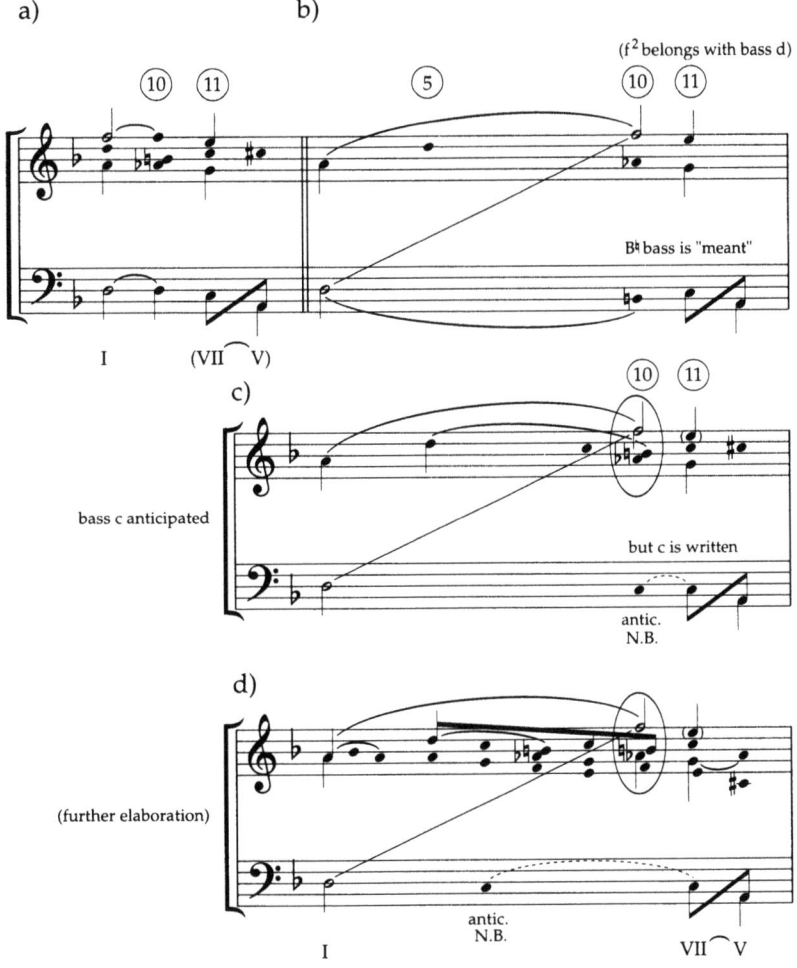

f^2 arrives, the bass should have moved to B♭. But, as Example 5c shows, Schubert writes a bass c, an anticipation of the real c of bar 11. Example 5d shows a further elaboration. Here is a musical symbol expressing Gretchen's inner agitation, her anxious reaching out toward her lover – getting ahead of actuality, as it were, in hopeless anticipation.

These techniques are not specifically Romantic devices. One can find them in Bach as well (see Example 6). In the C minor Prelude from the *Well-Tempered Clavier*, Book I, the harmony being composed out in bars 21–34 is the V. The bass c (bars 32–34), though occurring within the realm of this V, must be heard as an anticipation of the tonic C in bar 35. Only at bar 35 do the foreground changes in texture and motivic detail mark the arrival of the tonic.

Example 6 Bach, Prelude in C minor, *Well-Tempered Clavier*, Book I

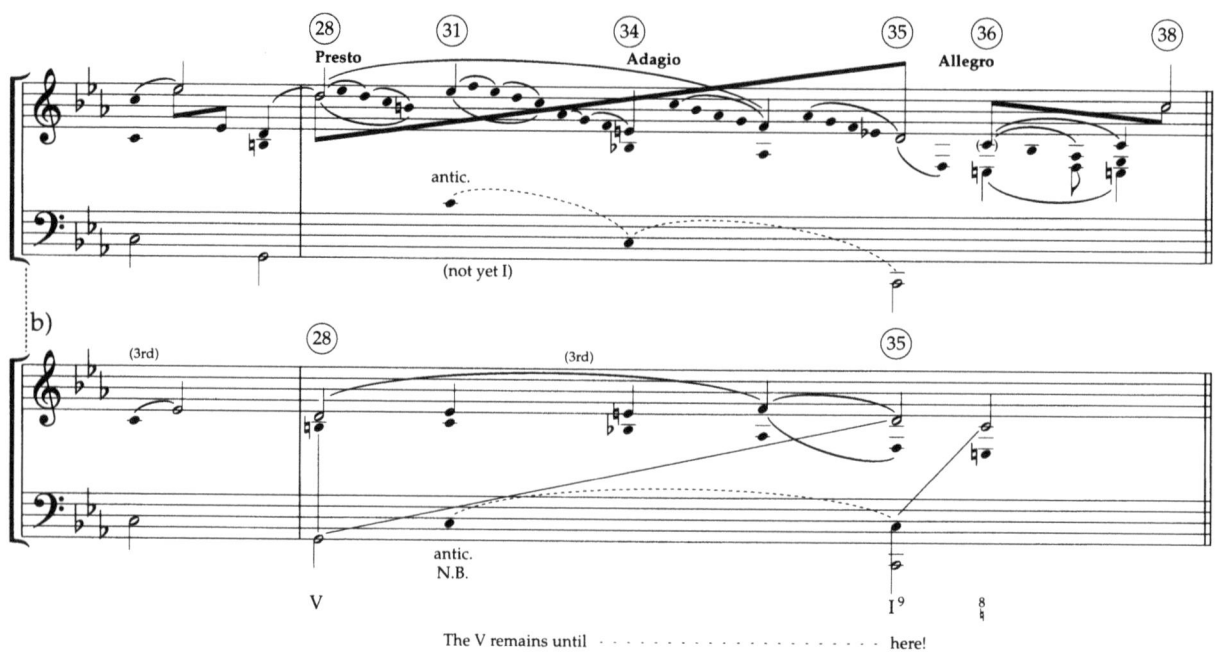

Another beautiful instance of anticipation is given in Example 7. The reading of this passage from Beethoven's Sonata Op. 31, No. 2, is dependent upon what may be called "respecting the integrity of the motive." Example 7a shows the first eight measures of the movement and the middleground origins of the four- (then three-) note figure. This figure (Example 7b) unifies the passage of bars 22–26: continuing throughout, it binds these measures together motivically as a single entity. The change of pattern in bar 27 indicates a new prolongation, but one that begins only there. So we cannot take an intermediate point, such as bar 23 (marked "N.B."), as the beginning of a new prolongation (see the sketch in Example 7f). The c in bar 23 (Examples 7c and 7d) is therefore to be read as an anticipation of the c in bar 27. Example 7e shows the underlying harmonic basis.

Example 8 presents my final example of anticipation and elision from the traditional literature, the opening of the second movement of Schubert's Sonata in A minor, Op. 143. The underlying progression of Example 8a is elaborated as in Example 8b. In Example 8c, it is as if the bass G (bar 26, marked "N.B.") were a passing note going to A♮; but since this A♮ does not actually occur, one could speak of an elision. The G of bar 26 remains, and thus takes on the guise of an anticipation of the succeeding G of bar 29 (shown in greater detail in Example 8d). Two different prolongations appear to be combined and

Example 7 Beethoven, Sonata Op. 31, No. 2, second movement

Example 8 Schubert, Sonata in A minor, Op. 143, second movement

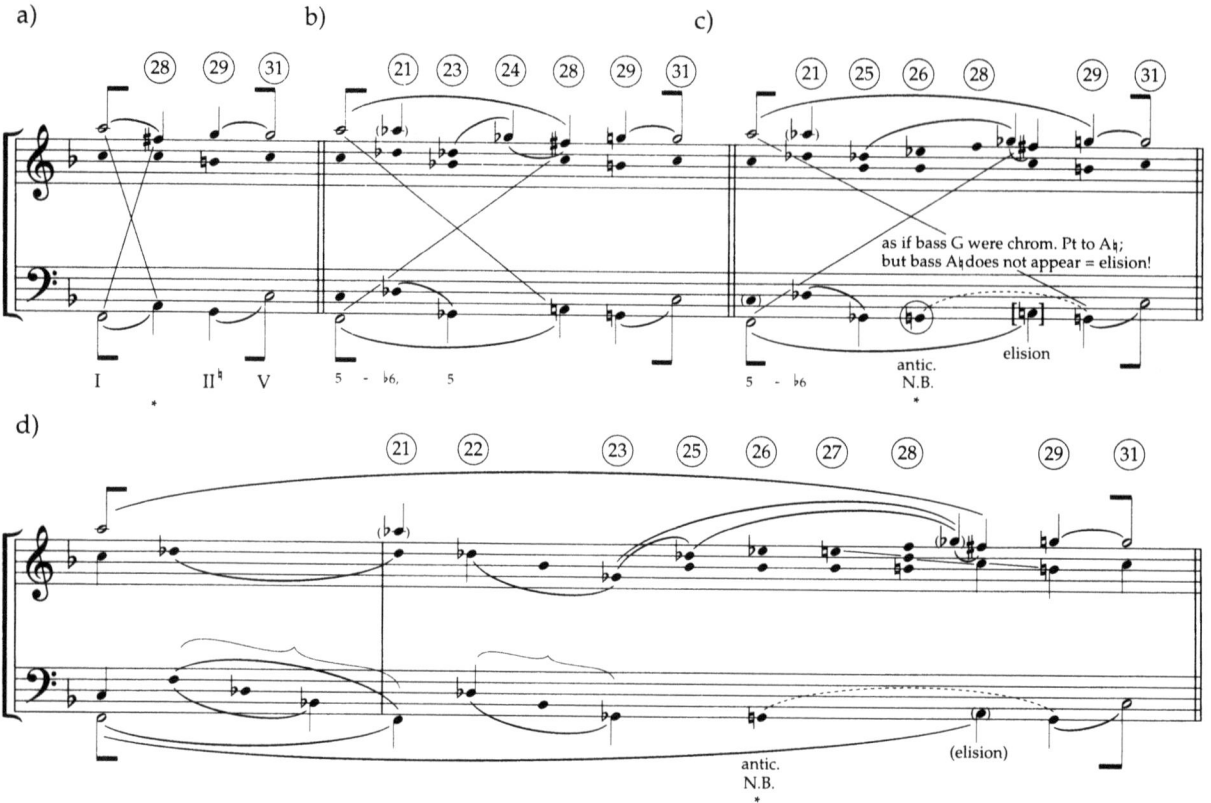

to overlap, clearly one purpose of this technical procedure. Another purpose is a programmatic one: to create a sense of *emerging*, as expressed by moving from a harmonically less distinct area in order to reach for a more distinct area and a definite goal. This programmatic notion is indeed also a feature of Sibelius's compositional thinking, as I shall try to demonstrate. Example 8e suggests how the bracketed five-note figure is gradually transformed: it continues in disguised fashion in the bass in bars 20–21, is abbreviated in bars 25–28, and becomes the second subject at bar 31. A foreground sketch (Example 8f) shows other motivic features, such as the play of mixture, D♯–C and D♭–C, and the initial rising sixth c^1–a^1 expanded to a^1–a^2 in bars 5–6.

One should bear in mind that procedures such as elision or anticipation serve not only a technical but also a psychological or programmatic purpose (which in fact called these procedures into being); they are much more than mere technical devices. These techniques convey, for example, in the Schumann song, something of the poignancy of the text – the composer's inner commentary; in the Brahms Ballade, a sense of urging onwards by overlapping; in Schubert's "Gretchen," the girl's lovesick yearning for her lover; in Beethoven's Op. 31, No. 2, a sense of inner agitation which will contrast with the serenity of the ensuing second subject.

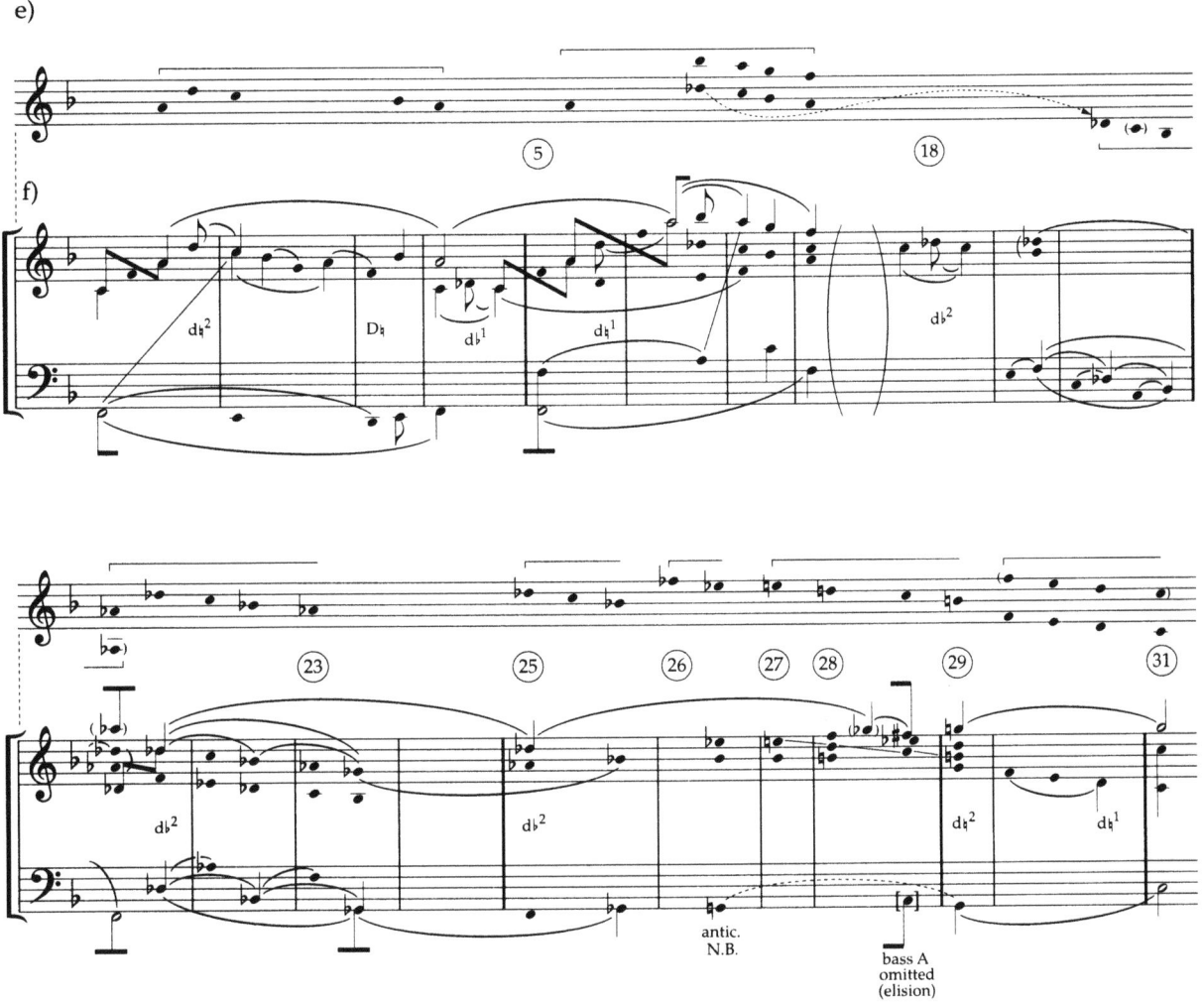

Before turning to Sibelius's Fourth Symphony, we may briefly consider the Schenkerian concept of the auxiliary cadence, partly because this concept is important to the understanding of the large-scale design and underlying programmatic aspect of the first movement of the Sibelius Symphony, and also because Schenker explained it rather cursorily, with the result that this concept is frequently misunderstood.[2] Example 9a presents a typical complete harmonic progression: a hypothetical work starts on the tonic, extends it via some

2. See Schenker, *Free Composition*, pp. 88–89.

136   Edward Laufer

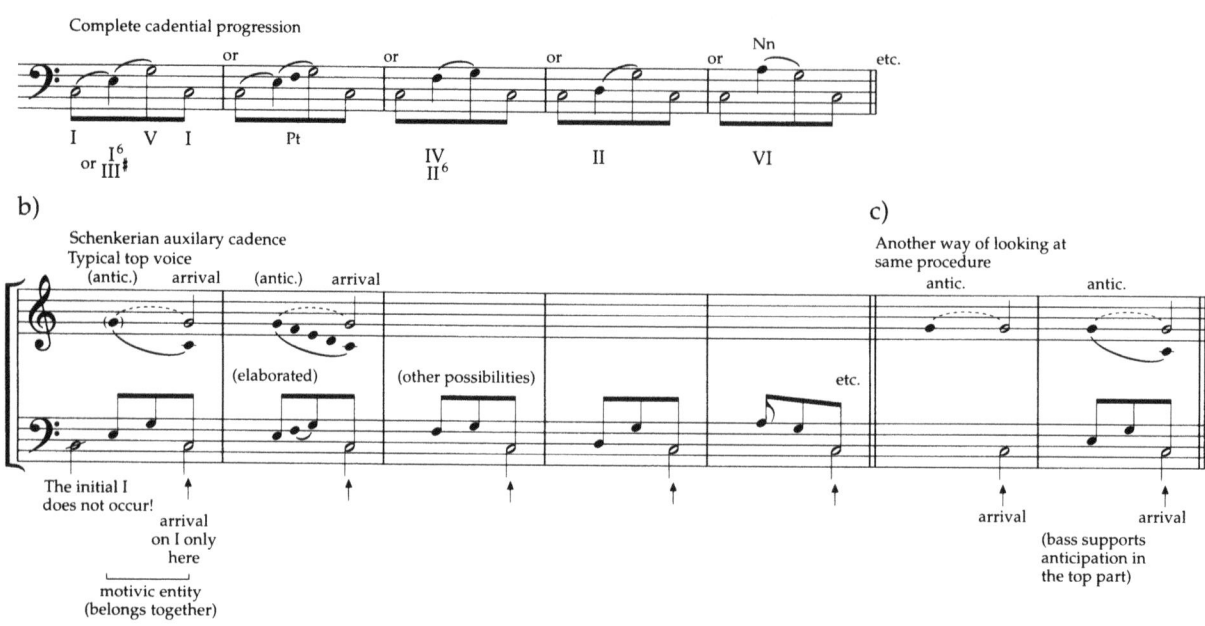

Example 9 Schenkerian concept of the auxiliary cadence

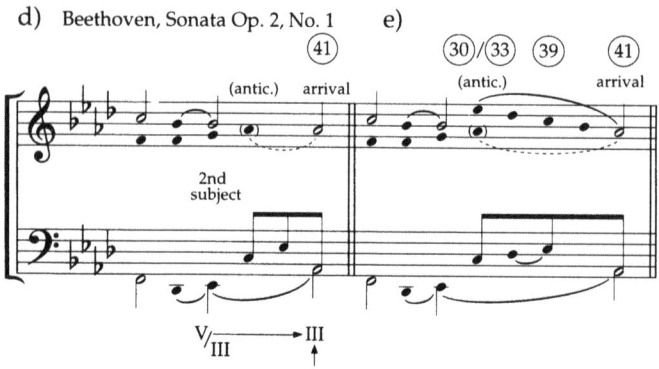

intermediate chord, such as I^6, $III\sharp$, IV, II^6, or VI, and proceeds to V and I. But what if the initial tonic does not occur? In Example 9b the harmonic progression cuts off a firm opening tonic, beginning *in medias res*. (It is important to note that the crossed-out initial tonic is *not* to be understood as being conceptually present.) As a result, the psychological effect is altogether different from that of Example 9a: the moment of arrival is now decisively directed to the tonic at the end of the progression, and only there. The sense is that of starting at

Example 10 Chopin, Prelude in E minor, Op. 28, No. 4

some less definite place and moving toward the point of tonic arrival. Another way of regarding the same procedure is to read an anticipation of the goal note (Example 9c). This anticipation is then itself supported by its own harmonies. The compositional *intent* is all important, namely the notion of reaching for the eventual point of arrival.

An illustration of this intent as expressed by means of an auxiliary cadence may be seen in the second subject of Beethoven's Sonata Op. 2, No. 1, first movement (Examples 9d and 9e). The real arrival on III (A♭) does not take place until bar 41. What precedes is a species of anticipation, still within the realm of the preceding V. Such a procedure can extend over three chords, as in Example 9b, or over an entire composition, as in Chopin's Prelude in E minor (Example 10). Here the music sinks down from the highest to the lowest registers, as if from quiet melancholy to hopeless despair, and the real tonic arrival – the tragic conclusion – occurs only at the last chord.

A similar procedure underlies the first movement of Sibelius's Fourth Symphony.[3] As shown in Example 11a, the real tonic arrival is withheld until the beginning of the recapitulation. As simple as this may seem, it is the simplicity of a master. I do not know of a single symphony in the tonal repertoire whose underlying plan corresponds to Example 11a – spreading an auxiliary cadence out over an entire symphonic movement. A possible traditional procedure *might* have been that shown in Example 11b. But why would Sibelius do this?

Santeri Levas quotes Sibelius as saying that all his symphonies "were pure, absolute music. . . . They had no programme element at all – although many people *say* that they have. . . ."[4] However, not everything Sibelius had to say

---

3. One must, however, acknowledge the necessity of considering a Sibelius symphony as a whole, since typically movements are linked by motivic associations and by a sense of cumulation carrying over from one movement to the next.
4. Santeri Levas, *Sibelius: A Personal Portrait*, trans. Percy M. Young (London: Dent, 1972), p. 84 (emphasis added).

about his work is to be taken at face value: he was very aware of his status as a public figure, which did not necessarily correspond to his private persona, and he might have said what he wanted people to believe. If one interprets the first movement of the Fourth Symphony as symbolizing a struggle to victory, from darkness to light, from nothingness to life, or from turmoil to serenity (somehow all the same poetic idea), then this idea is not really an *extra*-musical symbol: it is intrinsically part of the compositional idea, an idea which is technically set forth by the vast auxiliary cadence spanning the entire movement – starting as if from nowhere, to attain its goal only at the recapitulation.

Moreover, the primary tone e^2 shown in Example 11c does not occur in this register at first, and when it does appear it is not strongly marked. So there is a sense that this e^2 primary tone, too, is not really achieved until the recapitulation. Sibelius also deliberately obscures the course of the fundamental line (e^2–a^1) by a curiously unsupported $\hat{4}$ (d^2 in bar 25), which appears in the "wrong" register as d; the $\hat{3}$ (c♯ in bar 27) is not supported by *tonic* harmonization – the tonic is withheld until later. The obscurity of the development section also enhances the sense of tonic arrival in the recapitulation. All these features combine to mark that eventual goal. Technically, Example 11c does not show a fundamental line at all but rather a fifth-progression, because the bass does not provide firm *background* support for the top line's descent: an actual background here would only show A.[5]

How beautifully are motivic aspects integral to the larger design! The opening tritone-motive (Example 11d), in a fantastic enlargement, gives rise to the course of the bass line of the entire exposition, and then reappears in enlargement and transformation in the recapitulation, underlying the second subject. This is what one could term the *structural* use of a motive: a foreground motive becomes a middleground motive.

One might argue that the initial bass C is of such short duration that it cannot assume the significance accorded to it in Example 11c. And yet, just here resides the paradox. Just because the C *is* short and therefore seemingly tentative and indecisive it stands out as memorable in this sense, and can cast its shadow over the entire bass line that is to come, until "resolved" at the recapitulation. The bass C♮ stands, figuratively, for indecisiveness, turmoil, and unrest; the c♯ opposed to it (bar 27) stands for resolution and serenity – not fully attained until the recapitulation.

Example 12 sketches the exposition in various stages, from the basic framework (Example 12a) though successive elaborations (reading upwards). In Example 12b (bar 27) the bass c♯ anticipates the goal chord (bar 32); the f^1 passing tone (bar 29) is extended as f^1–a^1–c♯^{2}. This constitutes a transformation of the

---

5. Example 10, the Chopin E minor Prelude, is similar in this respect. It will be noted that in the Sibelius Symphony there is *no* interruption in the Schenkerian sense (no $\hat{5}$–$\hat{4}$–$\hat{3}$–$\hat{2}$, $\hat{5}$–$\hat{4}$–$\hat{3}$–$\hat{2}$–$\hat{1}$), a concept integral to Schenker's understanding of sonata form. Although there are certain sonata movements in which one cannot read an interruption, I can think of no other symphonic sonata-form movement in which this is the case. Here, truly, is a most striking modification of sonata form, not only in this respect but also in the manner in which the first subject appears, the key area of the second subject, and the omission of the first subject in the recapitulation – points which will be noted later.

On the first movement of Sibelius's Fourth Symphony

Example 11 Sibelius, Symphony No. 4: an overview of the first movement

Example 12 Sibelius, Symphony No. 4, exposition

opening fifth motive A–c–e. Examples 12c and 12d show how this fifth is filled in. Given the foreground of bars 27–32 (Example 12d), how bold and magical is the effect of this "extraneous" c♯ which has nothing to do with the foreground harmonies above it. Perhaps the reason for placing the d (the $\hat{4}$, bar 25) in the "wrong" register was to continue to the c♯ (the ♯$\hat{3}$ of the fundamental line) in the "wrong" register as well; and the purpose of this c♯ in that register was to clash with its opponent, the low opening C♮. This is the fundamental opposition of the movement, which is to be reconciled and "corrected" only in the recapitulation.

At this point, it may be well to consider certain motivic features. Santeri Levas writes: "Cecil Gray and a number of other musicologists after him have remarked that Sibelius first stated his thematic ideas in fragments, so as to assemble them into actual themes later on." Levas recounts that he discussed this with Sibelius, who must have started up at this remark, and "quite categorically said: 'That's not true at all. I do not build my themes out of small fragments.'"[6] The point may be emphasized: the themes are not built out of small fragments. Rather, different themes may be associated by their having fragments in common; that is, certain components recur in the various themes. This does not mean that all the themes are somehow the same. Like brothers and sisters in the same family, they have certain features in common – yet each theme is different and individual.

Thus the neighbor-note figure (Example 13a) from the opening tritone-motive later underlies the second subject and also associates with the closing theme. The tritone-motive (Example 13b) relates to the rising fifth-motive (Example 13c) which is answered by the descending fifth (bars 10–12): the rising and descending fifths then associate with the horn's fifth-motive (bar 37) and the closing theme (bars 41ff. and 50ff.). How subtle is the association of the rising fifth-motive (Example 13c) to its filled-in transformation in bars 29ff. and 32ff. (Example 13d)! Beautifully concealed, too, is the transformation of the descending fifth (Example 13c) into a sixth (bars 43ff., Example 13e), the last two notes of which (f♯^{1}–c♯^{1}) become the fourth-motive (bars 40ff., Examples 13c, 13f, and 13g). As seen in Example 13f, this fourth-motive is in reality a transformation (or better, a transfiguration) of the tritone-motive. Here we already find a programmatic expression of the metaphor: struggle to victory, from nothingness to being. The fourth-motive (Example 13f) at the end of the exposition foreshadows a "resolution" of the opening tritone-motive: the chromatic C♮–F♯ is momentarily "corrected" to the diatonic f♯^{1}–c♯^{1}. Poetically, here is a promise of the serenity only to be found later.

Example 14 presents analytical sketches of the exposition. Example 14d shows an overview; more detail is given in Example 14c, and various motivic features are shown in the other sketches. Thus Example 14b indicates certain transformations of the opening tritone-motive: how it becomes the second subject (bars 31–32), and how it is "corrected" and reordered (bars 40ff.) as the closing theme. The characteristic neighbor-note feature of the tritone-motive, in enlargement (Example 14a), governs the top line of the second subject area. Example 14e indicates certain concealed transformations of the first subject's

---

6. Levas, *Sibelius*, p. 88.

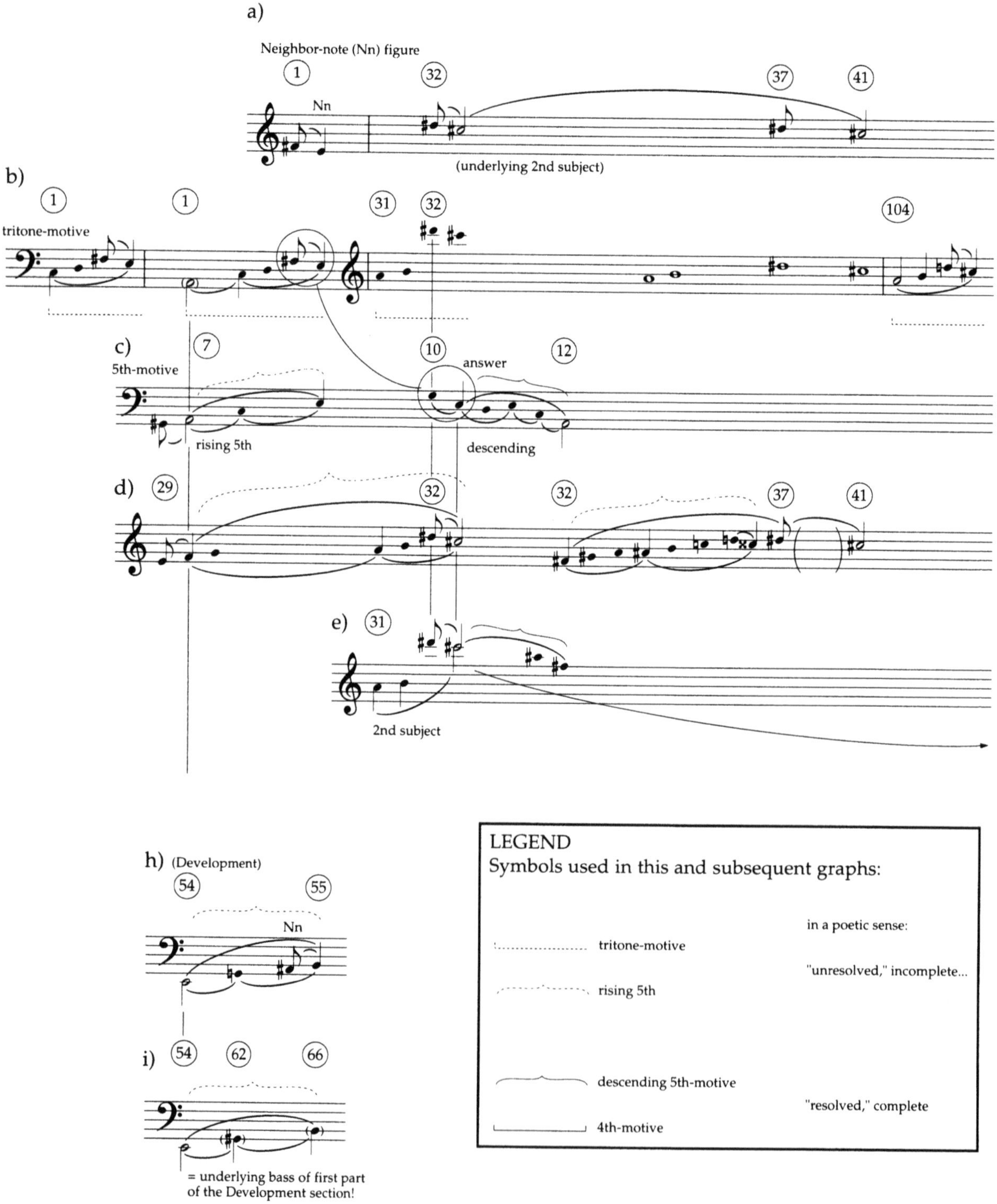

Example 13 Sibelius, Symphony No. 4: some instances of association of themes through common motivic components

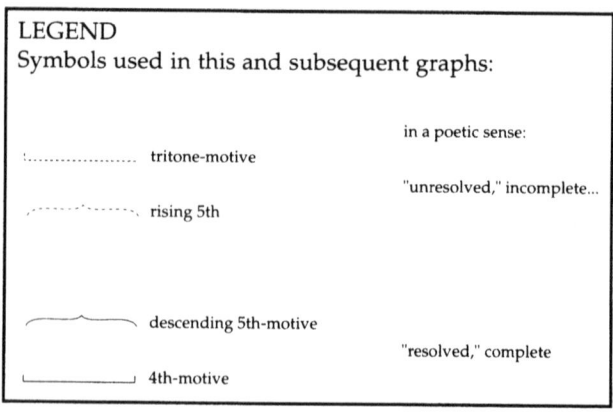

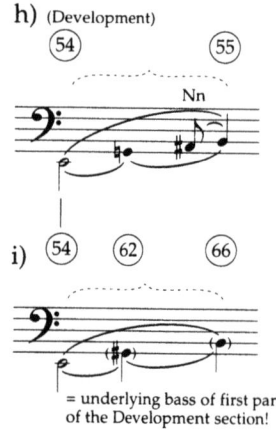

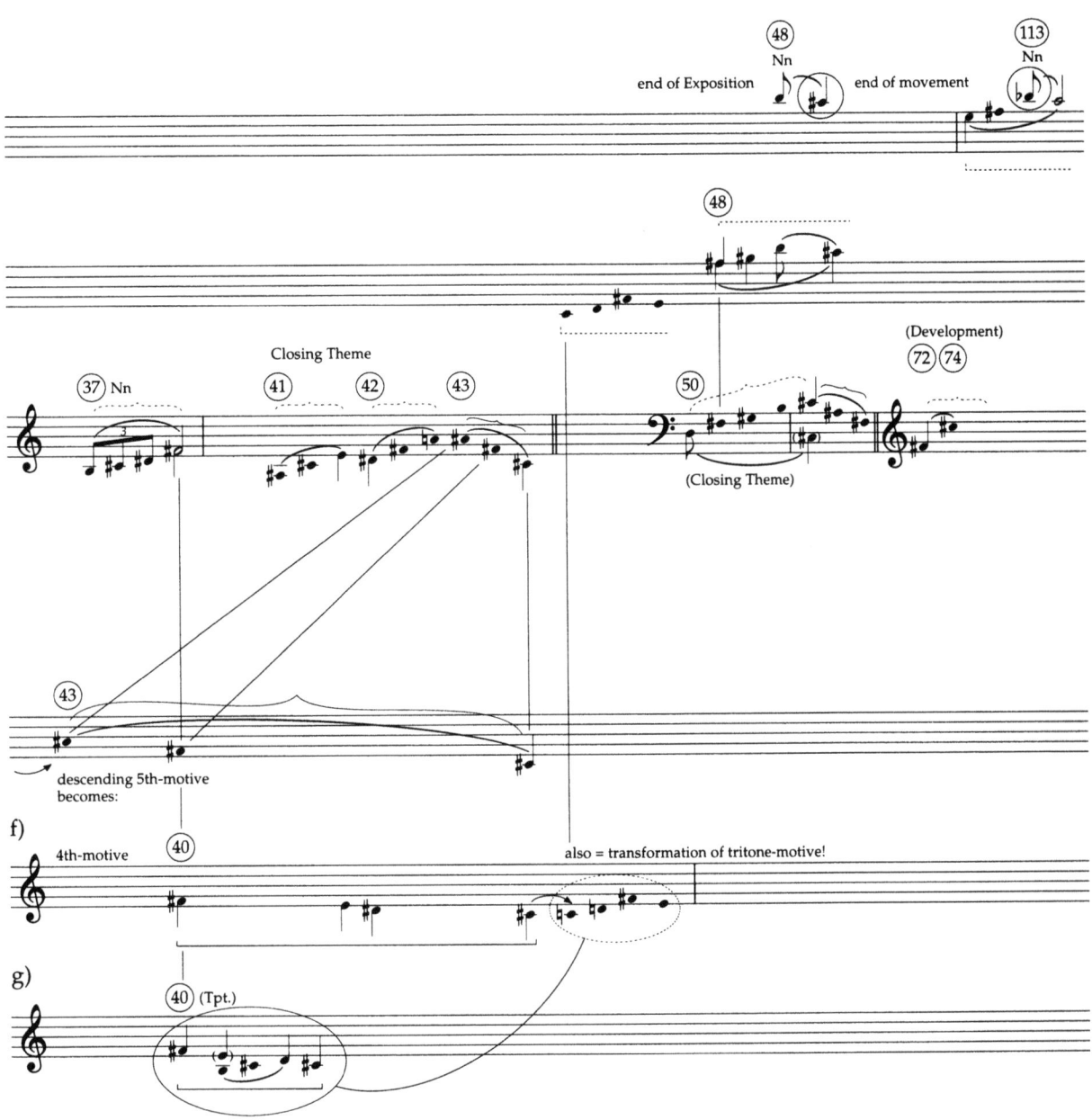

fifth-motive into the sixth a#² –c#¹ (which will later be distorted to a#²–c♮² in the development, bars 69ff.). As also shown in Example 11, the tritone-motive in enlargement (Example 14f) gives rise to the bass line of the entire exposition – an amazing compositional inspiration!

Example 15c (with reductions shown in Examples 15d and 15e) indicates

Example 14 Sibelius, Symphony No. 4, exposition

On the first movement of Sibelius's Fourth Symphony

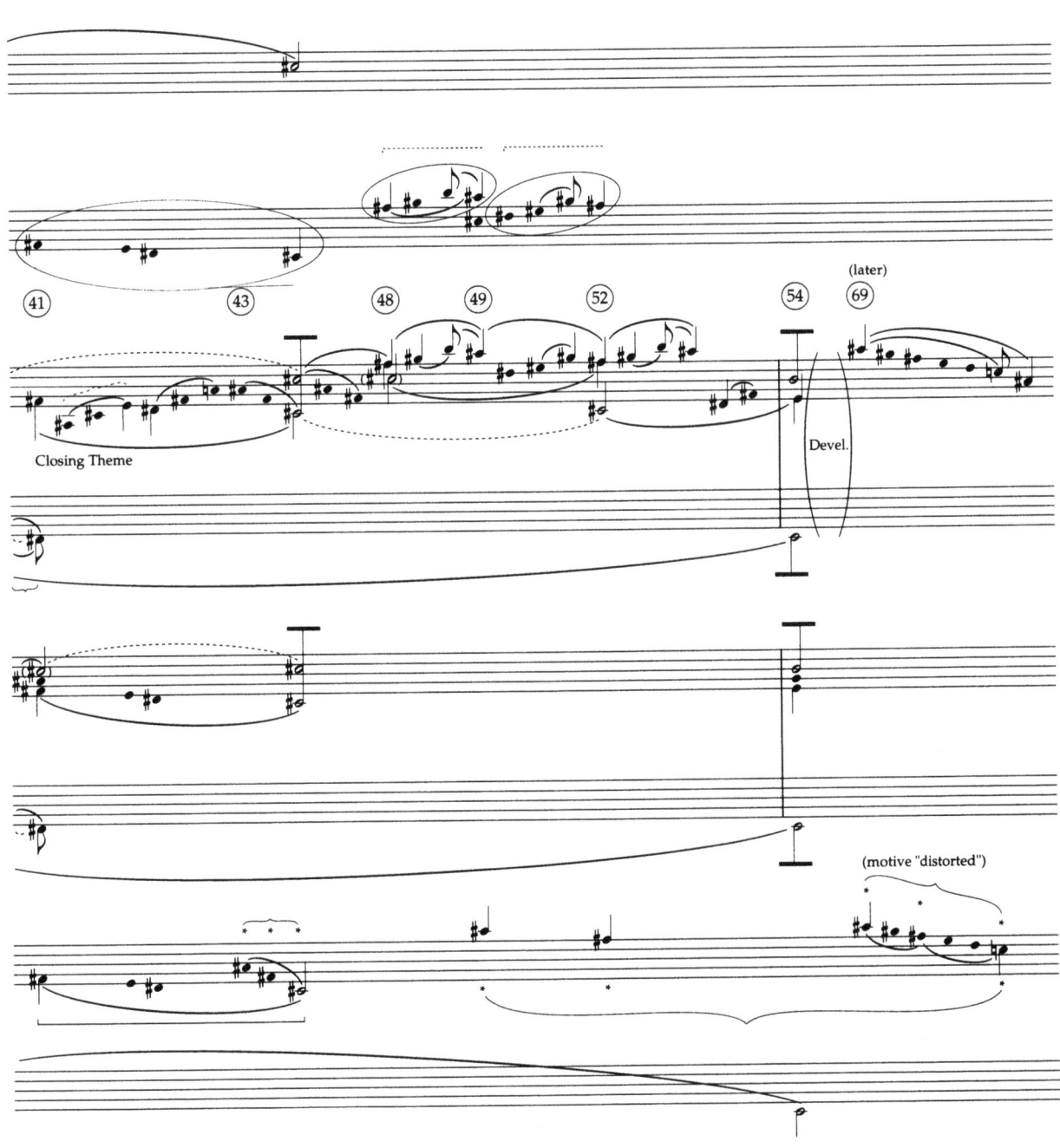

146   Edward Laufer

Example 15 Sibelius, Symphony No. 4, exposition

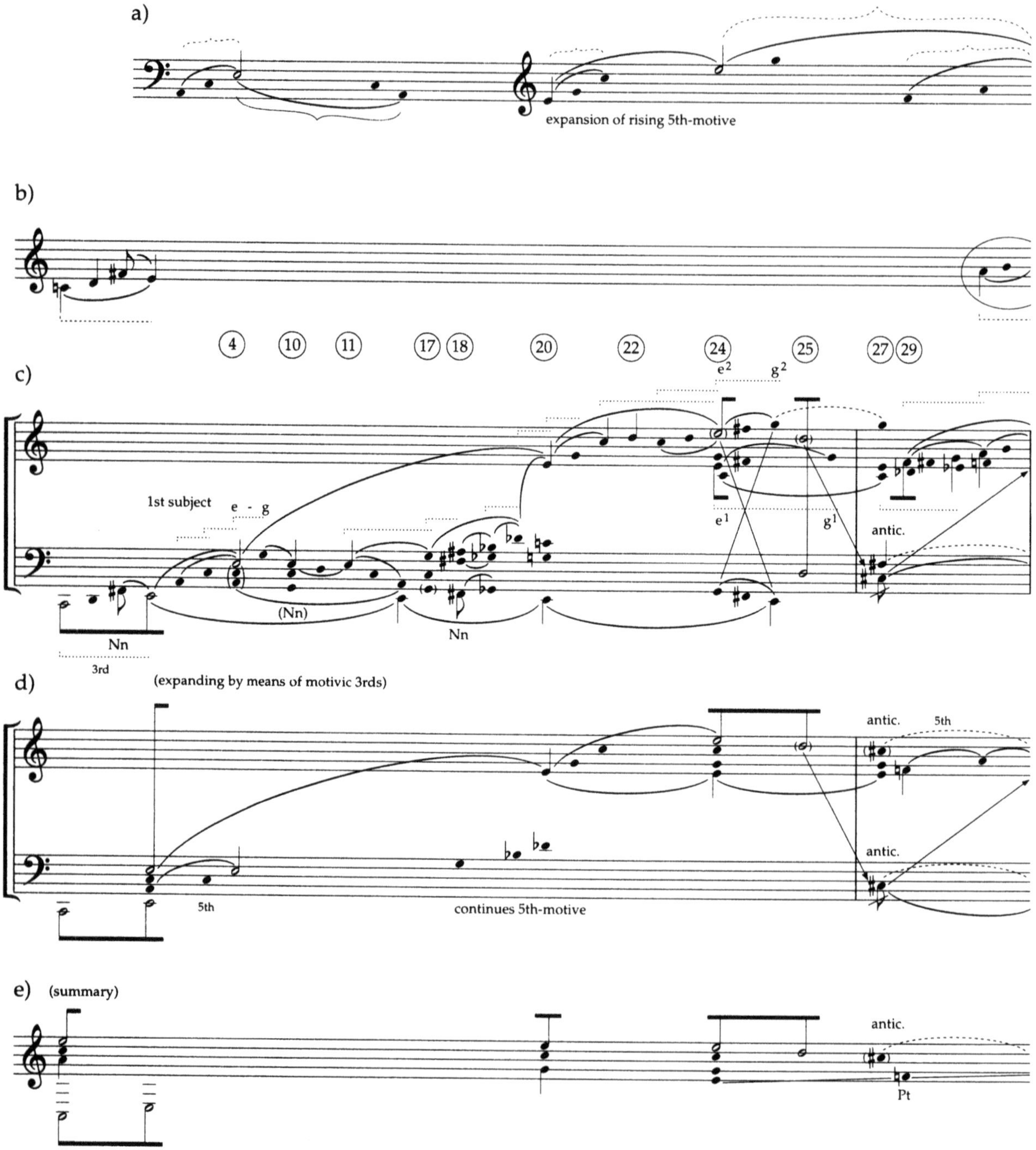

Example 16 Sibelius, Symphony No. 4: some rhythmic transitions

Sibelius's remarkable compositional procedure of moving step by step, as it were, from the first to the second subject: the rising fifth-motive (bar 4) organically becomes the second subject (bar 32). The rising thirds (at the dotted brackets) of the rising fifth-motive expand upwards (bars 4–25), becoming a filled-in transformation of the fifth-motive f^1–a^1–$c\sharp^1$ (bars 29–32). This "false" augmented fifth is in turn answered by the "corrected" perfect fifth of $c\sharp^2$–$a\sharp^1$–$f\sharp^1$ (bar 32), part of the second subject. What wonderful point-to-point continuity: one subject gradually being transformed to become another – what I referred to earlier as *developing transition*.

A few more points concerning Example 15c: the characteristic third e–g–e (starting in bar 4) perhaps comes about as an expansion of the opening neighbor-note figure F♯–E. Because of this third-figure, the e^2 in bar 24, shown as the primary tone $\hat{5}$, goes on to g^2; therefore the e^2 itself is not very strongly marked. (Because it hardly seems like the primary tone it is shown in parentheses.) A more strongly marked e^2 does not appear until the recapitulation (bar 88), by which time it serves rather as a reminder of the e^2 primary tone. In this way, too, Sibelius expresses the sense of moving toward a goal and the eventual arrival. The emphasis on $f\sharp^2$ (bars 32ff.), an inner voice placed above the $c\sharp^2$ top voice as a consonance, certainly refers to the opening F♯, which was then a dissonance: the programmatic intent has already been suggested. Examples 15a and 15b sketch the transformations of the rising fifth-motive and the opening tritone-motive.

Sibelius's masterly use of the technique of developing transition also extends to rhythmic events (see Example 16). One hears, for instance, how the rhythmic figure of bar 36 is transformed, by degrees, into the quite different rhythmic shape of the figure in bar 48.

The development section of this Symphony is without question among the composer's boldest and most enigmatic achievements, if not the boldest altogether. Many commentators have respectfully shied away from it, declaring it "atonal"; and even so perceptive a critic as Simon Parmet almost gave up, considering this development section unanalyzable.[7] It is neither atonal nor unanalyzable; its logic is formidable, if obscure. And the "obscurity" is indeed deliberate, having to do with the same poetic idea of complexity moving toward clarity.

Example 17a sketches the harmonic framework for the first part of the development; Examples 17b and 17c include more detail. We can again consider how Sibelius composed middleground motives upon this framework. As seen in Example 17d, the rising fifth-motive from the opening, now E–G–B, in enlargement becomes such a middleground motive, the carrier of the bass for the entire first part of the development section. The braces in Example 17c show how the fifth-motive, in various guises, is constantly worked in. Moreover, the fourth-motive reappears at bar 60, marking the main bass notes (the e–g♯–b enlargement). But now the fourth-motive is "distorted," shortened to a third. What is the point of this intense motivic concentration of the fifth-motive and the deliberate distortion of the fourth-motive? Surely the intent of this concentration and complexity was to make the recapitulation, with its contrasting simplicity and clarity, stand out even more as the goal.

Example 18a suggests one possible traditional procedure for extending the dominant in a development section.[8] Example 18b would be a plausible elaboration, although hypothetical; I cannot think of any work that actually does this. Let us suppose that the dominant chord which is due (shown in parentheses in Example 18c) is omitted or elided, and the progression is elaborated as in Example 18d. The top voice $b\flat^2$ is a passing tone on its way down to the a^2. This brings us closer to what Sibelius has done (Example 18e). Then consider a further elaboration (Example 18f): a descending inner voice is added, as is a bass anticipation of the goal note A. The rather straightforward basic progression of Example 18a has been overlaid with complications. It may also be noted (Example 18g) how the bass E–G starts to restate the same rising fifth as had just been heard in the first part of the development, though the fifth is not completed because of the onset of the recapitulation.

---

7. See Simon Parmet, *The Symphonies of Sibelius*, trans. Kingsley A. Hart (London: Cassell, 1959), p. 53, and Murtomäki, *Symphonic Unity*, p. 90.
8. I consider procedures in traditional development sections, from a Schenkerian standpoint, in "Voice-Leading Procedures in Development Sections," *Studies in Music from the University of Western Ontario* 13 (1991), pp. 69–120.

150 Edward Laufer

Example 17 Sibelius, Symphony No. 4, development section, Part 1

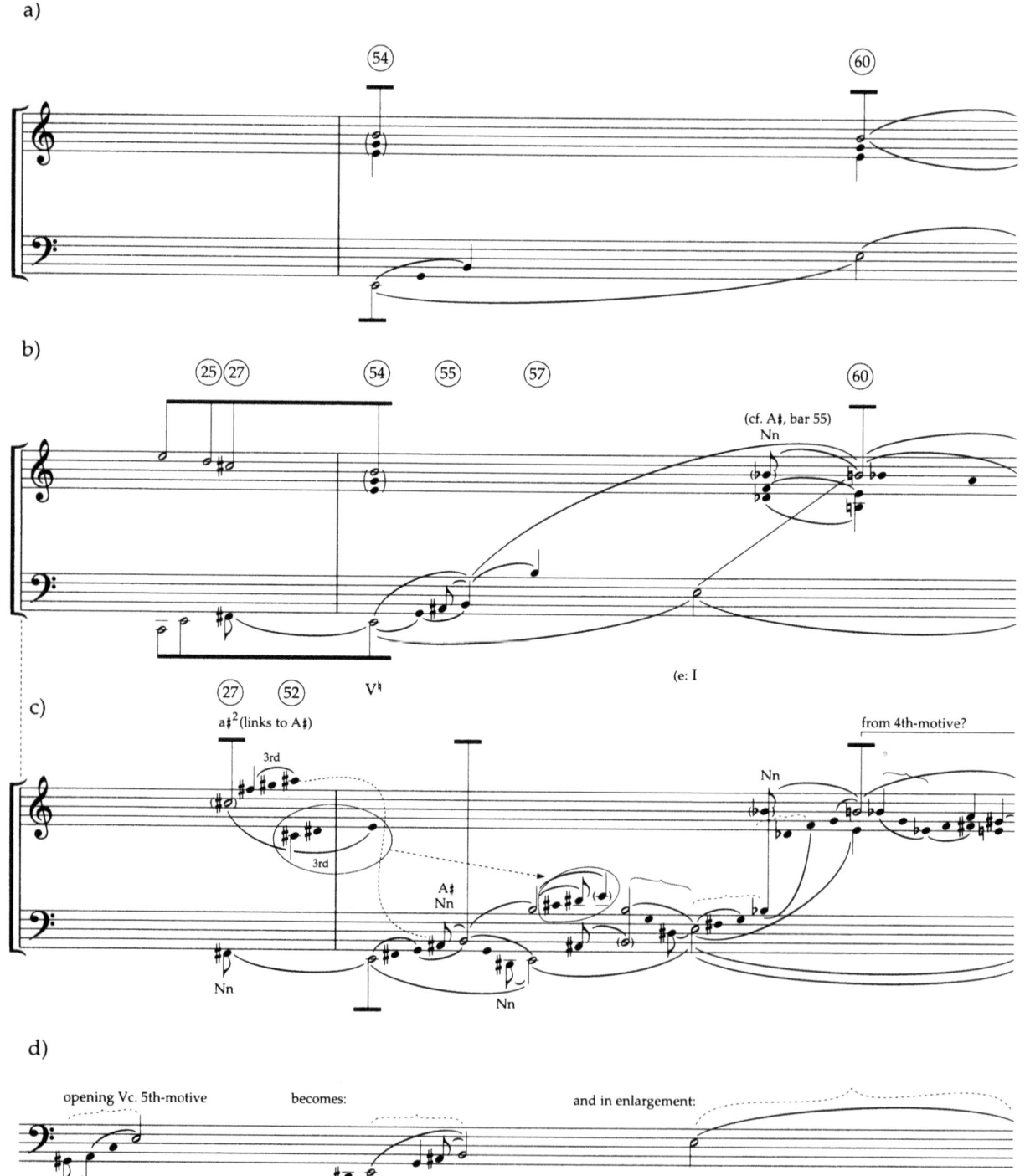

On the first movement of Sibelius's Fourth Symphony

(underlying bass motion for Development, Part 1, is the motivic 5th!)

Example 18 Sibelius, Symphony No. 4, development section, Part 2: general harmonic basis

If we look again at the rising top line of Example 18f (Example 18h being the underlying basis), then we see in Example 19d that the rising fifth-motive is applied to each note of the rising top line, and to each note of the bass line as well! Example 19a provides an overview of the development section, showing these applications of the rising fifth-motive. Example 19b shows the rising top line e^2 to e^3 (cf. Examples 18d–18f) superimposed over the descending inner voice b^1–$c♮^1$ ($c♯^1$); cf. Example 18f. This descending line (Example 19e) derives from the second subject's descending line (cf. Examples 13e and 14e) which, in turn, had originated in the descending fifth-motive! Example 19c combines these various lines. Example 19f suggests how the rising top line e^2–e^3 (shown in Example 19b), perhaps also comes from the rising fifth-motive. The motivic concentration is astonishing, as is the resultant complexity of the various motivic superimpositions.

It will be recalled that a feature of the exposition was the reaching up to the (not strongly marked) primary tone e^2 in bar 24, by means of rising motivic thirds (see Example 15c). Now, as the development moves toward the recapitulation, an important question arises: how does Sibelius find an equivalent way of reaching for the primary tone once again? How beautifully has he solved this compositional problem: the rising top line e^2–e^3 of the development recomposes the idea of the exposition's rising line leading up to e^2 (Example 15c, bars 4–24), and the motivic rising thirds of the exposition, which derived from the rising fifth-motive, have been recomposed as the rising fifth-motive of bars 65–88 (Examples 19a and 19d).

Example 20 attempts to put additional foreground features into perspective. Thus Example 20e shows the underlying framework once again, and Example 20d shows the superimposed descending line, first as a derivative of the descending fifth- (sixth-) motive, then filled in, then composed in enlargements! Example 20c indicates the superimposed rising and descending lines, with the rising fifth-motive applied as well. Example 20b shows how the main notes of the enlargements of Example 20d are themselves elaborated, organically, through expressions of the descending motive of Example 20d. Example 20a further clarifies this: the sixths (bars 69ff.) become the tritone-motive, now serving as accompanying figuration. The descending fifth-motive (Example 20a, bars 73ff.) is filled in (Example 20b). And as if these multifarious superimpositions were not enough, Sibelius adds further complexities: the anticipation in bar 77, and the oblique relationship whereby the $e\flat^3$ in bar 86 technically belongs with its bass note G in bar 82 – a rhythmic shift of sorts (see Example 20e). The motivic elements throughout bars 69–88 are all transformations of the rising and descending fifth-motive and the tritone-motive. Not a note is empty filler: every aspect is organic. The result is one of the most remarkable inspirations in twentieth-century music.

Finally, the recapitulation (Example 21) presents the resolution of the agitated complexities just heard. With tonal resolution, poetic resolution has been achieved. Thus in Example 21c (with a reduction shown in Example 21d) the sustained A of the timpani (bars 88ff.) harks back to the same note's anticipation in the development, but now with a new meaning: no longer is the A an element of dissonance and turmoil, but instead, within the A major tonic context, it provides consonance and serenity. And, as shown in Example 21e, the chromaticism of the exposition's a^1–b^1–$d\sharp^3$–$c\sharp^3$ is also revalued, now within a clear tonic. Example 21a shows how the rising fifth-motive is recomposed. Since this first-subject motive had been worked in throughout the development section, there is no need for a return of the first subject, and the recapitulation begins in bar 88 directly with the second subject.[9]

9. Compare, for example, Chopin's Sonata in B♭ minor, Op. 35, for a similar procedure (not that Sibelius was influenced by this work).

Example 19 Sibelius, Symphony No. 4, development section

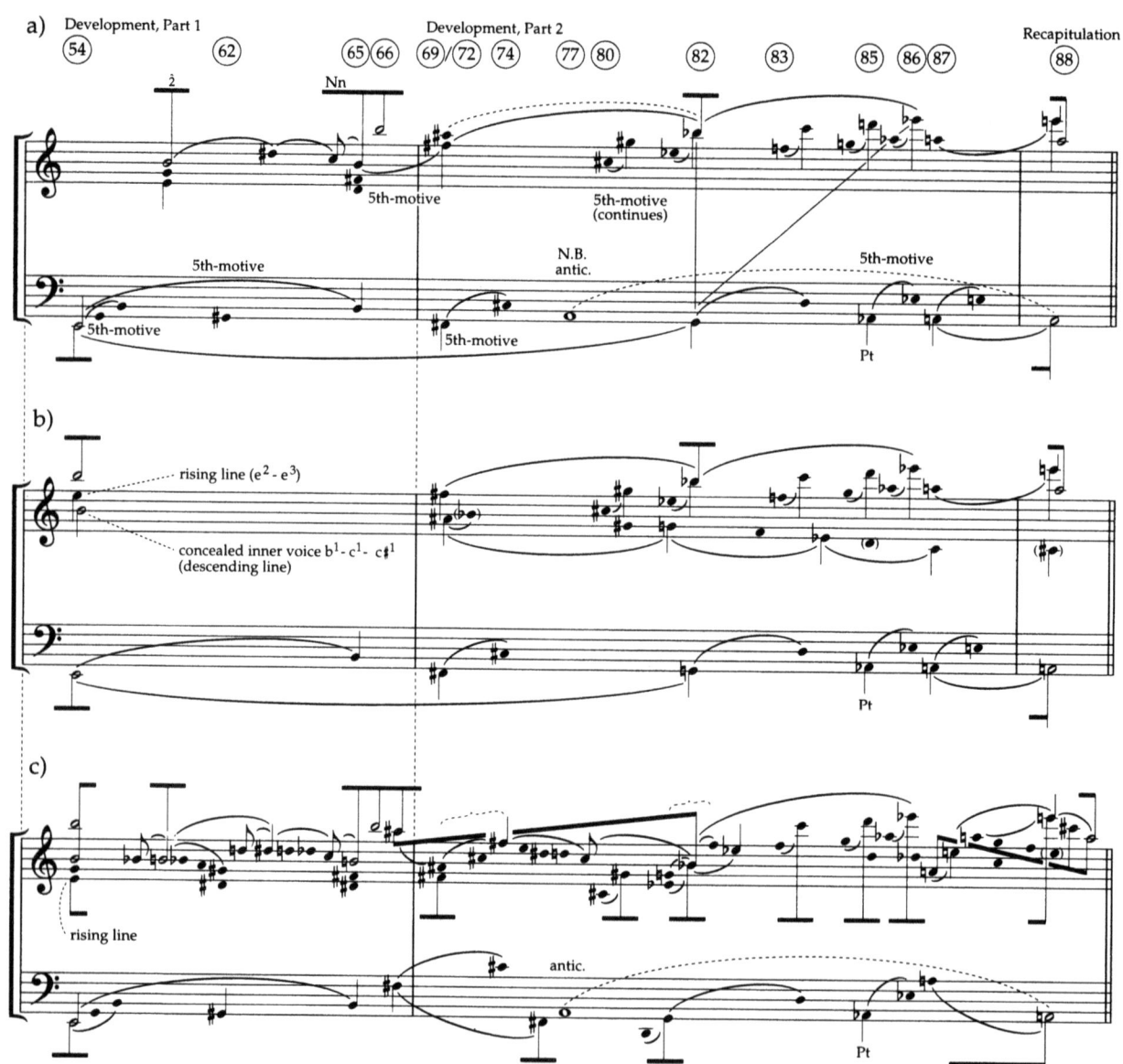

At the coda (bars 110ff.; see Examples 21b and 21c), there is a reminder of the opening tritone-motive with its bass C♮. The motive that was shown in Example 11d is reordered and transformed. The exposition's opposition of C♮ and C♯ is now reversed, with C♯ emerging as the "correct," triumphant form and C♮ only a subdued recollection. As seen in Example 21d, the final neighbor-note figure b♭²–a² (bars 111–13) is also a reminder of past events, recalling the b♮²–b♭² of the development section's top voice (see Examples 18e and 20e) and the a♯² which had closed the exposition (see Examples 14c and 15c).

On the first movement of Sibelius's Fourth Symphony

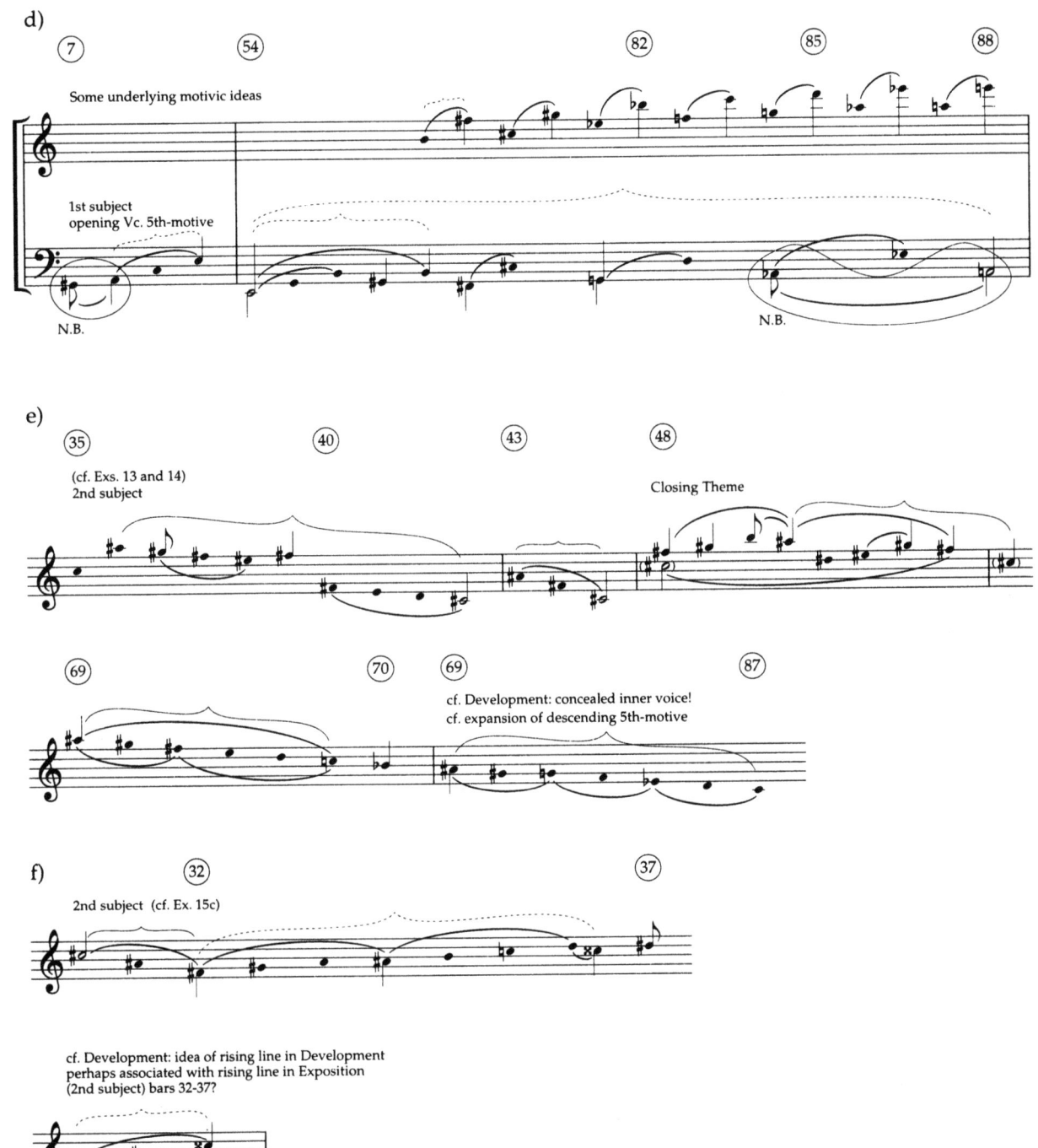

156 Edward Laufer

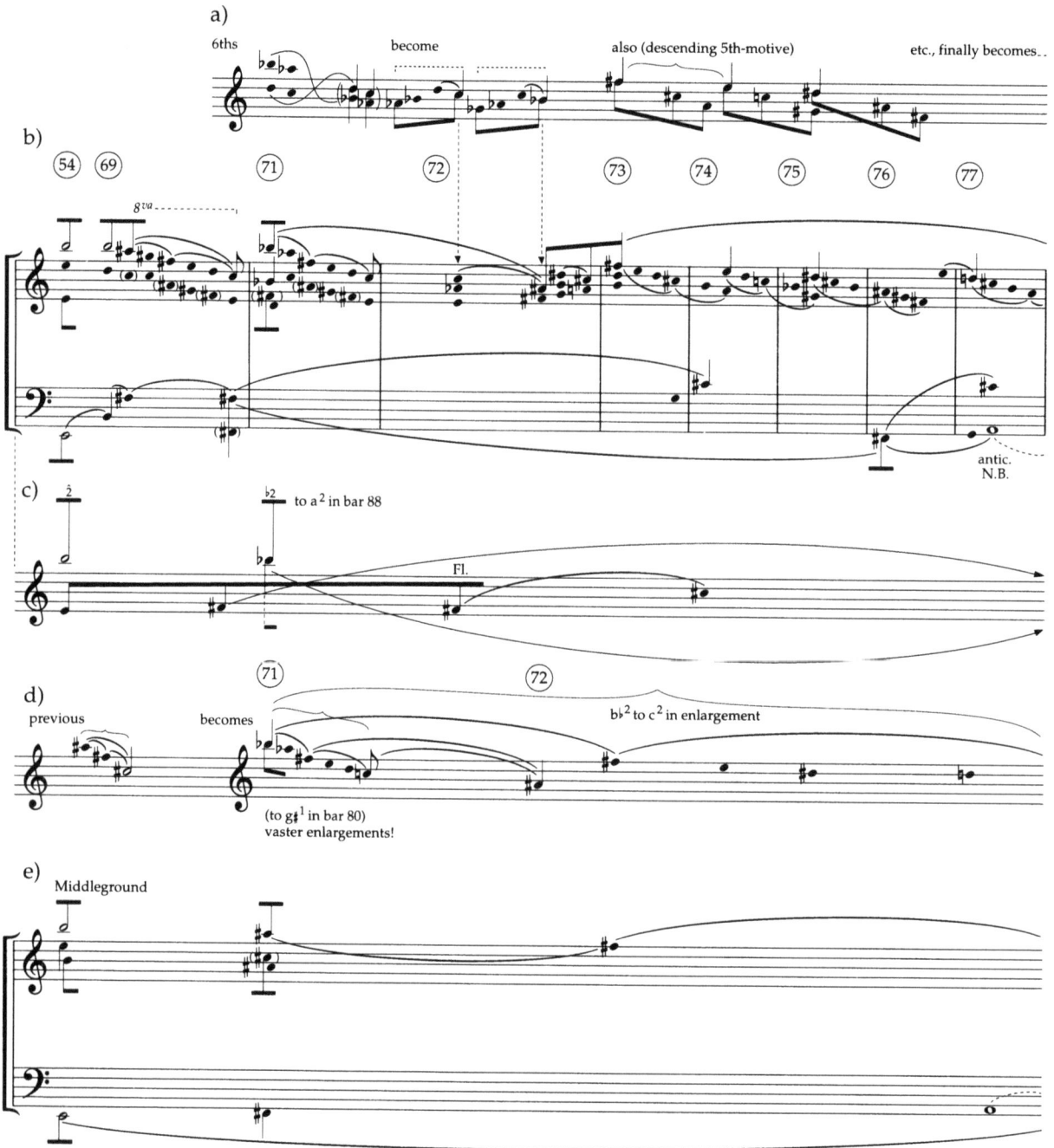

Example 20 Sibelius, Symphony No. 4, development section

On the first movement of Sibelius's Fourth Symphony

Example 21 Sibelius, Symphony No. 4, recapitulation

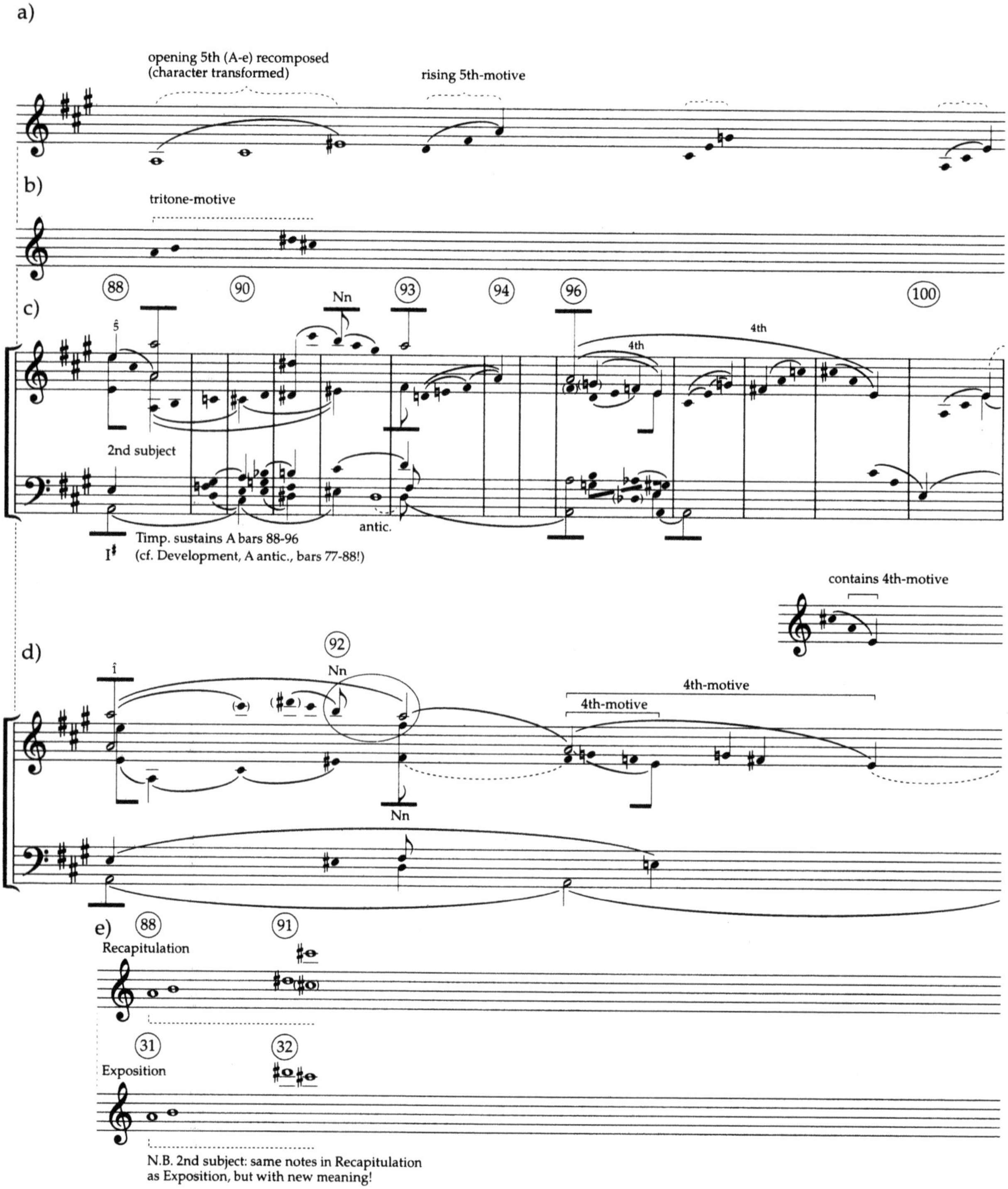

On the first movement of Sibelius's Fourth Symphony

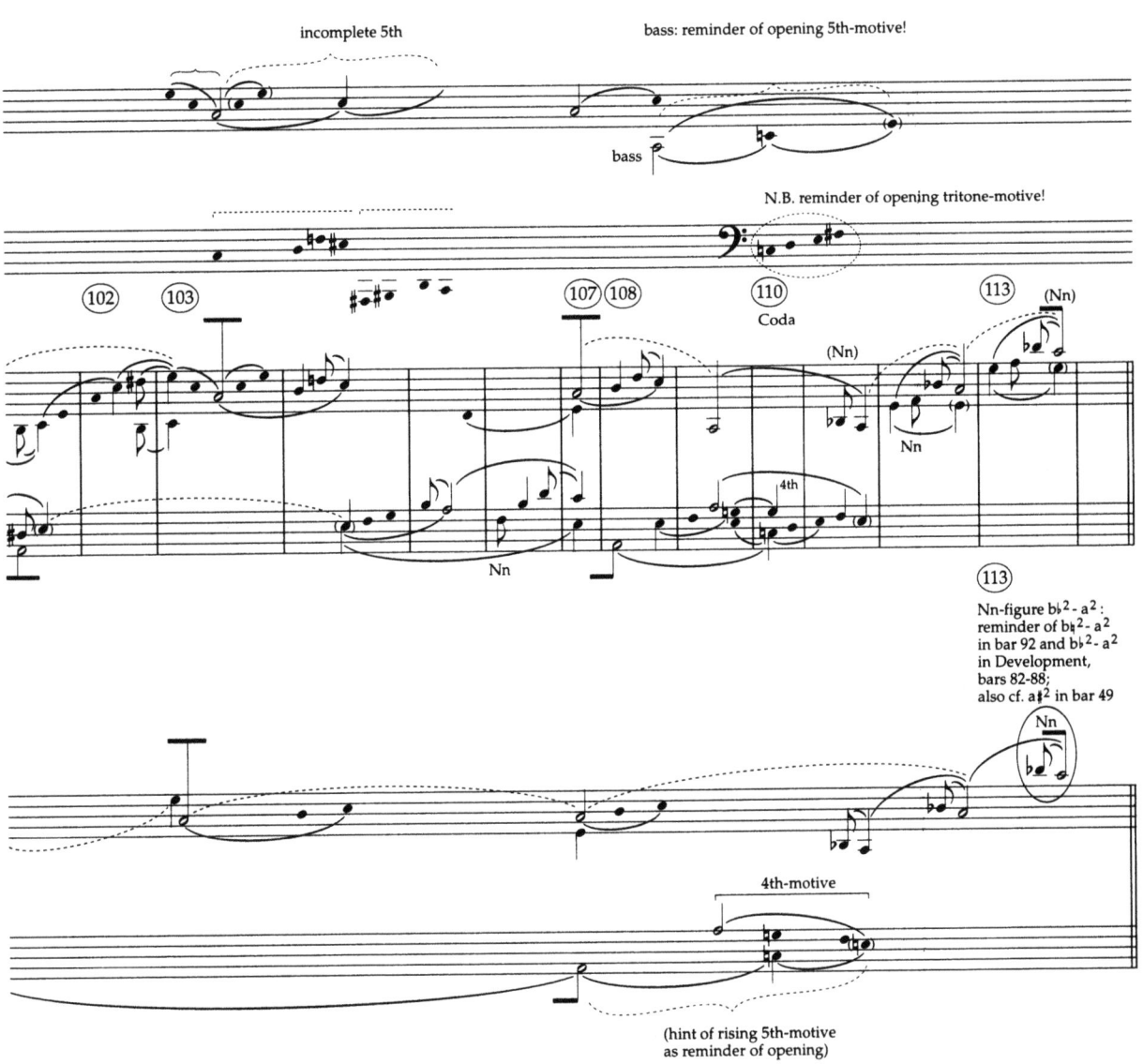

It is a testimonial to Sibelius's greatness and versatility that each of his symphonies explores a different sound-world. Each, in its own way, is concerned with integration of contrasts and with cumulation over the entire span. Perhaps in no work is this accomplished with such cohesiveness and concentration as in the Fourth Symphony. Sibelius himself could indeed refer to "that wonderful artistic logic that I seldom notice as I compose but can recognize afterwards,"[10] and say: "When a work of art which is intuitively created is scientifically analyzed, it reveals amazing requirements."[11]

for Catherine

10. Quoted in Levas, *Sibelius*, p. 46.   11. Quoted in *ibid.*, p. 83.

Voice leading as drama in *Wozzeck*

Arthur Maisel

Einer nach dem Andern!

Alban Berg's *Wozzeck* has been widely discussed since it was first performed – in fact, discussion began before the premiere – and a number of analyses, some going into great detail, have been published. What is perhaps most surprising is the degree of unanimity among analysts, given their divergent analytical approaches; despite some heat, there is sufficient light to speak of a consensus. This is a tribute to the clarity of Berg's musical thought, which is remarkable considering how complex and how new his idiom was. Leaving aside the truism that there will always be something to say about such a work, the consensus also begs the question of whether much is left to be said.

Given this situation, I must acknowledge that my essay appears to draw more heavily on the work of others than it does. Claims of priority are not the issue; I only hope to have a unity of vision (and not a singularity) about things that a number of us have noticed – a view that illuminates issues that have not been addressed previously.[1] Among these issues is prolongation in posttonal music, which is of interest in connection with many works written in the first quarter of the century, and which ought not to be so settled as it has seemed.

Concerning my title, the question may be raised as to how voice leading can be viewed *as* drama. The expected, paratactic "Voice leading *and* drama" is a more typical title after all. The allusion to Joseph Kerman's famous book is of course intentional – but it is far from being facetious. I do mean to assert that much of the musical expression of the drama in *Wozzeck* takes place in the voice leading, and this cuts to the quick of the difference between my approach and previous ones: others have tended to view some of the same entities that I discuss as static musical symbols submerged in the voice leading; I hope to show that the voice leading itself derives from these symbols and allows them to enact basic elements of the drama in musical terms. To do this, I will focus my discussion on a pair of symbols, the first two chords of the opera.

Classic leitmotive technique, long used by dramatic composers and codified for Berg's generation by Wagner and his epigones, has been discussed a number of times in connection with *Wozzeck*. In this technique a musical entity is made

---

1. I cite only the first publication of important insights. Minutiae or self-evident points that have long been common currency in analyses of *Wozzeck* are presented sans apparatus. Whether this paper sinks or swims depends on the reader's familiarity not just with the opera but to some extent with the analytical literature as well; Appendix A provides an overview.

to represent or refer to a character or theme in the drama, usually by *association*.[2] Association is the most reliable and, indeed, almost inevitable means of connecting musical and dramatic elements. What we might call a *precompositional transformation* is also sometimes used to connect ideas; examples may be found in Wagner's *Ring* cycle, for instance, in the way the "covenant" (descending scale) becomes the "love of the Wälsungs" (descending scale that rises through intermittent leaps of an upward seventh). But in *Wozzeck* the musical element's connection to the drama is frequently reinforced by its *structural embodiment* of the dramatic idea. To cite a well-known example: the five-tone chord associated with Wozzeck consists of four pitches from one whole-tone collection and one from the other, which seems to symbolize the man's status as a misfit. (In contrast, the Drum Major's motive works through *imitation* of his preening and slightly ludicrous – though at the same time creepy – goose step.)

Berg's practice is thus a consolidation of and an advancement over Wagnerian technique: Wagner's motives themselves seldom extend even to imitation of an idea; probably the majority work through mere association, the musical symbols having little inherent dramatic meaning. They accrue their great store of meaning by creating a complex web of associative links over time. Furthermore, it ought to be borne in mind that Berg's project is very different from Wagner's, especially in scale. No one could sustain the sort of density Berg achieves over vast Wagnerian stretches of time. But Berg creates density not so much by filling in with more of the same kind of detail as by folding the structure back upon itself – a qualitatively different kind of density that a Schenkerian approach is uniquely able to address. Pitch-class set analysis can reveal significant sets buried like *Muscheln* in the musical texture (it may even be too good at that), but it is less able to address the ways Berg moved beyond what he inherited from the Wagnerian tradition. Where Berg goes furthest beyond his predecessors (and I hope to go beyond mine) is with a process of *compositional* transformation of one or more of the musical symbols that mirrors a dramatic transformation.

Linienkreise, Figuren – Wer das lesen könnte!

Alban Berg was given to introducing symmetries of all kinds into his music – whether or not they could be consciously perceived by listeners – to a degree that one could describe as compulsive. Such games might have been conducive to allowing deeper connections to work themselves out in the music just because the composer was otherwise occupied consciously. In the case of *Wozzeck*, where all the characters seem trapped in their fates, the symmetries drive home that point, too. Perhaps the drama and Berg's developing musical practice meshed so well because he could muster his penchant for symmetry by treating symmetry itself as a symbol – for nature, for the hierarchical social

---

2. George Perle, "Representation and Symbol in the Music of *Wozzeck*," *The Music Review* 32/4 (1971), pp. 281–308; repr. in Perle, *The Operas of Alban Berg*, Vol. 1: *Wozzeck* (Berkeley: University of California Press, 1980), pp. 93–129.

order, or for Wozzeck's obsessions (*idées fixes*, in the medical terminology of Büchner's time). And perhaps the opera appeals to analysts because we identify with the way Wozzeck sees the world as aflame with deeper meaning.

Yet, despite any seemingly arbitrary features of the structure, the wonderful thing about Berg's music is how "natural" it is, how expressive: he was, of course, the first member of the second Viennese school to gain some acceptance by the general music-loving public as a result. And – *pace* Kerman – another reason for Berg's accessibility is that he endeavors to highlight significant symmetries for the listener.[3] Berg seems to have realized very early that atonality required alternative means for the listener to predict the next event; that the omnisymmetrical chromatic scale needed to have axes of symmetry imposed on it compositionally – thus his use of interval cycles that converge on important pitches at key structural points as early as the Op. 3 String Quartet.[4] It is noteworthy that Wozzeck's "projection" of his obsessions onto nature resembles in this way the composer's imposition of "meaningful symmetry" on a musical universe that may be too symmetrical to have meaning. At any rate, although the question remains as to how much the ubiquitous symmetries enhance one's experience of the music, there is no doubt that for the analyst a symmetry may emit the first glimmer of some part of the work's musical and dramatic meaning.

. . . zwei auf einmal.

The first two chords of *Wozzeck* have a number of salient features. They are both five-tone chords. They are mutually exclusive in pitch-class content.[5] Each voice

---

3. See Joseph Kerman, *Opera as Drama*, rev. edn (Berkeley: University of California Press, 1988), p. 183, for his complaint – apropos *Wozzeck* – about "analytical abracadabra." Kerman mentions the connection he finds difficult to accept between the low B at the end of act II and the B pedal in act III, scene 2, which ends in the famous unison crescendos. His mocking of the possibility of actually making the connection seems eminently reasonable – until we notice that the B at the end of act II and the last B before the crescendos are both played on the lowest string of the harp. Surely this is distinct enough a sound to aid the memory, particularly since the notes are the last sounds of their respective sections. See also the discussion of J. Peter Burkholder's "Berg and the Possibility of Popularity" in Appendix A.
4. Charles Porter, "Interval Cycles in Alban Berg's String Quartet Opus 3," *Theory and Practice* 14–15 (1989–90), pp. 139–77 (an article drawn from his Ph.D. dissertation, "Interval Cycles and Symmetrical Formations as Generators of Melody, Harmony, and Form in Alban Berg's String Quartet Opus 3," The City University of New York, 1989). The seminal article on the subject is Perle's "Berg's Master Array of Interval Cycles," *The Musical Quarterly* 63/1 (1977), pp. 1–30. Such interval cycles do not play a major role in *Wozzeck*, but see Appendix B and Example 4c. Moreover, Dave Headlam (see Appendix A) believes that Berg's mature harmonic language is founded on interval cycles.
5. In other words, they are *complementary* in the only musically meaningful sense – as opposed to the set-theoretical sense. Perle's keynote address at the 1989 meeting of the Society for Music Theory in Austin, Texas (published as "Pitch-Class Set Analysis: An Evaluation," *The Journal of Musicology* 8/2 [1990], pp. 151–72) does make a good point concerning the generalization from the hexachordal sets of twelve-tone theory to the variously sized sets of pitch-class set theory: twelve-tone sets can be distinguished only by ordering (Schoenberg) or segmentation (Hauer); we must assume transpositional equivalence because the sets exhaust the universe of tones. Smaller sets, in contrast, can be distinguished by pitch content alone because transpositional equivalence is not necessarily applicable to them. I do not believe Perle is questioning the applicability of transpositional equivalence to smaller sets; he is only questioning whether it is axiomatic. For an example of the peculiar results of the peculiar concept of complementarity as defined by pitch-class set theory, see note 12 below.

Example 1

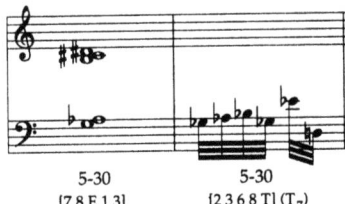

moves through a different linear interval from the first chord to the second. If we follow the convention of numbering pitch classes ("pc" for "pitch class" hereafter) so that C is 0, then in the second chord the "odd" whole-tone collection predominates, the chord being a type long recognized as characteristic of the opera, a "whole-tone chord with one extraneous note" ("whole-tone plus" hereafter);[6] in the first chord the two whole-tone collections are as evenly represented as they can be in five-tone chords, with the "even" whole-tone collection having the simple majority (see Example 1a).[7]

Douglas Jarman was the first analyst in print to link the first two chords of the opera with the two main characters, Marie and Wozzeck, respectively.[8] In *The Structure of Atonal Music*, Allen Forte had noted the connection between the second chord (pc set 5–30) and what George Perle has called "Wozzeck's entrance and exit motive" (see Example 1b, adapted from Forte, and compare

---

6. The longer formulation is Perle's, the shorter is mine; Dave Headlam also uses it. Janet Schmalfeldt uses "almost whole-tone"; see *Berg's "Wozzeck": Harmonic Language and Dramatic Design* (New Haven: Yale University Press, 1983), a book based on her Ph.D. dissertation, "Berg's Wozzeck: Pitch-Class Set Structures and the Dramatic Design" (Yale University, 1979).
7. A fuller treatment of the constraints governing Berg's choice of chords is given in Appendix B.
8. Douglas Jarman, *The Music of Alban Berg* (London: Faber and Faber, 1979; repr. Berkeley: University of California Press, 1985), p. 66.

Examples 1c and 1a).[9] In his book on the opera, Perle takes no note of this idea; other students of the work, however, have no doubts about the identity of the content of the first two chords and the passages during which we see Wozzeck and Marie together for the first and last times. On both occasions, the leitmotive that Perle, taking a cue from Berg, calls "Marie's aimless waiting" (as a collection, pc set 5–20) precedes Wozzeck's entrance leitmotive.

In digging for symmetry, Jarman unfortunately goes too far, to my mind. Linking the first two chords with the two leitmotives involves transposition of the chords by the same interval and some quite straightforward composing-out of their respective pitches; Jarman, however, wants to connect the first two chords with the cadential chord (or "chords," as he has it) with which all three acts close (see Example 2a). In order to demonstrate the identity of his "cadential chords A and B" with Marie's and Wozzeck's chords (hereafter, M and W), he has to transpose each of his two chords by a *different* interval; he then has to add to the first an extra tone that is not always present – never at the ends of the acts – as well as having to leave out two other tones. This is his "cadential chord A^1," a seven-tone chord that includes all the tones of M.[10] The first instance of his cadential chord sounds more like an appoggiatura chord to the actual last chord of the section where it appears, the transition between act I, scenes 2 and 3 (see Example 2b). Of the pitches in the latter chord that resolve embellishing tones in the former, three – D, G, and B♭ – are the only pitches *not* included in the three-chord sequence ("X–Y–Z," to use Perle's labels) that underlies the preceding scene (see Example 2c). In any case, as intimated, I find questionable Jarman's premise of considering the cadential music to consist of *two* separate chords.

Appoggiatura chord or no, it is more appropriate, I think, to treat Jarman's chord A^1 as what might be termed a "nonce chord" – that is, one that forges a relationship between two chords not otherwise related, for a local (in this case, programmatic) purpose: Marie is about to appear for the first time in the following scene. (The Captain has alluded to her in scene 1, and she is referred to very obliquely in the chords of scene 2, as Jarman and Janet Schmalfeldt have shown; see the discussion of Example 3a below.) As far as there being any connection between M and the cadential chord, it is perhaps most to the point

---

9. Allen Forte, *The Structure of Atonal Music* (New Haven: Yale University Press, 1973), p. 24; Perle, "Representation and Symbol," p. 292 (*The Operas of Alban Berg*, Vol. 1, pp. 106–7). Forte finds "Wir arme Leut" (4–19) to be a subset of the chord associated with Wozzeck (5–30), and Jarman concurs (*The Music of Alban Berg*, p. 54). While literally true, this is not convincing to me because the leitmotive always sounds like a "minor-major seventh chord," which has so little whole-tone character. (It even recurs in chordal form in act II, scene 4.) See the discussion of my Example 3b (pp. 167ff.), where five-tone chords are created from the four-tone subsets of 5–30 that *preserve* its "whole-tone plus" character. One of these subsets is indeed 4–19, but it is expressed as a "$^4_2$" and thus maintains the family resemblance. In the opera we hear the characteristic "whole-tone plus" sound only because of the bass that accompanies "Wir arme Leut"; unfortunately, adding the bass yields set 5–26, not 5–30 (W). Set 5–26, being a member of the "whole-tone plus" family, is therefore aurally related to the chord associated with Wozzeck. It might in fact even be mistaken for that chord; compare the two sets in normal order: 5–26 (0148T) and 5–30 (01468).

10. Jarman, *The Music of Alban Berg*, pp. 62ff. Jarman's transpositions are labeled with the assumption that his cadential chords A and B are at T_0; my labels always take M and W at T_0 as the referential transposition. Therefore the numbers complement each other (e.g., his T_7 is my T_5).

Example 2

a) After Jarman

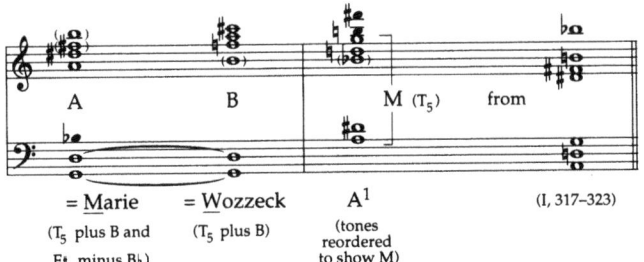

d)

b)   c)

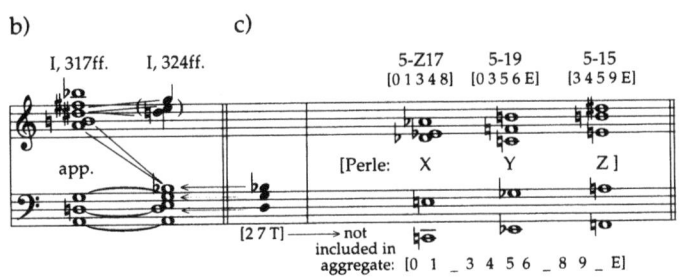

e)

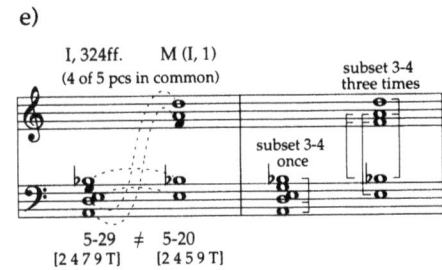

that W can be related to the cadential chord as a tritone transposition – an idea I will discuss further. That Jarman can relate M to the cadential chord is then an inevitable result of the latter's transpositional relationship to W and another more significant feature of the first two chords already mentioned: they are literally complementary, having no pitches in common. As Milton Babbitt and David Lewin showed in the 1960s, mutually exclusive six-pitch sets are often convertible into each other either by transposition or by transposition and inversion. The same would apply to mutually exclusive five-pitch sets if we supply the missing tones – which is what Jarman does (see Example 2d).

The question is, of course, whether the composer actually uses any abstract relationship. As a number of my examples show, Berg frequently relates other chords to W or M by common pitch content. In contrast, he seems to want to keep W and M distinct from each other; for example, in the open spacing of the first chord of the opera and the close spacing of the second, or in the extreme gestural difference between the "Marie's aimless waiting" and the "Wozzeck's entrance" motives. Perhaps just because the two chords are so similar as sets, Berg poetically prefers for most of the opera to keep hidden their broken symmetry – that is, that Wozzeck and Marie have more in common than appears on the surface.

Let me pursue this concentration on the characteristics of the two chords a bit further. Just as W is one of a number of chords of a type that pervades the opera, M is part of a family that might be characterized ad hoc as "major seventh chords (plus)." This is even less precise than the "whole-tone plus" description of the W family, and a closer approximation of the source of the family resemblance is the presence of pc set 3–4 (015) as a subset: a "major seventh chord" can be described as 3–4 twice, in prime and inverted forms, with two tones in common.

Oh! meine Theorie!

A digression is now in order, to discuss the issue of pc sets as discrete entities in this music. My impression is that Berg uses chords in looser associative pairings than is allowed by classical set theory – although Forte's introduction of genera is undoubtedly intended to address the issue of similarity.[11] Set-theoretical approaches to similarity are, however, problematical. When the pcs of two sets are almost the same, basing similarity on interval content gives trivial results. Conversely, it seems counterintuitive that two transpositions of the same set with no common pcs would be said to be more similar than two different sets with many pcs in common. This is like saying in a tonal context that A major and B♭ major are more similar than A major and A minor. There are really two kinds of similarity, and in a given piece of music both can be equally interesting. For this reason, Perle's less specific characterizations might be more apposite to the way Berg composes. For example, twenty-six apparently distinct pc sets fit the "whole-tone plus" description.

In the past, pc set theorists like Schmalfeldt attempted to come to terms with this difficulty by using the inclusion relation; Jarman, though not using Forte's numbers, takes a similar tack. There is a problem with this approach: when the source sets are large – the cadential set of *Wozzeck*, for example, has eight members – it becomes very likely that smaller sets will be included. In theory, the inclusion of a smaller set in a number of permutations within a larger set signifies a stronger inclusion relation, but the opposite could as reasonably be maintained when the theory is applied to analysis: if there are a number of ways that a given trichord might be derived from a certain octachord, a specific occurrence in a piece of music is that much more likely to be coincidental (or even unavoidable) than it is to be musically significant. I do believe that the *maximal* inclusion of 3–4 in M (5–20) has some significance. However, the chord at the end of the interlude between scenes 2 and 3 of act I (the one that resolves Jarman's A^1) is reminiscent of the first chord of the opera (M) in part because the chords share four of their five pcs, not because they are reducible

---

11. Forte, "Pitch-Class Set Genera and the Origin of the Modern Harmonic Species," *Journal of Music Theory* 32/2 (1988), pp. 187–270. An interesting precursor is Robert Morris, "A Similarity Index for Pitch-Class Sets," *Perspectives of New Music* 18/1–2 (1979–80), pp. 445–60. To quantify similarity, Morris subtracts interval vectors and weights the results according to the size of the sets compared. See the useful discussion of this and other related issues accompanying Martha Hyde and Andrew Mead's bibliographic overview of the current state of research in twelve-tone and atonal theory in *Music Theory Spectrum* 11/1 (1989), pp. 35–48.

to the same set, and despite the fact that 3–4 occurs only once in the former as opposed to three times in M (see Example 2e).[12]

Accordingly, I often find it at least as helpful to pay attention to actual pitches in this music as to the more abstract set relations. This also corresponds to Berg's practice in the opera of singling out certain pitches as symbols, the dyad B–F being a well-known instance. At any rate, a "flexible" set-theoretical approach is especially appropriate to analysis – as distinct from theory – because it responds to a fact of the compositional process: that musical relationships that were unsought or unplanned sometimes "come to hand" in the course of composition.

Man kann viel seh'n, wenn man zwei Augen hat und wenn man nicht blind ist, und wenn die Sonne scheint.

Such a flexible approach is better illustrated in practice than described: to do so, I will discuss the sequence of three chords ("X–Y–Z") underlying act I, scene 2. While both Jarman and Schmalfeldt have demonstrated that the first of the three chords combines elements of W and M (see Example 3a), I have not seen a satisfactory explanation of what Perle calls the "curious 'rightness'" of the sequence, though his example goes some of the way.[13]

A flexible set-theoretical explanation begins with the fact that each of the chords contains a different one of the three possible four-tone subsets of W that preserve its "whole-tone plus" character (see Example 3b); the addition of the fifth tone of each chord makes it inversionally symmetrical! This suggests the following programmatic explanation: W is eminently unsymmetrical, being characterized by the inclusion of a "wrong note" in the symmetrical whole-tone collection – again, to symbolize Wozzeck's role as a misfit. In act I, scene 2, Wozzeck projects his own obsessions onto the natural world; thus the use of three different subsets of his chord that preserve its essential character and their conversion into symmetrical – that is, "natural" – chords. Chords Y and Z also contain four-tone subsets of M (see Example 3c), but none of the three chords contains a subset of 5–20 that characteristically maximizes 3–4 (either 4–20 or 4–8). So I find no special significance in the presence of the subsets of 5–20 or in the fact that Z contains the shared subset of W and M (4–16).

One ought to be cautious about asserting the significance of inversional symmetry unless the composer uses it compositionally – but here Berg does just

12. Another aspect of the inclusion relation as defined by set theory that leads to musically awkward results is the proposition that a small set is related to a larger one by inclusion even if it is not a subset of the larger set but only a subset of the larger set's complement (a direct consequence of making transpositional equivalence axiomatic; see note 5 above). For example, set 3–1 (012) is not a subset of 5–20 (01568) but it is a subset of 7–20 (0124789), the complement of 5–20, so one is supposed to see a relationship to the "complex about 5–20 and 7–20." It is something one can *see* but not something one can *hear*. When one is hearing 5–20, one is not hearing 3–1 (nor does one say to oneself, "If I were hearing the seven tones that I'm not hearing right now, I would be hearing 3–1").

13. Perle, "The Musical Language of *Wozzeck*," in *The Music Forum*, Vol. 1 (New York: Columbia University Press, 1967), pp. 204–59, Example 23 (p. 221). The article is republished (in expanded form) in *The Operas of Alban Berg*, Vol. 1, pp. 130–87, and there one should refer to Example 109 (p. 143).

Example 3

a)
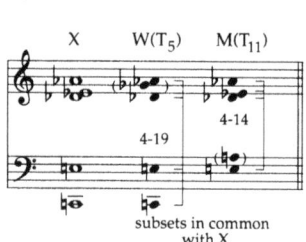

c)
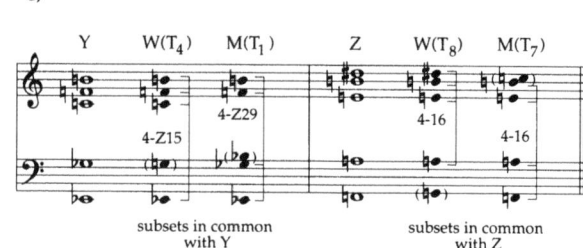

b)

d)
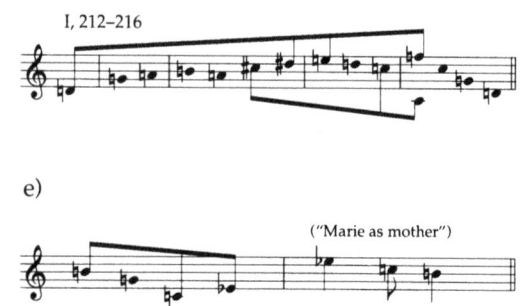

e) ("Marie as mother")
"Wir ar - me Leut"

that. There are explicit references to the axis of symmetry of X – that is, D – in bars 201ff., and the music in bars 210–12 converges symmetrically on the D that commences Andres's first arioso.

Even though inversional symmetry has been an important topic of the literature concerning this repertoire, I am not aware of much attention paid to its *perceptibility* – in particular, the perceptibility of the axis of symmetry; even less, *shifts* in the axis of symmetry. Yet this passage persuades me that these things may be perceptible and that they account in part for both the "rightness" that Perle finds and its "curious" quality (which I take to imply "hard to explain or put into words").

How are we to understand the choice of the three transpositions of W that become the basis of X–Y–Z? Perhaps some of the factors involved are the following: E♭(D♯) is the one pitch in common to all three chords, and it is also the axis of symmetry *of* the shifting axes of symmetry of the sequence: D–D/E♭–E♮ (refer again to Example 3b). This "motion" is recalled by the beginning of Andres's song in bars 212–15 (see Example 3d). In his 1929 lecture on the opera, Berg says that the tenths were "the basis" of the three chords, comparing the effect of the individual members of the sequence to the tonal I, V, and IV, respectively.[14]

14. Published in English translation in H. F. Redlich, *Alban Berg: The Man and His Music* (New York: Abelard-Schuman, 1957), pp. 261–86, and newly translated in Jarman's Cambridge Opera Handbook on *Wozzeck* (Cambridge: Cambridge University Press, 1989), pp. 154–70.

f)

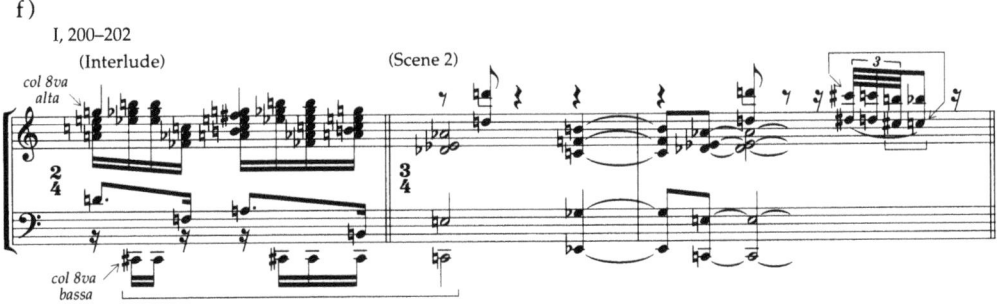

g)

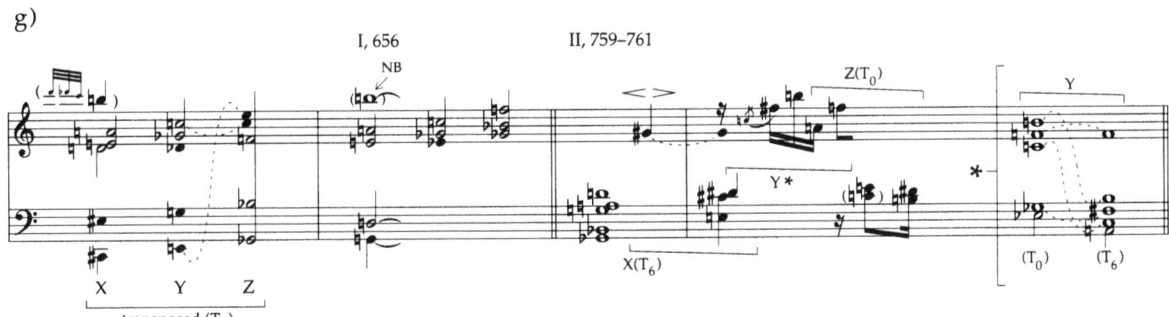

Berg's reasons for invoking the tonic for X, based on C–E, and the subdominant for Z, based on F–A, are obvious enough; describing Y – with E♭–G♭ for its lower tenth – as a dominant seems odd, though it is perhaps comparable to some sort of "applied-dominant function" chord like a diminished seventh.

Even if one doesn't hear the specific functions Berg ascribes to the chords, it is clear that if X is tonic, then Y and Z are both nontonic. As Perle mentions, both chords Y and Z contain the tritone B–F, while X does not: X is based on an odd transposition of W and so features the *even* whole-tone collection; the others, being based on even transpositions, feature the same *odd* whole-tone collection as both W in its original transposition and the cadential chord at the end of each act.[15] It may or may not be a coincidence, therefore, that what we may call (for want of a better term) the "roots" of the three transposed subsets of W – C, B, and E♭(D♯) – are themselves a characteristic subset, 3-3 (014), of W, figuring in both the "Wir arme Leut" and "Marie as mother" leitmotives (see Example 3e). Chords Y and Z represent harmonic motion away from chord X – as the dominant and subdominant do from the tonic in tonal music – because they are built on the other whole-tone collection. So Berg's comparison with a tonal progression is less superficial than it might seem at first: the sort of subtlety that characterizes harmonic relations in tonal music is here imported into an atonal context, within the structural unit (the scene) but, more important, also at a higher structural level because the local "tonic," C, is a member of the "nontonic" even whole-tone collection.

---

15. Perle, "Musical Language," p. 221; *The Operas of Alban Berg*, Vol. 1, p. 143.

The choice of C–E as the lowest notes of chord X may have been conditioned by the presence of B–F in Y and Z, being the traditional resolution of that tritone. Of greater significance, though, is that the C of scene 2, as a member of the "nontonic" whole-tone collection, also inflects the C♯ that governs act I, scene 1, and ends the interlude between the scenes in the bass; then, in the motion from X to Y the innermost voice echoes the bass, D♭(C♯)–C♮, and the motion is echoed again in the triplet thirty-second-note figure (see Example 3f). When the chord sequence recurs in disguised form in the interlude that precedes act I, scene 5 – where nature in the form of Marie's sexual attraction to the Drum Major really does threaten Wozzeck's domestic arrangement – pitches of X–Y–Z recur a half-step higher because scene 5 is, like scene 1, organized around the G–C♯ tritone (see Example 3g).[16]

This transformed repetition (which to my knowledge has previously escaped notice) of the X–Y–Z sequence as the opening chords of the interlude acts as a link between the second scene of the opera and later scenes. Jarman (*The Music of Alban Berg*, p. 68) points out that the opening chords of the interlude before the last scene of act I prefigure the Drum Major's motive, then recur in the tavern scene, act II, scene 4 (played by the onstage band), and provide the basis for the rondo motive of act II, scene 5. The X–Y–Z sequence recurs in the latter scene as well, initially as the "breathing" of the sleeping soldiers, and then as the pitch source for the rondo theme. (And notice how the B above the staff in bar 656 links scene 5 of act I to its dramatic fruition in act III, scene 2!)

This cycle of motivic links helps make an unusual dramatic structure at the end of act II more convincing. The bass of the nightmarish conclusion of the tavern scene in the interlude between act II, scenes 4 and 5, could have led to what would have been a conventional second act curtain: it unfolds the cadential set (bars 724–35) in two interlocking transpositions, T_0 and (T_{11}) – E♭ (D) F (E) G (F♯) A (A♭) C♯ (C) F♯ (F) B (B♭) – but stops just short of the last two tones, D (C♯). Then the last scene begins with the chorus of sleeping soldiers (X–Y–Z at T_6). The staccato Ds of the oboes in act I, scene 2, is now a swell on $g\sharp^1$, first by a solo contrabass and then by Wozzeck, crying out in his sleep. Wozzeck awakens and reiterates the bass pattern of the preceding interlude (bars 746 and 750), but completes the unfolding of the cadential set to D (C♯) – on the word "Messer!" (bar 751) – at which point X–Y–Z comes back in the orchestra at its original pitch (bar 755).

The pairing of G♯ and D here is related to the function of D in the cadential chord of the opera as an "extraneous" element like the A♭(G♯) in W (the cadential chord being based on W at T_6). The link adumbrates harmonic features of the final scenes: the D is the last tone of the embellishing harmony (based on W at T_0) to be unfolded in the middle section of the orchestral interlude (refer to Examples 4a and 4b below); its relationship to A♭ in W is also made explicit by the voice exchange in the final scene, in which C♯ and G trade positions (refer to Examples 6 and 7a below).

As the final scene of act II continues, the chord sequence is stated X–Y–Z–Y–X at its original transposition (bars 755–57), then a descending

---

16. Bass organization in scene 1 coincides with axial organization; in contrast, scene 2 is organized around C in the bass but axially around E♭.

chromatic series of parallel X chords restores the tritone transposition, with the contrabass swell on G♯ (bar 760) signaling that Wozzeck has gone back to sleep (although the stage directions do not say so). The G♯ acts, however, as a harmonic pivot because the opening motto of the rondo, accompanying the Drum Major's entrance at bar 761, is based on X–Y–Z at T_0. (The Y is actually both T_0 and T_6, but these have four tones in common, the subset 4–9 [0167] which has the same pcs at T_0 and T_6; refer back to Example 3g.)

We have seen that classical pitch-class set theory can hinder certain kinds of insight into voice leading because of its focus on the identity of pc sets, while a more flexible approach allows other connections to be revealed. We can now return to our main topic, voice leading as drama, and examine an illustration of the application of such an approach.

With the inflection of the C♯ of act I, scene 1, to C♮ in scene 2, C comes to represent Wozzeck himself.[17] Although the "extraneous" note in W was originally A♭, C plays the role of misfit more often throughout the opera, having been established in act I, scene 2. Even at the start, C is the first note after the introductory chords and the first and last note in the solo oboe phrase that corresponds to the rise of the curtain – though distinctly extraneous to the prevailing odd whole-tone harmony and clearly a melodic appendage of the C♯ and B that frame the ambitus. When, later in the first scene, Wozzeck asserts himself, breaking out of the military discipline of the reiterated C♯s of "Jawohl, Herr Hauptmann," his aria, "Wir arme Leut" (bars 136ff.) moves from C♯ to C in the bass. At the beginning, C♯ is the lowest note of a twelve-tone harmony arpeggiated upward and ending on c^3; this is answered in bar 147 by a downward arpeggio on the same chord except with C♯ on top and the C in the bass. The high $c♯^4$ in the solo violin corresponds to the line, "It would be a fine thing to be virtuous" ("Es muß was Schönes sein um die Tugend"). Then the music plummets to C in the bass for the line, "But I'm just a poor guy" ("Aber ich bin ein armer Kerl!"). The bass then moves on to B, foreshadowing the end of the action, as Wozzeck sings, "The likes of us suffer in this world and the next" ("Unsereins ist doch einmal unselig in dieser und der andern Welt!").

With such associations of pitch and of the *motion* between pitches in mind, one can hear the bass motion from C♯ to C at the beginning of scene 2 as depicting Wozzeck's release from military discipline – whereupon he is possessed by his visions.[18] In act III, when Wozzeck tries to pull himself back to normality

17. Though, to paraphrase Dorothy Parker's famous description of the young Katharine Hepburn's acting, Wozzeck's behavior runs the gamut from the C♯ of "Jawohl, Herr Hauptmann" to the B of the murder scene. The tone most associated with B is F – right from the linear motion in the first two chords, f^1–b – and Perle points out ("Musical Language," p. 218; *The Operas of Alban Berg*, Vol. 1, p. 140) that F is associated with Marie in many ways: as the tonal center of the sonata-allegro movement, act II, scene 1; as the tonality of one of the two passages in the opera notated with a key signature (act III, scene 1, bars 33–42 – the other is the final orchestral interlude); and as the note that dominates Wozzeck's death scene (act III, scene 4), as his B dominates Marie's (act III, scene 2).

18. Leo Treitler's idea that the first and last scenes of the opera represent everyday reality and are therefore detached from the drama, while dramatically apt, is thus not supported musically; see "*Wozzeck* and the Apocalypse," in *Music and the Historical Imagination* (Cambridge, Mass.: Harvard University Press, 1989), pp. 242–63). Moreover, the first two scenes are linked in another way. Treitler's new motive in scene 2, the top voice of X–Y–Z, is an unfolding of the pitches of W minus the tritone G–C♯: note the identical spelling, A♭–B–D♯.

after the murder, the B of the murder scene, scene 3, moves up to C in the bass at the start of scene 4.[19] The motion C♯–C♮–B then recurs in the bass in the final scene of the opera (see Example 6 below).

He, bist Du toll?

Having broken ranks with set theory, we can now turn to several large-scale features of act III that relate to the first two chords. Another of Berg's symmetries, a programmatic one, was first noted by Perle.[20] The orchestral interlude between scenes 3 and 4 of act III omits any reference to leitmotives associated with Marie, although it recalls material associated with everyone else of any consequence in the story – especially material connected with Wozzeck, naturally; the final scene then concentrates on Marie's leitmotives (and a key chord from two of her earlier scenes – act I, scene 3, and act III, scene 1 – is featured; refer to bar 385 in Example 7d). Taking Perle's perception a step further, it seems to me that the last two musical sections of the opera are a gigantic expansion of the first two chords. If none of Marie's leitmotives are heard in the interlude, it is only because the entire section prolongs *her* chord, M; even if her leitmotives make up most of the material of the final scene, W is the underlying harmony.

Perhaps the idea of prolongation in the interlude will not seem as problematic as it does in the final scene (see below). Many would agree that the interlude is tonal, if only in some very loose sense (its beginning and ending derive from an early uncompleted piano sonata in D minor).[21] As my graphs will show, I think it is tonal in quite a strict sense; Berg evidently thought it tonal enough to use a key signature of one flat (despite continuing to follow the atonal style of ubiquitous accidentals – including B♭).

Turning to the analysis of the final interlude, note that a skeletal I–III–V–I still governs this section (see Examples 4a and 4b), but there is more than just an intense chromaticism obscuring the tonal organization: quintessentially atonal processes are superimposed on the structure; for example, the converging and diverging semitone cycles implicit in the first period (ending with the tonicization of V of III, motivically marked, in bars 333–34; see the cycles in Example 4c). Perle has pointed out the importance of whole-tone collections to this interlude, noting how the two whole-tone collections are combined to give the complete chromatic collection in bars 368–70 (see Example 4d).[22]

Moreover, the structural motion from I is paralleled in the foreground by a carefully gradual dissolution of tonality (which in fact is only a seeming dissolution) that culminates in the twelve-tone chord of bar 364. The chord is then

---

19. On an autographed picture of himself, Berg once used the C major chord of act II, scene 1, as a "quotation." This could be taken for a witticism, or, seen in the light of the meaning of C outlined above, it could have – typically – deeper significance. The picture is reproduced in the photo insert of Perle's *The Operas of Alban Berg*, Vol. 1 (No. 20).
20. Perle, "Representation and Symbol," p. 303 (*The Operas of Alban Berg*, Vol. 1, p. 122).
21. The first page of the autograph of the sonata is reproduced in Jarman's Cambridge Opera Handbook on *Wozzeck*, p. 91.
22. Perle, "Musical Language," pp. 243f.; *The Operas of Alban Berg*, Vol. 1, pp. 158f. I have emended Perle's example slightly.

made to serve as V by the marked bass A in the trombones and timpani on the upbeat to bar 365 – maybe the most extreme illustration in the repertoire of Schenker's idea that the *Stufe* can be represented by the bass alone.[23] The process of dissolution leading up to the twelve-tone chord can be summarized in this way: after the first four introductory measures (bars 320–23), which are almost diatonic, the next four end with a D♭ major chord standing for I, D minor (it supports the arrival of the top voice on $\hat{3}$). The $\hat{4}$ is obscured by being transferred down an octave; this is compensated for by the reiteration of $\hat{4}$–$\hat{3}$ in the violins, bars 328–30; later, $\hat{2}$–$\hat{1}$ is reiterated in a similar way in bars 342–45. Motivically, these reiterations help tie the early piano sonata to the climactic statement in bars 365–67 of Wozzeck's fugue theme from act II, scene 2 (bars 313–14 of that act).

After bar 327, the chromaticism intensifies, and by bar 335 the foreground is largely whole-tone – though a vestigial I–IV–V–I tonicizing III, F, is still audible in bars 335–38. In structural terms, the upper voice has reached an interrupted $\hat{2}$ and the bass has reached III at this point (the seventh over III having been consonantly prepared by V of III – the middleground being, as one might expect, far more conservative than the foreground). On the surface, tonality seems to have been dissolved, but a motion to an inner voice, $\hat{2}$–$\hat{1}$–$\hat{7}$, continues in the deep middleground. (If D minor represents Marie in some sense, the assertion of the equivalence of D and D♭ in bar 327 and then its reinterpretation as a motion, D–C♯, is highly suggestive, particularly given the perorative context. Berg draws Marie and Wozzeck together, via M and W, even more explicitly in the final scene, as the discussion of Example 7d below will show.) After a doubly chromatic exchange of voices, D–C♯(= D♭) and B♭–B♮ (bars 342–46), the main tones of the outer voices unfold a seven-tone collection that includes all the pitches of W at T_0 (bars 346–64). The two added pitches are F, a member of the whole-tone collection that predominates in W, and D, which is the last pitch unfolded and acts as an anticipation of the return of the tonic. In bars 352–59, the three "diminished seventh" chords (4–28) are unfolded in the same order as they are subsequently "stacked" to form the twelve-tone chord of bar 364 (see Example 5). If we take the bass pedal G of bars 352–59 into account, as we surely must when listening, a hierarchy is willy-nilly created in which G♭ moving to G♮ in bar 355 is heard as a resolution. Once we are hearing this way – and I think we can hardly keep ourselves from doing so – it is a slight leap to hearing the motion of F to E in a similar way, especially given its quasi-traditional rhythmic displacement of the "tone of resolution." Thus, in bar 355 we hear the embellished unfolding of a subset [47T] of 4–28$_1$ [147T] and not 5–4 [4567T] at all.[24]

---

23. As far as the tonality of the interlude goes, is it a gesture toward tradition on Berg's part or some kind of ploy that he ends in the same key as he began? (It "works," on the surface at least, to substitute A♭ for A in the bass of bar 364 and proceed with everything transposed down a half-step.) The outer "diminished seventh chords" do, however, seem to function like applied chords to a dominant A: the lower acts like a common-tone diminished seventh, the upper like a VII^7 of V.

24. It can limit pc set theory as an analytical tool to accept its positivistic outlook too wholeheartedly because the basis of analysis is an act of hearing, which is typically contextual. Context is admittedly a slippery slope on which to build an argument and can therefore make for bad theory – but experience is so conditioned by context that avoiding the slippery slope can just as readily make for bad analysis.

174 Arthur Maisel

Example 4

a) Middleground

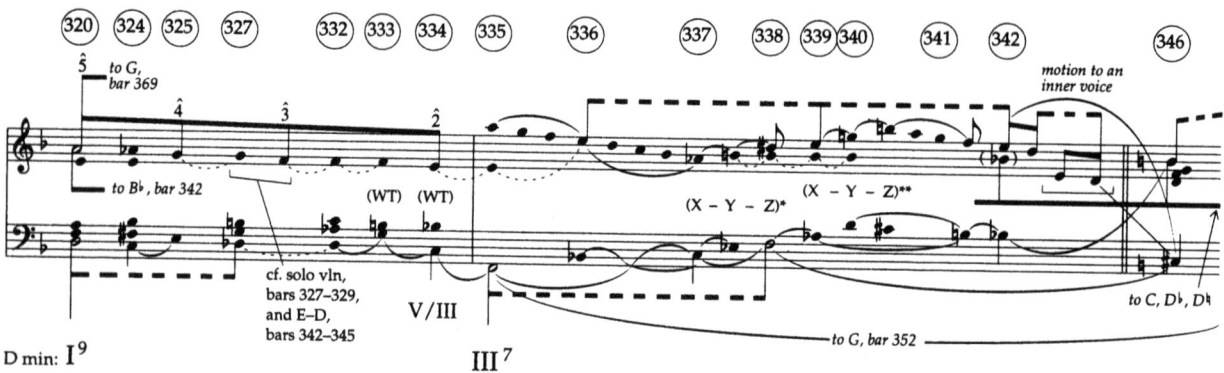

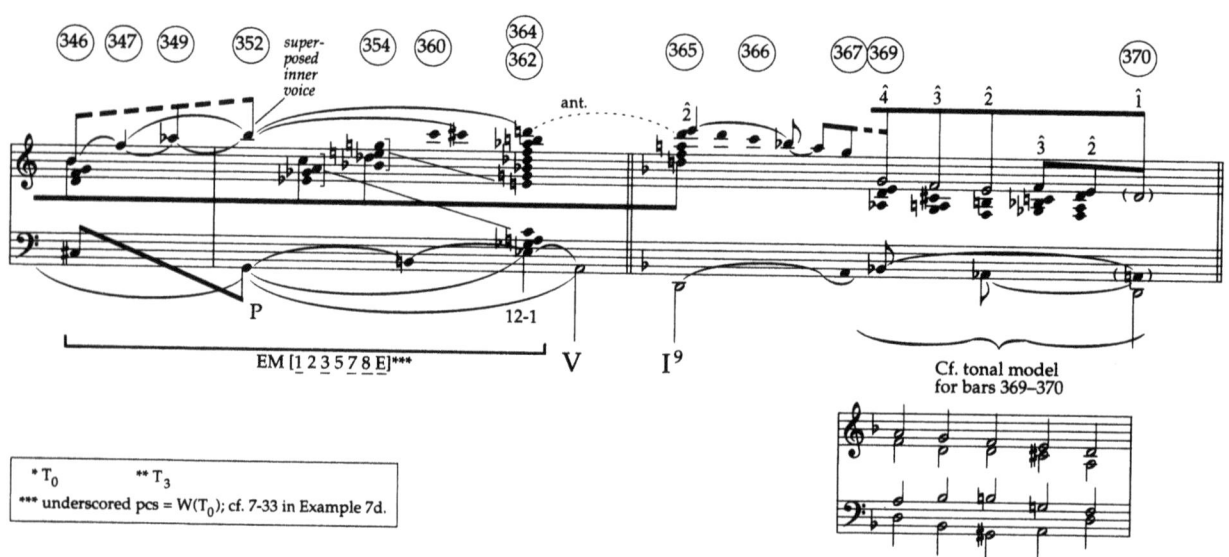

b) Background

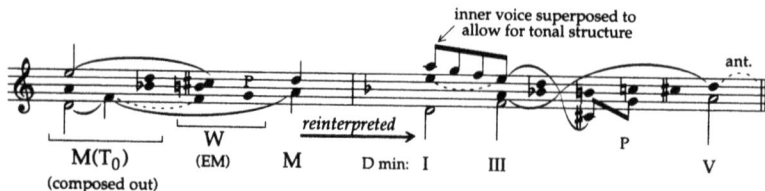

c)

d) After Perle

An aspect of tonality that allows us to connect distant events, discounting intervening ones, or even to disconnect simultaneous events (Schenker poetically calls it "aural flight"), also continues to hold for this music. The result is that a note can belong more to a set that is not present than to one that is. The three transpositions of 4–28 are prominent in bars 352f., 354f., and 356f., respectively. While they are seldom explicitly present in the intervening measures (bars 358–61), they are sustained (in three distinct registers) as the 12–1 of bar 364 is built up over the course of the two preceding measures. Therefore it makes sense to segment the intervening measures in ways that take into account the context established by the three 4–28s, even if this contradicts the more obvious segmentations on the surface of the music, such as 4–17 (0347).[25]

The canonic entrances in bars 349–51 of the Captain's theme from act I, scene 1 (used as his fugue theme in act II, scene 2), have established a duple meter. This persists with the introduction of the three 4–28s successively on downbeats of the implicit rather than the notated bars. When both the 4–28s and the motivic references begin to pile up phantasmagorically in bar 356, the

25. With traditionally tonal music, for instance, few objections would now be raised to describing $\hat{3}$, supported by III♯ when it arrives after an initial ascent, as being more associated with I, even though the tonic is not sounding and would be dissonant if it were, and even though the $\hat{3}$ is the *root* of the chord that is sounding. This is so in part for the simple reason that the piece probably begins and certainly ends with the I.

Example 5

4–28s already occupy discrete registers (which do, however, continue to shift). So the line that carries G (a member of 4–28$_1$) from the bass to an inner voice in bars 356–58 is initially embellished by members of 4–28$_0$, but then by members of 4–28$_2$ as it ventures into the middle register (see Example 5c). The embellishments of this ascent derive from the top voice in bars 323–25 and twice adumbrate the contrapuntal setting of the climactic quotation of Wozzeck's aria "Wir arme Leut" in bars 361–62.

The end of this passage parallels quite closely the first phrase of "Wir arme Leut," in act I, scene 1 – except that the aria is at T_{10}, if the orchestral passage is arbitrarily considered to be T_0. In the aria, too, the melody is accompanied by the stacking of the three 4–28s. The first phrase of the aria ends with the words "Wer kein Geld hat" set to the "Marie as mother" leitmotive and accompanied by M – also at T_{10}. This supports the identification of the D minor ninth chord of the final orchestral interlude with M because it takes the same role as M does in the earlier scene: the resolution of the twelve-tone harmony. The climactic passage of the orchestral interlude is paralleled even more closely – because of the canonic imitation of the melody – by the end of the development section of the sonata form of act II, scene 1: there the twelve-tone chord abruptly disappears to reveal Wozzeck's C major triad (V of F, the tonic of the scene).[26]

Ohne den Segen der Kirche!

The "problem of prolongation in posttonal music" has been well summarized by Joseph Straus in his article of that name.[27] He finds the difficulty to be in essence one's inability to distinguish between harmonic and nonharmonic events. I feel he is mistaken in assigning the difficulty to the music, however – it is rather a problem of the state of our theory of posttonal music. For tonal

---

26. Allen Forte provides a detailed analysis of the last interlude in "The Mask of Tonality: Alban Berg's Symphonic Epilogue to *Wozzeck*," included in *Alban Berg: Historical and Analytical Perspectives*, David Gable and Robert Morgan, eds. (Oxford: Clarendon Press, 1991), pp. 151–200. I find many of the local set unfoldings at least potentially convincing (the unfolding of 5–30 [W] in the bass, bars 324–27, for instance). Overall, however, I disagree with Forte's analysis, which rests on his belief that chromatic motivic features and tonal structure are necessarily in conflict, and with his conclusion that only by removing "the mask of tonality" (p. 193) can the motives be analytically integrated (p. 176). This represents a shift from the position expressed in his earlier study (see the quotation in note 27 below). To be sure, some of the motivic references Forte discovers would not find a "congenial setting" in a tonal analysis (p. 176), but a number of them are unconvincing in themselves, apart from any structure, tonal or not. For example, to find 5–19 in bars 320–24 entails leaving out the big upbeat a–a¹ but including a♭¹; it then entails changing the "preference rules" and picking b$^{(1)}$, which corresponds gesturally to the omitted A♯, as well as b♭¹, which corresponds to the A♭.
27. Joseph N. Straus, "The Problem of Prolongation in Post-Tonal Music," *Journal of Music Theory* 31/1 (1987), pp. 1–21. Some of Fred Lerdahl's comments in regard to this article are similar to mine (see Appendix A), although his conclusions are quite different.
    Christopher Lewis, in "Tonal Focus in Atonal Music: Berg's Op. 5/3," *Music Theory Spectrum* 3 (1981), pp. 84–97, attempts to reassert the possibility of a kind of tonal prolongation in atonal works but proposes an unconvincing dual structure. I find Forte's conclusion regarding the variations of act III, scene 1 (in "Tonality, Symbol, and Structural Levels in Berg's *Wozzeck*," *The Musical Quarterly* 71/4 [1985], pp. 474–99), more congenial: "[The music is a] synthesis: ... the main structural pillars of the variations are tonal ... while the foreground and middleground are a composite of atonal and tonal elements, with precedence at the middleground level given to the tonal voice-leading structure" (p. 499).

music, we have two theories that stand in a metatheoretical relation to each other: that is, harmony and counterpoint. While we have in set theory a working theory of harmony for posttonal music, we hardly have the barest beginnings of a theory of counterpoint. Straus rightly describes prolongation as the sense of the continuation of a musical object, particularly when it is not literally present – in other words, prolongation is a cognitive act of the listener, not something that inheres in the fluctuations of atmospheric pressure we refer to as music. Therefore, I find it reasonable to start with the assumption that we process posttonal music in a manner at least akin to the way we process tonal music, which means including prolongation and the concomitant structural levels.

The putative prolongation in the final scene of *Wozzeck* cannot be said to rely on the presence of a tonal structure – this clearly is atonal music. Yet it relies on features that, though found in tonal music, can be said to be a priori to it. Neighbor-note motion, for instance, while clarified by a tonal context, does not really depend on tonality so much as on a more general gestalt phenomenon. Passing motion, in contrast, would seem to entail some sort of tonality (as would incomplete neighbors, for that matter). An uninflected exchange of voices could be said to be a priori to tonality (whereas chromatic inflection requires a tonal context). Another voice-leading effect usually associated with tonality that could well be a priori to it, at least in part, is the difference in interpretation we give to the following two cases: (1) alternation of a minor $^6_4$ with a major $^5_3$ caused by a half-step motion in the bass; and (2) alternation of a major $^5_3$ with a minor $^5_3$ caused by half-step motion in the top voice. Although when the triads are viewed as sets the two cases are identical, in fact we interpret them in opposite ways: Even out of context we tend to hear the $^5_3$s as more stable. It might be objected that the different interpretations are not a priori to tonality, and I must admit that our tonal upbringings have much to do with them. What is a priori to tonality is the fact that motion in the bass and motion in the top voice with the same "sets" causes different resultant harmonic intervals.[28] In sum, I think one can refer to prolongation in atonal music if one can show two things: first, that a large structure seems to be organized around a single musical object – be it a chord, an interval, or a single pitch; second, one must be able to show on the surface of the music how the listener could, in principle at least, cognitively organize the intervening music so as to be able to connect distant points.

As the graphs in Example 6 show, the final scene of *Wozzeck* involves the unfolding of a subset – G, A♭, C♯ – of W at the same pitch level as that chord first appears, the only level that preserves the pitches of both characteristic and unique intervals: the tritone G–C♯ and the semitone G–A♭ (see Example 7a below). More interesting, the unfolding takes the form of an exchange of voices.

28. Of course, set theory asserts the identity of these inversionally equivalent intervals with respect to atonal music. The history of music shows, however, that fourths were perfectly consonant until thirds started to be used as consonances as well, which seemed to "force" composers to treat fourths as dissonances. An ancestor of a set theorist in the fourteenth century might have asserted that there was no reason why we couldn't just assume that fourths were still as consonant as thirds, but surely it is the case that there are certain facts of how we perceive that art (and theory) cannot escape.

The label "PR" is used to avoid "I" – but it means the governing harmony, that which is *prolonged*, in a closely analogous way to what the tonic represents in tonality.[29] It is worth noting that the structural embellishing chords (EM) in the last scene belong to the same family as M. In other words, just as W served as the goal of motion away from D minor in the interlude governed by M, chords of the M family serve to embellish the prolongation of W in the last scene.

The listener can draw the connections implied (and can therefore be said to experience the prolongation) because on the surface the twelve tones are divided into pairs of pitches a half-step apart: F♯ and G, A♭ and A♮, B and C (though on a deeper level B is paired with C♯), C♯ and D, E♭ and E♮ (see the foreground graph in Example 6a). The voice leading consists largely of oscillations between the members of each pair, and in most of these pairs, one of the pitches wins out in the end; for instance, A♭ disappears in favor of A, C in favor of B, and so on. Because the oscillations occur at different moments, many different combinations result. It could be argued that the listener has no means to predict the eventual outcome of the sum of all the oscillations and so has no way cognitively to organize the prolongation, but providing a secure basis for prediction is precisely the role of context – played here by the exchange of voices.[30] The larger structure is also clarified on the surface by the hemiola that marks the two outer members of the voice exchange. (The brief appearance in bars 380–81 of a related chord as an embellishment *of* the central embellishing chord is also marked by hemiola.)

In set-theoretical terms, the cadential chord can be understood as W at T_6 with three added pcs. Of these three, F♯ is merely an embellishment of F♮, D♯ can be heard as embellishing the D♮ of the G–D pedal point, and B adds a note in common with the original transposition, that is, in addition to the pitches G and C♯. (These last two form the only tritone of the original chord; the only other transposition that preserves them is T_6.) Two tones that continue to be involved in embellishing motion and therefore maintain ambiguity till the end, D and F♯, are the tones whose motions in the bass, respectively to C♯ (bars 370–72) and G (bars 385–90), frame the final scene (refer again to Example 6a).

Even though the cadential chord is based on the tritone transposition of W, it is voiced with G in the bass, as W was (see Example 7b). The voice exchange in effect restores the position of the voices to that of the opening chords – E–D, G–C♯ – after their inversion in the interlude and at the beginning of the final scene – D–E, C♯–G (see Example 7c). The objection that W has D♯ rather than

29. My assumption is that the somewhat static bass in Berg's music is functional in the sense that it is intended to act as an anchor amid the extreme chromaticism. While not usually functional in the full tonal sense of defining *Stufen*, it still has a more than equal share in defining the harmony. Even though Berg "liberates" inner voices to greater significance at times, the total equality of voices usually assumed in set theory does not yet obtain in this music. For the same reason that Berg imposes inversional symmetries on his chromatic palette, he is loath – as a practical theater composer – to give up the cognitive assistance the bass gives the listener.

30. Besides, inability to predict the outcome of a prolongation is often the case with tonal music as well. It is usually masked by our mostly unconscious repertoire of reasonable expectations, based on our early exposure to other tonal music. "Dropping the needle" in the middle of this prolongation would indeed make it very hard for a listener to predict the outcome, but perhaps no more so than in the case of a tonal prolongation heard by a listener who is as lacking in early life experience of tonal music as most of us are of atonal music.

Example 6

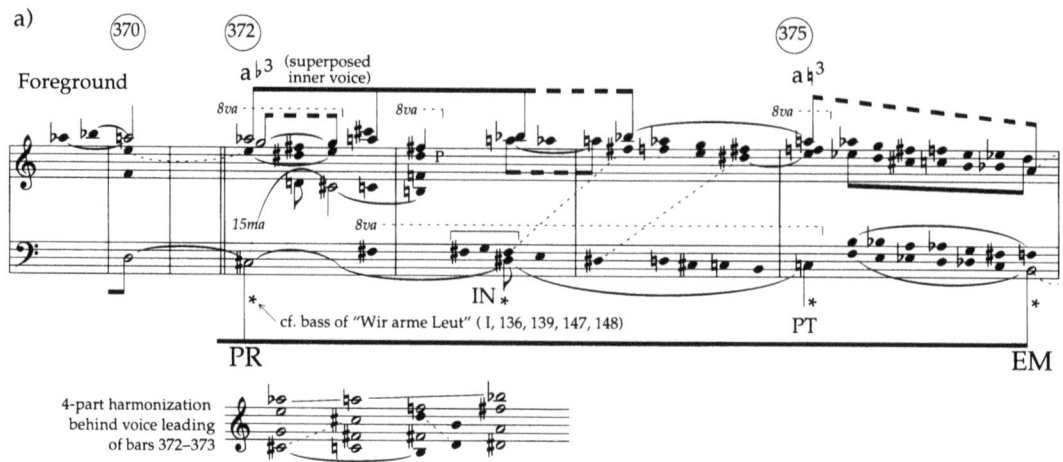

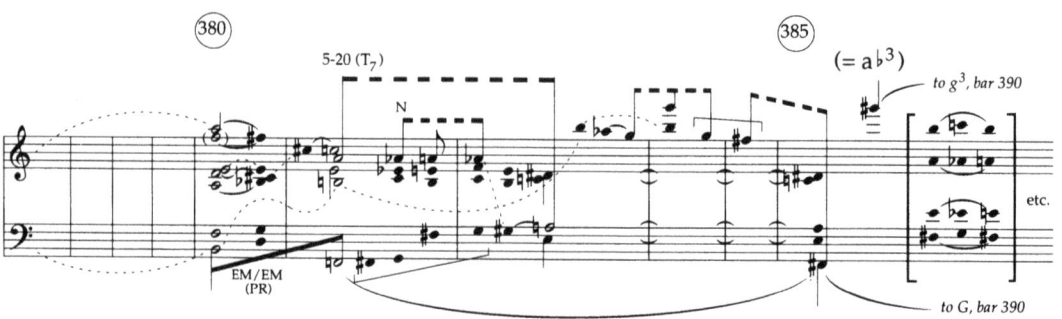

C♯ on top is worth addressing, if only to remind the reader that the tritone G–C♯ is of much greater significance in all that follows the first appearance of W than is the interval between the literal outer voices.

The embellishing harmony (EM) unfolded in bars 379–85 comprises a number of sets associated with Marie (see Example 7d). M itself, at T_7, is featured as the resolution of its own embellishing chord (6–Z28), whose pc makeup relates it more to the harmony prolonged by the voice exchange (PR) – note the common tones, indicated by asterisks, C♯, E, and G. The later appearance of the same set a whole-step higher, however, is the last stage of the unfolding of the embellishing harmony. In other words, two transpositions of the same set here have markedly different structural functions based on their transpositions (i.e., their pc content). The chords that constitute the unfolding harmony are arranged so that each succeeding chord contains four common pcs with the previous chord. Several of the pcs are retained throughout and several are dropped; the latter all come back in the final cadential chord (which is 7–33, not 8–24, as in Jarman and Schmalfeldt: I cannot hear the F♯ as integral to the last chord after its resolution to G in the bass and its reiterated resolution to F♮ in the closing oscillation).

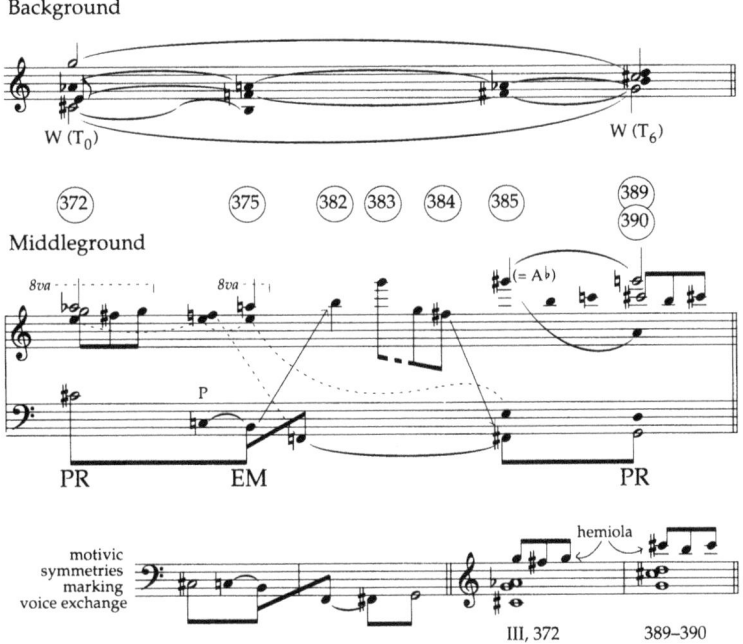

The transposition (T_7) of the central chord of the embellishing harmony, M, seems designed to maximize its similarity to W at T_6 (plus B♭) while avoiding C♯, one of the pcs involved in the voice exchange being embellished. (Obviously T_6 would maximize its dissimilarity.) The only transposition with more common pcs, T_9 [E1267], includes C♯; two other transpositions have the same number of common pcs: T_0 [2459T], which has already been featured in the orchestral interlude, and T_5 [79T23], which includes G, the other pc involved in the voice exchange. By maximizing the common pcs of M and related chords with W in the final scene, Berg emphasizes their closeness, where previously he has disguised it. What is more, he lays out the similarity by in effect turning M into W note by note.

Further evidence for a quasi-traditional role for the bass can be found in bars 381–86. The descending lines of these bars are composed so that almost any four consecutive tones include at least once the trichord, 3–4, associated with the M family. There are twenty-four unordered trichords 3–4. Of these, twenty occur in the descending lines; two others sound as a result of the descending line in combination with the sustained chord (4–18). Example 8b shows the descending line in "exploded" form to reveal the various transposed occurrences of 3–4. The two trichords 3–4 that do not occur at all are those that include both F and F♯, [56T] and [156]. Since the bass is governed by a motion from F to F♯ in the passage (refer back to Example 6a), this exclusion is understandable. Note also how the motivic parallelism F–E–D♯ and F♯–E–D♯ (bars 383 and 384) echoes the prevailing bass motion.

Example 7

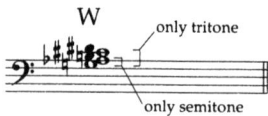

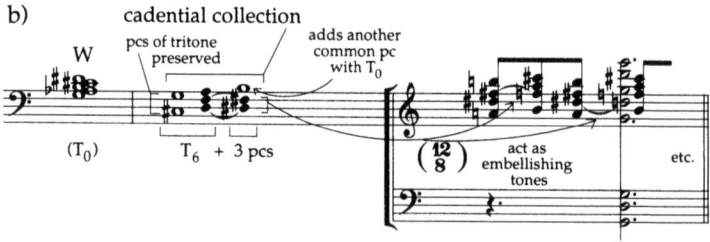

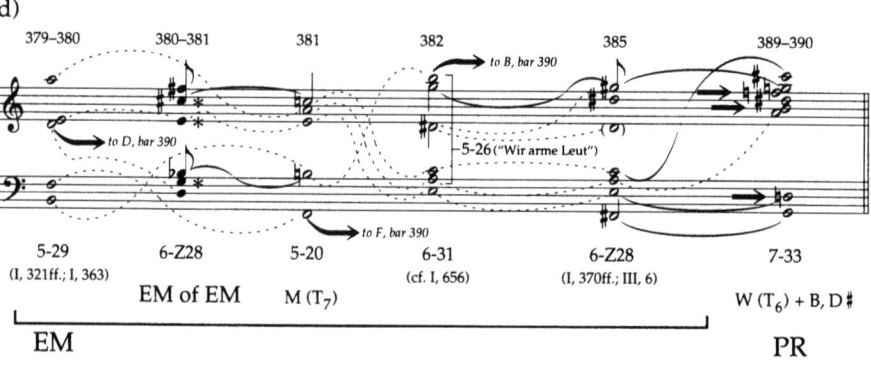

Another trichord, 3–3 (014, i.e., "Marie as mother"), associated with Marie in her relationship to Wozzeck – both Wozzeck's "Ach, Marie" (act I, scenes 1 and 4) and Marie's "Komm, mein Bub" (scene 3) – occurs repeatedly in the same passage. This trichord is not included in M, being a characteristic "whole-tone plus" subset of W and the smallest member of the W family (a Bergian joke perhaps). It is introduced in tandem with 3–4 in the first music Marie sings (the trio of the military march played by the offstage band in act I, scene 3; see Example 8a), which Schmalfeldt convincingly proposes as the source of "Marie's pitch-structural matrix."[31] The pit orchestra's first chord, however, is

---

31. See Schmalfeldt, *Berg's "Wozzeck,"* pp. 123ff.

Example 8

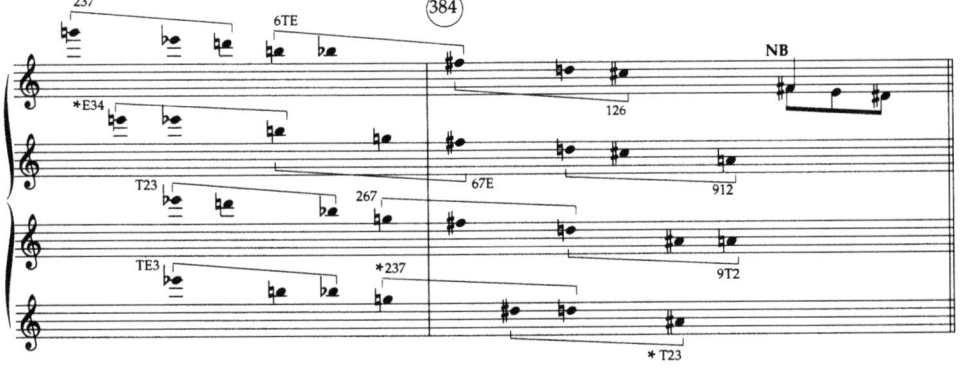

*set repeated

not M (5–20). Schmalfeldt relates the first simultaneity to M as a subset (4–16) – literally true – but she can only do so by ignoring the second note in the melody, f^2, which is clearly part of the same harmony, being approached by leap and occurring within the same metric subdivision as the first chord. Berg could have composed the passage using M, either by making the lowest note of the first chord D♭, or by changing the second melody note to E♭. The latter would have eliminated "Marie as mother" but would have referred to Marie's characteristic perfect fourths, including the child's last words in act III, scene 5, "Hopp, hopp" – at precisely the same pitch level, a♭²/g♯² – e♭²/d♯²! The chord we actually do hear when the orchestra enters at bar 363 of act I is 5–29, the chord of resolution at the end of the interlude preceding this scene, now at T_{10}. The reader will recall that at T_0, 5–29 shared four of five pcs with M at T_0 (refer back to Example 2e).

Hopp, hopp!

Joseph Kerman attempts to undermine the effect of the final orchestral interlude by revealing that it is a slow and rather Mahleresque waltz,[32] but this is really quite beside the point. The pathos bordering on bathos of the interlude is effective in the theater, especially after the distancing of the audience that Berg enforces by various means throughout the opera. If it is granted that M is being prolonged in this section, the verging on bathos seems apt in another way: this is how the sentimental and self-pitying Marie would have us see the story – as a romantic tragedy. (Note the distant echo of her line from act I, scene 3, bars 456–57, "Der Mann! So vergeistert!" at bars 343–44 of the interlude.)

Although Berg identified with his protagonist on some levels, the ironic (*echt* modernist) last scene shows that he ultimately does not see the story as a tragedy. The second chord of the opera had a similarly ironic effect – made more comic by extreme compression: the first chord, the yearning M, spanning an octave and a minor seventh and consisting of thirds, fourths, and fifths, was suddenly deflated into W, spanning an augmented fifth and consisting of seconds. Berg's music gives the last scene the inevitability lacking in the drama by making it the needed deflation of the overblown rhetoric of the interlude. Then at the end, the stage is left empty, a world suspended between the poles of Wozzeck's behavior, B and C♯. In this state of suspension one last symmetry unfolds.

Earlier interpretations of both the play and the opera tended to see the theme as the destruction of the individual by the social order (not an unlikely interpretation given Büchner's political radicalism and Berg's own statements about the work). Recently, Jarman has proposed that it is more the natural world with its mechanistic cycles and its indifference to human affairs that is Wozzeck's true nemesis – pointing out how the ubiquitous symmetries symbolize such a natural order (also convincing, given Berg's interest in the theories of Wilhelm Fliess).[33] In fact, I think it is precisely *between* these forces that we see Wozzeck trapped – one might say a Freudian rather than a Fliessian interpretation.

The obsessive guilt Wozzeck feels over the murder is symbolized by the *Hauptrhythmus* of act III, scene 3: Wozzeck cannot escape his consciousness of guilt – practically every note in the orchestra and every word he or anyone else utters is contained by the obsessive rhythm (every single instance is labeled in the score by Berg, as well). The rhythm is introduced subliminally by the staggered entrances of the instruments during that first crescendo on B at the end of scene 2. After scene 3 it is dissolved though still recognizable in the first

---

32. Kerman, *Opera as Drama*, pp. 188f.
33. See Jarman's Cambridge Opera Handbook on *Wozzeck*, pp. 67f.

Example 9

a)

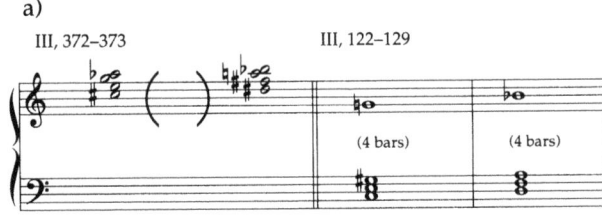

b)

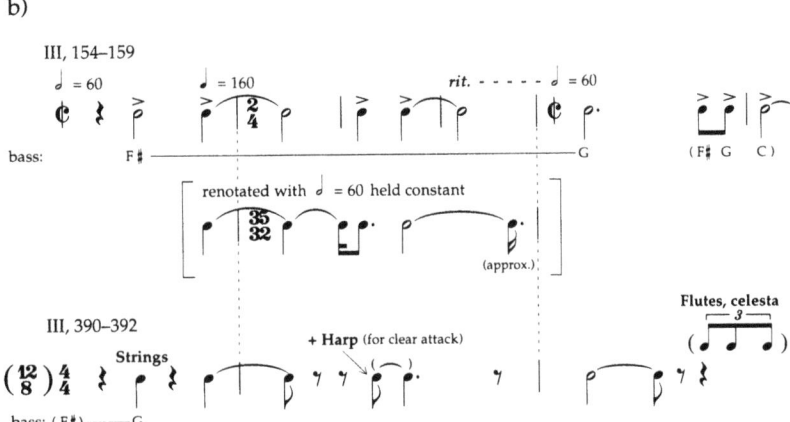

rhythm of scene 4.[34] The rhythm is marked by Berg only once more, during scene 4, at the moment when Wozzeck realizes that he must find the knife and dispose of it. The rhythm would then seem to die with Wozzeck, naturally enough.

Yet, isn't it recalled – as subliminally (and as unmarked by Berg) as it was introduced – by the octave Gs in the final measures of the piece? This recollection is prepared by the similarity of harmonies between the openings of scenes 3 and 5 (see Example 9a);[35] moreover, the first consciously audible pitched rendition of the rhythm was on G (in association with a prominent G♯/A♭), in the pianola solo at the beginning of scene 3.

The circle closes – like a trap. This very cinematic opera ends like one of those science-fiction movies in which the monster survives (and the final title asks

34. Perle shows how this variation on the rhythm is in fact derived from the last overlapping statements of the rhythm in the brief orchestral interlude between the scenes. See *The Operas of Alban Berg*, Vol. 1, p. 181, Example 186, in the section on rhythm and tempo added to the reprint of "Musical Language."
35. Although the rhythm is somewhat distorted in the final recollection, it has in fact appeared in a number of variants (see Perle, *The Operas of Alban Berg*, Vol. 1, pp. 174–81). The distortion of the rhythm as it surfaces at the very end was prepared at a point in scene 3 where F♯ moves to G in the bass (see Example 9b, and cf. Perle's Example 184) – just as it does before the putative recollection.

"The End?"). The murder will continue to follow the child – can we doubt that he will grow up to be another Wozzeck? Berg's obsessively exact prescription of the stage movement fits: the curtain is to begin to fall as the child rides off on his hobbyhorse; the stage should be empty on the beat that the oscillation of B and C♯ begins; the curtain must hit the stage at precisely the moment when the recollection of the *Hauptrhythmus* starts. The anguish that haunted Wozzeck from the beginning, which was only crystallized in the guilt over the murder, does not die with him but continues to hang over the world like a pall: Berg's empty stage seems to draw the audience in, and then the closing curtain keeps us from escaping the plight of the characters, as if to say that we are all suspended between the C♯ of society's constraints and the B of instinct.

APPENDIX A

An overview of the analytic literature on *Wozzeck*

Of all the treatments of the opera, the first extensive and analytically sophisticated study remains in many ways the best: George Perle, "The Musical Language of *Wozzeck*" (first cited in note 13 above). Douglas Jarman's treatment comprises several sections in his book *The Music of Alban Berg* (see note 8 above); both the book and the sections on the opera are models of their kinds. I discuss my areas of disagreement with Jarman in the main body of this essay. Though considerably longer, Janet Schmalfeldt's book (see note 6 above) represented something of a retrenchment – despite the author's evident musicality and sensitivity to all aspects of the work – because of its too rigorous reduction, also discussed above. More recently, Allen Forte has published studies on two sections of the opera, "Tonality, Symbol, and Structural Levels in Berg's *Wozzeck*" (cited in note 27 above), and "The Mask of Tonality: Alban Berg's Symphonic Epilogue to *Wozzeck*"; the second study's analysis of the orchestral interlude between scenes 4 and 5 of act III is briefly discussed in note 26 above. Most recent of all is another survey, *The Music of Alban Berg* by Dave Headlam (New Haven: Yale University Press, 1996), which discusses *Wozzeck* at some length, if not in the depth that Jarman does.

For reviews of Schmalfeldt, see Douglass Green and Stefan Kostka, untitled review, *Journal of Music Theory* 29/1 (1985), pp. 177–86, and Anthony Pople, untitled review, *Music Analysis* 5/2–3 (1986), pp. 265–70; for reviews of Forte, see Anthony Pople, "Secret Programs: Themes and Techniques in Recent Berg Scholarship," *Music Analysis* 12/3 (1993), pp. 381–99, and Dave Headlam, untitled review, *Music Theory Spectrum* 15/2 (1993), pp. 273–85.

Although some find Perle's approach too ad hoc, among his strengths as an analyst are a willingness to treat different elements separately – "tone centers," "vertical sets," "chord series," and so on – and an admittedly old-fashioned flexibility of terminology that responds to the music instead of trying to make it respond to fixed theoretical categories. For myself, I do not find pitch-class set theory sufficient as an analytical tool, as my being in the present company may have already led the reader to suspect. (Others, including Headlam, who are not primarily Schenkerians have also felt the lack of a distinction between the harmonic and the nonharmonic in set theory.) I think I ought to establish what status pitch-class set theory has in my own work, since I do make use of it, at least as a lingua franca. This is done to clarify for the reader my orientation, not to suggest any revision of the theory – a job already well undertaken by others, including Forte.

A thread running through the debates between Forte and others, notably Richard Taruskin and George Perle, has been what Forte rightly sees as a misapprehension of his purpose in creating the theory and a more general misunderstanding of the relationship between music theory and analysis. The strongest suit of pitch-class set theory is its abstraction. In his article, "Pitch-Class Set Analysis Today," based on his talk at the King's College London Music Analysis Conference, 1984), and published in *Music Analysis* 4/1–2 (1985), pp. 29–58, Forte put it bluntly: "Music theory is abstract; music analysis is concrete. The power of a theory resides in its ability to provide a general background against which an analytical statement may be measured." I believe I differ from Forte in thinking that theory and analysis can have no such settled relationship; that there is always the need in analysis for the ad hoc. In effect, I question whether theory really is a priori to analysis.

Be that as it may, pitch-class set theory can be seen as Forte's attempt to avoid the epistemological issues that, as an eminent Schenkerian, he well knew plagued the early reception of that theory in the United States. Yet criticisms have fallen back on a recurring question. Does set theory tell us anything about what we hear? I have left my work open to this sort of criticism because I believe an analysis must do so, but set theory is not open to it, and I hope to have avoided spotlighting some of the *analytical* problems that result from the theory's rigor as if to imply that they invalidate the theory. For it is beyond question that a theory does not stand or fall on a given analytical application made of it. Perle's work on *Wozzeck* was criticized by Kerman on just such grounds (see note 3 above), so it is ironic that Perle allowed himself to use perceptibility as a criticism of set theory in his 1989 SMT keynote address (see note 5 above).

There is, however, a related issue in the analytical application of pitch-class set theory to *Wozzeck* in particular that, as far as I know, has gone unraised. What is the status of the supposed *representation* of a character in a music drama by a given set, if the set cannot itself be perceived as such? This is not to question whether sets can act as leitmotives, which it will be evident I fully accept, but whether a particular instance of a given set can have any *dramatic* relevance if its identity cannot be heard but can only be seen by putting it inside a closed curve. Both Schmalfeldt's and Forte's analyses are full of such instances. It is understandable and appropriate that one wants to talk about dramatic issues in discussing an opera, and the equivalence of set and leitmotive works well in musical terms, but sets that are imperceptible have at least theoretical respectability, whereas imperceptible leitmotives are ludicrous.

In connection with prolongation in posttonal music see Straus (the citation is in note 27 above) and Fred Lerdahl, "Atonal Prolongational Structure," in Stephen McAdams and Irène Deliège, eds., "Music in the Cognitive Sciences: Proceedings from the Symposium on Music in the Cognitive Sciences, 14–18 March 1988 Paris," *Contemporary Music Review* 4 (1989), pp. 65–87. Straus is discussed briefly in the body of this essay. Lerdahl declares that any prolongational theory that applies to atonal music must "shed its Schenkerian origins" (p. 68). His reason for saying so is explicitly that he prefers his own generative theory of tonal music (GTTM) to Schenker's as a cognitive theory. It ought to go without saying that if Schenker's is a cognitive theory (as I believe it is) – and not merely a theory of tonal music – it is at best a cognitive theory *in ovo*. It does, however, give better analytical results than GTTM, in part because it calls for a *performative integration* of both top-down and bottom-up analysis. In contrast, GTTM is almost exclusively top-down and, as a result, relatively static, responding with less agility than an analytical method requires when dealing with art music. (Diana Raffman's *Language, Music, and Mind* [Cambridge, Mass.: MIT Press, 1993] adopts GTTM as a theory of modular first-order cognition, which shows how we parse music as a kind of "natural language" but tells us little about how we perform the higher-order cognition required by art music.)

Headlam, despite his welcome acknowledgment of the analytical limitations of set theory's exclusive concentration on harmonic structure, explicitly eschews prolongation (pp. 63–64) and as a result has to be content with offering an alternative harmonic explanation that relies on cyclic sets (though not entirely following Perle). He does thereby make a needed distinction between harmonic and nonharmonic tones but has to conclude his book with a frank admission that he cannot explain the latter (p. 388).

It ought to be borne in mind that in Berg's case at least, the "break" between late nineteenth-century tonal music and what is assumed to be "atonal" music is far from clear. Berg obviously was involved in rethinking the basic means at his disposal, and the resulting music is very innovative – but it is an extension of the tradition nonetheless and tonal in some way yet to be adequately defined. (Forte, in the earlier of his two studies cited above, makes this point.) J. Peter Burkholder's essay, "Berg and the Possibility of Popularity," in Gable and Morgan's book (cited in note 26 above), pp. 25–53, addresses the issue of Berg's links to the past, taking off on Mozart's trope about writing to please both the general public and the connoisseur, and finding a key element of Berg's solution to be his reliance on associations with older music. There is little to disagree with in the essay, but superficial resemblances to older music cannot be the extent of Berg's connection to tradition, for dozens of his contemporaries maintained such resemblances without either the popular success or the scholarly attention Berg has received. Burkholder's essay seems subject to a prevalent oversimplification that innovation has to be radical. Berg not only retained much that was traditional but also was innovative on *all* levels of structure. Therefore, we cannot build a theory of the music from scratch but, what is more demanding, must rethink the best existing theory in much the way Berg and others rethought tonality.

APPENDIX B

Constraints on Marie's chord (M)

If we assume that Berg started with the second chord (W) – since it is of a type so characteristic of the opera – and that he deliberately imposed the features mentioned above as constraints on the constitution of the first (M), we can narrow down his choice of M from hundreds of possibilities to a more manageable number. By adding a few other, less obvious constraints, the choice can finally be narrowed down to the one Berg in fact made, with the assertion that just those constraints were determinative. The supposed process is sketched in what follows.

Given the constitution of the second chord, there are fifty-one possible initial chords if we assume the constraints mentioned in the text, to wit: the chords have to be mutually exclusive with respect to pitch class, there are to be the maximum number of linear intervals in the motion between the two chords, and one of the linear intervals has to be the tritone F–B (see Perle, "Musical Language," pp. 210–18; *The Operas of Alban Berg*, Vol. 1, pp. 135–41); Perle always refers to this as B–F because of the characteristic vertical position of the pitches, even though the first chord, Marie's chord, contains Marie's note F and the second, Wozzeck's chord, Wozzeck's note B – see also note 17 above).

Since there are six linear intervals but these are five-tone chords, one linear interval has to be left out. Berg evidently wanted to include all the pitches of the "tonic" (odd) whole-tone collection, meaning that he had to have six odd and four even pitches in the ten-tone aggregate of the two chords. In other words, the total *number* of both the even and odd pitches is *even*. If we think of intervals as the results of subtraction, it is clear that even-even and odd-odd subtractions will have even results, and even-odd and odd-even subtractions odd ones. With an even number of both even and odd pitches, each even-odd or odd-even subtraction will necessitate another, so odd results will always come in pairs. Since there are three odd intervals, this means that one odd interval will have to be either duplicated or omitted. Omitting linear interval 5 – which is what Berg did – brings the number of possible initial chords down to thirteen.

If we extrapolate interval cycles from the outer voices of the thirteen two-chord progressions that omit linear interval 5, only four converge on G and C♯, the members of the cadential tritone, and of those four only one initial chord contains no F♯. As I have shown, the initial chord can be identified with D minor – a key that had special significance for Berg, according to Jarman (*The Music of Alban Berg*, p. 18, note 1), so the lack of F♯ – a pitch that would create modal ambiguity – is a good possibility as the deciding factor.

Even though interval cycles do not play a major role in the opera, several succeeding intervals of the putative cycle in the outer voices of the first two chords do mark points of stasis in the first six measures: B♭–E, bar 3, and D♭–F, unfolded in bars 4–6. The poles of the melody in bars 2–5 are C♯/D♭ and G, the tones on which the cycle converges to a unison.

Though the linear tritone between the first two chords is in the innermost voice, it is subtly exposed: it is played by the undivided second violins, while the two higher lines are played by the divided firsts; and the largest vertical interval of both chords lies below this innermost voice.

Sequential expansion and Handelian phrase rhythm

Channan Willner

Introduction: the basic pace

In the second part of the Allemande from his Suite in C, K.399, known as the "Suite in the Style of Handel" (an inauthentic but not inaccurate title), Mozart follows the practice of Baroque composers in elaborating on the sequential spinning he had begun in the first part (see Example 1).[1] The early sequence of bars 3 and 4 moves essentially in quarter notes, following what one might call the *basic pace* of the composition – marked by the even, largely stepwise motion of its outer voices in their normalized, unexpanded state.[2] Just after the central double bar, Mozart complements the first sequence with a slower moving one, advancing in half notes (bars 15 and 16). He then continues with a still slower sequence, one that progresses basically in whole notes, in bars 18, 19, and 20. (The music is quoted in Examples 1a and 1b; the gradual expansion in sequential duration is shown by means of asterisks and rhythmic notation above and below each system. These symbols mark the points at which the underlying motion takes place. The parentheses in each system enclose the ancillary chords that extend the time span of the more structural adjacent chords.)

If we examine the motion between the outer voices of the three sequences, we will readily observe that it is *stepwise* motion, highlighted by the aforementioned asterisks and rhythmic notation in Example 1, that articulates the changes in pace: the steps of the second sequence broaden those of the first, and the steps of the third broaden those of the second. In so doing each sequence

---

1. This study is based on material presented in my doctoral dissertation, "Durational Pacing in Handel's Instrumental Works: The Nature of Expansion in Music of the High Baroque" (The City University of New York, in preparation). I should like to thank Charles Burkhart, Floyd K. Grave, William Rothstein, and Frank Samarotto for their helpful and generous comments on several earlier versions.
2. The notion of basic pace should not be confused with the even, steady flow of the surface that marks much of the Baroque repertoire. It should be noted that in bar 1 of Example 1 (in keeping, perhaps, with Mozart's Classic transformation of Baroque style), the basic pace of quarter notes is defined by the left hand's arpeggiated comments (beats 2 and 4) on the melody's ascent from c^2 to $e\flat^2$ (beats 1 and 3). The textural and registral ramifications of the basic pace *vis-à-vis* its representation by polyphonic unfoldings and inner-voice motions are described in my dissertation.
    The tonal properties of the basic pace are, to be sure, backed up by the underlying voice leading at deeper levels. As Baroque phrase rhythm gradually gives way to pre-Classical periodicity, the underlying tonal support grows while the significance of the local tonal properties wanes. Though a detailed treatment of shifts in balance between and among layers of voice leading and duration is beyond the purview of this paper, I try to present a sense of it in my closing examples.

Sequential expansion and Handelian phrase rhythm

Example 1 Mozart, Suite in C, K.399, Allemande: compound 4/4 time

a) Bars 1–4

b) Bars 13–21

disrupts the flow of time established earlier in a way that a similar but isolated group of two chords could not.[3]

Let us now observe how similar durational enlargement, which exemplifies what Carl Schachter has called "tonal rhythm,"[4] guides the presentation of three sequences, whose essential stepwise movement ranges from eighth notes to half notes, in the Allemande from Handel's Suite in F minor, from the 1720 collection (see Example 2). In particular, the second and third sequences shown in Examples 2b and 2c slow the pace in much the same way as did Mozart's sequences; given the similarity in motivic design of the two pieces, one could even surmise that these sequences might have served as Mozart's point of departure.

Handel's three sequences provide us with a valuable glimpse at the thematic as well as the durational significance of Baroque sequences. The first sequence, in bars 3–4 (Example 2a), describes a rapid descent in eighth notes from a high A♭ in the upper voice; it is supported by a corresponding descent in parallel tenths from F in the bass, and by a series of 7–6 suspensions in the inner voice that mimic parallel fifths against the upper voice.

The second sequence, in bars 20–21, several measures after the double bar (Example 2b), repeats much the same progression but moves in quarter notes and begins on a high F, omitting the first two steps of the progression (they are briefly represented, however, in the upbeat to bar 20). The second and fifth of the repetition's steps, on bass tones C and G, are broken into two chord patterns each (the curly brackets under Example 2b): the second chord in each pattern, though an applied dominant to the chord that follows, remains ancillary to the first and resides, as it were, in the first chord's time span.

The third sequence, in bars 27–29 (Example 2c), acts as a closing motivic reminiscence and moves still more slowly, in half notes. Most important, it supplies the high A♭ and G missing from the second sequence. Like Mozart's, Handel's gradual twofold augmentation points to a fundamental task of Baroque sequences: a great many (but certainly not all) introduce some sort of durational expansion and show at least the potential for altering the composition's basic pace. In the broad compound 4/4 time typically outlined by allemandes the basic pace progresses in quarter notes; in the more robust simple 4/4 (which we shall encounter in Example 5) it moves in half notes; and in 3/4 time it advances in dotted half notes as well as in alternating half notes and quarter notes (rarely in quarter notes alone).

The overview offered in Example 3e shows the relation of the basic pace and its expansions to other levels of pace in a piece set in what some eighteenth-century musicians called "simple 4/4 time" (a relatively straightforward metrical type with a weaker accent on the third beat, as distinct from compound 4/4,

---

3. A single instance of a chord preceded or followed by an ancillary chord is usually not enough to occasion expansion. Two patterns – a minimum of two chordal pairs – are required for the time-span encompassed by the subservient chords to compete effectively with that of the principal chords within the framework of a hypermetrical structure. From an empirically analytical (and compositional) vantage point, the elimination of just one short time-span alone during durational reduction will cause havoc in the alignment of the durational levels.

4. Carl Schachter, "Rhythm and Linear Analysis: A Preliminary Study," in *The Music Forum*, Vol. 4 (New York: Columbia University Press, 1976), pp. 313–15.

Example 2 Handel, Suite in F minor (1720), Allemande: compound 4/4 time

a) Bars 1–4

b) Bars 20–21

c) Bars 27–29

Example 3

a) Sequential contraction and expansion in compound 4/4 time, summary*

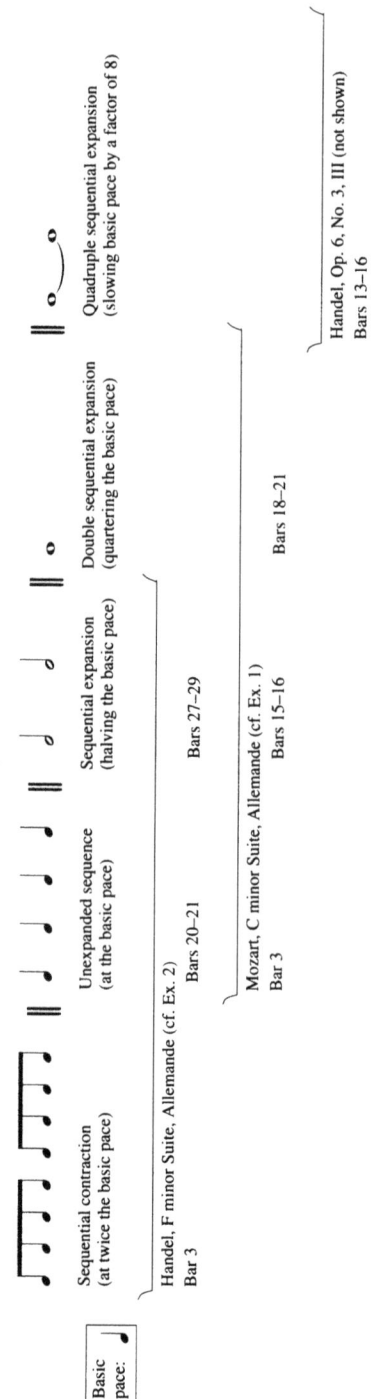

*Halved notes in simple 4/4 (cf. Ex. 5)

b) Basic pace profile in simple and compound 4/4 time, summary

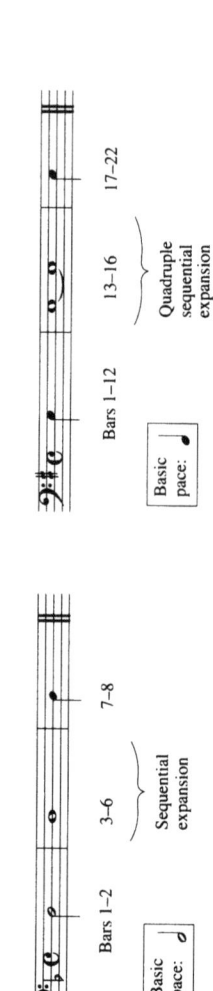

c) Sequential expansion in 3/4 time, summary

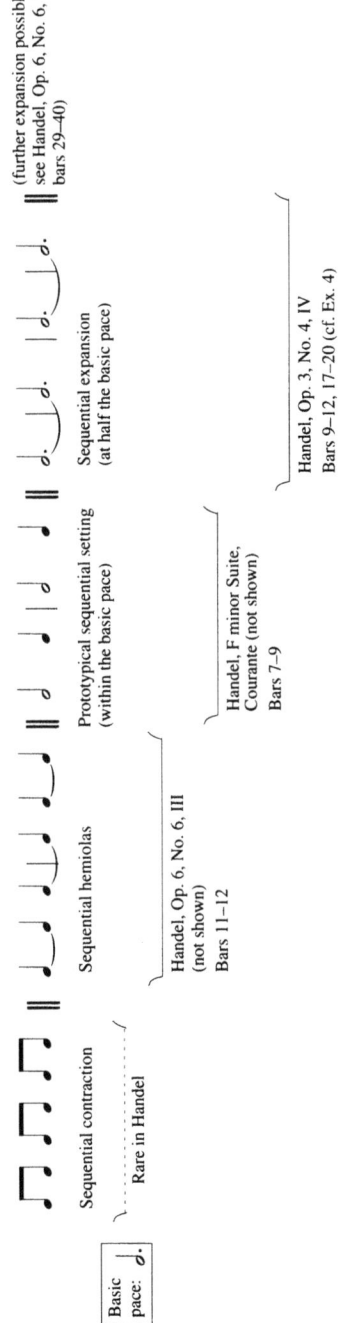

Basic pace:

Sequential contraction   Sequential hemiolas   Prototypical sequential setting (within the basic pace)   Sequential expansion (at half the basic pace)   (further expansion possible; see Handel, Op. 6, No. 6, V, bars 29–40)

Rare in Handel

Handel, Op. 6, No. 6, III (not shown)
Bars 11–12

Handel, F minor Suite, Courante (not shown)
Bars 7–9

Handel, Op. 3, No. 4, IV
Bars 9–12, 17–20 (cf. Ex. 4)

d) Basic pace profile in 3/4 time, summary

Handel, Op. 3, No. 2, II, ritornello (not shown)

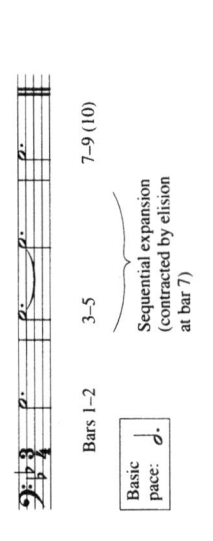

Bars 1–2   3–5   7–9 (10)

Basic pace:

Sequential expansion (contracted by elision at bar 7)

e) Tonal rhythm: Levels of pace and pace expansion in 4/4 time (simple 4/4; cf. Ex. 5)*

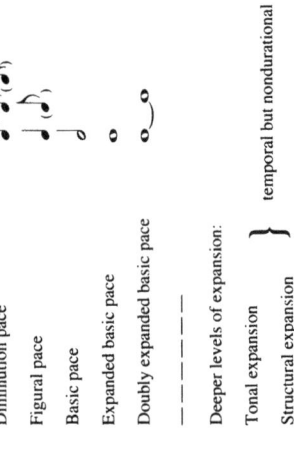

Diminution pace
Figural pace
Basic pace
Expanded basic pace
Doubly expanded basic pace
- - - - - - - -
Deeper levels of expansion:
Tonal expansion   } temporal but nondurational
Structural expansion

*Doubled notes in the compound 4/4 (cf. Exs. 1, 2)

in which each measure often comprises two shorter measures of 2/4).[5] The two lower levels of pace shown at the top of Example 3e comprise, respectively, the level at which linear progressions most often move at the surface (the *figural pace*) and the level at which their composing-out in turn governs the pace of diminutions at the very surface. Fluctuations of the basic pace that involve acceleration, fragmentation, or contraction engage these lower levels, sometimes with far-reaching consequences. The relation among all the levels shown in Example 3e and their relation to the underlying hypermeter will become clearer as we proceed. For now it will suffice to note that each level up to the double (and, in some cases, quadruple) expansion of the basic pace provides a durational and often stepwise framework for the level(s) below.[6] From this vantage point, pace at a given durational level may be defined as the rate at which the design at that level progresses; the hierarchic nature of the definition perforce prevents the lowest levels of diminution – usually sixteenth or thirty-second notes – from participating as full-fledged paces.

On account of the intensity with which sequences pervade the fabric of Baroque style, sequential expansion as such must be considered one of its fundamental procedures. Unlike discrete durational expansion, sequential expansion comprises a string of expansions that can stretch over a considerable span of time and therefore occupy substantial areas of the piece. In the course of this article, I shall focus on sequential expansion over increasingly long spans of time in relation to these resources but especially in relation to pacing. I shall attempt to define Handelian phrase rhythm on several levels *vis-à-vis* the resolution of seeming contradictions in the sequential realization of durational expansion.[7]

---

5. The substantial differences between simple and compound 4/4 time are described by Johann Philipp Kirnberger in *Die Kunst des reinen Satzes*, trans. by David Beach and Jürgen Thym as *The Art of Strict Musical Composition* (New Haven: Yale University Press, 1983), pp. 390–403. I have adopted the term "simple 4/4 time" from among several interchangeable terms Kirnberger employs in referring to this type, including "small 4/4," "simple common 4/4," and "common even meter."

6. Double sequential expansion is discussed, under the name "double augmentation," by Christopher Wintle in "'Skin and Bones': The C minor Prélude from J. S. Bach's Well-Tempered Clavier, Book 2," *Music Analysis* 5/1 (1986), pp. 85 and 91–92. We have encountered an example of it in Mozart's third sequence (Example 1b, bars 18–21). In such expansions, each step of the basic pace undergoes enlargement above and beyond the addition of the time span provided by the ancillary chord.

7. An early description of sequential expansion (in everything but name) appeared already in 1752, in Vol. 1 (*De Rhythmopoeia, oder Von der Tactordnung*) of Joseph Riepel's *Anfangsgründe zur musikalischen Setzkunst* (1752–68), pp. 53–54; though supporting harmonies are absent and Riepel couches his observations in terms of implicit temporary changes in meter from the notated 4/4 to *alla breve*, the idiom he presents is clearly that of sequential expansion. Riepel's example is quoted and the changes in tempo are discussed by Justin London in "Riepel and *Absatz*: Poetic and Prosaic Aspects of Phrase Structure in 18th-Century Theory," *The Journal of Musicology* 8/4 (1990), pp. 507–508; it is also cited by William Rothstein in *Phrase Rhythm in Tonal Music* (New York: Schirmer Books, 1989), p. 322, n. 93. See Rothstein's discussion of changes in pulse, pp. 177–80; for a more explicitly sequential example from Riepel see Elaine R. Sisman, *Haydn and the Classical Variation* (Cambridge, Mass.: Harvard University Press, 1993), p. 84, Example 4.1.

Within Schenkerian circles, the first explicit description of the principles of sequential expansion appears in William Rothstein's Ph.D. dissertation, "Rhythm and the Theory of Structural Levels" (Yale University, 1981); see Rothstein's interpretation of Schenker's reading in *Meisterwerk* II of the second theme from the first movement of Mozart's G minor Symphony, K.550 (Rothstein, pp. 195–96, and especially Figures 8.7 and 8.8). Clear intimations of such expansion appear also in Schenker's various publications. See, for instance, *Meisterwerk* II, pp. 16–17 (*Masterwork* II, pp. 4–5), Figure 7, bars 9–12 (cited by Rothstein, pp. 84–85, in a discussion of reducing out auxiliary dominants), and *Free Composition*, Figures 110/a4–5 (cited in Rothstein, p. 85, n. 10), with the attendant explanation in §245, pp. 88–89.

Though Schenkerian theory has traditionally been rooted in the concept of a fundamental structure and the generation of the foreground from the background through a series of structural transformations, it has recently encompassed a growing body of hierarchic theories concerned with levels closer to the surface as well. Within this framework, the notions of basic pace and levels of pacing – which offer a necessary first step in formulating a theory of phrase rhythm for Baroque music – in some ways reflect Schenker's own notion of melodic fluency (*fliessender Gesang*), the shapely progress of voices in strict counterpoint below the surface. They also echo William Rothstein's *imaginary continuo*, a texturally and registrally comprehensive summary of the composition's voice leading grounded in figured bass, and, above all, Frank Samarotto's idea of modulating from one *temporal plane* to another.[8]

While constraints of space preclude the presentation of a complete analysis that would demonstrate the larger, movement-long context in which sequential expansion occurs, mention should be made of the increasingly periodic framework within which both Handel's and Bach's phrase rhythm evolved, a framework that allowed periodic and aperiodic passages to appear side by side, sometimes within the same phrase. Later on, I shall take up the challenges that the basic pace began to encounter during the transition to Classical periodicity; here I should like briefly to enumerate the different types of periodic writing that Baroque phrases as such might incorporate.

Paraphrasing Carl Schachter's "tonal rhythm" and "durational rhythm," one might refer to tonal and durational periodicities. Tonal periodicities, which prevail in Baroque style (when periodicity is in evidence), establish an even division of time through the manifestly even movement of their outer-voice structures at several levels, primarily that of the basic pace (at the higher levels such periodicity might become durational; for a familiar example see the opening four bars of the Gavotte from Bach's G major French Suite).[9] Durational periodicities, which appear more rarely, fill in a metrically hierarchic grid (however small in scale) of the type that gradually became standardized during the pre-Classical era. A Baroque composition describes durational periodicity when the expansion and contraction of its basic pace is subservient to the repeated articulation of four-bar and eight-bar groups (a good example is the Corrente from Bach's G major Partita for Clavier).

As it happens, both tonal and durational periodicities may not only comprise a variety of sequential expansions but may also serve as a point of departure for further enlargement and repetition, thereby fostering larger hidden rhythmic repetitions that in turn realize what Carl Schachter has called "hidden periodicities."[10] Most important, many Baroque pieces (prompted by early changes in

---

8. Schenker, *Counterpoint* 1, pp. 94–95; Rothstein, "Rhythmic Displacement and Rhythmic Normalization," in *Trends in Schenkerian Research*, ed. Allen Cadwallader (New York: Schirmer Books, 1990), pp. 87–113 (see especially pp. 101–109); Samarotto, "Temporal Plasticity in Beethoven's Late Music" (Ph.D. diss., The City University of New York, in preparation). I am grateful to Frank Samarotto for sharing his ideas with me.
9. For a particularly lucid account of evenly articulated tonal rhythm in Bach see Rothstein, *Phrase Rhythm*, pp. 136–37. I discuss the different types of Baroque periodicities in "Bach's Periodicities Re-Examined," *Irish Musical Studies 4: The Maynooth International Musicological Conference, 1995, part 1*, ed. Patrick Devine and Harry White (Dublin: Four Courts Press, 1996), pp. 86–102.
10. Carl Schachter, "Rhythm and Linear Analysis: Aspects of Meter," in *The Music Forum*, Vol. 6, Part 1 (New York: Columbia University Press, 1987), pp. 17–22.

pace and early premonitions of larger grouping) tend to increase the size of their durational components – their segments, subphrases, and phrases – as they proceed, by means of changes in grouping and through expansions, not infrequently in ways that were soon to be codified by Joseph Riepel; in so doing they often double or even triple the length of these groups (compare, for instance, the two four-bar subphrases that open the Gavotte from Bach's G minor English Suite with the two eight-bar subphrases that close it). Large-scale, deeply embedded periodicities may thus emerge over the span of an entire piece without our being immediately aware of their existence. It is within this milieu of continual – and highly improvisatory – durational enlargement and nascent as well as hidden periodicity that sequential expansion most often takes place, and it is this expansional environment that provides the backdrop for (and, indeed, sometimes embodies the essence of) phrase rhythm during the high Baroque.[11] I shall return to these issues in the closing sections of this paper, but will ask the reader to keep them in mind throughout.

A principal instrument in establishing this environment is the underlying rhythmic continuum provided by the basic pace, which is largely responsible for the characteristic motoric thrust of the repertoire. The repeated disturbance and suspension of the basic pace through expansion and the frequent thematic, registral, and textural emphasis on weak beats in Baroque style in turn play an essential role in balancing the very same continuum.[12]

Sequential expansion and Baroque style

While sequences in later repertoires are by nature highly expansional, as several writers have noted, they are more stylized than their Baroque ancestors: the figurations they support tend to be lighter and more neutral than those of their surroundings, in emphasis of their transitional and prolongational character. The expansions they foster, though often durational, strike us primarily as tonal in nature.

Baroque sequences, by contrast, reflect much the same compositional density as their surroundings. Though they frequently play developmental, transitional, and episodic roles in concertos, fugues, and arias, they do not necessarily signal a different or less concentrated way of writing at the surface. The durational enlargements they embody attach a rarefied quality to a common compositional resource because they are apt to be more concealed than in later styles.

The sequential expansions we already observed in Examples 1 and 2 are at once tonal and durational – the subservient chord in each two-chord pattern expands the principal chord by extending either the beginning or the end of its duration, or time span. When the ancillary chord appears first, it often acquires

---

11. In emphasizing the durational nature of enlargement the present essay's focus differs from that of Brian Alegant and Don McLean's paper, "On the Nature of Enlargement," presented at the annual meeting of the Society for Music Theory in New York, 1995.
12. I discuss these issues in "Stress and Counterstress: Accentual Conflict and Reconciliation in J. S. Bach's Instrumental Works," *Music Theory Spectrum* 20/2 (1998), pp. 280–304.

the quality of a suspension or appoggiatura.[13] Shorter ancillary chords, such as those in Mozart's first sequence and Handel's second sequence, do not alter the basic pace of the piece; they merely reside in the time span of the principal chords and occasion no durational expansion. In such cases the principal and ancillary chords together occupy one beat (or, as in Handel's first sequence, which is in fact contracted, half a beat) of the basic pace. Only ancillary chords that occupy a full beat of the basic pace – and thereby double the span of the chord they prolong – occasion a durational expansion.[14] From the perspective of the compositional process, it is sequential expansion that causes the basic pace to fluctuate; from the analytical point of view, conversely, it is the fluctuation in the progress of the basic pace and its supporting harmonic rhythm within the context of the entire movement that allows one to determine if expansion – signalled by small parentheses in the reductions by two and large parentheses in those by four – has in fact occurred.[15]

One should keep in mind that expansion in later periods often sublimates chords that are implicitly extended over long spans of time. No matter how far flung, the expansion does not completely obscure the underlying triadic presence of the home sonority. When expansion in Baroque style occurs, it remains primarily contrapuntal: the expanded sonority recedes into the background while largely stepwise progressions, acting on its behalf and under its domain, occupy and work out its time span. The effect or suggestion of tonal stasis, quite characteristic of Classic and Romantic expansions, may not necessarily materialize, at least not to the same degree. Furthermore, the steady movement of the surface tends to inhibit the explicit temporal articulation of the tonal ebb and flow. In precadential progressions, for example, the subdominant is quite often repeatedly expanded, first by I^6 from below, then by motion to the inner voice VI above the bass (see the Allemande from Handel's C minor Concerto Grosso, Op. 6, No. 8, bars 12–13, for a typical example, in the temporary key of E♭). Save for its frequent metrical accentuation, the subdominant in these progressions shares wholly pluralistic emphasis with both I^6 and VI; that the same progres-

13. Detailed discussions of the appoggiatura's incursion into the time span of the tone it delays vis-à-vis the normalization of displacement occasioned by suspensions appear in Rothstein, "Rhythm and the Theory of Structural Levels," Chapters 2 and 5 (especially pp. 84–86), and "Rhythmic Displacement," pp. 87–91 (especially Example 6.2). Particularly valuable is Rothstein's extensive treatment of normalizing the time span of the principal tone; it is the account of normalization in his dissertation that served as my point of departure in preparing the present study. As Rothstein observes, dealing with time spans of embellishing chords that appear *after* the principal chord is, by contrast with appoggiatura chords, a relatively straightforward matter: "With unaccented linear chords, normalization occurs automatically when we 'reduce out' those chords" ("Rhythmic Displacement," p. 91).
14. Once the principal chord and the ancillary chord have combined to extend the span of each step of the basic pace, there emerges some leeway in the articulation of their time span. Very often, the ancillary chord in its appoggiatura-like setting is extended by half a beat while the principal chord is reduced by half a beat, resulting in the seemingly topsy-turvy situation whereby the ancillary chord, like an extended appoggiatura, might occupy the span of a dotted quarter note, dotted half note, or even one and a half measures, while the principal chord lasts only an eighth note, quarter note, or half note; see, for instance, the third movement, Allegro, from Handel's E minor Concerto Grosso, Op. 6, No. 3, bars 13–16.
15. Gauging the various levels of harmonic rhythm is a good way to find out whether expansion has taken place, though the interplay between the genuine bass line and the inner voices immediately above often complicates matters considerably.

Example 4 Handel, Concerto Grosso in F major, Op. 3, No. 4, Allegro (fourth movement)

a) Score

sion sometimes supports the expansion of I⁶ rather than IV is emblematic of both the malleable and the fragile qualities of Baroque expansions. The excerpts I present will illustrate how even under such chordally ecumenical circumstances durational expansion may nonetheless take place. The closing Allegro from Handel's F major Concerto Grosso, Op. 3, No. 4, offers an apt illustration in triple meter (Example 4).

During the opening ascent of the tune in bars 1–3, from f^2 through g^2 to a^2, one tone governs each measure and establishes a basic pace of dotted half notes. This ascent clearly undergoes expansion right after the central double bar, where both f^2 and g^2 govern two measures each and in so doing expand the

Sequential expansion and Handelian phrase rhythm

b) Durational reduction

basic pace (see the asterisks and rhythmic notation above and below each staff in Example 4a and the square brackets in Example 4b). Appearances to the contrary, it is the first, accented chord of each two-chord pattern in bars 9–12 – and in the corresponding, descending sequence of bars 17–20 – that is ancillary to the second: the chord acts as an enlarged and harmonized consonant appoggiatura (the apparent tonic in bar 9, especially, must not be regarded as a return to the tonic of the piece).

In facilitating motivic enlargement and penetrating the deeper levels of tonal and durational structure, sequential expansion provides an essential link

Example 5 Handel, Concerto Grosso in F major, Op. 6, No. 2, Allegro (second movement), ritornello: simple 4/4 time

a) Bars 1–9

between the diminutions at the surface and the extensive, purely tonal augmentation they often undergo in the course of the piece at deeper levels of structure. I shall explore this important role in a later study; for now, the summary outline in Example 3e will tacitly suggest how sequential expansion offers such a link *vis-à-vis* the expansion of the basic pace.[16]

16. The role sequential expansion plays in fostering long-span motivic enlargements hinges on the changing relation between the composition's outer voices and on shifts in the priority of one voice over another (at the surface as well as below), and also on the composition's articulation of the long-range harmonic structure. It is the complexity of the ties between these seemingly disparate and sometimes intractable elements of the design that requires postponement of their consideration.

b) Durational reduction

Vordersatz

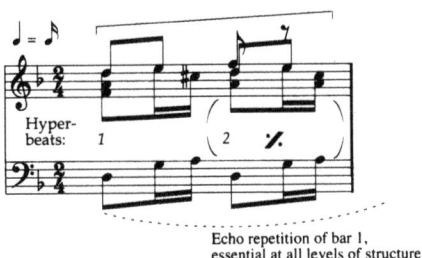

Echo repetition of bar 1,
essential at all levels of structure

Fortspinnung

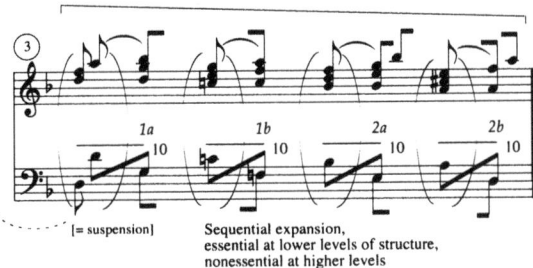

[= suspension]   Sequential expansion,
essential at lower levels of structure,
nonessential at higher levels

Epilog

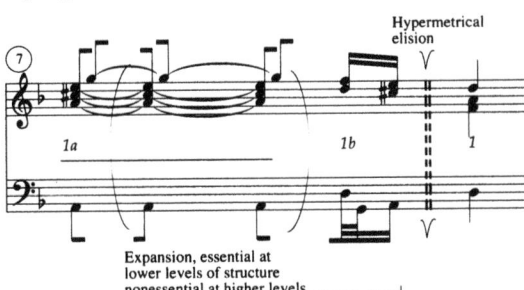

Expansion, essential at
lower levels of structure
nonessential at higher levels

Essential and nonessential expansion

The sequential expansions in the F major Allegro are not difficult to detect because their prototype – the initial ascent from f^2 to g^2 and a^2 – has just been presented. Very often, though, the prototype is either less apparent or altogether absent from the surface of the music, and the expansion must then be inferred from changes in the basic pace. Such inference is found in our next example, the opening ritornello of the second-movement Allegro, in D minor, from Handel's F major Concerto Grosso, Op. 6, No. 2 (Example 5).

In this ritornello, which unfolds in simple 4/4 time, the opening melodic ascent from d^2 to e^2 and f^2 in bars 1–2 and its echo in bars 2–3 introduce a basic

Example 5 (*cont.*)

c) Combined-species counterpoint reduction

Vordersatz

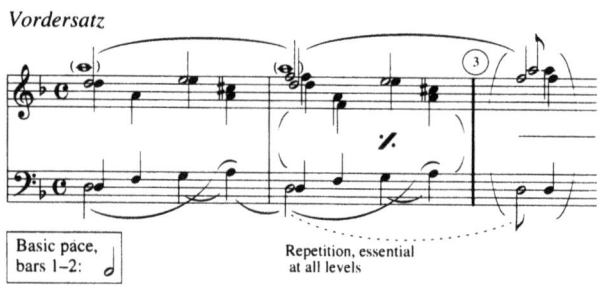

Fortspinnung (at the deeper level)

Fortspinnung

Epilog

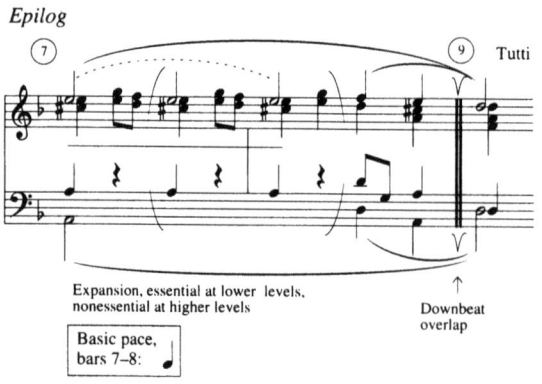

pace of half notes (eighth notes in the fourfold reduction of Example 5b);[17] statement and echo constitute the *Vordersatz* of the three-part ritornello.[18] During the *Fortspinnung* that ensues, in bars 3–6, a more deliberate descent, essentially in whole notes (quarter notes comprising tied eighths in the reductions) follows; each tone of the descent is displaced from the downbeat to the middle of the bar by its lower neighbor and by the neighbor note's supporting applied dominant or upper fifth, which occupy half of its time span – see the asterisks and rhythmic notation above and below the system in Example 5a, as well as the square brackets over the reduction in Example 5b. From the high B♭ in the middle of bar 3 to the F in the middle of bar 6, the upper voice descends in parallel tenths with the bass at an expanded pace that is particularly characteristic of the developmental middle section of tripartite ritornelli and ritornello-like structures.[19] In decidedly Handelian fashion, this expansion leads to still further enlargement, through expansion at a deeper level, in the *Epilog*, bars 7–8; at the surface, however, the basic pace, as such, accelerates its movement to quarter notes.[20] (In subsequent sections of the Allegro it is in fact the *Epilog* that undergoes the most interesting expansions, in the manner of a developing variation. Indeed throughout many concerto movements, such as

17. In establishing the basic pace of bars 1 and 2, I allowed for the occupation of the entire second half of each measure by one half note on account of the overlap between the melodic ascent d^2–e^2–f^2 and its echo, which helps sustain the motion in half notes. The II^6 on the third beat of each bar is absorbed by the dominant on the fourth beat, whose time span is moved back to the third beat at the higher levels.

18. I find it is most efficient to retain the original German terms introduced by Wilhelm Fischer in his path-breaking study of the Baroque ritornello's internal scheme, which occupies a short but highly influential segment of his article "Zur Entwicklungsgeschichte des Wiener klassischen Stils," *Studien zur Musikwissenschaft* 3 (1915), pp. 22–33. According to Fischer, ritornello form divides essentially into three parts: an introductory *Vordersatz* that lays out the thematic material, a developmental *Fortspinnung* that spins it out sequentially, and a closing *Epilog*, which provides tonal closure. The existence of many variants of this three-part kernel has been amply documented in the literature.

19. Despite their outward similarity to the ritornello scheme, the eight-bar Schoenbergian sentence structure and its longer offshoots show profound durational differences, especially in the fragmentation realized by the sequences that appear in their developmental measures (usually bars 5–6 or corresponding measures in more extended formations). Intensification that comprises fragmentation or contraction is usually foreign to the orchestral Baroque ritornello but appears with some frequency when the ritornello scheme is freely adapted to instrumental style (see the contraction in bar 3 of Handel's F minor Allemande, Example 2a). A valuable comparison of the sentence and the ritornello on the basis of the presentation, continuation, and cadential functions of their three parts is found in William E. Caplin, "Funktionale Komponenten im achttaktigen Satz," *Musiktheorie* 1/3 (1986), pp. 256–58, with further references.

20. Here a taste of hierarchically periodic writing appears: the basic pace accelerates to quarter notes (with a concomitant, quite Handelian, change from simple to compound 4/4, as Floyd K. Grave has suggested in a private communication) while a competing pace introduces further expansion to movement in two whole notes, realized in bars 7 and 8 by the dominant. See, in this connection, the account of surface acceleration coinciding with harmonic deceleration in Rothstein, *Phrase Rhythm*, pp. 83–87, and the discussion of different levels of surface activity in Joel Lester, *The Rhythms of Tonal Music* (Carbondale: Southern Illinois University Press, 1986), pp. 219–20. When a substantial increase in surface activity takes place, as it does in bars 7 and 8 (note the consistent doubling between the *concertino* violins and the intensification of their figural diminutions) the ear will recognize the effect of contraction at one level yet will tend to organize the greater activity in longer blocks of duration at a deeper level, thereby setting a natural stage on which hierarchically periodic writing might step in and introduce itself.

Though often hidden, similar coexistence of periodic and aperiodic writing involving simultaneous contraction and expansion (which may extend to duration and grouping paces) pervades much of Handel's music from the later 1730s and 1740s; I shall take it up later on.

the closing Allegro from the A minor Concerto Grosso, Op. 6, No. 4, *Fortspinnung* and *Epilog* join together and offer a major source for further developmental expansion, which often takes place in clusters of sequences and might be named "progressive expansion.")

A glance at the notes written into Examples 4b and 5b will disclose that, borrowing an adjective from Kirnberger's treatment of suspensions, I distinguish between *essential* and *nonessential* expansion (and, along the same lines, between essential and nonessential repetition, extension, and the like).[21] To say that sequential expansion is essential at a given level of structure (usually, but not exclusively, at levels close to the surface in the twofold reductions) is to regard the entire contents of the sequence, both its principal and ancillary chords, as full-fledged members of the phrase or subphrase in question. Thus, at the surface, the durational span of Handel's ritornello is eight bars, extending by means of overlap to the downbeat of bar 9; both the sequential expansion of bars 3–6 and the extension of bars 7–8 are reckoned fully in our count.

To say, on the other hand, that the expansion is nonessential (usually, but not necessarily, at the higher levels of the fourfold reductions) is to leave out the ancillary chords altogether – this above and beyond reducing the note values of the material that remains. The advantage of such thoroughgoing omission and the attendant reduction in duration resides in its clarification of the composition's highly individualized, underlying phrase rhythm. Within the confines of the phrase, Handelian phrase rhythm shapes and articulates the composition's slow-moving, overarching hypermetrical structure. Through the thematically engendered realization of expansions and repetitions, and particularly through sequential expansion, it transforms the relatively abstract durational contours defined by the underlying movement of two-bar hypermeasures into discrete and shapely durational segments at the surface. The basic pace and its fluctuations articulate this transformation.[22]

The distinction between essential and nonessential expansion – a theoretical tenet applicable also to later tonal styles – derives from the length that phrases, subphrases, and smaller segments assume at the surface. Fully periodic writing (in later styles) and incipiently periodic writing as well as contextual, piece-specific segmentation of time (in Baroque style) will often dictate the length of a phrase (say, eight, ten, twelve bars or more, including "irregular" lengths), a subphrase (two, four bars or more, including incomplete bars) or a segment (a half bar, one bar, one and a half bars or more). Essential expansion provides the material that extends the length of the unexpanded structure to the length required by the periodic or contextually segmented framework.[23] The issue is

---

21. Kirnberger, *The Art of Strict Musical Composition*, pp. 44–45 and 79–98. In his Ph.D. dissertation, "Rhythm, Meter, and Phrase: Temporal Structures in Johann Sebastian Bach's Concertos" (University of Michigan, 1993), Mauro Botelho also employs a distinction between essential and nonessential expansion, within the somewhat larger framework of the basic phrase.
22. This is a more localized and "internal" view of phrase rhythm than what one usually associates with the term. See Rothstein, *Phrase Rhythm*, p. 12, for an overview of the more common, long-range usage of "phrase rhythm." I shall discuss the more extended rhythmic relations among Handel's phrases – their large-scale phrase rhythm – later.
23. In so doing, it summons up the manifestation of both explicit and hidden periodicities; see note 9 above. In considering units smaller than the phrase (and sometimes the phrase as well) it is a bit misleading to speak of length or even of duration. It will become evident later why grouping pace is preferable. The changes in duration around which Baroque phrase rhythm revolves are essentially rhythmic in nature.

explained quite thoroughly (if without recourse to new terminology) in Carl Schachter's analysis of the two short phrases that make up the Minuet from Domenico Scarlatti's Sonata in F, K.78: each phrase's basic length of six bars is enlarged by what I would call "essential expansion" in order to realize eight bars at the foreground.[24] (A similarly essential expansion is accomplished by the sequential expansions in Example 4, above.) It is also illustrated succinctly in William Rothstein's observations on Kirnberger's transformation of a three-bar group into a four-bar group, by what I would regard as the "essential repetition" of the third measure.[25]

In Handel's D minor ritornello, the sequential expansion of bars 3–6 is essential at levels close to the foreground inasmuch as it extends the basic length of these measures from two to four bars; the expansion in bars 7–8 is equally essential in that it transforms one bar into two. The cumulative purpose of both expansions is the procurement of an introductory eight-bar phrase (extending, as I have observed, to the downbeat of bar 9) that is to become the object of considerable repetition and further expansion in the course of the movement. (The sequential expansions in Example 4, similarly, help procure the eight bars required by the second and third phrases.)

In sharp contrast and seeming contradiction to the expansion in pace and duration, there is also a sense that a contraction takes place in bars 3–6. The two-bar articulation of bars 1–2 is replaced, at the very surface, by one-bar articulation (marked by the rising-step figures, $a^2-b\flat^2$, g^2-a^2, and f^2-g^2). The change involves an altogether different type of pace but one that is intimately related to the basic pace, namely a tonally articulated but largely durational *grouping pace*. As we shall later see, an ad hoc hierarchy of grouping paces (to which the four-bar group, bars 3–6, also belongs, but at a higher level) helps organize the movement of the basic pace into larger durational units, yet can at the same time contradict it; the emergence of long-span periodicity is facilitated by the growing regularity of the grouping hierarchy and the diminishing prominence of the basic pace.[26]

Expansion and species counterpoint

If we now compare the *Vordersatz* of Handel's Allegro with its *Fortspinnung*, we shall find that, despite the expansion of the basic pace in bars 3 to 6, the surface design of bars 1 and 2 as such – namely the figurations in eighths and sixteenths and the supporting movement in quarter notes in the outer voices (represented by the first two levels of duration in Example 3e) – prevails as if expansion has not really taken place. This seeming contradiction informs many Baroque expansions, perhaps most; to explain how it is to be resolved, we must consider the dependence of Baroque expansions on the supporting role, durational as well as tonal, that contrapuntal progressions deriving from the *stile antico* (or

---

24. Schachter, "Rhythm and Linear Analysis: Aspects of Meter," pp. 45–49.
25. Rothstein, *Phrase Rhythm*, p. 66, Example 3.2; Kirnberger, *The Art of Strict Musical Composition*, p. 410, Example 4.34. For a particularly vivid example, compare the brief orchestral introduction to the "Hallelujah" Chorus from *Messiah* with the entrance of the chorus.
26. The fundamental study of grouping and grouping structure remains Fred Lerdahl and Ray Jackendoff, *A Generative Theory of Tonal Music* (Cambridge, Mass.: MIT Press, 1983), Chapter 3.

prima prattica) and resembling those of combined-species counterpoint play just under their surface.

Many theorists have noted the simultaneous operation of various durational strata in tonal music. The durations and rhythms of these strata – expressed through the pace of each stratum – animate their tonal counterparts: like the tonal strata, they are realized either explicitly or implicitly. The eighths and sixteenths in bars 1 and 2, for instance, are apparent at the surface; the half notes of the underlying ascent from d^2 to e^2 and f^2 in bars 1 and 2 are apparent just below; but the whole notes that articulate the implicit, repeated a^2 shown hovering over bars 1 and 2 in the contrapuntal reduction of Example 5c are decidedly latent. (They are represented at the lower octave by repeated figural sixteenths.) What I believe has not been previously expressed is that the pace of each of the underlying, partially implicit durational strata also describes a partially implicit, largely stepwise tonal motion (modified of course by at least some arpeggiation, repetition, and suspension), and that all the strata – tonal and durational, from the diminutions at the foreground to the slow, sustained tones of the middleground – work smoothly together because (at least in Baroque style) their paces realize a series of stepwise progressions essentially identical to the movement of voices in combined-species counterpoint. The all-important proliferation of implicit tones and durations is made possible by the harmonic framework of the music.[27] The durational properties of the strata reside in the opportunities their constellation presents for seamless shifts in emphasis – often collapsed into one unbroken melodic line – from one group of constellations of explicit and previously implicit tonal and durational strands to another, this without necessarily altering the fabric of the contrapuntal design at the surface in any appreciable way.[28]

As Example 5c demonstrates, the stratum of implicit whole notes occupied by the high a^2 of bars 1 and 2 in Handel's ritornello is activated in bars 3 to 6 by the now familiar whole-note descent from $b\flat^2$ to f^2 and by its supporting motion in parallel tenths in the bass and the supporting parallel motion in the other instrumental strands. The shift in stratum, which allows the overlapping ascents in half notes from d^2 to e^2 and f^2 in bars 1–2 and 2–3 to be directly continued by the fall in whole notes from $b\flat^2$ to f^2 in the same melodic line, also allows the expansion to occur without interfering with the continuation of the more active strata of bars 1 and 2, whose cascading quarter notes and half notes, as well as figural eighths and sixteenths, are superimposed now over the more deliberate motion in whole notes. Furthermore, it allows the basic pace to combine sets of pitches (the two dovetailing ascents d^2–e^2–f^2, then $b\flat^2$–a^2–g^2–f^2) and sets of durations (half notes, then whole notes) in one

---

27. The most comprehensive study of implicit tones and the circumstances under which they can play a tangible compositional role is William Rothstein, "On Implied Tones," *Music Analysis* 10/3 (1991), pp. 289–328.
28. Much the same explanation holds for changes in grouping pace (discussed below) when these assume significance in Baroque style. As we shall see, the stepwise support that linear progressions afford the basic pace in later styles remains undiminished at the level of the phrase and subphrase (and especially the period), but it is supplanted by larger harmonic motions that support broader, more periodically conceived grouping paces, and a more pluralistic textural distribution of figural elements.

continuous tonal and durational gesture. If uncovering the basic pace represents a necessary first step in constructing a theory of phrase rhythm for Baroque music, retracing the shifts among its supporting contrapuntal and durational strata is a close second.

The basic pace and longer durations

Looking now at the changes the basic pace undergoes within the span of a phrase, such as our Concerto Grosso ritornello, we see that in expanding and then contracting at the turn of the *Fortspinnung* and the *Epilog* the articulation of the pace acquires a distinct profile, that of a closed durational design; a summary of such profiles, along with a summary of their articulating sequential expansions, is offered in Example 3. Over the course of a complete movement, profiles such as those shown in Examples 3b and 3d will tend to repeat several times, often in the manner of hidden rhythmic repetitions, in correspondence with the number of phrases in the movement (unless some phrases are very short or contain no expansion), promoting a rhythmic ebb and flow that belies – and, I think, supersedes – the motoric thrust of the surface. Such ebb and flow reflects the uniquely spatial quality of the basic pace, a quality it assumes through its union of duration and pitch. It also accounts for the coherence of large-scale phrase rhythm in the Baroque repertoire, a phrase rhythm that may be viewed less as an additive chain of durationally independent phrases than as the balanced sum total of long-span fluctuations in the basic pace.[29]

Indeed, one might define large-scale Baroque phrase rhythm as a play of equal and unequal durations and paces at several levels of durational structure that is governed by tonal and durational enlargement and is articulated by fluctuations in the basic pace. If Classical and Romantic phrase rhythm hinges (flexibly) on the stability of its periodic hierarchy and on the ready alignment of its durational levels, Baroque phrase rhythm revolves around the network of changes in the length of its constituent phrases, and on the frequent readjustment and realignment of its durational hierarchy. These changes and adjustments – which, I believe, derive from improvisatory practice – are particular to each piece and therefore will not yield a crop of theoretical generalizations. While they represent the core of Baroque phrase rhythm, they effectively prevent us from completing the formulation of a theory that will explain it. Nonetheless, the narrative compositional purpose (or, quite likely, simulated improvisatory scheme) they serve may be clear enough to allow us at least to characterize the rhythmic profile of the piece in question. Our closing excerpt, from Handel's Royal Fireworks music, will offer an example (and a particularly complex one) of how such characterization may be undertaken.

A Schenkerian Pandora's box will open if we attempt to discover whether the basic pace is a phenomenon that originates and resides in the outer voices

---

29. A similar view of large-scale phrase rhythm, couched in terms of pacing and implicit tempo changes, is offered by Ivan Waldbauer in "Riemann's Periodization Revisited and Revised," *Journal of Music Theory* 33/2 (1989), pp. 342–43, 369, and 375.

equally or in one of them principally. Because this issue hinges on long-span harmonic and thematic articulation its consideration cannot detain us here. Within the present confines, it will suffice to observe that even though the upper voice predominates in determining the pace, both of the outer voices express the pace jointly in the course of a movement: the essential motions of bass and upper voice often interlock, and despite changes brought about by expansion and contraction the basic pace remains unaffected by either movement within the inner voices or by the figural patter of diminutions at lower levels throughout the texture.

The thoroughgoing conflation of diminutions, slower unfoldings, and still slower basic pace and its expansions within a single, essentially stepwise melodic line (and often slower but largely stepwise bass) sets apart the realization of temporality in Baroque style from its articulation in the Classic and Romantic repertoires.[30] The diminutions, unfoldings, and basic pace (such that it is) of later compositions are more equitably distributed throughout the texture, and the melodic as well as accompanimental lines in which they take part show decidedly lighter collections of strata. Though pitch and duration are still bound by interacting strata of pace, they are far less intimately linked; and sequential expansion, though still an important resource, must now share the limelight with seemingly similar idioms that may not necessarily introduce any alterations in the durational design.

Levels of pace in later styles

That the basic pace operates effectively but under dramatically different circumstances in later styles is a matter of concern to us here because many of Handel's later instrumental works, among them several of the Concerti Grossi, Op. 6, some of the posthumously published organ concertos, Op. 7, and the Music for the Royal Fireworks (from which an example will be offered presently) already show it working in somewhat the same way it would later in the music of Mozart and Haydn (and, for that matter, Beethoven and Brahms).

While on a small scale stepwise motion in later styles still realizes a basic pace that expands and contracts at the level of the phrase, the subphrase, and their division into segments, it will not necessarily allow such a pace to continue across phrase and section boundaries. Each phrase, in other words, will tend to establish its own basic pace, which articulates the movement of the local contents, and (at least from this perspective) the composition's larger phrase rhythm will accommodate a dialectic among closely related but quasi-independent basic paces. More important, even local changes in pace may not necessarily involve the basic pace directly, or necessarily occasion genuine durational expansion and contraction; most often they will rather signal a shift from one constellation to another of purely durational, hierarchically periodic paces – figural and grouping paces – that are made available by the overwhelmingly duple durational framework and are often supported by underlying chordal

---

30. Baroque conflations of the strata in one melodic line and the strata's wider textural distribution in later styles are taken up by Joel Lester in *The Rhythms of Tonal Music*, pp. 138–45.

prolongations. Substantial expansions and contractions in harmonic rhythm – typically from one-bar harmony to two-bar or even four-bar harmony (and, in later styles, sometimes to an underlying eight-bar harmony) – may therefore be due to changes in the priority of pacing within the group of available paces, rather than to the onset of durational or sequential expansion as such.[31] Their origin will, in other words, be purely durational rather than tonal.

These observations apply largely to pieces at moderate to rapid tempi. It appears that the basic pace, along with the expansion it supports, continues to prevail in slow movements throughout the Classic and Romantic eras, when the maintenance of a deliberate pace from beginning to end is an important durational feature, but the matter requires further study.

The basic pace represents the most significant pace in a chain of paces that are collapsed onto one melodic line; it is a contrapuntally and metrically supported *tonal* construct and, allowing for expansion and contraction, it remains essentially unchanged for the duration of a movement (in Baroque style) or a phrase (in later styles). By contrast, the *principal grouping pace* of the periodic *constellation of paces* just described supports the most significant movement of groups of figures or diminutions and groups of measures that are active at the surface; it is a metrically (and, often, hypermetrically) supported *durational* construct that may move either slowly or rapidly, and may or may not coincide with the basic pace.[32] Its speed fluctuates widely because it may draw on any of the paces, usually three to five in number, available in the constellation. The frequent alternation among these paces will bring about *exchanges of pace* within the constellation, and it is these exchanges that will simulate expansion and contraction at the level of one to four (or, in later styles, eight) bars.

Unlike the diminutional and contrapuntal levels of pace shown in Example 3e, the constellation's paces are distributed among the various strands of the texture: the shorter paces support figural and accompanimental material, and the longer paces establish both the harmonic rhythm at several levels and the hierarchy of grouping at the one-, two-, four-, and (in some cases) eight-bar levels. The priority of paces depends on local (usually thematic) circumstances; the importance of the constellation resides in the opportunities for mercurial changes in pace it presents within a relatively strict periodic framework. Durational expansion, in Schenker's sense of *Dehnung*, and sequential expansion along the lines I have drawn earlier, all continue to appear side by side with these mercurial changes, but should not be equated with them.

Example 6, a schematic interpretation of the extended sentence that opens

---

31. We have already encountered premonitions of such changes, acting in competition with the basic pace (and, in typically Baroque fashion, still within the confines of an expansion), in Example 5, bars 7–8; see note 20 above. On a modest scale, such changes also appear with some frequency in Bach's music (compare, for example, the quarter note and dotted half note paces in the Sarabande from the E minor English Suite) and throughout the keyboard works of François Couperin.

32. In a recent article, Floyd K. Grave has employed the term *modular rhythm* (after Jan LaRue's notion of the module) to describe much the same phenomenon as the principal grouping pace; see Grave, "Metrical Dissonance in Haydn," *The Journal of Musicology* 13/2 (1995), pp. 168–202. A similarly rhythmic approach to grouping structure is followed by Arnold Feil in "Rhythm in Schubert: Some Practical Problems – Critical Analysis, Critical Edition, Critical Performance," in Eva Badura-Skoda and Peter Branscombe, eds., *Schubert Studies: Problems of Style and Chronology* (Cambridge: Cambridge University Press, 1982), pp. 327–45.

Example 6 Mozart, Sonata in C major, K.330, Allegro, bars 1–16: sentence structure, basic pace, and pace constellations

Mozart's Piano Sonata in C major, K.330, illustrates the foregoing observations.[33] The principal grouping pace is shown at the top of each constellation, the subordinate paces in decreasing order of importance below. Insofar as the figural motion in quarter notes in bars 1–2 and 3–4 (a compound melody comprising the motions g^2–f^2–e^2–g^1, e^2–d^2–c^2–g^1, and c^2–b^1–c^2–g^1 under an implicitly sustained g^2) gives way to a descent in half notes in bars 5–8 and (abbreviated) in bars 9–10 (from a^1–g^1 to an implicit f^1–e^1, underlying the surface arpeggiations), Mozart's sentence retains the sense of an expanded basic pace (if without effecting a genuine sequential expansion) in much the same way as did the descent from $b\flat^2$ to f^2 in bars 3–6 of Handel's D minor ritornello (Example 5).[34]

But Mozart's simultaneous and more conspicuous presentation of fragmentation in the design – his replacement of the two-bar grouping pace of bars 1–4 with a one-bar grouping pace at the beginning of bar 5, the fundamental requirement of sentence structure – is in fact due to an exchange of paces within the constellations shown in the diagram. As the arrows indicate, the one-bar pace that played only a minor role in bars 1–4 assumes the position of principal grouping pace in bars 5–16, while both the two-bar grouping pace and the quarter-note figural pace of bars 1–4 recede to secondary positions. In bar 11 – at the middle rather than at the beginning of a four-bar group – two internal figural paces exchange places within the constellation while the one-bar grouping pace remains primary. The motion in eighth notes, shown partly by means of grace notes in the diagram, assumes precedence over the motion in quarter notes; the two-bar grouping pace remains active in a supporting capacity, at a deeper level.

For its part, the basic pace, too, accelerates in bar 11, resuming its original motion in quarter notes, which is signaled by the $\begin{smallmatrix}8-7\\6-5\\4-3\end{smallmatrix}$ progression in bar 11. Important though they obviously are, the basic pace's expansion and contraction are, in the long run, ancillary to the exchanges of pace that take place within the constellation. It is the exchanges of pace – rather than the fluctuations of the basic pace – that articulate the familiar sentential design and the unusual twist it encounters in bar 11. It is no accident that later on several precipitous exchanges of pace (at the beginning of bars 25 and 26, and again

---

33. The sentential parsing here follows (with some ad hoc modifications) the terms offered by William E. Caplin in "The 'Expanded Cadential Progression': A Category for the Analysis of Classical Form," *The Journal of Musicological Research* 7/2–3 (1987), pp. 215–57, and in *Classical Form: A Theory of Formal Functions for the Instrumental Music of Haydn, Mozart and Beethoven* (New York: Oxford University Press, 1998). I wish to thank William Caplin for making his typescript available to me before the book's publication.

    A sentential analysis of the theme from Mozart's K.330 appears in Schoenberg's *Fundamentals of Musical Composition*, ed. Gerald Strang (New York: St. Martin's Press, 1967), p. 74, Example 59f; a reading of bars 1–8 different from the interpretation offered here appears in Caplin's *Classical Form*, pp. 38–39, Example 3.5. For sentential analyses of extended sentences see also Caplin, "Hybrid Themes: Toward a Refinement in the Classification of Classical Theme Types," in *Beethoven Forum*, Vol. 3 (Lincoln: University of Nebraska Press, 1994); see especially pp. 154–55.

34. To a greater degree than in the Baroque repertoire, the basic pace alone cannot account for the uneven pacing of mixed note values that articulates the thematic design at the surface of K.330. An account of *composite pacing*, as one might call it (referring to thematic pace fluctuations that do occur in Baroque style but thrive in the more harmonic, prolongational environment of later styles) is given in my dissertation.

Example 7 Handel, Concerto Grosso in D minor, Op. 6, No. 10, Allegro (first movement), bars 1–7: fugue subject

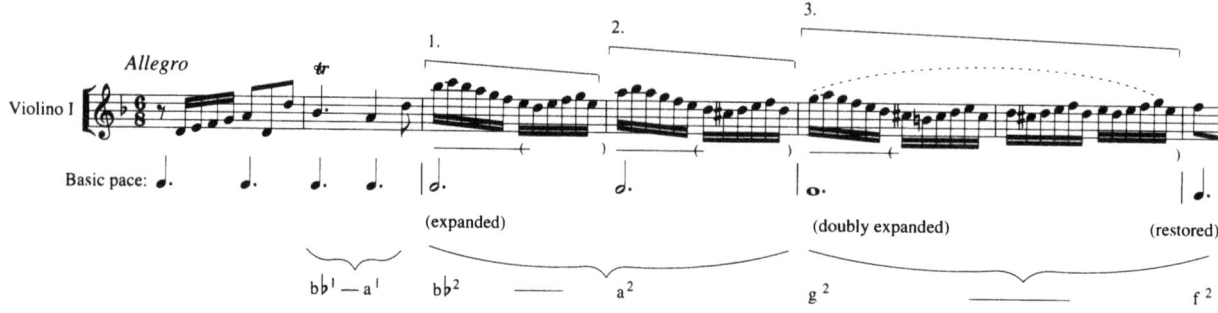

in bars 31 and 32) emerge as the exposition's most memorable rhythmic quirks.

Brief as it is, Mozart's sentence illustrates how the Classically periodic balance among the various paces leaves little room for tonally derived pacing save for its employment as a compositional idiom.[35] The large-scale sequential expansions in Handel's late compositions illustrate vividly the high Baroque's arrival at the outer limits of such pacing. As it happens, both tonal periodicity and its supporting basic pace are most vulnerable when allowed to flourish in the large because, at that level, their tonal identity becomes obscured by their wide compass.

Nascent periodicity and large-scale sequential expansion

I should now like to present a pair of examples illustrating the long-span projection of sequential expansion and, in the second example, its appearance within a nascently periodic framework. Example 7, from Handel's D minor Concerto Grosso, Op. 6, No. 10, shows the further enlargement typical of many three-pronged sequences in their closing measures. Through the addition of one measure, the enlargement provides a durational bridge to the resumption of the prevailing unexpanded design by superimposing a larger duple grouping over the three-part sequential structure. In this instance it also expands the fugal subject's characteristic motive, b♭^{1}–a^1, several times, progressively; see the brackets atop Example 7.[36]

Similar enlargement, on a much larger scale, pervades much of the

---

35. I discuss the ramifications of the new balance in periodic and tonal pacing in "Beethoven and Handel: The Significance of a Borrowing," a paper delivered at the conference "Austria, 996–1996: Music in a Changing Society" (Ottawa, January 1996), to be published in the conference proceedings, ed. Walter Kreyszig (Vienna: Wilhelm Braumüller Universitäts-Verlagsbuchhandlung, in preparation).

36. Floyd K. Grave (private communication) has pointed out that the fragmentation of the figure comprising six sixteenths in bar 5 represents sequential acceleration. Like the acceleration in bars 7–8 of Example 5, it takes place at a level closer to the surface than the expansion that occurs at the same time at the deeper level, although in this instance the basic pace joins the expansion, not the acceleration (see note 20, above).

Example 8 Handel, Music for the Royal Fireworks, Ouverture

a) Bars 66–89, tonal reduction

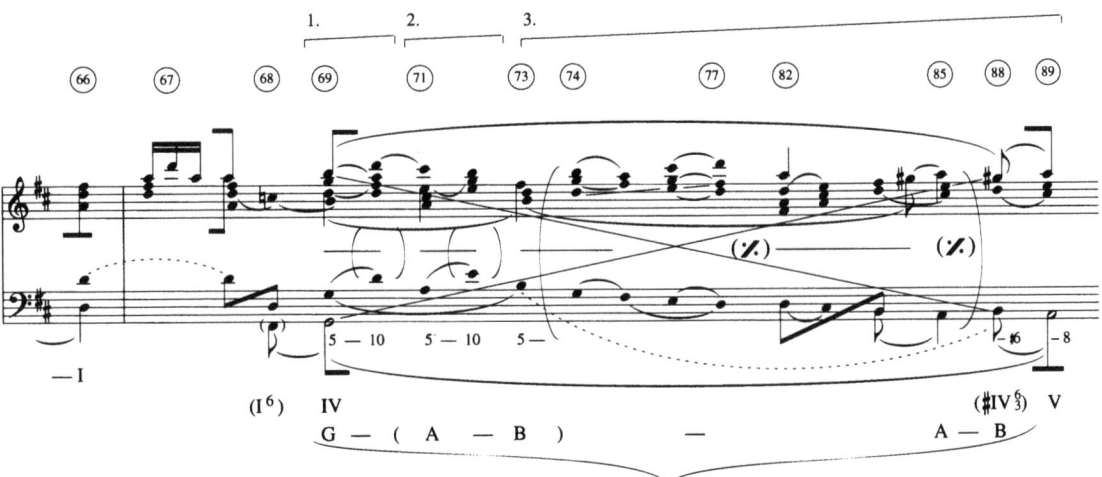

b) Bars 48–89, and source of bass outline

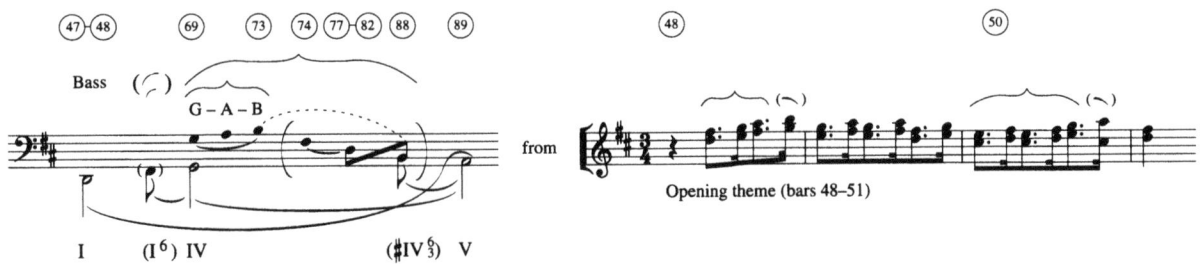

Opening theme (bars 48–51)

Ouverture from the Music for the Royal Fireworks and repeatedly accounts for its projection of great breadth and grand effect. The first such enlargement is shown in tonal as well as durational reduction in Example 8.

At the beginning of Example 8a, bar 68, we find the tonic in first inversion, the principal theme having already been stated four times (bars 48–63) and followed by a sequential transition (bars 64–69). The sequence in question enters, overlapping, in bar 69. One measure after the introduction of its third and last two-bar pattern, in bar 74, a complete and precipitous change in design takes place that interrupts and delays the completion of the pattern: the previously wide-ranging parallel motion in all instruments is replaced by descending chords in the upper parts and by rising unison arpeggiations in the lower parts, which span sixteen measures (bars 74–89), overlapping with the sequential progression that begins in bar 89.

Hinting at the emerging Galant and Classical styles, this apparently periodic and foursquare sixteen-bar group, whose repeatedly descending fourth-pro-

Example 8 (*cont.*)

c) Bars 67–89, durational reduction

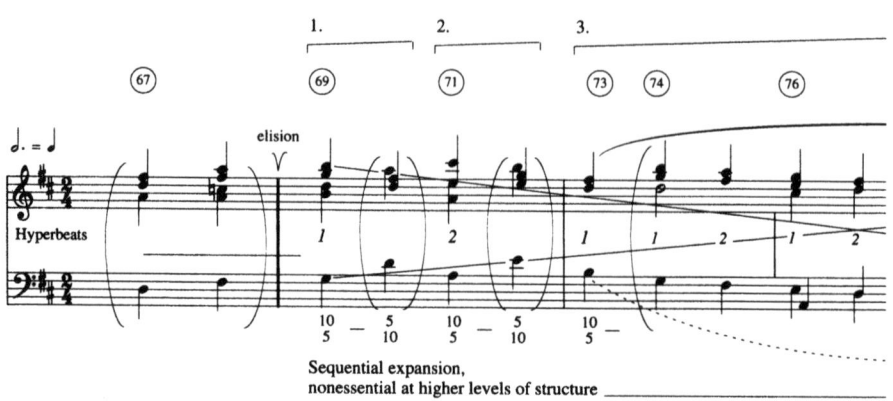

gressions articulate a tonal periodicity at the four-bar level and a durational periodicity at higher levels, effectively suspends our sequence's expanded two-bar basic pace and establishes its own internal temporality; it does so by giving up the principal theme's characteristic one-bar extended upbeats and adopting instead a straightforward grid of emphatically hierarchic downbeat accents. Yet enclosed as it is by the larger sequence the group possesses no genuine tonal or durational independence. As the reductions in Example 8 show, it is absorbed by a voice exchange that spans all three patterns of the sequence begun in bar 69. The exchange is designed to unfold – and in the last moment to chromaticize – the subdominant, before the goal of the passage, the dominant, enters in bar 89, at which point the Ouverture's characteristic upbeat chains briefly reappear.

It is important to note that the descending passages in bars 82–85 and 86–89, though largely identical in their opening two measures, proceed quite differently in their closing measures, each passage leading to a destination identical in pitch but different in tonal significance. While the last component of the expanded sequence, over the bass tone B, is expanded from bar 74 to bars 88 and 89, a third progression, G–A–B, ascends at a deeper level from the bass G in bar 69, at the beginning of the sequence, to the B in bar 88, filling in the voice exchange shown in Example 8a with a large-scale passing tone A that enters in bar 85. (A corresponding a^2, part of a matching descent from b^2 to $g\#^2$ in the upper voice, enters already over D in bar 82.) It is the passing A in bar 85 that serves as the goal of the bass descent from D to A in bars 82–85. The descent from D to A in bars 86–89, by contrast, aims first at the B in bar 88, the conclusion of the voice exchange and the rising third G–A–B, and then proceeds to the structural A in bar 89, where forward tonal motion resumes. One might say that the sequential expansion and the stepwise realization of the voice exchange are two essentially separate events that are collapsed into a single extended progression.

The large square brackets in Examples 8a and 8c summarize the sequential enlargement; the curly brackets in Example 8b show its origins in the opening motive of the Allegro. Within this larger framework, the "visiting" periodicity of bars 74–89 may be viewed as something of an improvisatory mirage, in keeping with the state of suspense and controlled freedom that the irregularity

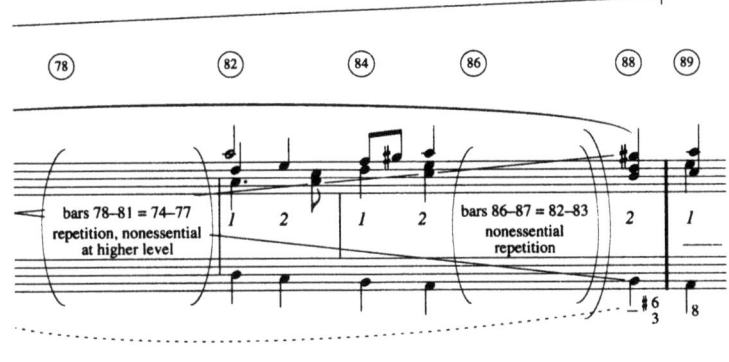

of the enlargement has engendered. The grand effect of the enlargement is due to the spatial quality of the basic pace: the ebb and flow of its tonal and durational components, and especially its retardation to the point of suspension by the enlargement, suggest an expanse of majestic proportions.[37]

However unreal it may appear within the frame of the embracing sequential expansion, the periodic hierarchy of bars 74–89 must nonetheless be dealt with as such, especially given its proximity to the opening sixteen-bar thematic area (bars 48–63), whose broad durational periodicity is also articulated by a tonal periodicity at the four-bar level. The schematic analysis in Example 9 outlines the constitution of both groups and that of the connecting, overlapping sequence in bars 64–69, which undergoes expansion as well.

As in Mozart's K.330 (and, for that matter, any Baroque piece that is partly periodic), the one-bar basic pace, its expansions, and its baggage of contrapuntally durational strata must compete here with a fluctuating constellation of periodically based grouping paces. Ironically, these owe their initial articulation to the movement of the basic pace. Throughout bars 48–63, the one-bar stepwise basic pace repeatedly outlines both the double-neighbor figure, $f\#^2-g^2-e^2-f\#^2$, and its transposition, $c\#^2-d^2-b^1-c\#^2$, and in so doing establishes a solid tonal periodicity; the four-bar principal grouping pace atop the constellation of paces, by contrast, regulates the thematic articulation that takes place at four-bar intervals and provides the basis for the higher-level durational periodicity. During the transitional sequence of bars 64–69, the basic pace expands threefold (see the parentheses in the reduction in Example 9) while the principal grouping pace contracts to three-bar movement; the two paces briefly coincide, forcing the less significant two-bar pace out altogether. (Though it intensifies the Ouverture's forward drive, this meeting of paces compromises both the tonal periodicity at the surface and the durational periodicity at higher levels.)

Our long-span, three-pronged sequence, which enters in bar 69, at first expands the basic pace only twofold, momentarily quickening its progress

---

37. I discuss the hemiolic implications of bars 74–89 in "The Two-Length Bar Revisited: Handel and the Hemiola," *Göttinger Händel-Beiträge* 4 (1991), pp. 209–12.

Example 9 Handel, Music for the Royal Fireworks, Ouverture, bars 48–89: sequential structure, basic pace, and pace constellations

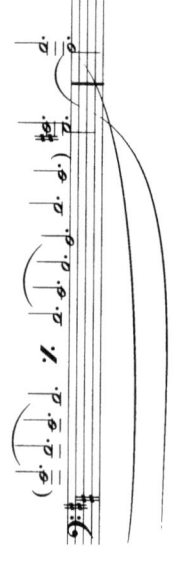

(relative to the preceding sequence) to two-bar movement and heightening the Ouverture's drive still more. The principal grouping pace accelerates similarly, and for the duration of bars 69–73 the two paces continue together.[38]

During the transformation of bars 74–89 from one measure to sixteen (the sequence proper closes in bar 88 but the sixteen-bar expansion extends to bar 89) the basic pace, as we have seen, slows to the point of complete suspension. This temporal suspension, in turn, opens a window that allows the periodicity of the principal grouping pace – now restored to its original four-bar movement – to reassert itself (and in so doing to reify the potential for extended duple ordering inherent in the phenomenon of expansion).[39] Though few exchanges have taken place within the constellation of grouping paces, the principal grouping pace has succeeded in establishing its presence and in holding its own against the fluctuations of the tonal basic pace. While both paces, with their attendant periodicities, seem to rule the passage in equal measure, the basic pace and the tonal periodicity it articulates ultimately yield their exclusive control over the design's temporality.

Conclusion: the nature of Baroque temporality

Interesting and valuable as theoretical concepts, the notions of sequential expansion, basic pace, principal grouping pace, and pace constellations offer an empirically instructive contribution to the study of Baroque performance practice, for they provide substantial internal evidence that the articulation of Baroque temporality, despite its motoric thrust, is just as flexible and diverse as the realization of later durational frameworks, sometimes even more so. Recognition of this diversity will help us rethink our traditionally one-dimensional and contradictory views of Baroque metrics as irregular and relentless. Supported by stepwise motion at levels close to the surface and enriched by early premonitions of Classical periodicity, the temporality of the high Baroque sustains a vigorous improvisatory impulse that resides well within the reach of both the receptive listener and the alert performer.

Although the maintenance of a similar impulse remained something of a cherished ideal during the Classic and Romantic eras, it became much harder to achieve and sustain within the confines of the relatively strict hierarchic periodicity that soon took over. The extraordinarily frequent recourse to durational expansion and shifts in pace constellations – and the perpetual search for new forms – that we find throughout the later repertoires are due in no small measure to the emergence of this new challenge.

---

38. Harald Krebs offers a penetrating account of somewhat similar changes (couched in very different terms) in "Some Extensions of the Concepts of Metrical Consonance and Dissonance," *Journal of Music Theory* 31/1 (1987), pp. 108–10. Particularly valuable is Krebs's suggestion that a complete movement could be analyzed in terms of its adherence to and diversion from metrical consonance, and the relation of such consonance and dissonance to pitch structure (p. 119).

39. The multiplicity of levels inherent in the onset of expansion provides for a built-in, if hidden, periodicity; see note 20, above. The periodicity of the principal grouping pace can reassert itself quite readily on account of the similarity in four-note kernels between bars 48–63 and bars 74–89 (G–F♯–E–D and D–C♯–B–A in the bass of bars 74–89, corresponding to the upper-voice kernels F♯–G–E–F♯ and C♯–D–B–C♯ in bars 48–63).

Strange dimensions: regularity and irregularity in deep levels of rhythmic reduction

Frank Samarotto

The guiding idea for this article is well expressed in a famous quotation from Renaissance philosopher Francis Bacon: "There is no excellent beauty that hath not some strangeness in the proportion."[1] This statement is excerpted from one of Bacon's forays into what was then a developing literary form, the essay. Like Montaigne, who invented this form, Bacon sought in his essays to encapsulate a world of observation in a handful of pithy statements.

In many ways, modern-day music theorists do something similar in that they often seek to summarize complex artistic statements with simpler aphoristic models. Also like Montaigne and Bacon, some theorists are testing a new form of summary, an essay into rhythmic structure. I refer of course to the application of Schenker's theories to the analysis of rhythm, as developed by Carl Schachter and William Rothstein.[2] The aim of this method of rhythmic reduction is to create a hierarchy of rhythm both analogous to and closely in rapport with the hierarchy of tonal structure: groups of measures are combined to form groups of hypermeasures, while their significance is evaluated in coordination with the underlying voice leading.

Hierarchies in Schenkerian theory are generally assumed to have a structure that proceeds in a uniform progression from complexity to simplicity, that is, from a complex surface to ever simpler explanatory models.[3] In this way irregular features are resolved into regular schemata, individualities are consumed

---

1. From the essay "Of Beauty," first published in 1612.
2. See Carl Schachter's series of three articles collectively titled "Rhythm and Linear Analysis" and subtitled (1) "A Preliminary Study," *The Music Forum*, Vol. 4 (New York: Columbia University Press, 1976), pp. 281–334; (2) "Durational Reduction," *The Music Forum*, Vol. 5 (1980), pp. 197–232; and (3) "Aspects of Meter," *The Music Forum*, Vol. 6, Part 1 (1987), pp. 1–59. See also William Rothstein's "Rhythm and the Theory of Structural Levels" (Ph.D. diss., Yale University, 1981), and his *Phrase Rhythm in Tonal Music* (New York: Schirmer Books, 1989).
3. One is reminded of Schenker's aphoristic statement: "My concepts show that the art of music is much simpler than present-day teachings would have it appear. However, the fact that the simplicity does not lie on the surface makes it no less simple." See *Free Composition*, p. xxiii.

    Richard Cohn and Douglas Dempster cite inconsistencies in Schenkerian hierarchy and suggest the possibility of introducing other models in "Hierarchical Unity, Plural Unities: Toward a Reconciliation," in *Disciplining Music: Musicology and Its Canons*, ed. Katherine Bergeron and Philip V. Bohlman (Chicago: University of Chicago Press, 1992), pp. 156–81. Richard Cohn pursues this issue further in "The Autonomy of Motives in Schenkerian Accounts of Tonal Music," *Music Theory Spectrum* 14/2 (1992), pp. 150–70, and "Schenker's Theory, Schenkerian Theory: Pure Unity or Constructive Conflict?" *Indiana Theory Review* 13/1 (1992), pp. 1–20. Though concerned with the specific issue of motivic relations, these articles look to the possibility of the sort of heterogeneous view of Schenkerian unity implicit in my present argument.

by generalities. In the following analyses I will challenge this assumption in order to demonstrate how the technique of rhythmic reduction can absorb – or express – some particularly significant irregular features in order to explore not *whether* but *how* models of deeper rhythmic levels can be related to the surface we experience.[4] To do so, I will take as test cases two short pieces that have many similarities: both are trio sections from middle movements of Beethoven's piano sonatas, and both are in D♭ major. Both embody rhythmic paradoxes, but of quite opposite sorts, one a distracted musing, the other a tangled knot.

My first example is from Beethoven's Op. 27, No. 2. The Trio provides an apparently simple example of rhythmic structure: it seems quite easily parsed into four-measure groups throughout the whole of its twenty-four bars.[5] Example 1 presents my reading of the voice leading, which shows a descending third in a delicate play between a lower, then higher register. This continues until the drop to G♭ in bar 53; the aimless meandering in parallel sixths that follows suggests that these measures (until the crescendo in bar 57) are little other than an expansion of the IV^6 harmony that initiates them. (These measures are also set apart by the change of figuration from anticipations to suspensions.) The implication is that bars 53–57 also represent a *rhythmic* expansion of IV. This is a technique that Schenker typically invoked to explain odd-numbered measure groups, though Schachter and Rothstein have each shown expansions within duple groups.[6] In addition, the expansion in question here does not derive from a prior model given earlier in the piece, a model of the sort that Rothstein has called a foreground prototype; one must assume an unexpanded model in the middleground.[7]

Example 2 presents a hierarchic rhythmic reduction to show how this might be done. Level c, at the bottom of Example 2, reduces each measure to a single quarter-note hyperbeat. This more or less literal reduction yields six hypermeasures. If we accept the expansion of the IV chord suggested by my dotted slurs, then we can reduce that span into the single hyperbeat above it, and thus reduce the six hypermetric groups of level c to the five shown in level b. Now this introduces an odd asymmetry of two plus three, and again the retained IV^6 seems to be the culprit. In the next move, to level a, I perform the same operation again and reduce out the expansion; this yields a more comfortably balanced group of four.

Before taking the final step to the top level, we must observe something anomalous about the process of reduction presented thus far. As the expansion passed through the sieve of analytic hierarchy, it produced irregularity not

---

4. Here regularity is associated with duple construction, for reasons of innate simplicity rather than aesthetic value. It is worth recalling that Schenker's assertion, "metric ordering based on two and its multiples is the most natural to us," was based on the principle of repetition and did not prevent him from identifying odd-number measure groups. See *Free Composition*, p. 119, §286.
5. Measure numbers are counted from the beginning of the Allegretto.
6. See for instance Schachter's analysis of Scarlatti's Sonata K.78 in "Rhythm and Linear Analysis: Aspects of Meter," pp. 45–49. An expansion can also *result* in a four-bar group that represents a single bar at a deeper structural level, as for instance in *Free Composition*, Fig. 148/1.
7. Rothstein, "Rhythm and the Theory of Structural Levels," pp. 150–80; the concept of a middleground prototype derives from a clarification made by Ernst Oster in a footnote to §297 of *Free Composition*, p. 124.

Example 1 Beethoven, Sonata Op. 27, No. 2, second movement, Trio: voice-leading sketches

a) Foreground

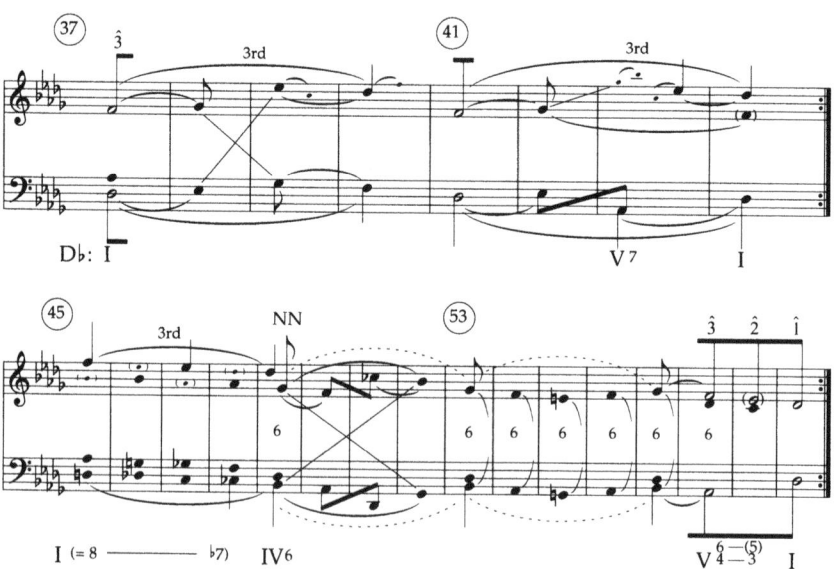

b) Middleground

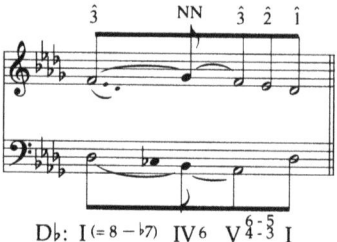

apparently present at the surface level: the group of six at level c is certainly more symmetrical than the group of five at level b, at least with respect to duple pairings. Here it seems that moving up the hierarchy introduces rather than removes complexity, somewhat in contradiction to what we expect higher levels to do. At level a, the balance is restored, especially between the two halves of the top voice. However, even here a significant irregularity remains: the IV⁶ is now reduced to one "hyperbeat," but it is the first beat. Thus it displaces the cadential $^6_4$ chord in the last hypermeasure from its usual position of relative metric emphasis, creating a sort of syncopation. (This metric placement reflects the syncopated harmonic rhythm of the first two hypermeasures of level c.) Reducing out the IV⁶ would allow greater symmetry. The top level, which I call level x, does this, as well as some further normalization, with the aim of

Example 2 Beethoven, Op. 27, No. 2, second movement, Trio: rhythmic reduction

showing an exact (and hidden) correspondence between the two halves of the piece.[8]

As attractive as it is to reveal hidden correspondences, level x seems to me to be a step too far: so lean a reduction seems rhythmically featureless and uninformative about the piece. It is proportionally the same as level a, but level a is more effective in encapsulating what I hear as a fundamental asymmetry in this piece and is more successful in placing that asymmetry within a regular framework.

To explore this asymmetry, I will again call on Bacon, who in the same essay placed "gracious motion" above all else as "... the best part of beauty[,] which a picture cannot express." This idea can be directly conjoined to the strangeness of proportion:

---

8. Normalization, an essential technique of rhythmic reduction, refers here to the evening out of note values to resolve the rhythm into a more basic state. See William Rothstein, "Rhythmic Displacement and Rhythmic Normalization," in *Trends in Schenkerian Research*, ed. Allen Cadwallader (New York: Schirmer Books, 1990), pp. 87–113, an essay derived from his dissertation (see note 2 above). This aspect of the reduction is incidental to the point in question.

Example 3 Beethoven, Op. 27, No. 2, second movement, Trio: hypothetical simpler version

... in the composition of excellent beauty there is something which is less consistent or coherent with other elements than those elements are with each other. I.e., if gracious motion is the best part of beauty, then the *proportions of a figure in action necessarily vary from normal static ones*...[9]

I will take a cue from this idea of gracious motion, and consider how our ineluctably temporal experience of music blurs the stability of the essentially static hierarchy through which we interpret our experience.[10] One way to capture the moment-by-moment perspective is to place my reading of the expansion in the context of a listener's possible expectations.

If we take the first two four-bar groups as a premise, how might we have expected the piece to continue? I will assume that both halves will be equal in size and that the basic rhythmic shape of the first four bars will be the model for subsequent phrases.[11] These assumptions yield a hypothetical simpler version given in Example 3. Though of course my rendering is not the only possibility, it is a necessary consequence of the mechanism of hierarchical reduction that the realization bear some similarity to level a of the rhythmic reduction.

To be sure, there is much that is deficient about this version. In comparing it to the real score, we see that the monotonous rhythmic shape of Example 3 is extended to cover the second part in a single gesture. This avoids a segmenta-

---

9. From the commentary by J. Max Patrick (who draws here on a later Latin translation that elucidates many passages in the original English text) in *Selected Essays of Francis Bacon* (New York: Appleton-Century-Crofts, 1948), p. 78, emphasis added.
10. The need for theory to address this aspect of musical experience has been eloquently argued by David Lewin in "Music Theory, Phenomenology, and Modes of Perception," *Music Perception* 3 (1986), pp. 327–92.
11. This shape resembles Edward Cone's model of a phrase as beginning- and end-accented, discussed in *Musical Form and Musical Performance* (New York: Norton, 1968); see especially p. 40. While I accept this as an accentual possibility, I do not regard it as metric or as a necessary characteristic of all phrases.

tion of the I♭⁷ from the IV to which it resolves. Still, we might well imagine that the IV first reached in bar 49 will proceed directly to the cadential $^6_4$, in other words, that bar 50 will turn out to contain the final dominant of the piece. Instead we are pleasantly surprised when the subdominant blossoms into a four-bar group that is clearly a variation by free inversion of the opening four bars. But notice that at the end of this four-bar group, we are back exactly where we started, on a IV⁶ chord. In fact, bar 49 is *identical* to bar 53. What will happen at this point?

We have a record of alternatives Beethoven actually considered. Plate 1 and Example 4 present a facsimile and transcription of the tenth page of the autograph, which contains this Trio.[12] Bar 49, the beginning of the G♭ area, may be found in the third system (third measure). At the end of this system, Beethoven began by repeating the previous four measures, then crossed them out, not even filling in the left hand, and indicated the jump with his usual "Vi- de." Having given up the possibility of the symmetry of immediate repetition, the piece finds itself back at the IV⁶ again ready to give way to a cadential $^6_4$. But in the measure after this $^6_4$ chord, Beethoven was uncertain how to continue: in the fourth system, three measures after the "de," the left-hand notes A♭ and D♭ are scratched out, and G♮ is substituted as the new bass. At some point, parallel sixths emerged here to sweep the voices past the $^6_4$ and again a cadence was thwarted.[13] At the end of the four-bar group of parallel sixths, the IV⁶ again reappears before finally moving to a cadence. Thus we reach the same place three times, each time with a different consequence. The first time (third system, third measure), a crescendo marking was written and crossed out; this happened the second time also (bottom system). The third time the crescendo was decisively placed in the fourth bar before the end, to clinch the progression to the final dominant.[14]

The importance of these alterations is that the rhythmic irregularity takes place at the point where the autograph shows the most uncertainty. The action of the piece itself inscribes an even greater play of indecisiveness, as if composing out a train of thought that wanders distractedly from the point and returns at its leisure.

This impression is confirmed by related events that occur in the surrounding Allegretto. The opening phrase begins with a flash of *maggiore* light emerging from the dark *minore* of the first movement and immediately seems to *act*, both playfully and unexpectedly. This dominant-cadencing phrase is built on an evasion: it slips past the cadential $^6_4$ chord before regaining its moorings and succeeding at a more sure-footed cadence. Example 5 shows the origin of this evaded cadence in the overlap of the hypothetical complete phrases, dis-

---

12. Lewis Lockwood presents an example of inferring the stages of compositional process in a similar autograph, that of Beethoven's Sonata Op. 26, in *Beethoven: Studies in the Creative Process* (Cambridge, Mass.: Harvard University Press, 1992), pp. 4–5.
13. The changes in the first system are related to this passage also: the bass was changed from root position chords to parallel tenths, which then serve to prepare the later sixths.
14. Schenker's commentary on this autograph notes that Beethoven frequently gave in to the impulse to place a crescendo mark too soon, later removing it in order to obey a higher law of synthesis. See *Ludwig van Beethoven, Sonate Op. 27, Nr. 2*, facsimile edition with an introduction by Schenker (Vienna: Universal Edition, 1921), p. v.

Plate 1 Beethoven, Op. 27, No. 2, second movement, Trio: autograph

tinguished by articulation.[15] This stumbling action comes to fruition in two subsequent phrases that instantiate the more straightforward kind of expansion where a literal model is expanded later in the piece. The foreground prototype is given at Example 6a with a rhythmic reduction next to it. The expansion shown at Example 6b begins by stating the first half of the phrase twice, then arriving firmly on the dominant through an expanded subdominant. As with the Trio, the impression is of the music trying out different alternatives before making a definitive arrival. The voice-leading graph below shows an underlying similarity to the Trio: the very same parallel sixths, with nearly identical harmonies, prolong the IV^6.[16]

15. This overlap also confers an accent on bar 2 in conflict with a hypermetric scanning that begins with the first bar; this ambiguity persists throughout the Allegretto. Rothstein also attributes the hypermetric ambiguity in this piece to stronger harmonic changes on even-numbered bars, but decides in favor of the melodic grouping, invoking what he calls the "rule of congruence." See his "Beethoven with and without *Kunstgepräng*': Metrical Ambiguity Reconsidered," in *Beethoven Forum*, Vol. 4 (Lincoln: University of Nebraska Press, 1995), pp. 173–74.
16. The connections among all the movements of this work figure prominently in Ernst Oster's analysis; see "The *Fantasie-Impromptu*: A Tribute to Beethoven," *Musicology* 1/4 (1947), pp. 407–29, reprinted in *Aspects of Schenkerian Theory*, ed. David Beach (New Haven: Yale University Press, 1983), pp. 189–207. See also the reading by Edward Laufer given in his review of *Free Composition*

Example 4 Beethoven, Op. 27, No. 2, second movement, Trio: autograph transcription

It is these quasi-improvisatory departures from our expectations that most strongly impress on us the sense of music as dramatic action. The fixed elements of regular metric and hypermetric patterning are more like a static architecture that we survey in time but which remains as still as a row of columns. The blurred motion of a figure in action is inextricably bound to the rhythmic irregularity and the strangeness of proportion. The G♭ expansion of Example 2 is not simply an important part of the piece – it is a fundamentally different kind of event. The equalization that results in level x represents the element of

in *Music Theory Spectrum* 3 (1981), pp. 167–69, Examples 12 and 13. Not noted by either is the similarity of the Trio (see my Example 1b) to the celebrated opening of the first movement.

A less obvious connection is more significantly tied to the idea of expansion itself. As just noted, the expanded passages in both the Trio and Allegretto involve a bass motion of $\hat{6}$–$\hat{5}$–$\natural\hat{4}$–$\hat{5}$. These tones recur in minor in the coda of the final movement, passing from top voice to bass at the end of bar 187 and continuing into bar 189. Setting off the final two tones is a poignant adagio which must surely recall the stretching out of time that is the essence of an expansion, albeit with a starkly different affect.

Example 5 Beethoven, Op. 27, No. 2, Allegretto: evasion in the first phrase

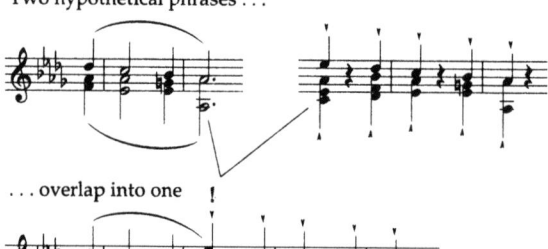

Example 6 Beethoven, Op. 27, No. 2, Allegretto: expansion in the final phrase

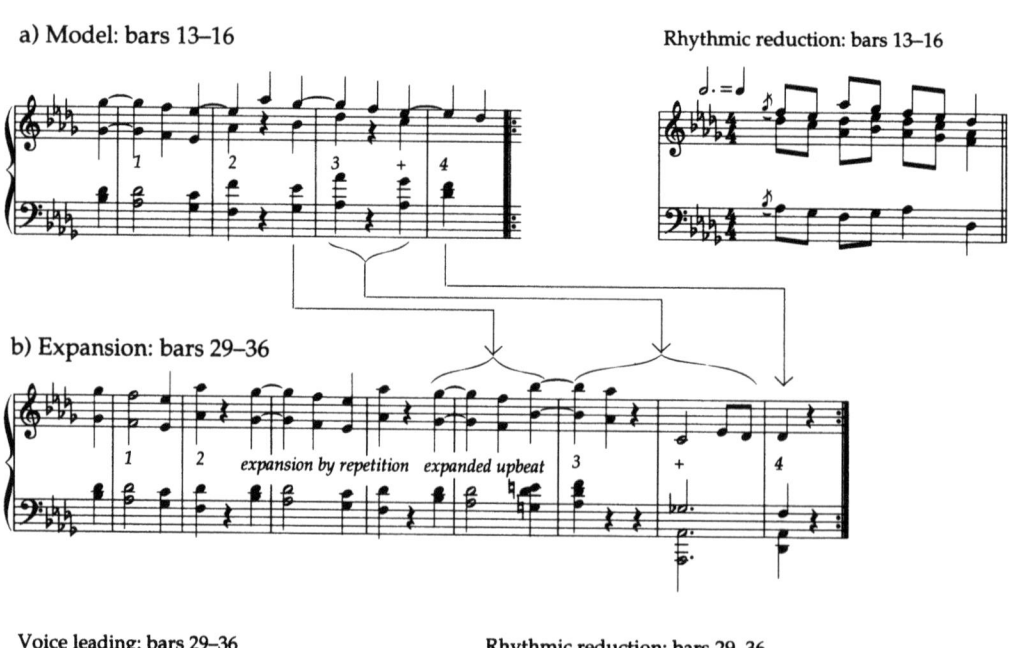

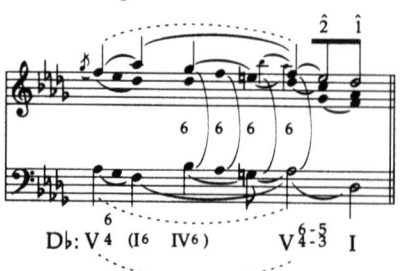

Example 7 Beethoven, Sonata Op. 110, second movement, Trio: voice-leading sketches

a) Foreground

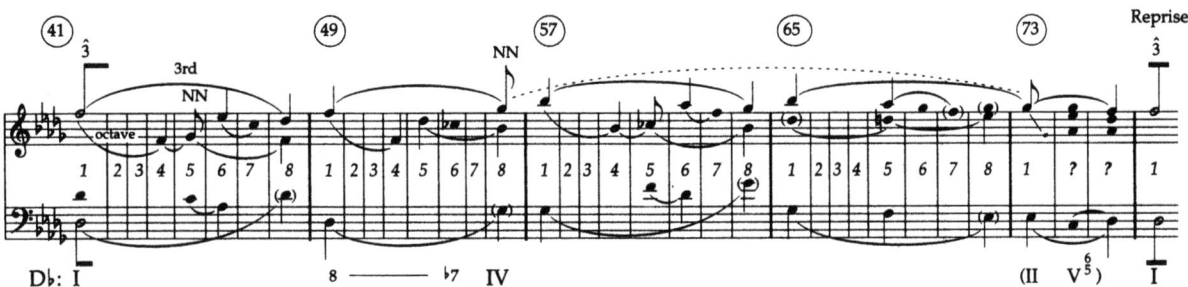

b) Middleground

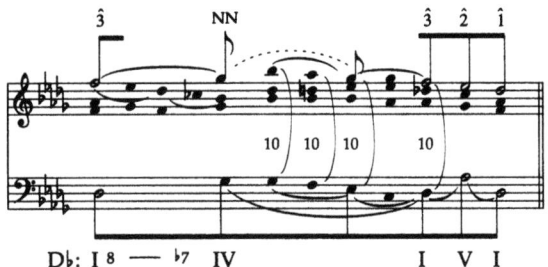

equilibrium, derived in principle from the ideal world of species counterpoint, the realm of logical relation. The G♭ expansion represents the element of disequilibrium, from the unmeasured world of free improvisation, the arena of performative action. While appearing to be regular on the surface it embeds itself deeply in the middleground as an element of irregularity.

The problems are more acute in my second example, the Trio from the Allegro molto, the second movement of Beethoven's Op. 110. Example 7 shows my reading of the voice leading of the Trio.[17] Example 8 is the rhythmic reduction. The piece moves mostly in eight-bar units; I have made these into hypermeasures by representing the original measures as eighth notes. (The echoing repetitions in bars 92–95 extend the basic structure while acting as a transition to the return of the Scherzo.) Level c gives the reduction rather literally. The problem is clearly set in relief: the fifth phrase, bars 73–75, is a lone three-bar group, shown by the change of meter signature.[18]

---

17. This reading differs somewhat (though not substantially) from that of Schenker in "Noch einmal zu Beethovens op. 110," in *Meisterwerk* I, p. 181 ("A Postscript to Beethoven's Opus 110," trans. William Drabkin, *Masterwork* I, p. 101). Another reading that includes comments about the rhythmic structure is given by David Beach in "Motivic Repetition in Beethoven's Piano Sonata Opus 110, Part II: The Trio of the Second Movement and the Adagio-Arioso," *Intégral* 2 (1988), pp. 75–97.

18. Beach, "Motivic Repetition," p. 94, suggests that the hypermetric downbeat is shifted by one measure from bar 73 to bar 74. I do not quite agree with this idea, but in any case it does not answer the question I pose here. Schenker refers to these bars as a *Takttriole* and makes the interesting

Example 8 Beethoven, Op. 110, second movement, Trio: rhythmic reduction

It might be tempting to read out these three measures as a parenthetical expansion attached to the previous phrase, but a comparison with Example 7 shows that I regard the events in these bars as essential parts of the voice leading, reaching into a deep level of middleground. Rhythmic expansions should comprise material which is inessential to the tonal structure. In addition, bar 73 clearly begins as if it were going to start a new phrase, which is abruptly cut off.[19] Thus, when level b effects some rhythmic normalization, the anomalous three-hyperbeat group gets a slightly larger value in accordance with its structural value.

> suggestion that the performer give special stress to bar 75 to make up for the lack of a fourth bar; see his *Erläuterungsausgabe, Op. 110*, p. 49; rev. edn, p. 58. Though Riemann sometimes applies the term *Takttriole* to groups of three bars that take the place of two, Schenker does not seem to be invoking any similar idea here; see Riemann's *System der musikalischen Rhythmik und Metrik* (Leipzig: Breitkopf & Härtel, 1903), pp. 107–11, cited in Rothstein, *Phrase Rhythm in Tonal Music*, p. 81.

19. This is also noted in Beach, "Motivic Repetition," p. 94.

Level a poses the most perplexing question: What would happen if we gave the odd hypermeasure a duration that renders it commensurate with the others in this piece? This hypothetical reading yields a perfectly regular construction of eight hypermeasures for the entire Trio. (Hypermetric numbering appears for the first time at this level because this regularity is so easily heard as metric.) However, moving from this deep level of hierarchy to the surface would require that the fifth and sixth hypermeasures be contracted by six and a half hyperbeats, or *thirteen actual measures*, to reach level c. One might well ask: Where are these thirteen missing measures?

It is, of course, a relatively mechanical job to fill out what might have occurred in this obsessively mono-motivic piece. Since bar 73 seems about to begin a new phrase tonicizing the II chord, one can simply follow the pattern of one subphrase prolonging the starting chord followed by a second subphrase that moves to the next goal. Example 9a presents one possible realization. (The original melodic figure, which was the subject of a good deal of last-minute tinkering by Beethoven, is rather awkward in minor; the fact that this possible transposition is sidestepped in an especially quirky manner suggests an interesting tangent to the idea of musical inevitability.) I will assume that my readers are as skeptical as I am of an analysis that requires the supposition of thirteen measures not actually in the piece. However, there are good reasons to think of the odd group as a contraction. The most important is seeded in the work's repeating melodic idea: a rhythmic shape that arches across the entire hypermeasure, as in the Op. 27 Trio, but this time with an even more pronounced emphasis on the first and eighth bars. In fact, the bars in between are so de-emphasized by the very much softer dynamics, the lack of pedal, the lack of the low register, and most of all, the ambiguous offbeats that they sound almost parenthetical. It is as if the inner measures of each hypermeasure are ready to collapse in under the weight of the outer pillars.[20]

Just this seems to happen in bar 73. Notice in Example 9a that the eight-measure double octave descent g♭^{3}–g♭^{1} is sharply condensed to a single abrupt octave in the actual piece. It is as if the record skipped (or the compact disc jumped). Or perhaps as if the pianist were momentarily lost: note that in Example 9a the right-hand figure at the beginning, which is bar 73 as it literally occurs, is duplicated later on in my realization. In fact, we have heard this figure before, in bar 45, as the beginning of dominant seventh harmony destined to return to the tonic, and I use it in my version of the "missing" measures to get back to the tonic. In bar 73 of the actual piece (see Example 9b), the music seems uncertain of whether it is in the right place: it scrambles to supply the bass note C that went with the figure in bar 45 and to somehow get back on track. This is once again the dynamic element I identified in the Op. 27 Trio, but used in an oddly opposite way. In Op. 27, the music returned to the same place three times and took a different path each time, expanding the content. In this piece, the melodic coincidence enables a jump over measures that might have happened.

---

20. This is graphically underscored in the picture provided by Beethoven's earliest sketch of this Trio (Artaria 197, folio 75), where the opening four notes, marked *fortissimo*, lead to a series of empty bars marked *piano*; transcribed in Karl Michael Komma, *Die Klaviersonate As-dur Opus 110: Beiheft zur Faksimile-Ausgabe* (Stuttgart: Ichthys Verlag, 1967), p. 12.

Example 9 Beethoven, Op. 110, second movement, Trio: the "missing" measures

a) Hypothetical version

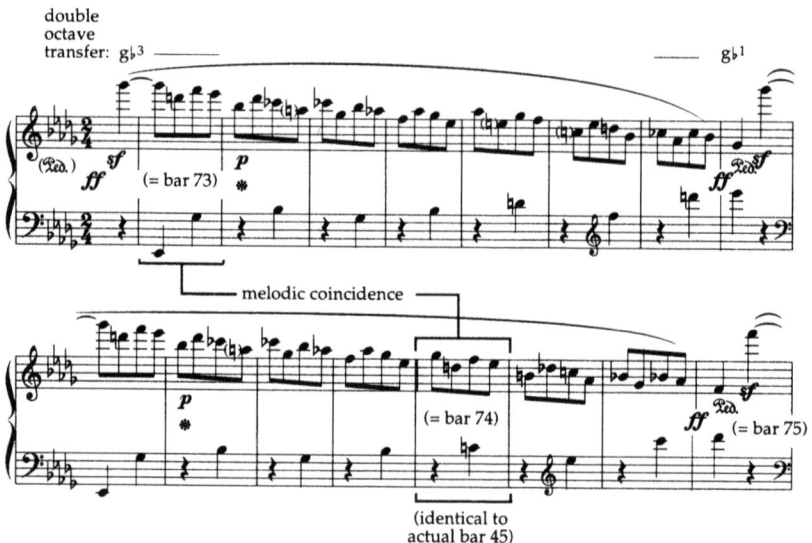

b) Contraction in the actual piece

Unusual as it is, this contraction forms part of a larger plot that encompasses the whole movement.[21] I will begin to unfold this story by comparing the overall rhythm of the Trio and the Scherzo. Example 10 shows the end of the Trio and the beginning of the Allegro and suggests that these two sections are on what I call different *temporal planes*.[22] The final third-descent is echoed in a quarter–eighth–eighth rhythm that is immediately juxtaposed against a basic pace of quarters and halves. In the return to the Scherzo, we experience a shift to a temporal plane mostly characterized by events moving twice as slowly as before. (Of course I am not referring to a change in tempo.) This feeling of deceleration seems to be continued in the ritardando that follows.

21. The sense of plot here is consonant with that of Fred Maus in "Music as Drama," *Music Theory Spectrum* 10 (1988), pp. 56–73; see also Richard Cohn, "The Dramatization of Hypermetric Conflicts in the Scherzo of Beethoven's Ninth Symphony," *19th-Century Music* 15/3 (1992), pp. 188–206.
22. Temporal planes are more fully discussed in my dissertation, "Temporal Plasticity in Beethoven's Late Music" (Ph.D. diss., The City University of New York, in preparation).

Example 10 Beethoven, Op. 110, second movement: transition between two temporal planes

Having established this relationship, we can consider the beginning of the Scherzo, which at first presents two rhythmically unproblematic four-bar groups.[23] Trouble starts in bar 9 with the third phrase, which seems to lose its balance momentarily. A normalized version is given in Example 11a: I have taken the 5–6 series and evened out the rate of its ascent. In Example 11b a rhythmic shift backwards contracts the second measure and creates in the piece what I call a "shadow" meter. The main meter, the meter as written, casts a shadow, as it were, of a subsidiary, displaced meter, which we are drawn to hear as real until it dissolves in the seventh measure. Notice that this shadow meter takes over more strongly in the first ending: the first chord comes in too early, effacing the written bar line. The ambiguous meter shifts the weight of the phrase onto the final A♭ chord.

Equilibrium is restored for the next four four-bar groups, but the final phrase, bars 33–40, is the most disruptive. Examples 12a and 12b give my hypothetical normalized version and its actual manifestation. The fifth bar of the model is shifted backwards with an almost violent contraction. As if shocked, the piece falls silent, quickly recovers and scrambles to squeeze in the dominant in contracted form. This time the effect is more profound than before: a shadow meter appears a full bar off the main meter, segmenting the eight-bar phrase into three plus four plus one.[24]

We are immediately thrown back into confusion at the first ending, as shown in Example 11c; the second ending (Example 12c) flies headlong into the kaleidoscopic rhythms of the Trio. Here the same shadow meter that takes over at the first ending is pervasively carried through in the right-hand *sforzandi* and the left-hand offbeats. The shadow meter explodes into sudden prominence just at the three measures (bars 73–75; see Example 12d) that severely disturb the symmetry of the Trio. Now the *sforzando* chords seem less of an anomaly

---

23. I leave aside the question of whether the even-numbered bars should receive metric accents in a sort of gavotte rhythm, a point which greatly concerns Donald Francis Tovey, who accepts the resultant rhythmic ambiguity as an inherent value; see *A Companion to Beethoven's Pianoforte Sonatas* (London: Associated Board, 1931), pp. 274–76.

24. Schenker also groups these bars in this way, without implying a manipulation of a more basic structure; see his *Erläuterungsausgabe, Op. 110*, p. 46; rev. edn, pp. 50–51.

Example 11 Beethoven, Op. 110, second movement, Allegro molto: contraction through rhythmic shift

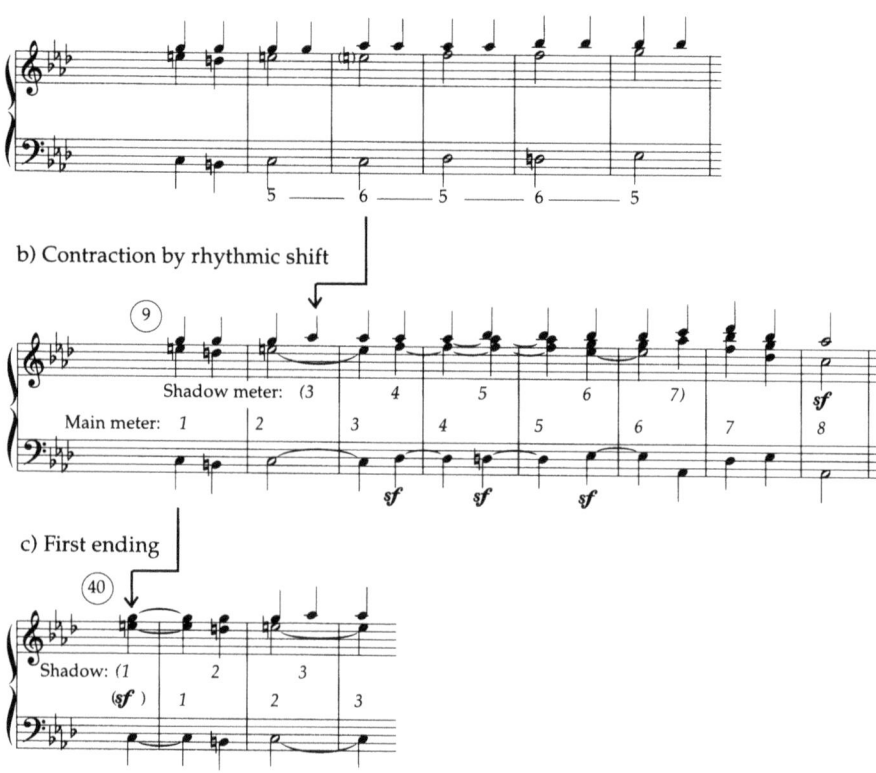

and more part of a gesture that has been disrupting the rhythmic surface since bar 10.

The disruption is not forgotten when the Allegro repeats, but this time, at the second ending, bar 143, the problem is dealt with. The final bar of the phrase (shown in Example 12e) is at last allowed, through elision, to be a strong first measure after which the *sforzando* chords of the coda sound as offbeats.[25] In the temporal plane of the Allegro, in which events occur twice as slowly as in that of the Trio, these hypermetric offbeats correspond to the *sforzando* metric offbeats of the Trio. In the complete coda (Example 12f), this offbeat gesture is allowed to come to a rhythmic resolution in the context of a large-scale eight-bar hypermeasure, while the continuous eighths of the cadenza-like ending fill out the last two hyperbeats by explicitly recalling the Trio.[26]

25. Both Schenker, *Erläuterungsausgabe, Op. 110*, p. 46 (rev. edn, pp. 50–51), and Schachter, "Rhythm and Linear Analysis: Durational Reduction," p. 199, remark that Beethoven's sketch notation tends to confirm the syncopated status of these chords; for a transcription of the sketch (Artaria 197, folio 74), see Komma, "Die Klaviersonate As-dur," p. 11, and Schachter, "Rhythm and Linear Analysis: Durational Reduction," Example 2b.
26. The resolution provided by the coda is heightened by a melodic conflict as well: two separate melodic characters seem to centrifugate from the opening c^2. The descending sixth of the opening

Example 12 Beethoven, Op. 110, second movement, Allegro molto: final phrase and coda

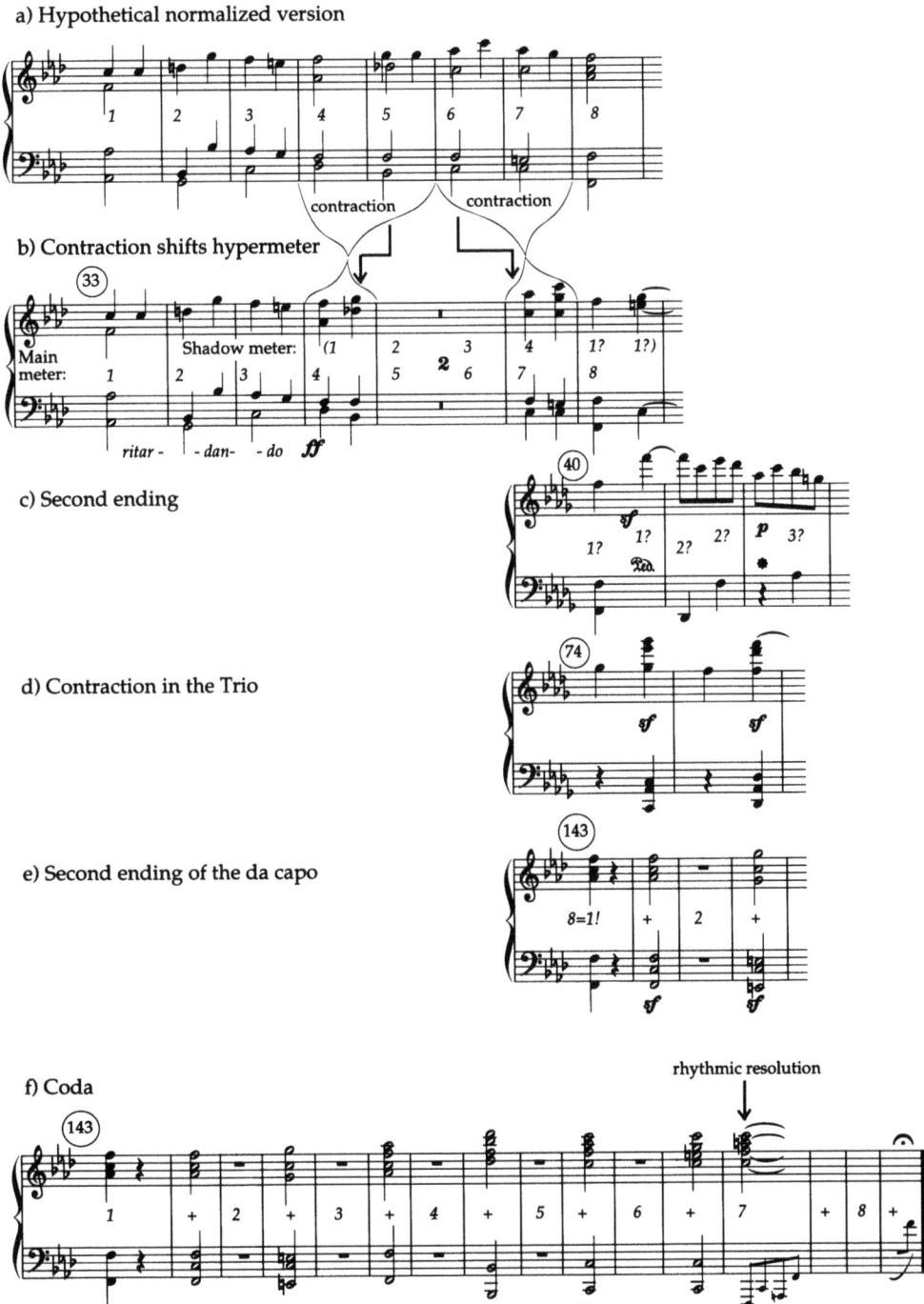

I am not saying that this coda makes up for the missing measures of this Trio (that seems rather artificial to me), but rather that the foreground rhythmic gesture is taken up again and resolved. More important, this foreground issue is essential to understanding the deeper levels of hierarchy. In tonal analysis, the analogous idea might be Schenker's concept of *Fühlungnahme*, the rapport or contact among the levels, the unifying impulses that span and connect and transform each level.[27] Schenker typically speaks of this rapport as emanating from background to foreground. It is perhaps essential to the nature of rhythmic analysis that the opposite seems to occur: immediate gestures penetrate to deeper levels and disturb their stability.

As to the problem presented by Example 8, the hierarchical presentation does a powerful job of setting the issue in clear relief. Nonetheless, this movement has such an individual and eccentric rhythmic wrinkle that a simple model cannot iron it out. Thus the top level, level x, is truly a falsification. The tension between levels a and b best captures the essential deeper structure, but the musical action here is so drastic in nature as to be fundamentally irreconcilable with regular patterning. It does not fit into an architecture; it collapses it.

I have shown instances of expansion and contraction that are embedded deeply into rhythmic structure and that represent impulses fundamentally at odds with the principles of regularity. The symmetries of rhythmic regularity must be experienced in time, but that very experience can blur those symmetries. The uses that composers made of this possibility is what rhythmic analysis must try to capture, since it is often the source of the most perfect beauty.

I began this essay with a quotation from Bacon; I will close with a more extended quotation from another source, jumping asymmetrically from about two centuries before Beethoven to about one century after. In her early diaries, Virginia Woolf expressed a concern about a contrast, similar to the one I have discussed, between the contemplation of beauty as statically proportionate and as jarringly conflicted. While in Italy in 1908, she wrote:

> I looked at a fresco by Perugino. I conceive that he saw things grouped, contained in certain & invisible forms; expression in faces, action . . . did not exist . . . not a hint of past or future.
>
> As for writing – I want to express beauty too – but beauty (symmetry? of life & the world, in action. Conflict? — is that it?
>
> I attain a different kind of beauty, achieve a symmetry by means of infinite discords, showing all the traces of the mind[']s passage through the world; & achieve in the end, some kind of whole made of shivering fragments; to me this seems the natural process; the flight of the mind.[28]

---

bars is associated with a decrease of intensity. Its opposite is the upward motion, pulling against gravity with a more intense *forte*; it begins at the c^2 in bar 6 and struggles to complete the sixth up to $a\flat^2$ in bar 16. These two qualities try to reconcile at bars 33–35, with explosive results at bar 36. But, at the coda, the rising tension is finally released as the *sforzandi* give way to a *decrescendo* to *piano* in a sort of *lieto fine* to the conflict.

27. Schachter discusses this concept in "A Commentary on Schenker's *Free Composition*," *Journal of Music Theory* 25/1 (1981), pp. 121–22.
28. Virginia Woolf, *A Passionate Apprentice: The Early Journals, 1897–1909*, ed. Mitchell A. Leaska (New York: Harcourt Brace Jovanovich, 1992), pp. 392–93.

Diachronic transformation in a Schenkerian context: Brahms's Haydn Variations

Timothy Jackson

In the *Cours de linguistic générale,* Ferdinand de Saussure distinguishes between "synchronic" and "diachronic" linguistic transformation. Synchronic transformation results from the application of logical, recursive operations. Diachronic transformation, by contrast, is neither logical elaboration nor reduction but – from a synchronic perspective – distortion. Saussure further identifies different "language states," which can be mapped, by synchronic and diachronic transformations, from one onto another. Jonathan Culler elucidates Saussure's use of the term "diachronic":

> Saussure argues that despite their different status, diachronic statements are derived from synchronic statements. What allows us, he asks, to state the fact that Latin "mare" became French "mer" ("sea")? The historical linguist might argue that we know "mare" became "mer" because here, as elsewhere, the final "e" was dropped and "a" became "e". But, Saussure argues, to suggest that these regular sound changes are what create the link between the two forms is to get things backward, because what enables us to identify this sound change is our initial notion that one form became the other.... Whence the importance of separating the synchronic and diachronic perspectives, even when the facts that they are treating seem inextricably intertwined.... Saussure is all too aware of the intertwining of synchronic and diachronic facts; indeed, for him the whole difficulty is one of separating these elements when they are mixed.... Linguistic forms have synchronic and diachronic aspects which must be separated because they are *facts of a different order* with different conditions of existence.[1]

The present study proposes that Saussure's distinction between synchronic and diachronic "facts of a different order" can illuminate the entelechy of musical structure as viewed from a Schenkerian perspective.[2] A musical work may embody in its endstate a conceptually prior state, which has become the endstate through a diachronic transformation (see Figure 1). From a synchronic perspective, the endstate is a "distortion" of the "previous" state and vice versa. Diachronic transformation is essentially different from voice-leading transformation. Voice-leading transformation assumes structure to be in a steady state, all structural levels embodied and undistorted in the endstate.

---

1. Jonathan Culler, *Ferdinand de Saussure* (London: Penguin, 1980), p. 29 (emphasis added).
2. This essay is based on studies of diachronic transformation in the context of Schenkerian analysis begun in 1984. I wish to thank Nicholas Marston for his valuable comments and suggestions, and I gratefully acknowledge support from a Canada Research Grant provided by the Social Sciences and Humanities Research Council of Canada (1989–91), which facilitated research at the Oswald Jonas Collection. Further research was conducted with support from a Senior Fulbright Teaching and Research Award (1994–95).

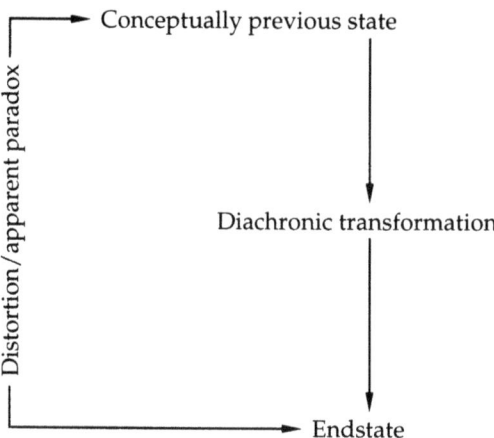

Figure 1 Diachronic transformation in a Schenkerian context

Diachronic transformation ruptures a steady state to create a duality of previous state and endstate and, from a single synchronic perspective, distortion and paradox.

An anamorph may provide, in the visual domain, a striking analogy for diachronic phenomena in music. To take one example, an observer facing the seventeenth-century mural by Emmanuel Maignan in the cloister of S. Trinità dei Monti in Rome sees a landscape with lakes, ships, towns, and mountains. Simultaneously embedded within this landscape, however, is a distorted image of a saint, who appears when the observer is shifted so as to view the fresco from the side.[3] The painting is "paradoxically dualistic"; it compels internally self-consistent but mutually exclusive interpretations. The work exists in two states, each a distortion from the perspective of the other: the saint is a distorted landscape, the landscape a distorted saint. The activation of one endstate over the other depends upon a spatial shift of the observer.

In a musical context, where the artwork is not a physical object in three-dimensional space, it is impossible to distinguish competing states through a spatial shift of the perceiver. Instead, from a synchronic hearing of a temporally unfolding endstate, the listener may intuit a conceptually earlier state which has metamorphosed into the endstate through a diachronic transformation. Tonal structures which seem paradoxical when heard exclusively from a synchronic perspective may not be self-contradictory when heard diachronically. In the discussion that follows, I shall attempt to show that apparently paradoxical passages in Brahms's Variations on a Theme of Haydn, Op. 56a and 56b, are produced by diachronic transformation.

---

3. See Fred Leeman, *Hidden Images, Games of Perception, Anamorphic Art, Illusion, from the Renaissance to the Present* (New York: Abrams, 1976); Jurgis Baltrusaitis, *Anamorphic Art* (Cambridge: Chadwyck Healy, 1966).

Apparent paradox in the theme of the Haydn Variations

In an essay entitled "Brahms and the Classical Tradition," first published in May 1897, the British music critic W. H. Hadow eulogizes Brahms as "the last great representative of the Classical tradition in German music."[4] The analysis to be presented here, however, calls attention to paradoxical, even anti-Classical aspects of the theme and Brahms's variations, aspects produced in part by diachronic transformation. Dualism and apparent paradox in the theme seem uncharacteristic of Haydn; indeed, the origins of the theme and the authenticity of Haydn's setting are uncertain.[5] The theme's contradictory implications perhaps provoked Heinrich Schenker to conceive differing readings. Contradictions between Schenker's analyses will serve as the point of departure for the technical discussion.

For the student of Brahms's Haydn Variations, there is an unparalleled wealth of source material. Not only are several of Brahms's *Stichvorlagen* extant, but also – quite remarkably, since Brahms habitually destroyed his working manuscripts – a folder of sketches is preserved in the Gesellschaft der Musikfreunde's Brahms collection. This autograph material has been discussed in considerable detail by Alfred Orel and more recently by Donald McCorkle and Ernst Hilmar.[6] A reexamination of the sketches for Variations 6 and 8, however, sheds new light on the genesis of Brahms's compositional strategy.

Schenker's analyses of the Haydn Variations, all of the orchestral version,[7] are preserved in several sources. Schenker's personal copy of the orchestral score, now in the Oswald Jonas Memorial Collection at the University of California, Riverside, contains an extensive series of analytical annotations in pencil and colored pencil. Graphs of the orchestral version of the Chorale, the variations, and the Finale (written in pencil, pen, and colored pencil) are in a private collection; they are among Schenker's papers that were in the possession of Felix Salzer. These graphs serve as the basis for a multi-level graph of the Chorale published by the editors of *Der Dreiklang*.[8] Hastily notated sketches on

---

4. W. H. Hadow, *Collected Essays* (London: Oxford University Press, 1928), p. 136. It is interesting that Brahms was described as a "Classical" composer just after his death but not – as far as I have been able to ascertain – during his lifetime, that is, by those critics for whom Brahms was a "modern" or "contemporary" composer. Angelika Horstmann's dissertation, *Untersuchungen zur Brahms-Rezeption der Jahre 1860 bis 1880* (Hamburg: Karl Dieter Wagner, 1986), pp. 234–49, suggests that contemporary critics do not seem to have identified the Haydn Variations, although based on a theme attributed to Haydn, as a "Classical" work.
5. See Donald M. McCorkle, ed., *Brahms: Variations on a Theme of Haydn*, Norton Critical Score (New York: Norton, 1976), pp. 27–32 (in the chapter "Genesis and the Creative Process").
6. See Alfred Orel, "Skizzen zu Johannes Brahms' Haydn-Variationen," *Zeitschrift für Musikwissenschaft* 5/6 (1923), pp. 296–315; McCorkle's opening chapters in the Norton Critical Score of the work (which includes facsimiles and transcriptions of the sketch pages); and Ernst Hilmar's facsimile edition of the two-piano version, *Johannes Brahms: Variationen für zwei Klaviere über ein Thema von Joseph Haydn, Op. 56b. Faksimile-Ausgabe nach dem Originalmanuskript im Besitz der Musiksammlung der Wiener Stadt- und Landesbibliothek* (Tutzing: Hans Schneider, 1989).
7. In the following discussion, the earlier two-piano version (Op. 56b, 1873) and later orchestral version (Op. 56a, 1874) will be assumed to be structurally identical, except in the eighth variation (see my discussion of Variation 8, below).
8. Schenker, "Urlinientafel zu Haydns 'Chorale St. Antoni,'" *Der Dreiklang* 6 (September 1937), pp. 138–39. I am grateful to Mrs. Felix Salzer, who kindly granted access to Schenker's manuscript graphs of the Haydn Variations in the collection now in her possession, and gave me permission to publish my transcriptions of some of them.

small slips of paper (*Zetteln*), which served as the basis for the graphs owned by Salzer and for the examples in *Der freie Satz*, are preserved in the Oster Collection of the New York Public Library.[9]

Generally speaking, the annotations in the score predate the graphs owned by Salzer. Analysis of the *Zetteln* suggests that they also predate some of the later annotations in the graphs owned by Salzer and the analysis published in *Der freie Satz*. Determining chronology is complicated by distinct layers of annotations and corrections in each of the sources, including the *Zetteln*, which reflect several passes through both the quick sketches and the worked-out graphs at different times.[10] In the score, the passages of detailed harmonic analysis may well be from an earlier period than the careted numbers, slurs, stems and beams indicating linear progressions. It should be noted that some of the pencilled harmonic analysis in the score seems to have been erased; when Schenker entered the careted numbers, slurs, stems and beams, he may have no longer completely agreed with parts of his earlier harmonic analysis. The use of careted numbers without brackets suggests that these particular annotations postdate 1926 and are probably from the late twenties.

While Schenker had arrived at the concept of interruption by the time item 35/81 in the Oster Collection and the graphs owned by Salzer were set down, the interruption symbol, which appears in the graphs of the variations (as seen in Example 9a) but not of the theme, is also absent from the annotated score. The analysis of the theme in item 35/81, which probably served as the basis for the early analysis of the Chorale in Salzer's collection, seems to be intimately connected with the development of the concept of interruption (around the years 1926–29). In this *Zettel* (shown in Plate 1 and Example 2) Schenker carefully studies the antecedent–consequent interruption form of the Chorale's initial ten-measure phrase, comparing it with the antecedent–consequent interruption form of the theme of the Adagio of Beethoven's Piano Sonata Op. 2, No. 1 (this is shown in Example 2f). At some point after setting down the graphs of the variations in pencil, Schenker went over them again in red pencil. The most important of these red pencil annotations (which will be marked "[r]" in my transcriptions) reinforce the reading of interruption (as seen, for example, in Schenker's analyses of Variation 5, Examples 10a and 11a; again, these annotations seem to be connected with the development of the concept of interruption. The graphs of the theme and variations that are in Salzer's collection were probably made in the late twenties or early thirties. Schenker's use of beams in these graphs to show third- and fourth-progressions is typical of the period of the *Fünf Urlinie-Tafeln* (1932). Significantly, the Chorale is included in Schenker's list of compositions for which he eventually planned to publish graphic analyses.[11] I shall argue that Schenker revised the graph of the

---

9. I shall refer to specific items in the Oster Collection by the numbers assigned to them by Robert Kosovsky in *The Oster Collection: Papers of Heinrich Schenker. A Finding List* (New York: New York Public Library, 1990). The first number identifies the file, the second the individual item. The relevant *Zetteln* are items 10/59, 22/40, 22/46, and 35/81.
10. In "Current Issues in Schenkerian Analysis," *The Musical Quarterly* 76/2 (1992), p. 250, I called attention to the importance of chronological distinctions in the Schenker manuscript sources.
11. Schenker prepared this list in connection with the work of an informal seminar he held during this time. Felix Salzer, who was a member of the seminar, relates its work to Schenker's preparation of

theme that is found in Salzer's collection – most likely in the years 1934–35 – in light of the analysis he set down in a late *Zettel* (item 22/40) associated with his work on *Der freie Satz*.

Examples 1a–1d, 1g, and 1j present the analysis of the theme published in *Der Dreiklang* (which was based upon the graph of the Chorale owned by Salzer). By indicating the simultaneous prolongation of tonic and dominant at the beginning of the B section (bars 11–14), this published analysis is self-contradictory. The fundamental contradiction is revealed by comparing middle-ground levels 1 though 4 (the numbering of these levels follows *Der Dreiklang*). Level 1 (Example 1c) asserts tonic prolongation until the arrival of the subdominant in the fifth measure of the B section (bar 15), which supports the neighbor-note $e\flat^2$. However, in level 2 (Example 1d), the slur I have marked x – from the f^1 in the bass after the double bar (bar 11) to the $b\flat$ (bar 19) – indicates dominant prolongation through the *entire* B section. This slur contradicts the notated *Stufen* IV and V^7, which presumably still come from the initial I. The contradiction between levels 1 and 2 intensifies in level 3 (Example 1g). In the upper voice, the dotted slurs I have marked u and v show d^2 and $b\flat^1$, both members of the tonic triad, being prolonged through the first four measures of the B section (level 1), while the slurs marked x and y, from f^1 to f^1 and from f^1 to $b\flat$ in the bass, signify dominant prolongation through the entire B section (level 2). The contradiction becomes even more striking when one compares the *Stufen* in levels 1 and 2 with those in level 4 (Example 1j). In levels 1 and 2, the indicated *Stufen* are IV–V^7, while level 4 shows the prolongation of V^7.

Turning now to Schenker's earlier harmonic analysis in his score, the beginning of the B section in the theme is unanalyzed. However, the parallel points in some of the variations are analyzed. In Variations 1, 3, 5, 6, and 8, Schenker places V in parentheses at the beginning of the B section. These parentheses indicate that Schenker understands the dominant at points analogous to bars 11–13 as totally dependent upon the tonic which follows at points analogous to bar 14. This reading is consistent with level 1 of the graph in *Der Dreiklang*, which shows tonic harmony prolonged through the first four measures of the B section (Example 1c). It is, however, inconsistent with those aspects of levels 2 through 4, which indicate dominant prolongation coinciding with the beginning of the B section.

In the *Zettel* in the Oster Collection, item 35/81 (which I date 1926–29; see Plate 1 and the transcription in Example 2), the reading of the B section is closely related both to the score analysis and to the analysis in level 1 of the graph owned by Salzer. In this sketch, *both* the dominant in bars 11–13 and the tonic in bar 14 are placed in parentheses. At least three chronological layers can be discerned in Schenker's reading of the top voice of the B section in item 35/81. Initially, Schenker seems to have read the $e\flat^2$ as a neighbor note to the d^2, which is supported by I (Example 2a). Then he considered the possibility of a $\hat{5}$-line (see Example 2b) whereby f^2 ($\hat{5}$) in parentheses leads down to a passing

---

graphs for publication and includes a facsimile of the list in the introduction to his edition of Schenker's *Five Graphic Music Analyses*, pp. 17–21. The graphs of the theme and the variations in Salzer's collection may have been prepared by Schenker for use in the seminar.

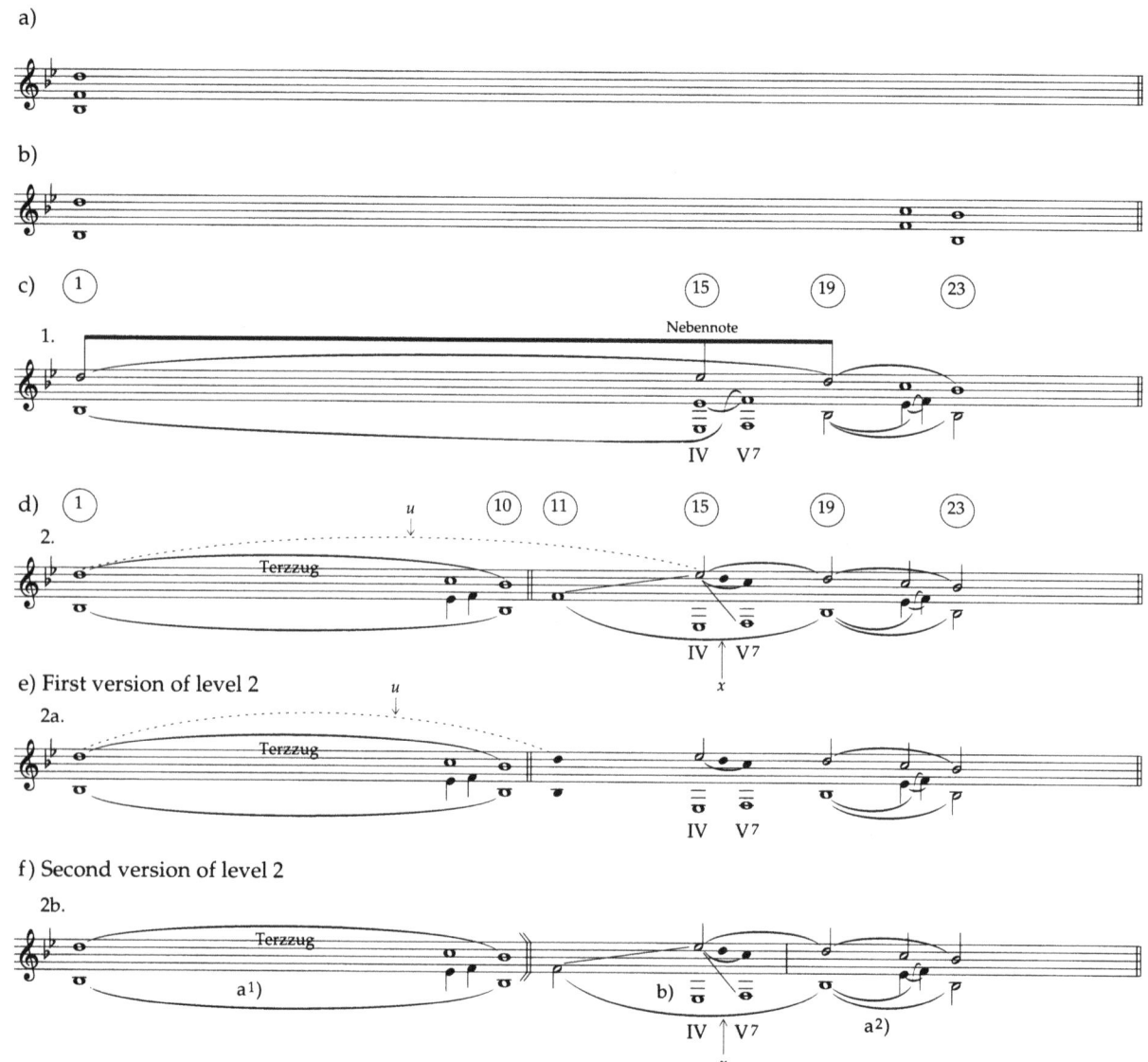

Example 1 Analysis of the theme as published in *Der Dreiklang* and transcription of Schenker's sketches as found in the collection of Felix Salzer

tone e♭² (4̂) and through d² (3̂) to c² (2̂). The comment "dann an 5" seems to refer to this reading; perhaps this observation implicitly signifies that 5̂ is placed above 3̂ rather than that 5̂ displaces 3̂ as *Kopfton*. Schenker subsequently rejected this interpretation in favor of his original reading of e♭² as a neighbor note, writing a large "4̂" in blue pencil above the e♭² (Example 2c). On the staves above the ascending sixth f¹–d² he added the note "aus der Mittelstimme."

In the lower left margin of item 35/81, Schenker then set down a background sketch (labeled "Ursatz") of the entire theme (Example 2e), showing the e♭² as a neighbor note (as in Example 2c); directly above, he circled the careted

numbers labeled "Urlinie" (Example 2d). The almost exact concordance between the *Ursatz* of item 35/81 and level 1 of the graph owned by Salzer (compare Examples 1c and 2e) suggests that item 35/81 served as a preparatory sketch for the early reading of the theme found in the Salzer graphs. On the other hand, another *Zettel*, item 22/40 (see Plate 2 and Example 3), emphatically contradicts item 35/81 by indicating dominant prolongation: a slur (marked *x* in Example 3) connects the Roman numeral Vs at the beginning and end of the B section. The foreground harmonic analysis published in Figure 42/2 of *Der freie Satz* (Example 4a) essentially duplicates the harmonic analysis of item 22/40. Notice, however, that Schenker further values the initial dominant and devalues the subsequent I–IV–II–V progression with the equal sign

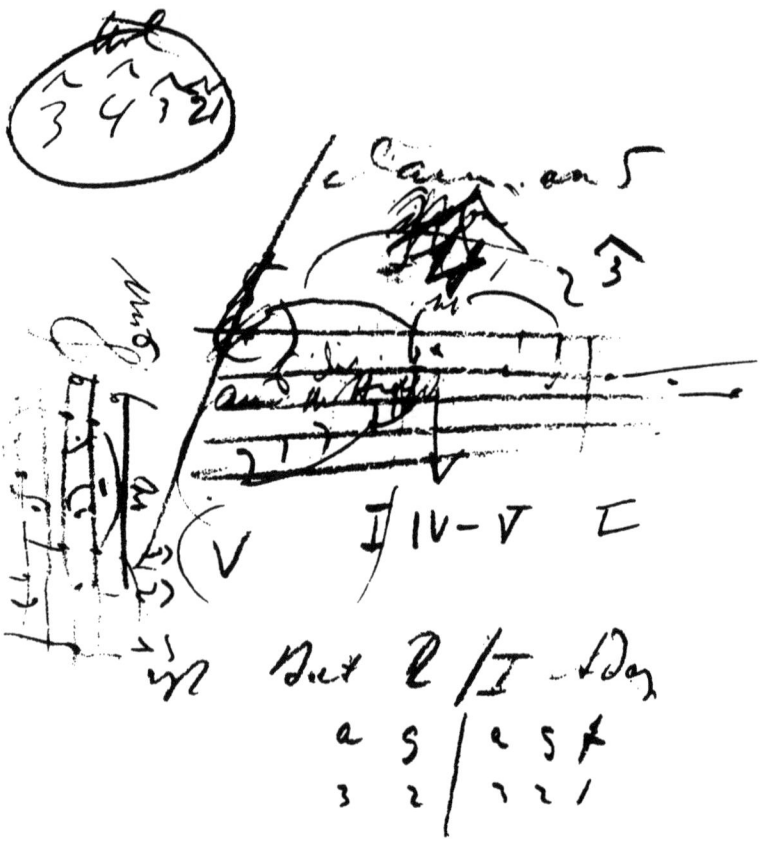

Plate 1 Schenker's sketch of the theme: the B section and the background as found in item 35/81, Oster Collection

and the parentheses. To summarize, the latest foreground harmonic analysis published in *Der freie Satz* inverts the earliest analysis found in the score and also in item 35/81. In the score analysis and in item 35/81, the initial dominant in bar 11 is dependent on a continuing tonic prolongation, whereas in item 22/40 and *Der freie Satz* the initial dominant is prolonged through bars 11–18.

Returning to the analysis of the Chorale published in *Der Dreiklang*, the above-cited contradictions result from the superimposition of elements from Schenker's earlier and later readings. Without crossing out or erasing elements of his earlier reading, Schenker appears to have made revisions – based on the analysis in item 22/40 – in his graph of the theme as found in Salzer's collection. The earlier readings of levels 2 and 3 preserved in the autograph sketches (which I have transcribed as levels 2a and 3a in Examples 1e and 1h) are clearly consistent with level 1 (Example 1c). In both levels 2a and 3a, the dotted slur I have marked *u* connects the initial d^2 with the d^2 in the B section (not with the neighbor note eb^2, as in level 2 of the graph in *Der Dreiklang*; see Example 1d). In the earlier version of level 3 (level 3a, Example 1h), the slur marked *u* is consistent with bass slurs marked *s* and *t*, which show tonic prolongation continuing through the beginning of the B section, supporting d^2. However, with the

Example 2 Schenker's sketch of the theme: the B section and the background as found in item 35/81, Oster Collection (transcription of Plate 1)

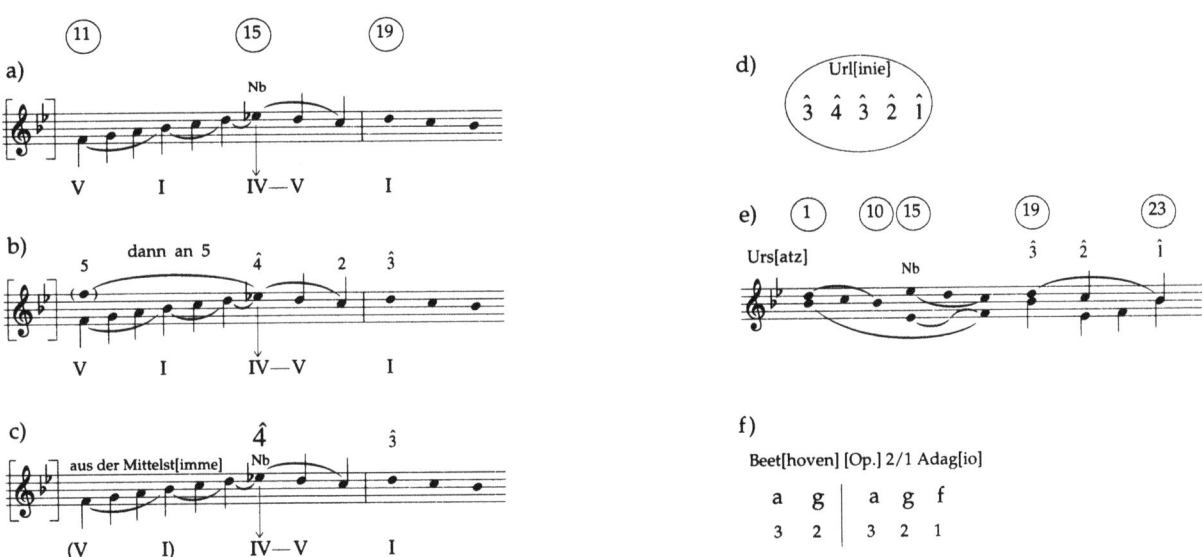

revision of levels 2 and 3 (transcribed as levels 2b and 3b in Examples 1f and 1i), the slurs marked *u*, *v*, *s*, and *t* were implicitly cancelled by slurs *x* and *y*. The slur marked *z*, which indicates a (dissonant!) seventh progression f^1–$e\flat^2$ (labeled "Sept" by Schenker) supported by a prolongation of V^7, must have been a very late correction, perhaps even postdating item 22/40.

While it is evident that Schenker decided in favor of the reading of the Chorale published in *Der freie Satz*, the graphs of the variations preserved in Salzer's collection remain consistent with the earlier reading of the theme. I find this discrepancy highly suggestive since it is my belief that, in this very special case, the contradiction highlights an essential aspect of the theme whereby *both* of Schenker's readings are simultaneously valid. This unusual situation results from *structural duality* created by a diachronic transformation embodied in the theme. Although the view of Brahms as a Classical composer (or at least as a Classicist) has persisted, in the past decade the term *ambiguity* – hardly a Classical characteristic – has enjoyed a certain vogue in reference to Brahms's music.[12] This study, however, is not concerned with ambiguity but with structural plurality in which internally self-consistent but mutually exclusive interpretations are simultaneously suggested by the same music.[13]

The contradiction in the sequence of Schenker's readings of the Chorale parallels a discrepancy in an unpublished reading of Brahms's Intermezzo in B♭

12. See, for example, Allen Cadwallader, "Foreground Motivic Ambiguity: Its Clarification at Middleground Levels in Selected Late Piano Pieces of Johannes Brahms," *Music Analysis* 7/1 (1988), pp. 59–91; in reference to Schubert, see Daniel Coren, "Ambiguity in Schubert's Recapitulations," *The Musical Quarterly* 60/4 (1974), pp. 568–82.
13. I tend to use the adjective "ambiguous" very circumspectly, not only because its connotations of indefiniteness, uncertainty, and vagary may be inappropriate, but because structural duality or plurality are frequently mistaken for ambiguity.

Plate 2 Schenker's sketch of the theme: the B section as found in item 22/40, Oster Collection

Example 3 Transcription of Plate 2

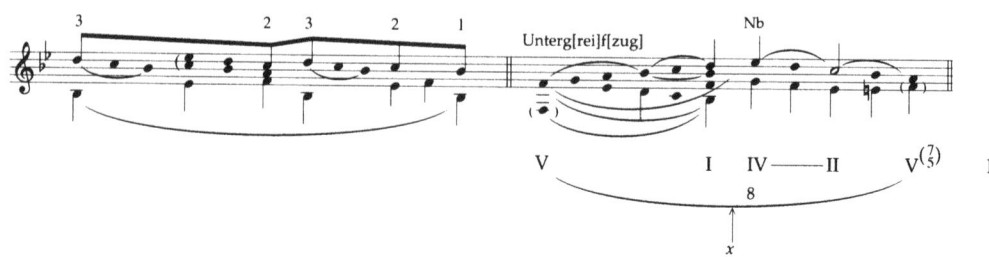

Example 4 Schenker's analysis of the theme in *Der freie Satz*
a) Figure 42/2

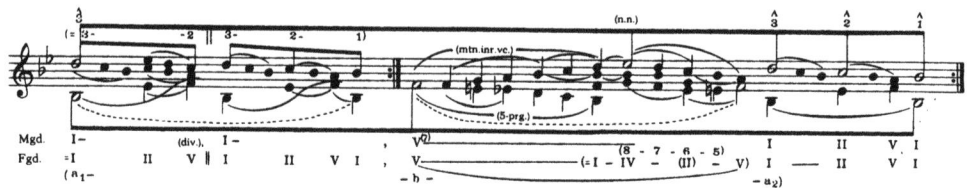

b) Figure 138/3

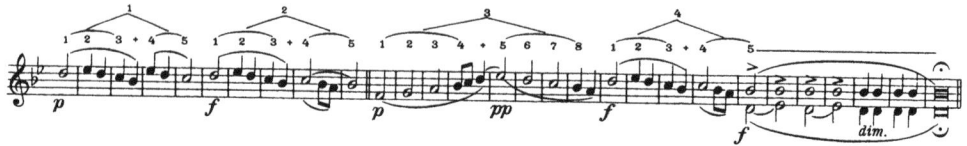

© 1935 Universal Edition AG Wien

minor, Op. 117, No. 2, transcribed by Allen Cadwallader.[14] Schenker had no conceptual way of dealing with such contradictions; therefore, when he came to publish a reading, he was compelled to eliminate them. Because they may document Schenker's intuitive, less rational hearing of a work, the unpublished graphs – with their internal contradictions – sometimes have an even greater richness and resonance than the rationalized, published graphs. Cadwallader's and my own work attempt to provide a conceptual framework in a Schenkerian context, which will allow for and explicate various kinds of pluralities, some of which are related to Schenker's unpublished graphs. However, the structural pluralities created by diachronic transformation are fundamentally different from the ambiguities identified in Cadwallader's article. To simplify matters greatly, Cadwallader is concerned with contradiction between motive and initial context. The present study investigates much more radical pluralities, which occur deep in the background and middleground. McCorkle observes that "with respect to the Haydn Variations, we may never know for certain what stimulated Brahms to compose the work."[15] Perhaps, however, Brahms's interest in the Chorale was piqued by the very contradiction which was later to provoke Schenker's contradictory readings. How Brahms understood the theme and exploited its special properties must be the subject of our inquiry.

Diachronic transformation and accentual reinterpretation in the theme

The Chorale provides an example of diachronic transformation in a musical context. It is certainly possible to analyze this theme as a ternary A1 B A2 form in which the antecedent of the A2 is omitted. To be sure, the omission of the antecedent in the A2 of a ternary form is not uncommon in the literature.[16] In my view, however, the Chorale does not simply omit the antecedent of the A2. Rather, the A2's antecedent is represented in the composition but in the guise of a diachronic transformation. In a hypothetical earlier state of the reprise, the antecedent is present in its "original" form, i.e., as equivalent to that of A1 (see Example 5a). The diachronic transformation of the A2's antecedent facilitates formal elision through superimposition of the antecedent of the A2 upon the latter part of the B (see Example 5e). The A2's antecedent appears in a diachronic rather than a synchronic transformation because the antecedent's structure is slightly distorted – not simply elaborated. This diachronic transformation of the antecedent is a form of variation already embedded within the theme itself reinterpreting the antecedent's tonal and rhythmic structures.

The metrical grids in Example 5[17] reveal accentual reinterpretation created by the diachronic transformation of the A2's antecedent and its superimposition

---

14. Cadwallader, "Foreground Motivic Ambiguity," p. 61, Example 1.
15. McCorkle, "Genesis and the Creative Process," p. 27.
16. The theme of Beethoven's *Ode to Joy* provides a famous example of this kind of abbreviation.
17. In the analytical examples featuring metrical grids, boldface squares represent hypermetrically accented measures. Arrows are used to indicate various kinds of accent. Accent may be produced by coincidence of tonal and metrical emphases; the so-called "structural downbeat" is indicated by arrows pointing downward. Non-coincidence of tonal and metrical emphases or syncopation is indicated by arrows pointing upward.

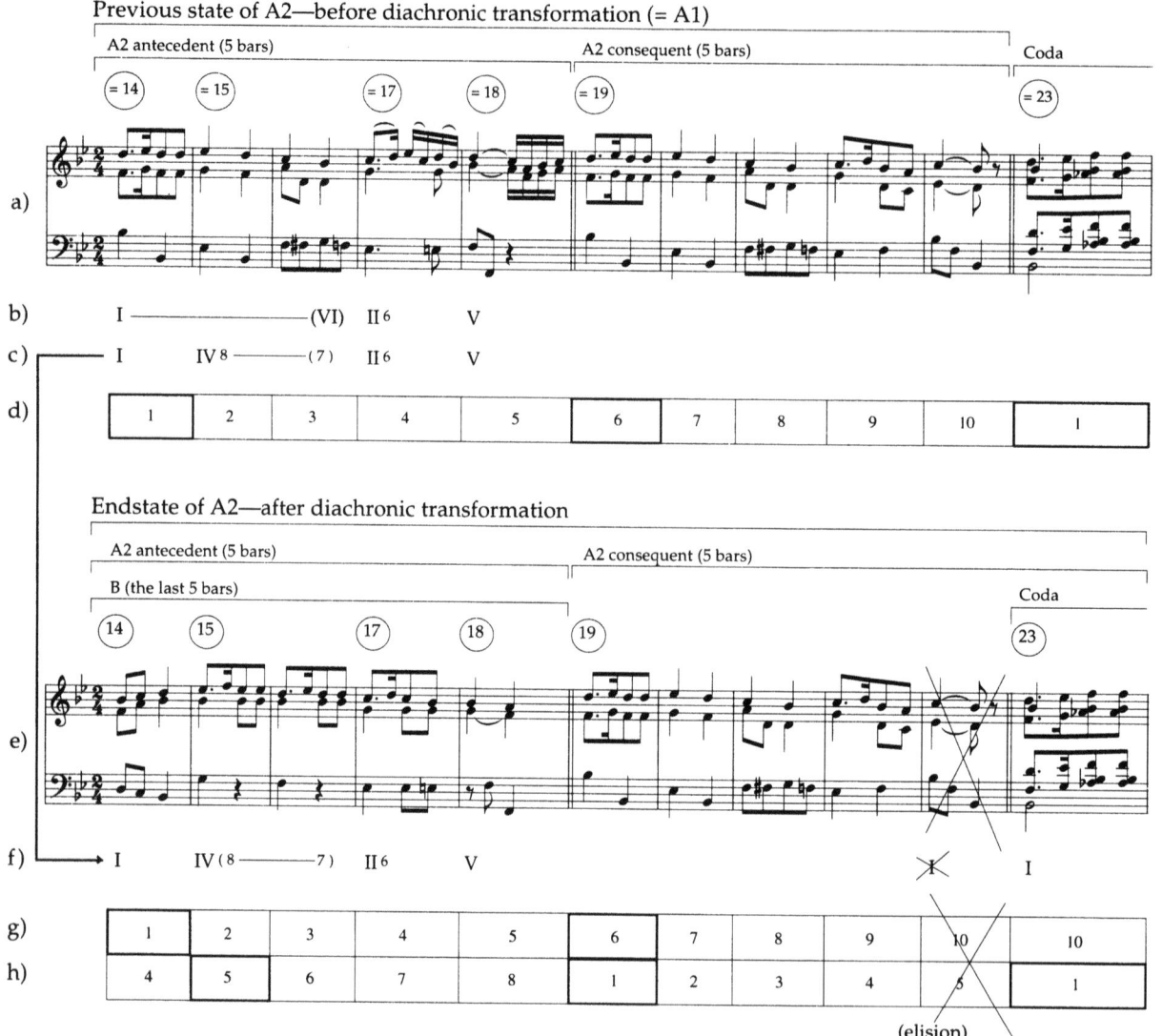

Example 5 The theme (bars 14–23): diachronic transformation of the A2's antecedent

upon the B. As shown by the grids, the diachronic transformation of the A2's antecedent preserves its five-measure durational envelope (Examples 5d, 5g, and 5h), but its superimposition on the last five measures of the B, which is organized as four plus four (equals eight) measures, necessitates accentual reinterpretation.[18] The initial, hypermetrically accented first measure of the A2's antecedent (see Example 5g) is revalued as an unaccented fourth measure, the accent being shifted to its second measure, reinterpreted as the fifth measure

---

18. The early critics noticed the contrast between four- and five-measure phrases. In a review written in 1874, Hermann Kretzschmar noted the theme's "sharply profiled metrical physiognomy" (see Horstmann, *Untersuchungen zur Brahms-Rezeption*, p. 234).

of the B's eight measures (see Example 5h).[19] The A2's consequent also preserves its five-measure duration. Notice, however, the elision of the first measure of the coda and the last measure of the A2's consequent, eliminating the redundant tonic chord (see Examples 5e–5h). Without the elision the total ten-measure duration of the diachronically transformed A2 exactly reproduces the ten-measure duration of the A1.

From a tonal perspective, the diachronic transformation in the theme creates *Ursatz* distortion. Examples 6a and 6b present views of the states of the *Ursatz* before and after the diachronic transformation. As shown in Example 6a, in the primordial version of the theme, the B section prolongs V^7 with the seventh, eb^2, functioning as an upper neighbor to the *Kopfton* d^2. This background structure (prior to the diachronic transformation) is identical to that of Schenker's final reading shown in the graph owned by Salzer (see the slur marked *z* in level 4, Example 1j); it is also the same as that shown in item 22/40 and Figure 42/2 of *Der freie Satz* (which is part of a demonstration of the difference between initial *Anstieg* and *Untergreifen*). However, if the A2's antecedent is represented in bars 11–14, albeit in the guise of a diachronic transformation, the rise to d^2 is latent but repressed by the force of dominant prolongation. Similarly, the interruption on C, which separates the A2's antecedent from its consequent, is present beneath the upper-voice neighbor note Eb. Thus – in conformance with Schenker's earlier readings in his score, with the earlier reading in the graphs in Salzer's collection, and with item 35/81 – bar 14 does, from a diachronic perspective, represent a return to the initial, structural tonic of the antecedent. Schenker's latest reading (in *Der freie Satz*) shows that, after the diachronic transformation, the structural tonic supporting a rise (with voice exchange) to d^2 ($\hat{3}$) is devalued, caught within the prolonged dominant (see the cancelled I and $\hat{3}$ in Example 6b).

Apparent paradox in the theme's larger tonal-formal organization is reflected in microcosm in the A's antecedent. The Chorale's first three measures paradoxically evoke two different, mutually exclusive interpretations. The first, which corresponds to Schenker's reading of these measures, may be reconstructed from the score annotations, the graph owned by Salzer (see Example 1j), and Schenker's remarks accompanying his rhythmic analysis of the theme in *Der freie Satz* (Figure 138/3, reproduced in Example 4b):

> ... in our example, which depicts the foreground, the interpolation of the neighboring note in the first third-progression gives rise to a 3-measure group. Since the second third-progression, eb^2–d^2–c^2, retains its fundamental 2-measure group, a 5-measure group results, clearly divided, however, into 3+2. Thus, this 5-measure ordering is based on a duple ordering, and the second third-progression in measures 4–5 has the effect of an acceleration.[20]

In Schenker's reading, the tonic is prolonged through the first three measures. Figure 42/2 of *Der freie Satz* and the two *Zetteln* in the Oster Collection,

19. Murray Gould, "A Commentary on Schenker's Analytic Sketches," in McCorkle's Norton Critical Score of the work, p. 147, hears bars 14–19 as a paraphrase of bars 5–9. This reading conflicts with my view that the A2's antecedent – not its consequent – is elided with the end of the B.
20. Schenker, *Free Composition*, p. 120. Item 10/59 in the Oster Collection serves as the basis for Figure 138/3 of *Der freie Satz*.

252 Timothy Jackson

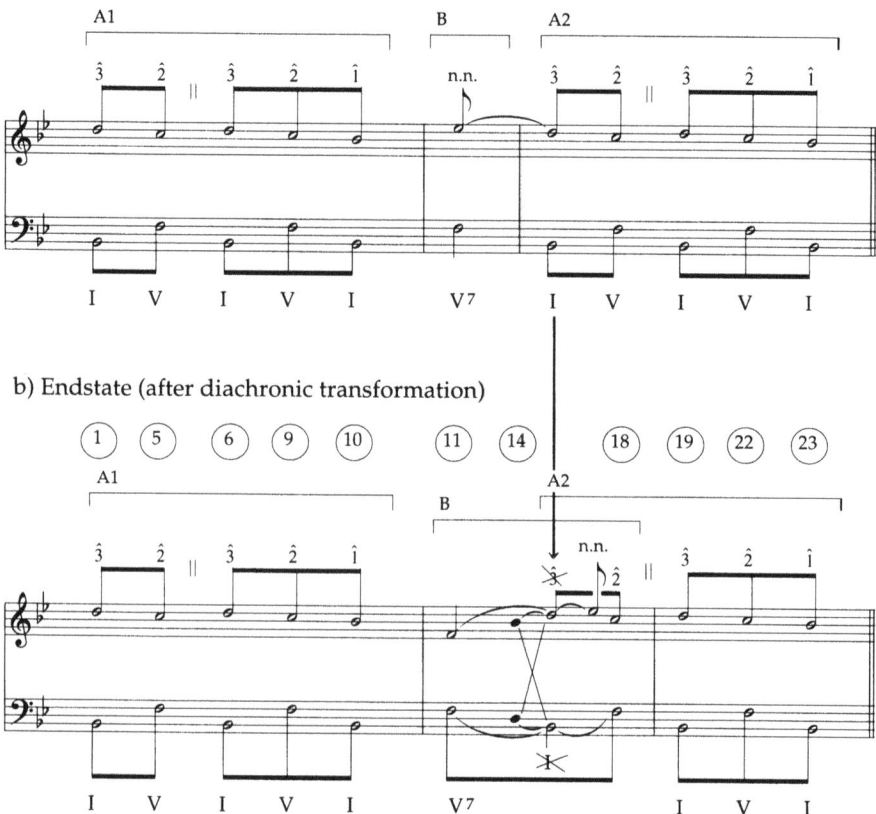

Example 6 The theme: diachronic transformation results in *Ursatz* distortion

a) Previous state (before diachronic transformation)

b) Endstate (after diachronic transformation)

items 35/81 and 22/40, do not show foreground upper voice detail, especially the neighbor note e♭² in bar 2 (mentioned in the commentary quoted above). Nevertheless, it is clear from the commentary, the annotated score, and the graph owned by Salzer that Schenker understands the upper voice in bars 1–3 as a third-progression d²–c²–b♭¹ embellished by an upper neighbor e♭² (see Example 7a and Example 1j). In the bass, Schenker connects the opening B♭ with the low B♭ in bar 2. The G minor chord in bar 3 is created by a 5–6 exchange over an implied B♭ root. In the course of bars 1–4, the bass descends in thirds, outlining the subdominant triad: B♭ (bar 1) to G (bar 3) to E♭ (bar 4).

But the theme simultaneously suggests a different reading of these measures (Example 7c). According to this alternative hearing, the harmony changes in bar 2 as the tonic in bar 1 moves to the subdominant in bar 2. The subdominant is then prolonged as the upper voice descends through the fourth e♭²–b♭¹ while the bass articulates a chromatically filled-in ascending third E♭–F–F♯–G. The G minor chord in bar 3 prolongs the subdominant as its upper third. The descending fourth e♭²–b♭¹ represents a motion into the inner voice, d² being understood (above b♭¹) as a passing seventh given consonant support by the G minor chord leading to c². As the bass regains E♭ in bar 4, the subdominant is

Example 7 The theme (bars 1–5): alternative readings of the tonal structure

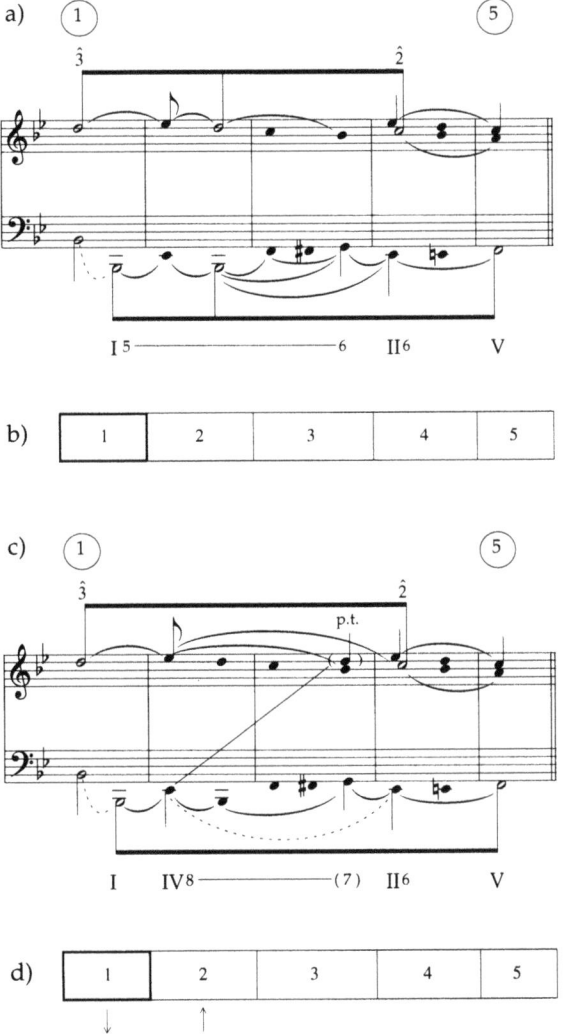

then converted, through an implied 5–6 exchange, into a precadential supertonic ⁶₃ chord.

Structural duality in the first three measures is reinforced by skewed design changes in the outer voices. Tonic prolongation in bars 1–2 (Schenker's reading) is underscored by a design change in the bass from quarters to eighths in bar 3, while subdominant prolongation in bars 2–3 is supported by a design change in the soprano from eighths to quarters in bar 2. "Tonic" and "subdominant" readings of bars 1–3 also suggest different rhythmic interpretations involving either interpolation or expansion. A four-measure prototype (Schenker's "duple ordering") underlies both interpretations. In Schenker's tonic reading, the second measure containing the neighbor note eb^2 is interpolated within a two-measure tonic prolongation, extending tonic harmony from two to three measures and the phrase as a whole from four to five measures (see Example 7b).[21] In the subdominant interpretation, the chord change on the second, weak, measure produces harmonic syncopation (marked by an arrow pointing upward), highlighting the motivically significant $e\flat^2$ (see Example 7d).[22] The syncopated subdominant is then expanded from one to two measures, thereby expanding the four-measure prototype to five measures and intensifying the effect of the syncopation.

Devaluation of the tonic in bar 14 has rhythmic consequences of great importance for the larger strategy in the variations. In Example 8, *a–b* represents the progression from the tonic in hypermetrically accented bar 1 to the subdominant in hypermetrically unaccented bar 2 (Example 8a). The progression from metrical downbeat on the tonic to syncopated accent on the subdominant at *a–b* is replicated at *c–d* and *e–f* (bars 6–7 and 19–20, Examples 8b and 8d). However, a different rhythmic situation arises at *x–y* (bars 14–15, Example 8c), the beginning of the diachronic transformation of the A2's antecedent. In order to preserve the five-measure duration of the A2's antecedent, the diachronic transformation must begin in bar 14, the hypermetrically weak fourth measure of the B's eight-measure phrase. At *x* (bar 14), the tonic forfeits its associated structural downbeat, which is suppressed (the arrow pointing downward is cancelled) and at *y* (bar 15), the subdominant's originally syncopated accent is converted into a metrical accent (the arrow pointing upward is cancelled and replaced by an arrow pointing downward).

The subdominant interpretation of bars 1–3 reinforces the connection between the A1's antecedent and the A2's diachronically transformed antecedent since the same harmonic progression I–IV$^{8-7}$–II^6–V is heard to underlie both passages (see the arrow linking Examples 5c and 5f). On account of this parallelism, I shall refer to the subdominant interpretation (Example 5c) as the "diachronic" reading, as distinguished from Schenker's "normative" tonic interpretation (Example 5b). As the graphs of Variations 3, 5, 6, and 8 in Salzer's collection show (see the transcriptions in Examples 9a, 10a, 10b, 11a, 13a, and 15a), Schenker retains his normative tonic reading at points analogous to bars 1–3. However, in the B/A2 section, he consistently reads a return to the tonic at points corresponding to bar 14, perhaps implicitly acknowledging the diachronic transformation of the A2's antecedent. Schenker could, of course, have revised his readings of the variations to reflect his final interpretation of the theme (i.e., to assert the prolongation of V^7 through the B/A2), although

---

21. In his discussion of the theme David Beach, following Schenker, observes that "the natural division of these five measures is 3 plus 2, not 2 plus 3"; see David Beach, "On Analysis, Beethoven, and Extravagance: A Response to Charles J. Smith," *Music Theory Spectrum* 9 (1987), p. 178. In the variations, however, Brahms is not wedded to the three-plus-two division, as the two-plus-three division in Variation 4 illustrates (see bars 146–50 and 151–55, which are clearly subdivided into two plus three).

22. In the *Erinnerungen* she published in 1925, Schumann's daughter Eugenie reports Brahms's fascination with syncopation; see *The Schumanns and Johannes Brahms: The Memoirs of Eugenie Schumann*, trans. Marie Busch (London: Heinemann, 1927; repr. edn, New York: Books for Libraries Press, 1970), p. 144. She writes: "Brahms gave much attention to syncopations. They had to be given their full value, and where they produced dissonances with the other parts he made me listen to the syncopated [parts] in relation to each one of the dissonant notes. He made the suspensions equally interesting to me; I could never play them emphatically enough to please him."

Example 8 The theme: metrical grid analysis showing accentual reinterpretation at *x–y*

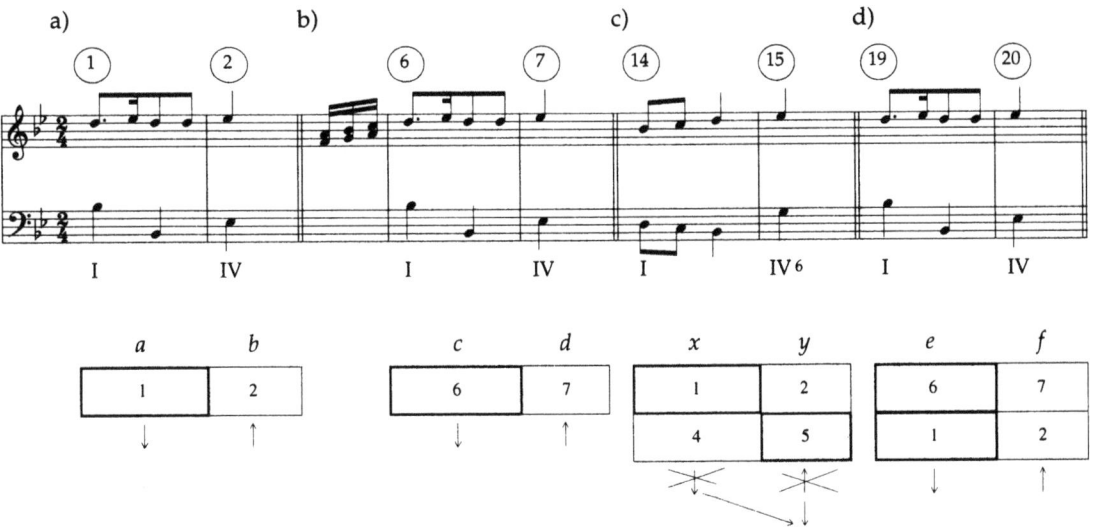

he did not do so. In my view, because of the theme's special "anamorphic" properties, the Chorale and Brahms's variations embody a very special kind of structural pluralism such that neither of Schenker's readings is "incorrect," nor is the diachronic interpretation. To favor any of these readings and reject the others would be like closing one's eyes to the saint in the landscape or vice versa.

From the diachronic perspective, Variations 3, 5, 6, and 8 suggest progressive destruction of normative antecedent–consequent interruption form by structurally devaluing tonic and dominant chords (which parallel the occurrence of these chords in the theme) and assimilating them within enlargements of the diachronic reading of bars 1–5. Where a tonic or dominant may be a structural harmony in the theme, in the diachronic reading of these variations this chord may become an apparent tonic or dominant, or even be totally revalued as an applied or passing chord.[23] In the following discussion and in the graphs, I shall place the indications "dominant" and "tonic" in quotation marks when referring to chords that parallel the functional dominants and tonics in the theme but do not retain this harmonic function in the variations. The juxtaposition of Schenker's normative readings with my own diachronic readings is intended to suggest – returning to the anamorph – that Brahms's larger strategy in these variations is analogous to making the saint and the landscape become increasingly distorted versions of each other.

---

23. Schenker's harmonic analysis in his score does not touch on this possibility. The synthesis advocated here is characteristic of the recent type of "Schenkerian–Osterian" analysis I described in "Current Issues in Schenkerian Analysis," pp. 245 and 256.

Variation 3: synthesis of antecedent and consequent in the A1

In his annotated score of Variation 3 and in his graph, Schenker connects the initial tonic chord in bar 88 with the tonic in bar 93 (see Example 9a).[24] This normative interpretation preserves the A1's antecedent–consequent form with interruption. However, the chord in bar 93 can be interpreted not as a structural tonic but as a V^7/IV caught within a descending fifth sequence of seventh chords $V^7/V^7/IV$ (bars 92–94, Example 9b). According to the alternative diachronic reading, subdominant prolongation supports an upper-voice enlargement of the neighbor-note motive, D–E♭–D, transposed up a fourth to G–A♭–G (see the bracket marked x in Example 9b). In this variation, then, an extension of the subdominant prolongation over the theme's bars 2–8 is strongly suggested. This prolongation would destroy the interruption, fusing the structural seam between the A1's antecedent and consequent to create a single, tonally undivided ten-measure enlargement of the subdominant reading of bars 1–5 (Example 7c). The diachronic interpretation is supported by Brahms's single broad slur, which runs all the way from bar 88 to bar 97, and by the crescendo, which, extending from bar 92 to bar 94, passes through the putative tonic in bar 93.[25]

As a result of passing through the "tonic" in bar 93, the structural downbeat associated with the tonic at the parallel point in the theme is suppressed and the syncopation beginning with the subdominant in bar 89 (corresponding to bar 2 in the theme, as shown in Example 9c) continues through the $V^7/V^7/IV$ chord in bar 92 (corresponding to bar 5 in the theme) to the subdominant chord in bar 94 (corresponding to bar 7 in the theme). Thus the structural downbeat associated with the tonic at the beginning of the consequent at point *c* is suppressed (bar 93) and its accent transferred to the syncopated subdominant at *d* (bar 94), a procedure clearly inspired by the theme's accentual reinterpretation at *x–y* as described above (see Example 8).[26]

Variation 5: synthesis of antecedent and consequent in the recomposed repetition of the A1 and B/A2

The synthesis initiated in Variation 3 is continued and intensified in Variation 5. For the first time, Brahms suggests fusion of the A2's diachronically transformed antecedent and consequent across the cadence at the end of the B. In this

---

24. In all of the transcriptions, the annotations placed in square brackets are mine. In some cases I have added annotations understood in Schenker's graphs, but not literally indicated by him, such as the Roman numeral I in bar 93 of Example 9a. Bar numbers have been added, as have my brackets and labels at the top of the transcriptions.
25. In the printed score, the violas have *two* slurs; the first extends from bar 88 to bar 92, the second from bar 93 to bar 97. This subdivision contradicts the *single* slur spanning bars 88–97 in all the other instruments. In his score, Schenker corrected the viola part, completing its slur in purple pencil.
26. In this variation, the A2's antecedent and consequent are not welded structurally into a continuous phrase, but a parallel synthesis to that in the A1 is suggested by the texture: the continuous third-species line beginning in bar 131 (corresponding to the second measure in the elided A2's antecedent) bridges over the cadence in bars 134–35 to continue through to the end of the consequent (bars 135–39).

Example 9 Variation 3

a) Schenker's normative reading of A1 (transcription)

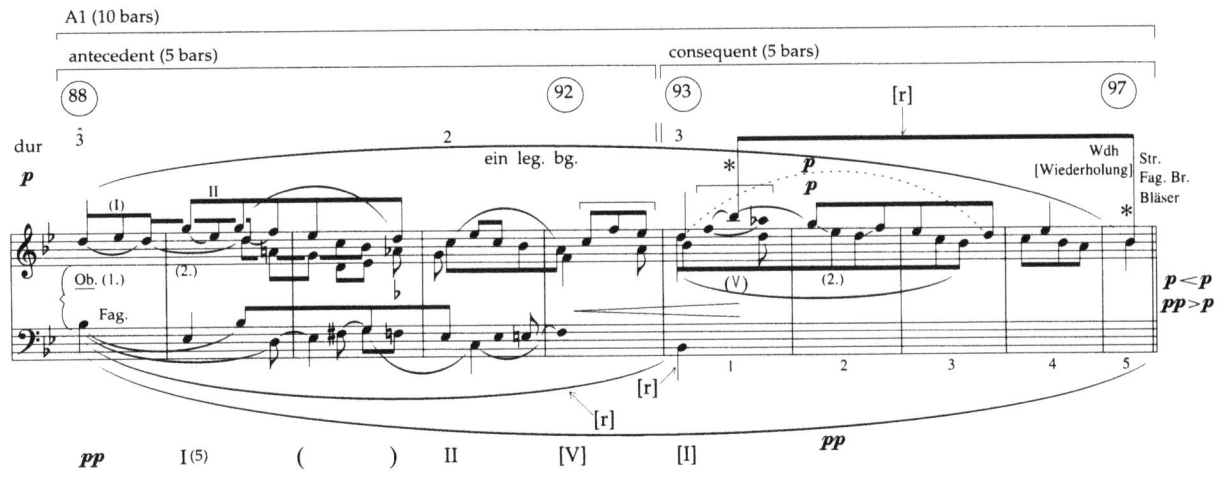

[r] = red pencil

b) Diachronic reading of A1

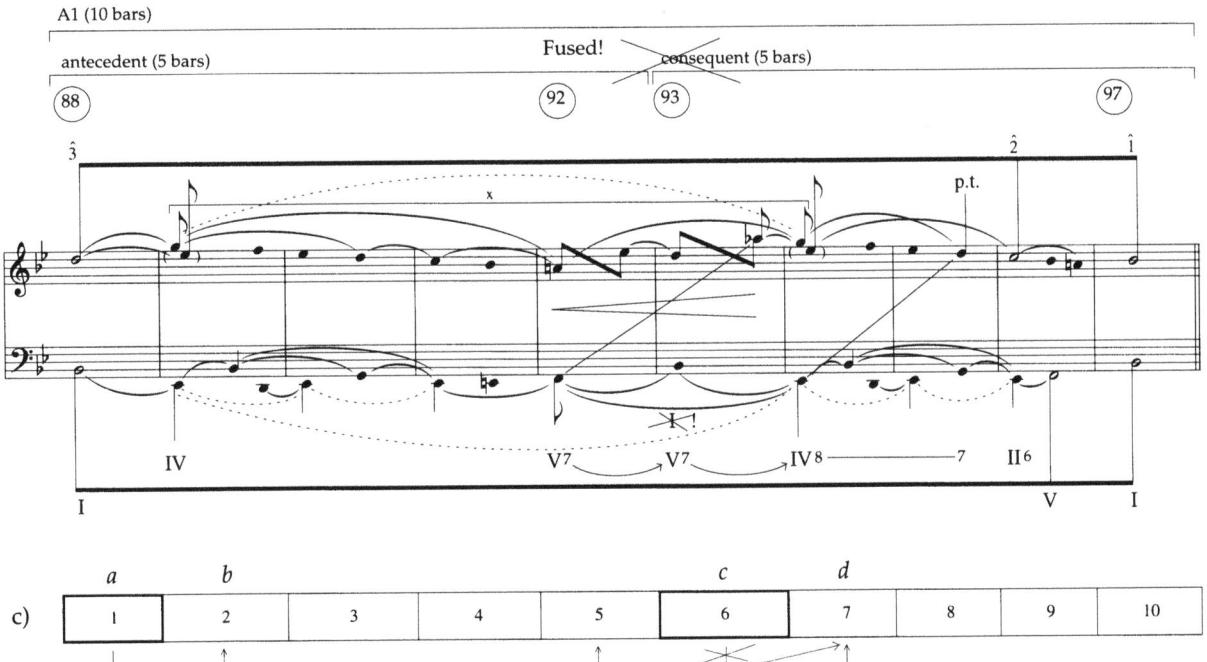

258   Timothy Jackson

Example 10 Variation 5

a) Schenker's normative reading of A1 (transcription)

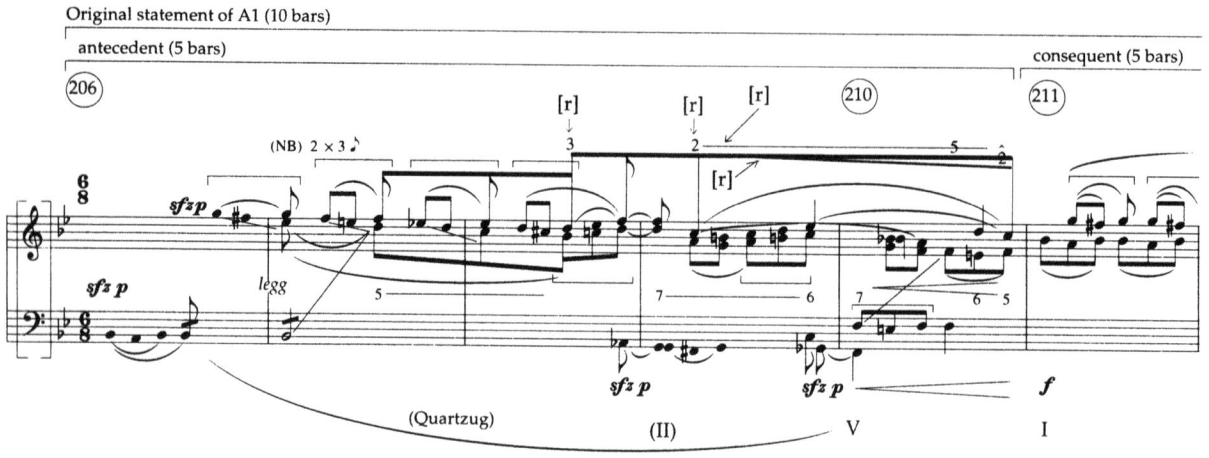

b) Schenker's normative reading of B/A2, original statement and recomposed repetition (transcription)

variation, he makes crucial modifications in the written-out repetitions of the A1 and the B/A2, which amount to recomposition contrasting normative and diachronic structures. In the initial statements of the A1 and the B/A2 the theme's tonal-rhythmic structure is retained: the clear-cut cadence on V followed by a new beginning on I in bars 210–11 and bars 233–34 evokes the antecedent–consequent interruption form within the A1 and B/A2. Schenker's normative readings are displayed in Examples 10a and 10b. However, in the

Diachronic transformation in Brahms's Haydn Variations

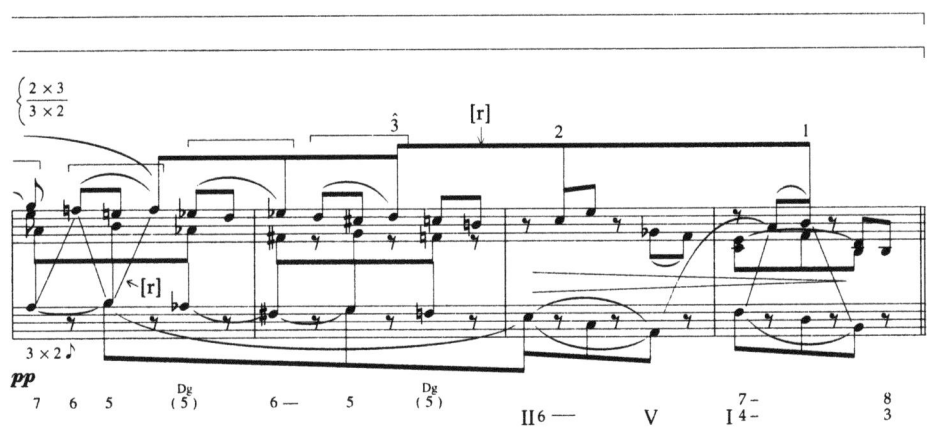

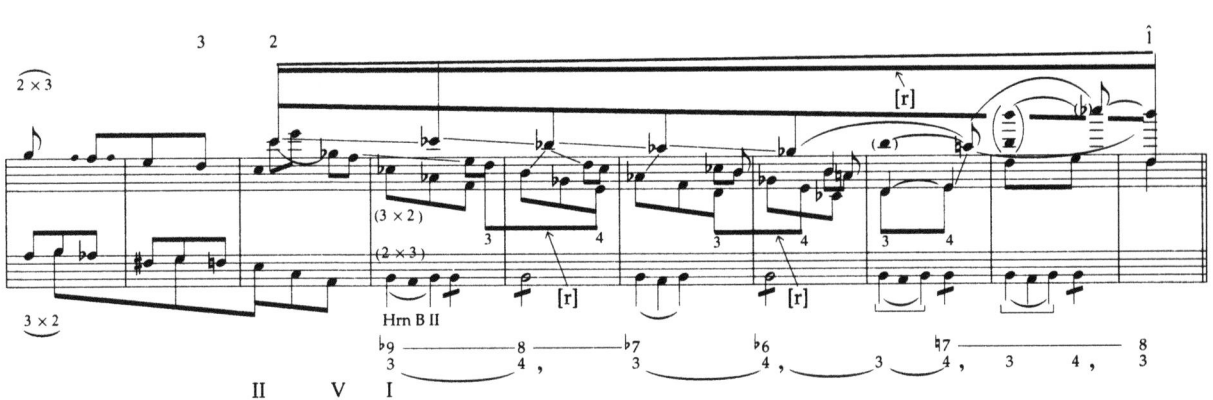

recomposed repetitions of the A1 and B/A2, the expected tonic at the beginning of the consequent is subverted by III$_{\sharp3}^{7}$ or III$_{\sharp3}^{\natural6}$ (or augmented B$\flat_{3}^{\natural6}$) chords in bars 221 and 253 respectively. Schenker does not allow the displaced tonic in bar 221 to fundamentally change his normative reading of interruption in the recomposed repetition of the A1 (see Example 11a); nor does he provide an alternative graph of the recomposed repetition (see Example 10b).

Several factors including hemiola, rhythmic shift, and change of harmony in the recomposed repetitions suggest the diachronic readings of the recomposed repetitions shown in Examples 11b and 11c. In the recomposed repetition of the A1 (bars 216–25), hemiola and rhythmic shift in bars 219–21 help to destroy the interruption, eliminating the seam between antecedent and consequent. The *sforzando* on the last eighth of bar 219 initiates a two-measure hemiola, which begins on the sixth eighth note of bar 219 (see Example 12a) rhythmically shifted against the notated meter. If we refer to the two-piano version to simplify the discussion, we see that Brahms shifts piano I an eighth note late relative to piano II to prevent parallel fifths between pianos I and II (see Example 12b). Hemiola, rhythmic shift, and tonal displacement suppress the expected structural downbeat on the tonic in bar 221 at point c, transferring its accent onto the syncopated subdominant on the downbeat of bar 222 at d (see the arrows in Example 12). In this way, hemiola and rhythmic shift play a significant part in suppressing the anticipated tonic's structural downbeat and transferring its accent onto the adjacent subdominant (c–d = x–y; see Examples 11b and 11c).

The striking contrast between interruption in the normative original statements and tonal synthesis in the diachronic recomposed repetitions appears to be the essential compositional idea in this variation. While in the normative initial statement (Example 10a, bars 206–15), I (bar 206) clearly moves to V (bar 210) and back to I (bar 211) to support interruption as in the theme (the ten-measure phrase is subdivided into five plus five), in the diachronic recomposed repetition of the A1 (Example 11b, bars 216–25), interruption is eliminated, fusing antecedent and consequent into a single, undivided ten-measure phrase.

In this variation, $\hat{5}$ (f^2) and $\hat{8}$ ($b\flat^2$) are placed above the primary tone $\hat{3}$ and function as cover tones. The neighbor-note motive d^2–$e\flat^2$–d^2 in the theme engenders neighbor-note embellishments of the cover tones: f^2–g^2–f^2 and $b\flat^2$–c^3–$b\flat^2$. The neighbor note f^2–g^2–f^2 is filled in chromatically with the passing tones $f\sharp^2$ and $g\flat^2$.[27] The motive f^2–$f\sharp^2$–g^2 (see the brackets marked x in Example 11b), taken from the bass in bar 3 of the theme, is recomposed in enlargement in bars 220–22 (after appearing in inversion; see the bracket marked x^i). The D seventh chord (bar 221) facilitates a top-voice enlargement of the upper neighbor-note motive, $b\flat^2$–c^3–$b\flat^2$ (see Example 11b). At the end of the variation the whole step C–B♭ is replaced by the semitone C♭–B♭, which exactly parallels the original semitone upper neighbor-note motive (D–)E♭–D (see Example 11c).

The recomposed repetition of the B/A2 (bars 245–63) sets up a parallelism with the recomposed repetition of the A1 (compare Examples 11b and 11c). In the recomposed repetition of the B/A2, the expected tonic at the beginning of the A2's consequent is once again displaced by a $D^{\flat 6}_{\sharp 3}$ or augmented $B\flat^6_3$ chord (compare bar 253 with bar 221). Schenker's annotations in his score reveal that he hears this chord as standing for the tonic. Brahms's harmonic displacement of the expected tonic also suggests the diachronic reading presented in Example 11c. The implied subdominant prolongation (involving voice exchange) in the

---

27. In Variation 5, as in Variation 6, F♯ is motivically associated with its enharmonic equivalent G♭.

Example 11 Variation 5

a) Schenker's normative reading of recomposed repetition of A1 (transcription)

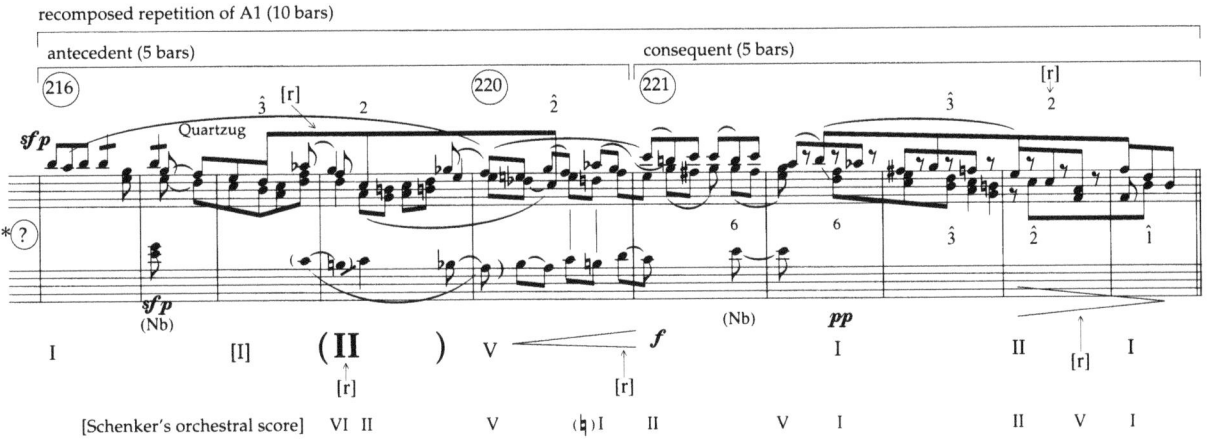

b) Diachronic reading of recomposed repetition of A1

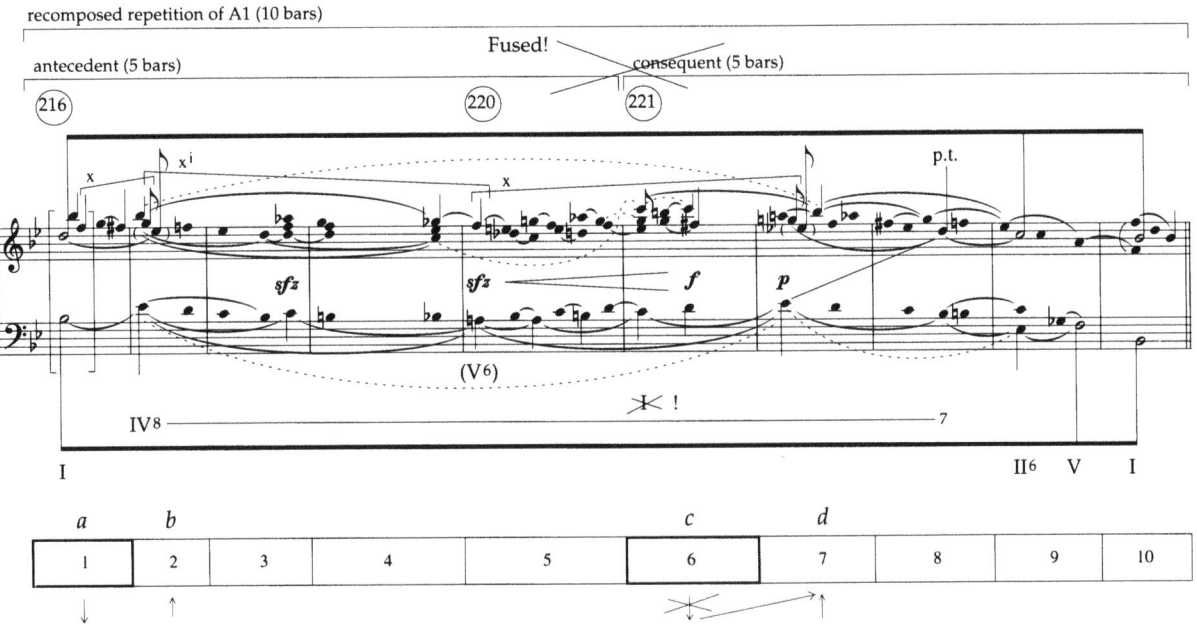

recomposed repetition of the A2/B destroys the interruption, structurally merging the A2's antecedent and consequent to parallel the fusion of antecedent and consequent in the A1's recomposed repetition. In conjunction with the tonal displacement of the tonic in bar 253, Brahms suppresses the expected structural downbeat at point e, conferring its accent upon the syncopated subdominant at f (e–f = x–y; see the arrows in Example 11c).

262 Timothy Jackson

Example 11 (*cont.*)

c) Diachronic reading of recomposed repetition of B/A2

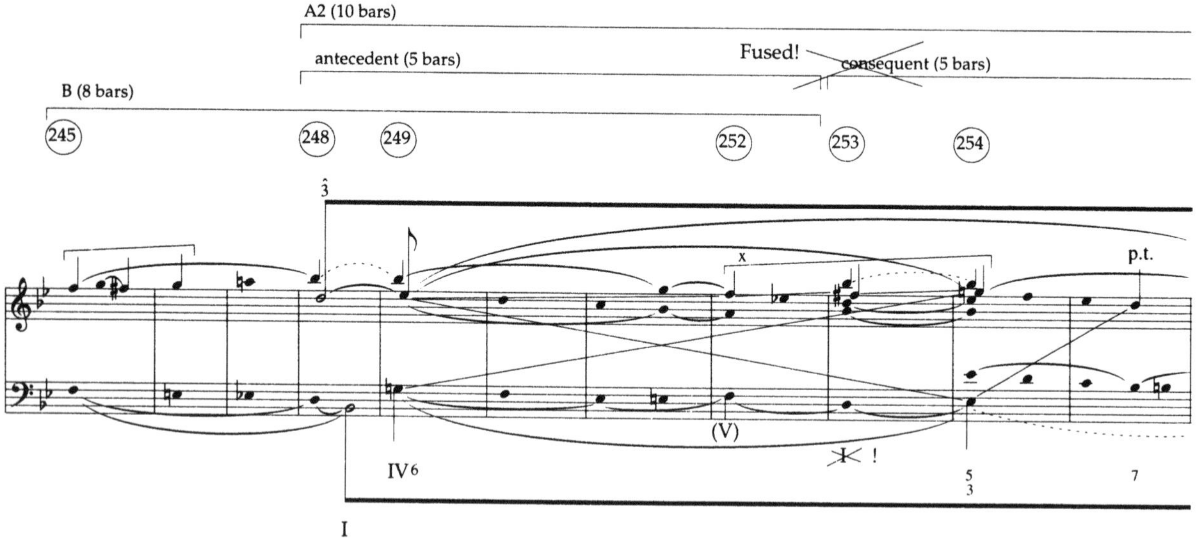

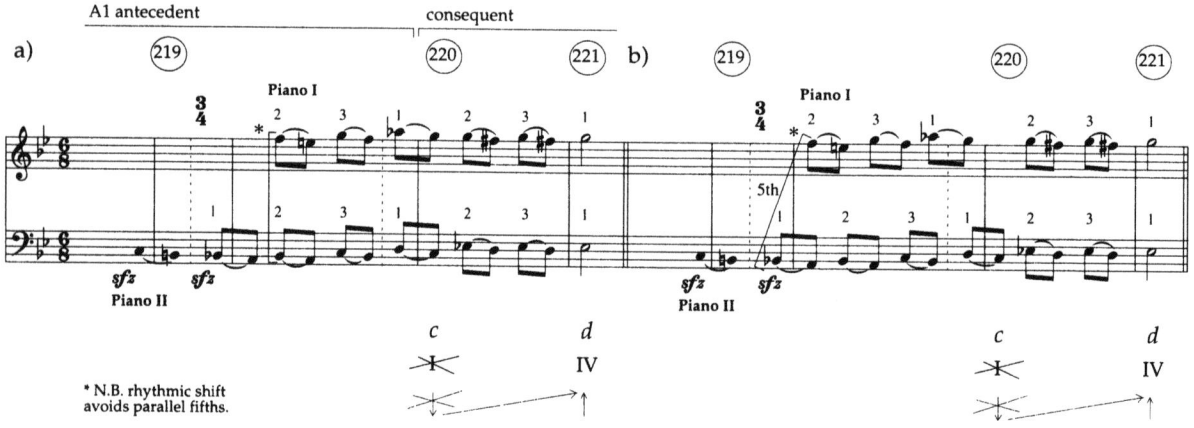

Example 12 Variation 5: suppression of the structural tonic at the beginning of the A1's consequent (two-piano version)

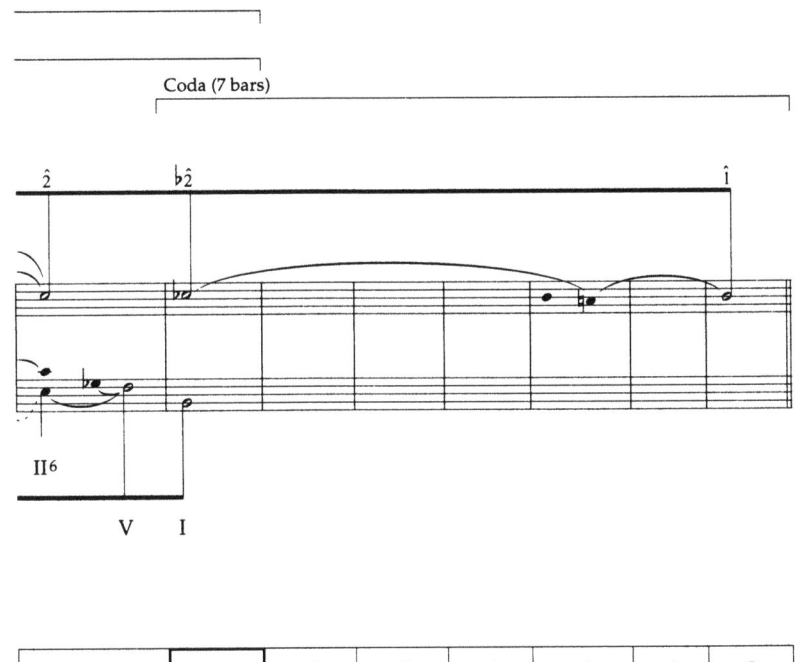

Variation 6: point *e* rhythmically shifted and its accent bounced onto *f*

In Variation 6, Brahms again focuses on the seams between the antecedent and consequent in the A1 (bars 268–69) and on the connection between the diachronic transformation of the A2's antecedent and the A2's consequent at the end of the B (bars 280–83). Examples 13a and 13b compare Schenker's normative reading with the diachronic interpretation. In both graphs of the A1, interruption is eliminated as $\hat{3}$ is sustained through the initial ten-measure phrase. In the B/A2, the primary focus of our attention, the dominant at the end of the diachronic transformation of the A2's antecedent and the tonic at the beginning of the A2's consequent are not displaced harmonically (as in

Example 13 Variation 6

a) Schenker's normative reading (transcription)

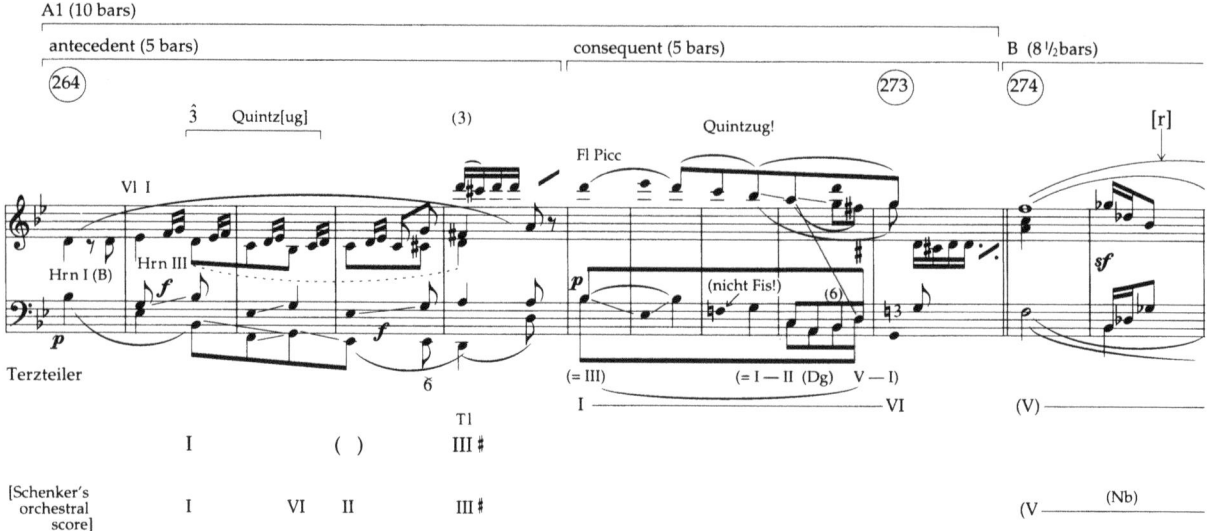

b) Diachronic reading

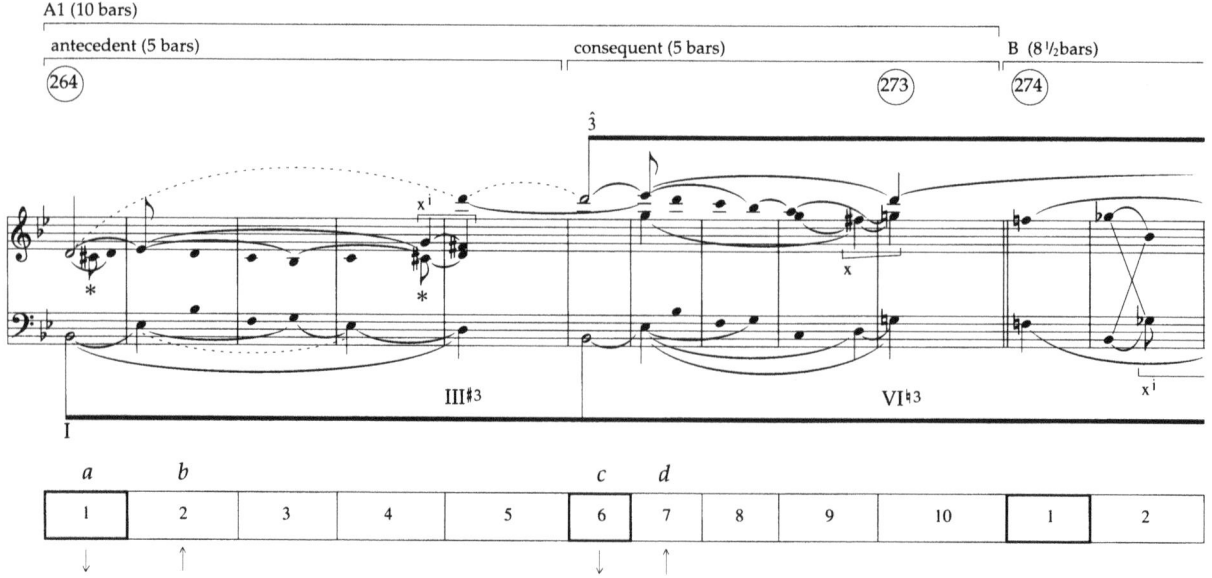

Diachronic transformation in Brahms's Haydn Variations

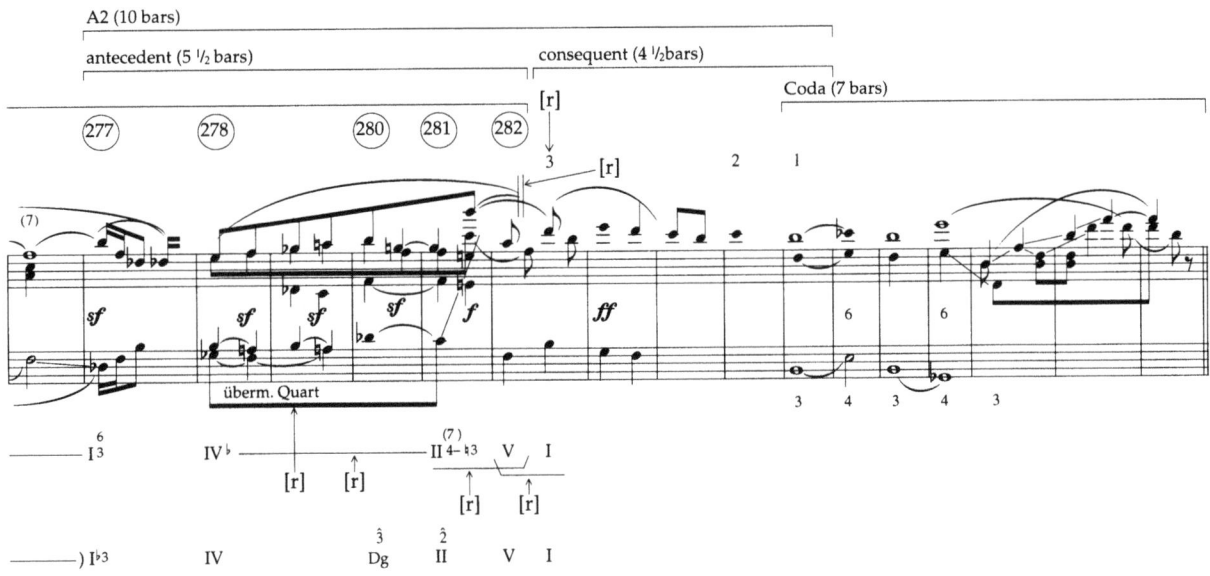

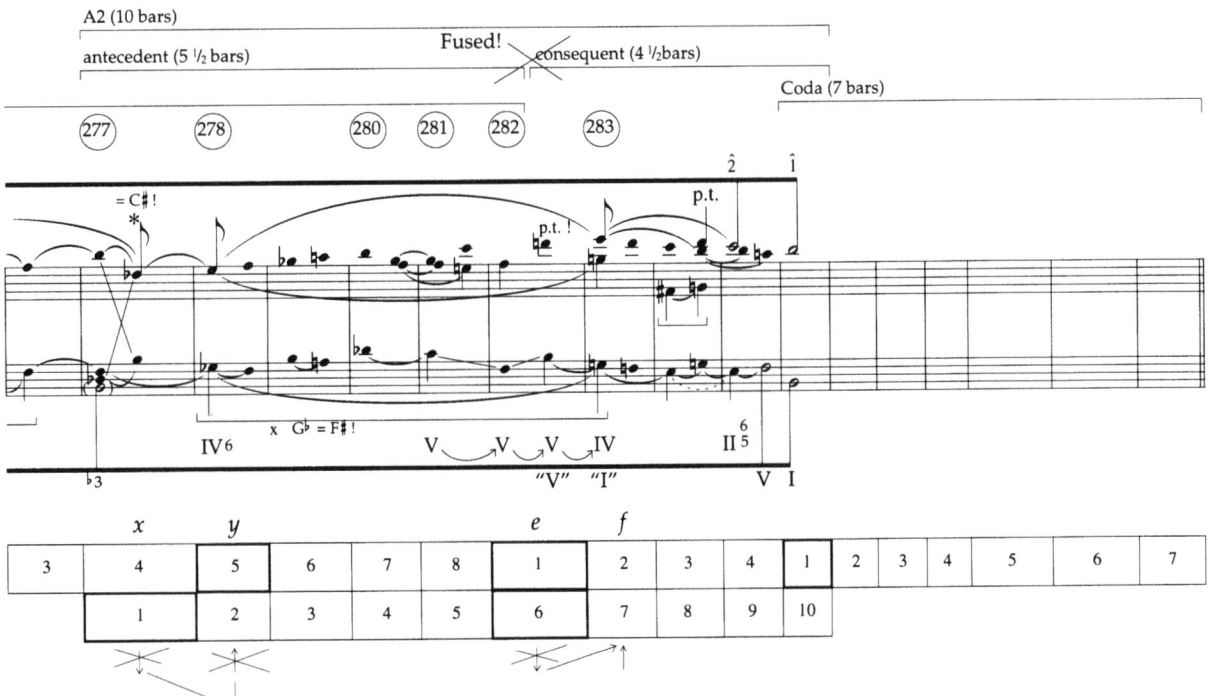

Example 13 (*cont.*)

c) Opening motive

d) Schenker's normative reading of the middleground (transcription)

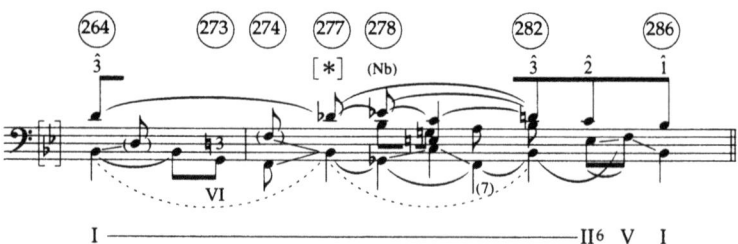

Variation 5), but rather they are displaced temporally – shifted to a point later than their predicted locations in bars 281–82. In his annotated score Schenker takes note of this shift with an exclamation point placed above the flute line. In Schenker's normative reading the effect of interruption is produced over the dominant (see the double lines in his graph) and the structural tonic is regained at the beginning of the A2's consequent (at the second quarter of bar 282, Example 13a). The overlapping brackets beneath "V" and "I" indicate temporal elision such that the dominant occurs in the time of the tonic and vice versa. In the diachronic interpretation, the "tonic" in bar 282 is reinterpreted as V/IV within a descending fifth sequence (V/V/V/IV), the resulting subdominant prolongation fusing antecedent and consequent within the A2 and destroying any sense of interruption (see Example 13b). This harmonic devaluation of the tonic is suggested both by the powerful momentum of the sequence, which seems to carry it through the putative tonic, and by the rhythmic shift, which squeezes the "dominant" and "tonic" chords into bar 282. In bars 278–83, the F♯–G segment of motive x of Variation 5 (enharmonically associated with G♭–F) is recomposed in enlargement as G♭(=F♯)–G, converting the minor subdominant into the major (see Example 13b). The vertical alignment of Schenker's graph of the middleground with the opening motive (see Examples 13c and 13d) seeks to propose that the upper voice of Schenker's normative reading constitutes a massive enlargement of the initial motive; D♭ (bar 277), which is partly responsible for the turn to the parallel minor, thus functions in the larger context as if it were C♯.[28]

---

28. This motivic connection is mine, not Schenker's.

In order rhythmically to shift the arrival of the "tonic" into the middle of bar 282, Brahms shifts the "dominant" chord onto the downbeat of bar 282 by expanding the sequence prolonging the preceding E♭ minor subdominant $^6_4$ (IV$^{♭3}$) an extra measure (see Example 13b). The sketches for the two-piano version, on folio 6 of the material in the Gesellschaft der Musikfreunde, provide a fascinating glimpse into the passage's genesis. Two different preliminary versions, shown in transcription in Examples 14a and 14b, and labeled Concepts 1 and 2 (with Concept 1 divided into Concepts 1A and 1B), show Brahms's initial uncertainty as to whether the sequence should be prolonged the extra measure. Concept 1, which closely parallels the final version of bars 278–79, suggests the expansion of the E minor subdominant (bar 278) with B♭ minor (bar 280) as its upper fifth. Brahms begins by sketching the rising scale passages in the outer voices for bars 278–80 (Concept 1A, Example 14a). Next, he probably enters the sustained B♭ and d♭^{1} in the inner voices, the syncopation foreshadowing the rhythmic shift in piano I (Concept 1B, Example 14a). Directly above this sketch, Brahms then notates his alternative for bars 278–80 (Concept 2, Example 14b, which appears below Concept 1 in the transcription).[29] The rhythmic shift in the inner voices of Concept 1B may have suggested the rhythmic shift in the uppermost voice in Concept 2. The figures in the top voice clearly anticipate the final version of piano II's right hand. Example 14c provides a hypothetical completion of Concept 2. Brahms quickly realizes that Concept 2 will cause him to reach the dominant in bar 281 (as in the theme) rather than in bar 282 (as suggested in Concept 1A) and he breaks off the sketch.

With two different concepts, Brahms is apparently in a quandary as to the precise location of the arrival of the "dominant" and "tonic" chords. Between these sketches and folio 7, where Variation 6 is laid out in ink, there may have been further studies, which are now lost. However, it is possible to infer Brahms's compositional thinking from the extant versions. The final version is a synthesis of elements of both concepts. The composer transposes Concept 2's bars 278–79 up a fifth to become Concept 1's bars 280–81 (see the brackets and dotted arrow in Example 14d). In this synthesis of the two concepts, the sequence prolonging the minor subdominant *is* extended an extra measure, forcing the arrival of the "dominant" onto the downbeat of bar 282 and displacing the "tonic" onto the second quarter of that measure. As a consequence of the shift of the "tonic," the structural downbeat associated with point *e* bounces onto the syncopated accent at *f* (a remarkable development of the accentual reinterpretation at *x–y*).

---

29. For McCorkle's transcription of this passage, see "Genesis and the Creative Process," pp. 37–38. Folio 6 is reproduced in facsimile on p. 142; folios 7 and 4, referred to below, appear in facsimile on pp. 143 and 140, respectively (selected transcriptions by McCorkle are included in his chapter).

Example 14 Variation 6: genesis of bars 276–83

Sketch transcription

Sketch analysis

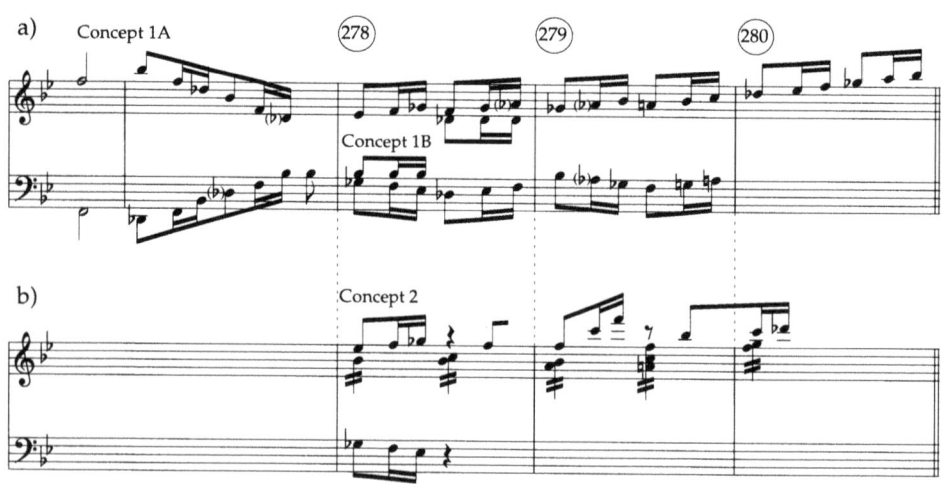

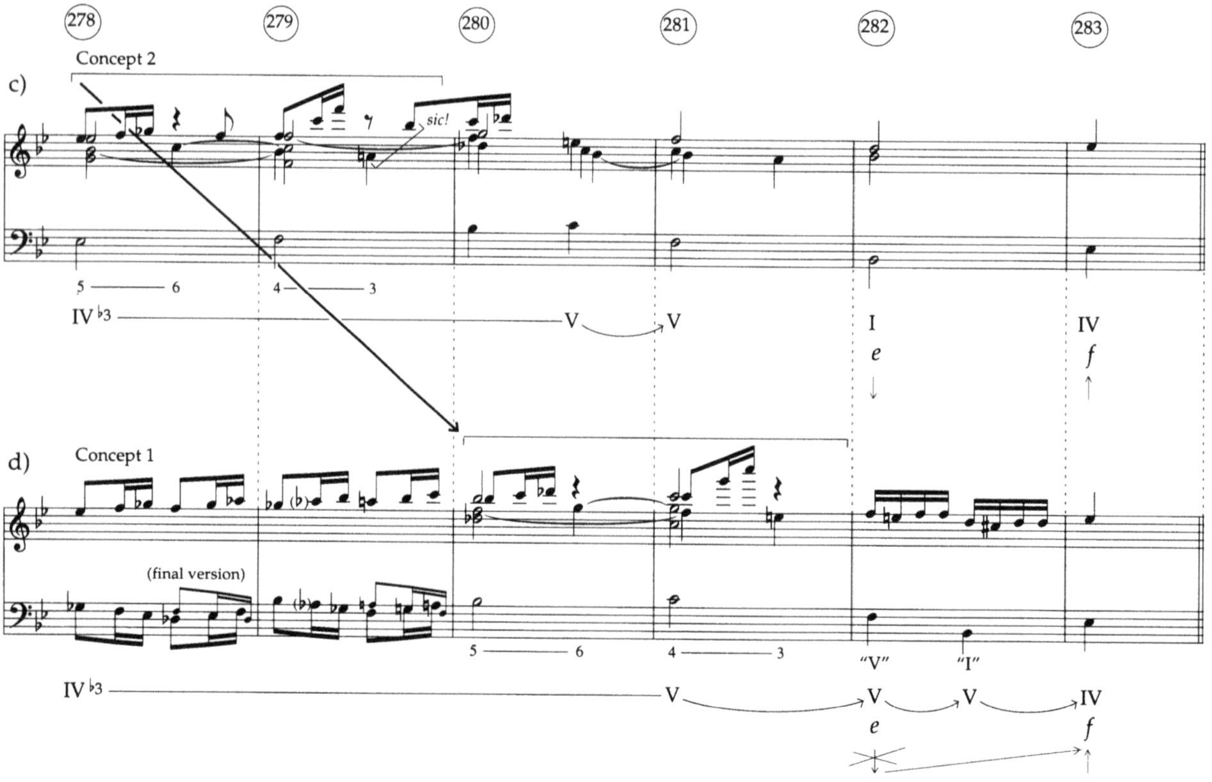

Variation 8: total synthesis in the diachronic reading

In this, the last variation, maximal conceptual distance between normative and diachronic readings is attained. The Finale, then, is assigned the task of reestablishing the original tension between the theme's normative and diachronic aspects. McCorkle reports that "Brahms's task in preparing an orchestral transcription was largely a matter of orchestrating the two-piano version.... It is likely that he accomplished the work with but a slight amount of additional compositional effort."[30] However, in the process of orchestration, Brahms did in fact make significant structural modifications in the eighth variation. In the two-piano version, the antedecent of the A1's recomposed repetition cadences on the tonic supporting an upper-voice descent to $\hat{1}$ (bar 336), while the orchestral version prolongs the dominant in this measure, as in the theme (see Example 15a). In the two-piano version, the consequent of the A1's recomposed repetition begins on the dominant (bar 337); the orchestral version restores the Chorale's tonic at this point. Furthermore, in the two-piano version, the consequent of the A1's recomposed repetition cadences firmly on the tonic supporting an upper-voice descent to $\hat{1}$ (bar 341, as in the theme) but in the orchestral version this tonic is displaced by an augmented ("German") sixth chord, which resolves directly into the dominant at the beginning of the B.

One of the most striking aspects of both versions of this variation is the deceptive cadence in bar 332, which displaces the expected tonic and obscures the seam between the end of the A1 and the beginning of the A1's recomposed repetition. The composer's sketches in the Gesellschaft der Musikfreunde reveal that the "synthetic" idea of bridging over this seam occurred very early in the compositional process. On folio 4, Brahms sketched the opening ten measures (bars 322–31). Directly below, on a separate staff, he entered a bass for the first six measures of the A1's recomposed repetition (bars 332–37). This bass sketch already implies a deceptive cadence in bar 332 and is identical with the two-piano version except for the tonic cadence in bar 337. Perhaps after writing out the two-piano version Brahms considered the substitution of dominant for tonic in bar 337 of that version to be a fortuitous modification of the model and, in the orchestral version, reverted to his original intention (shown in the sketch).

The substitution of the augmented sixth chord in bar 341 should be considered in the context of normative and diachronic readings (Examples 15a and 15b). In Schenker's normative reading, the submediant in bar 332 and the "German" sixth in bar 341 are both produced by 6–5 exchanges over the tonic; in the diachronic interpretation these same chords are built on the upper third of the subdominant. In the normative reading, the remaining internal tonics are all structural, while in the diachronic interpretation their primary function is to provide consonant support for the chromatic passing tones D and D♭ within the descending tetrachord E♭–D–D♭–C–C♭–B♭ (motive y). In the normative reading, the augmented sixth chord has a relatively local effect, simply substituting for the tonic in bar 341. In the diachronic interpretation, however,

---

30. *Ibid.*, p. 56.

Example 15 Variation 8

a) Schenker's normative reading of orchestral version (transcription)

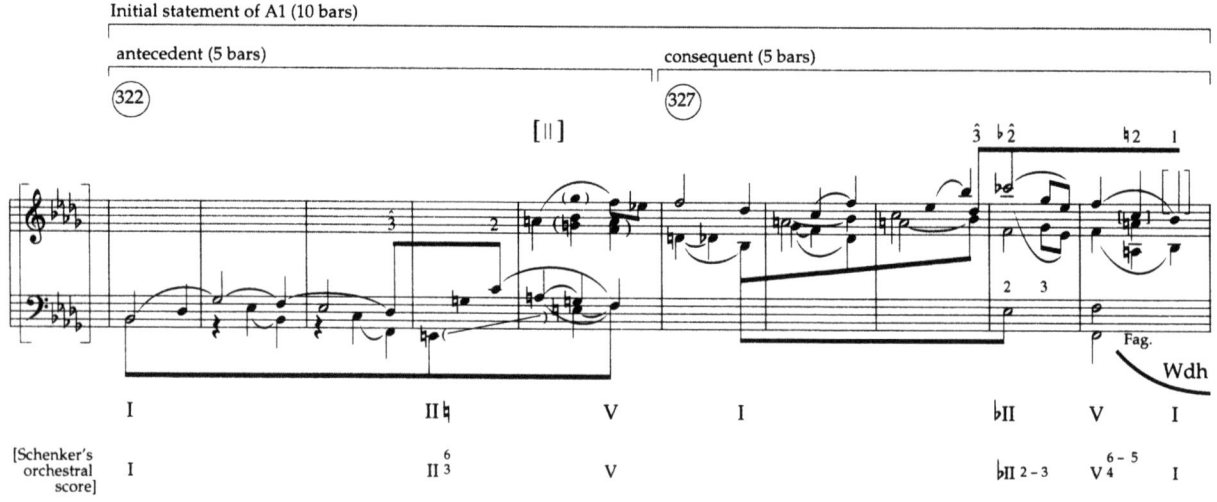

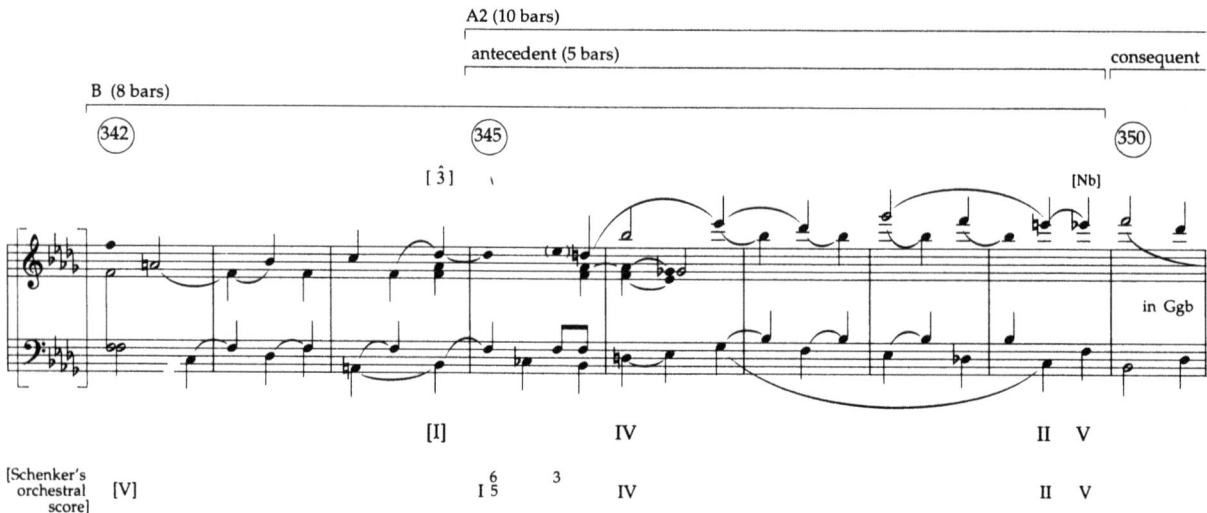

Diachronic transformation in Brahms's Haydn Variations 271

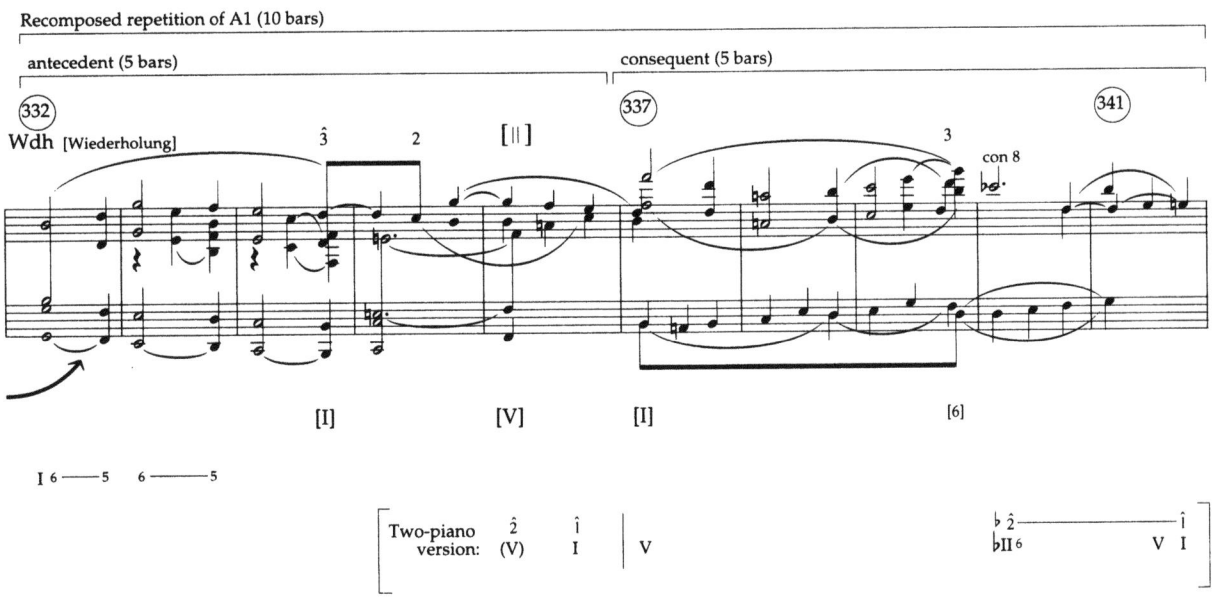

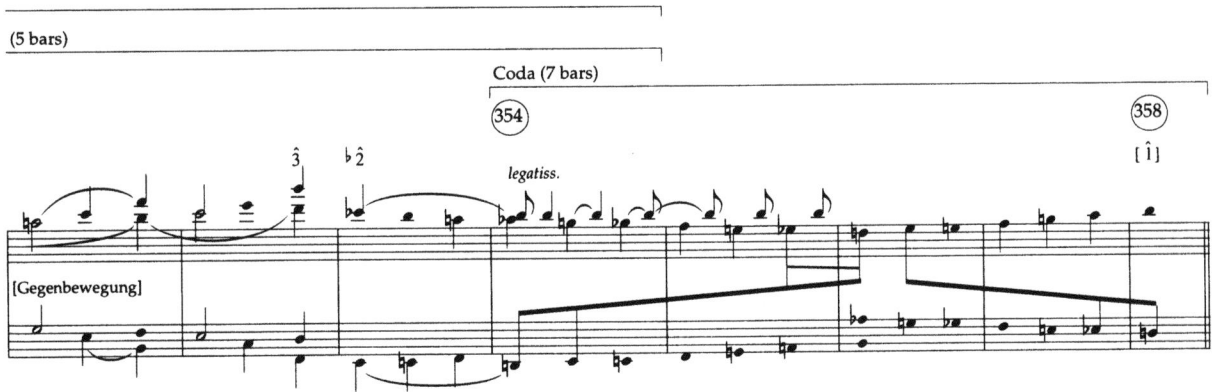

272   Timothy Jackson

Example 15 (*cont.*)

b) Diachronic reading of orchestral version

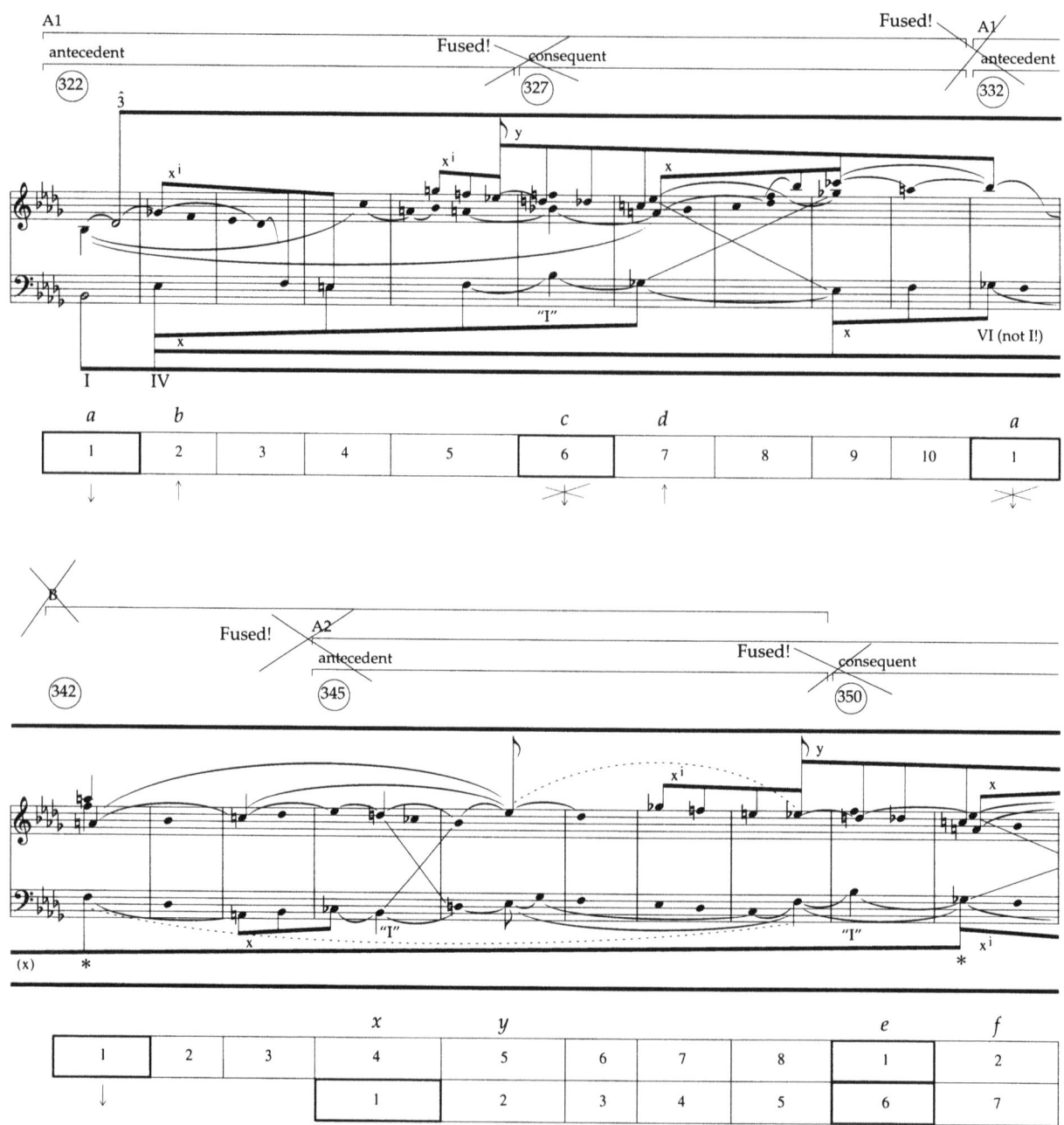

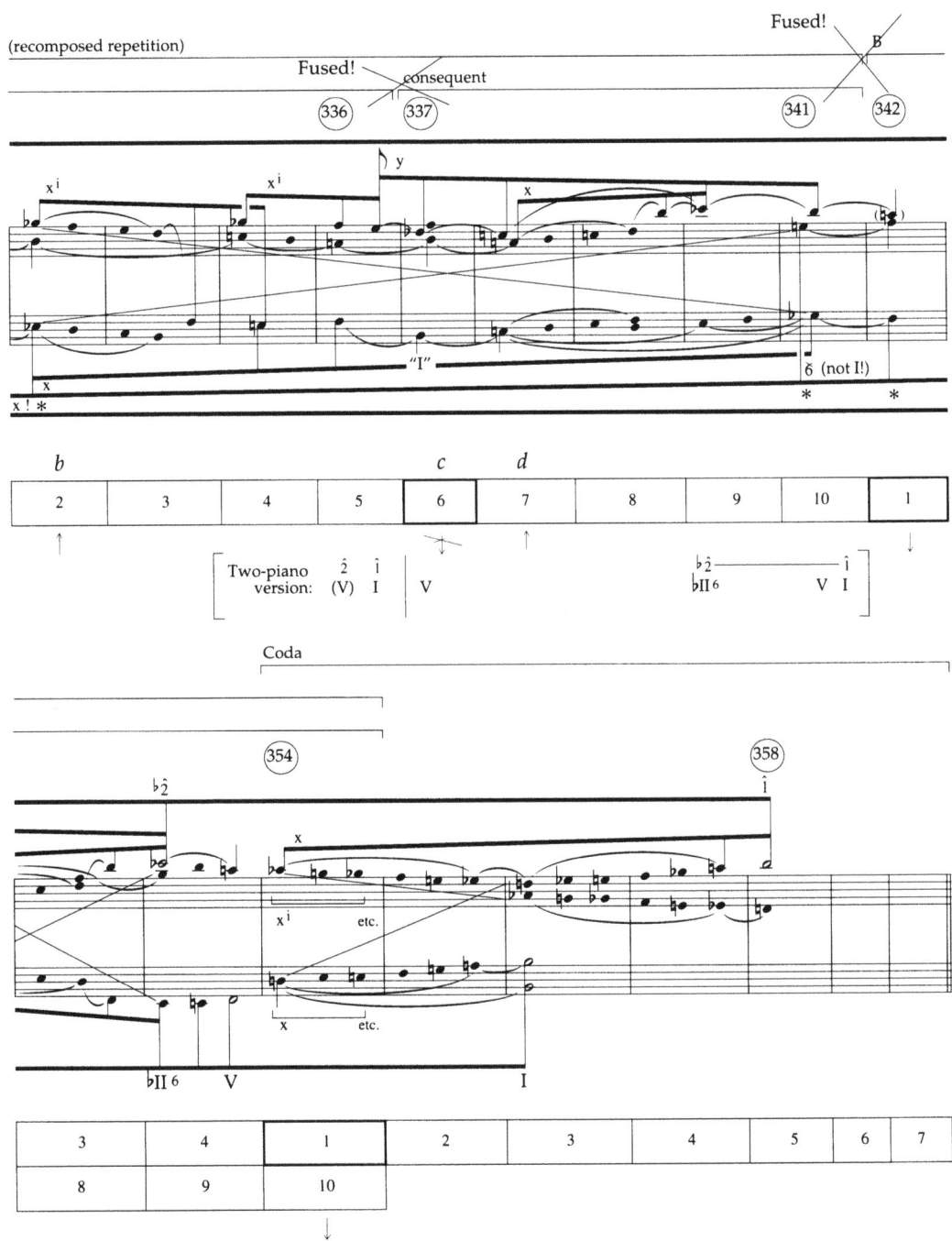

it creates a large-scale chromaticized voice exchange over the subdominant and thereby participates in a colossal expansion in the bass of the ascending-third motive x filled in chromatically (E♭–E–F–G♭). This motive, first stated in bars 323–28, now spans the entire variation.[31] Thus, viewed from the diachronic perspective, Brahms's substitution of the augmented sixth chord in the orchestral version suggests the complete elimination of internal closure and interruption – the fusion of initial statements and recomposed repetitions within a single undivided structure. As a result of this synthesis, structural downbeats at *a* (bar 332), *c* (bars 327 and 337), and *e* (bar 350) are suppressed and their accents transferred onto syncopated accents at *b* (bar 333), *d* (bars 328 and 338), and *f* (bar 351). Perhaps this effect of total synthesis was latent in Brahms's initial idea of the deceptive cadence at the beginning of the recomposed repetition.

To summarize: in the diachronic reading of Variations 3, 5, 6, and 8, the theme's accentual reinterpretation at *x–y* – produced by the diachronic transformation of the A2's antecedent – is progressively elevated to a structural principle; the accentual reinterpretation at *x–y* is mapped onto *a–b*, *c–d*, and *e–f*. While, in the theme, the accentual pattern of downbeat syncopation recurs at *c–d* and *e–f* (as shown in Examples 8a, 8b, and 8d), in the variations the theme's accentual reinterpretation at *x–y* (shown in Example 8c) becomes paradigmatic for suppressing downbeat accents at points analogous to *a*, *c*, and *e* and for "bouncing" these accents onto adjacent syncopations at *b*, *d*, and *f*. In other words, the accentual reinterpretation at *x–y* is "geographically" shifted to other parallel locations within the theme. This process of accentual reinterpretation, inspired by the diachronic interpretation of the A2's antecedent, develops built-in formal elision to eliminate remaining formal-structural boundaries and achieve the greatest possible synthesis.

In the essay quoted earlier in this article, W. H. Hadow defines Brahms the Classical composer as "[one] who aims before all things at perfection of phrase and structure, [and] whose ideal is simple beauty."[32] However, rather than "simple beauty" and "perfection of phrase and structure," the Chorale which Brahms selected as the theme for his variations contains a diachronic transformation which distorts Classical symmetry and balance. While Leon Plantinga regards the variation as a "vital testing ground for the development of [Brahms's] style," Walter Frisch detects a "neo-Classical retrenchment" beginning with the Handel Variations, Op. 24 (1862), and presumably continuing through the Haydn Variations, Op. 56a and 56b (1873–74).[33] While such "retrenchment" occurs overtly in Brahms's music, analysis discloses a

---

31. As shown in Example 15b, motive x is stated in both augmentation and inversion. The chromatic segment E♭–E–F in bar 353 clearly derives from the bass of the theme, bars 4–5.
32. Hadow, "Brahms and the Classical Tradition," p. 137.
33. Walter Frisch, "Brahms and Schubring: Musical Criticism and Politics at Mid-Century," *19th-Century Music* 7/3 (1984), p. 280; see also Leon Plantinga, *Romantic Music* (New York: Norton, 1984), p. 421.

compensating involution of Classical procedures behind the neo-Classical facade.

The traditional Schenkerian model presumes a work to be in a steady state in which structural levels tend to coexist and interrelate synchronically, each layer of background, middleground, and foreground being derived from the preceding layer, through either elaboration or reduction. The structural levels, moving from background to foreground, relate to one another as a series of anatomical projections, which show first the bone structure, then the muscles, and finally, the skin and surface appearance. However, the diachronic transformations studied here do not grow out of voice-leading transformations; on the contrary, they distort and realign voice-leading strata, modifying pre-existent relationships.

Diachronic transformations are not incipient at any structural level; rather, they disturb the synchronic relations between levels. Just as an earthquake realigns layers of rock in the earth's crust, diachronic transformation creates upheavals in a work's conceptual history. As has been shown, diachronic transformation is even capable of repressing *Ursatz* elements and destroying interruptions. It is therefore a much more radical type of transformation than synchronic. Whereas synchronic elaboration is embodied in later structural levels, diachronic transformation is extrinsic to synchronic evolution. Analysis cannot generate diachronic transformation from earlier levels; but it can identify when and where diachronic transformation has occurred. The concept of diachronic transformation suggests novel applications of traditional Schenkerian analytical tools and new avenues of future research.[34]

---

34. My forthcoming article "Diachronic Transformation in Schumann and Mahler" pursues this line of inquiry.

for Saul Novack, in memoriam

Bass-line articulations of the *Urlinie*

Eric Wen

One of the poignant moments in Brahms's Intermezzo in A major, Op. 118, No. 2, is the return of the opening theme in inversion (bars 34ff.). The distinctive features of the theme – the double-neighbor pattern and skip of a seventh – are instantly recognizable, despite the changes in their tonal meaning. Even before this point, however, there are several intimations of the opening theme. In bars 30–34 there is a fourfold statement of the initial upbeat figure in the bass. Furthermore, in bar 29 the melodic contour of the top voice is exactly the same as in bar 1.[1] Although this bar is not preceded by a literal repetition of the two-note upbeat (c♯^{2}–b^1) that begins the piece, the reiterated statements of the upbeat figure in the bass over the course of bars 30–34 would seem to compensate for its omission.[2]

The d^2 in bar 29 is preceded by an ascending chromatic line originating from g♯^{1} in bar 25, and a dominant pedal appears in the bass in bars 25–29. In bar 28, where c♯^{2} in the melodic line descends a third to a^1, Brahms's notation is significant: the a^1 at the end of bar 28 is tied into the next bar where it appears beneath d^2 at the beginning of bar 29. As a result of this transformation of a^1 from the soprano to the alto part, the upbeat figure is subtly recalled in the uppermost voice, allowing for a repetition of the entire opening theme in bars 28–30 (Example 1). This example shows how fluid and elusive the

Example 1 Brahms, Intermezzo in A major, Op.118, No. 2

---

1. In Allen Cadwallader's analysis of this piece in "Foreground Motivic Ambiguity: Its Clarification at Middleground Levels in Selected Late Piano Pieces of Johannes Brahms," *Music Analysis* 7/1 (1988), pp. 64–74, this rhythmically altered recollection of the first bar is designated as the formal recapitulation. Cadwallader comments further about Op. 118, No. 2, in "Echoes and Recollections: Brahms's Op. 76, No. 6," *Theory and Practice* 13 (1988), pp. 65–78.
2. The manifold appearances of this upbeat figure are examined by Robert Snarrenberg in "The Play of *Différence*: Brahms's Intermezzo Op. 118, No. 2," *In Theory Only* 10/3 (1987), pp. 1–25. In his deconstructionist journey through this work Snarrenberg associates the rhythmic gesture of the last two eighth notes in bar 28 (b^1–a^1) with the opening upbeat figure; see pp. 18–20 and Example 10.

concept of "top voice" can be. What seems at first to be a single linear entity splits into two components, and, in so doing, creates a remarkable motivic reference.

"Voice" versus "part"

In this essay we shall explore what is perhaps the most radical compositional application of this kind of "dematerialized" voice leading: the shifting of the top-voice structure into the bass so that a linear continuity bridges the registral gap between the highest and lowest sounds. Before examining the specific situations in which this can occur, however, I should like to establish a distinction between "voice" and "part." Although these terms are often used interchangeably (and indeed frequently overlap), it can be helpful to employ them in two different ways. In this divided usage, the term "part" is defined by a work's performing forces or textural elements, and is usually bound by the constraints of a particular tessitura (e.g., SATB). A "voice," on the other hand, is not dependent upon the limitations of the medium expressing the musical idea. A part can usually be identified by simply viewing the score; a voice is a linear succession that might traverse two or even more parts. Such an "ideal" conceptual entity can be an object of musical experience because its continuity results from basic properties of the tonal system: the melodic fluency produced by stepwise succession, the need to prepare and – especially – to resolve dissonances, the affinity subsisting between members of the same chord, and the connection of high and low registers effected by octave equivalence.

Example 2 Bach, Sonata No. 3 in C major for unaccompanied violin, Adagio

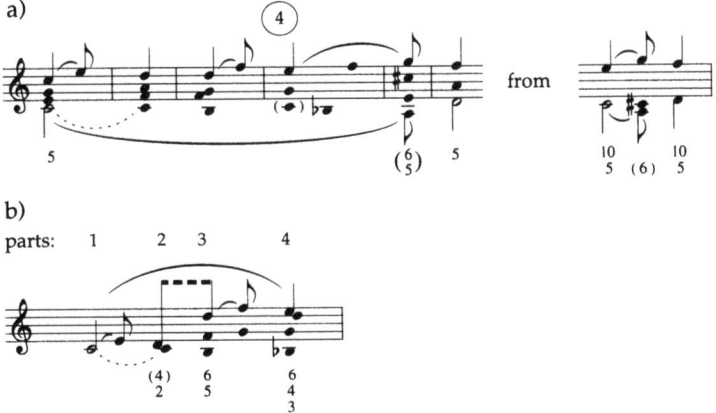

Thus Bach's Sonata No. 3 in C major for solo violin begins with one part on the G string, but in each successive bar a new string (and part) is added, enlarging the texture gradually from one to four parts. In the first four bars, as the melody is stated in turn on all four strings from the lowest to the highest, the "top" part is always superseded by a new one. Despite the addition of a new part (and string) at every bar, however, the voice leading of the top "voice" is contiguous (Example 2). There is continuity in the large-scale melodic line: a single top voice is expressed by four different "parts." Note that the unity of this top line is a composite unity – a river fed by tributaries. This is due to the presence of the voice-leading device of reaching-over in which ascending leaps in the upper voice have their origin in actual or implied inner-voice tones. Thus the top voice f^2 on the last beat of bar 3 originates in and resolves the "alto" f^1 (a diminished fifth) of the first beat.

In Example 2 a single voice encompasses several parts. Similarly, through the familiar device of "polyphonic melody," a single part can often express several voices. The registral placement of these voices in a polyphonic melody need not duplicate their placement in the underlying voice leading. In Bach's Passacaglia in C minor, Schenker (*Free Composition*, Figure 20/1) reads the adjacent notes f and g in bars 3–4 as two different voices. The f prolonged in bars 2–3 represents $\hat{4}$ in the top voice, whereas the g at the beginning of the following bar, despite its registral position above the f, articulates the dominant scale step (V). In the Sarabande from Bach's Cello Suite No. 5 in C minor (Example 3), the poignant dissonant intervals result from octave displacements in the voice leading. As shown in Example 3, the neighboring G–A♭ motion in the top voice of the opening four bars, which represents a contrapuntal 5–6 elaboration of tonic harmony, does not remain in the same tessitura.

Example 3 Bach, Suite No. 5 in C minor for unaccompanied cello, Sarabande

There are also situations where the bass line is not continuously stated in the lowest register. In the Sarabande of Bach's Partita No. 1 in B♭ major, for example, the fundamental voice leading of bars 23–24 is that of a descending sequence in parallel tenths leading from I to V. Despite the two-part texture of the music, the right hand articulates a segment of the bass line in its stepwise descent; the a^2 intended for the bass on the second beat of bar 23 appears in the highest rather than the lowest part (Example 4).

Example 4 Bach, Partita No. 1 in B♭ major, Sarabande

becomes

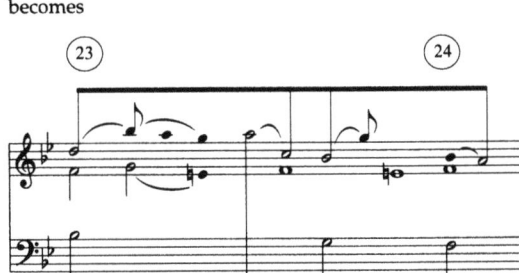

The voice/part dichotomy presented here is a kind of generalization of Heinrich Schenker's distinction between *Ursatz* and *Aussensatz* (outer-voice setting). It is important to note that he did not insist that the *Urlinie* necessarily be presented as the highest part. The notes of the *Urlinie* and scale degrees "remain at the same time pure idea, even if they crop up in the course of the treble and bass voices."[3] Schenker adds a caution: "The highest notes in the treble attract attention, arouse curiosity; and because they *are* the highest, they are exactly the ones that are always [mistakenly] considered to be the notes of the *Urlinie*."[4] While the *Urlinie* represents the basic melodic component of a composition, it need not be expressed by the part in the uppermost register.

The distinction between registral top voice (*Oberstimme*) and structural top voice

In his reading of the end of the first movement of Beethoven's "Moonlight" Sonata (*Free Composition*, Figure 54/3), Schenker reveals the distinction between registral and structural top voices. His graph shows the octave descent of the *Urlinie*'s 1̂ from c♯² to c♯¹ in bars 51–60. Although there is a skip from g♯¹ to c♯¹ in the melody (bars 59–60), the structural top voice does not break off; it continues in the highest notes of the accompaniment. The descent from 3̂ to 1̂ during these bars preserves stepwise continuity in the structural top voice despite the leap in the registral top voice.[5]

Structural descents in the inner voice can occur on a broader scale. Indeed,

---

3. Schenker, "Further Considerations of the Urlinie: I," trans. John Rothgeb, *Masterwork* I, p. 105.
4. *Ibid*.
5. Of course, this octave descent does not form part of the *Urlinie* proper, but it is the top-voice structure of this part of the movement. At an earlier stage of his career, Schenker would have considered it a segment of the *Urlinie*.

Example 5 Schubert, "Die liebe Farbe"

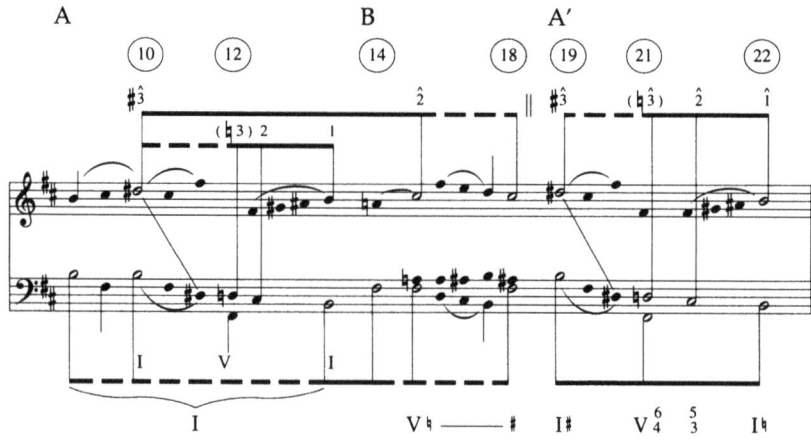

they can characterize the *Urlinie* itself. In Schubert's "Die liebe Farbe" from *Die schöne Müllerin*, part of the fundamental line of the entire work is presented in an inner voice. The expected primary tone would be D♮ ($\hat{3}$ in B minor), arrived at first in bar 10 after a stepwise initial ascent, and regained in bar 19. However, this expected minor $\hat{3}$ is raised to D♯ both times. This major form of $\hat{3}$ is taken over by the left hand of the piano part upon the arrival of the cadential $^6_4$ in the following bar, and is chromatically altered back into the minor mode before descending to $\hat{1}$ in the inner voice (Example 5). In this example, unusually, an inner voice of the piano accompaniment, not the melodic vocal part, articulates the structural top voice.[6] The occurrence of this structural melodic descent in the inner voice has a programmatic significance. In the phrase "Mein Schatz hat's Grün so gern" ("My beloved likes green so much") there is an intentional conflict of mode between the vocal part and piano accompaniment. The major form of $\hat{3}$ expressed by the singer serves as a metaphor for the outward joy normally associated with the words "mein Schatz," but the occurrence of the structural melodic descent in minor in the piano accompaniment expresses the inner pain felt by the narrator. Here the borrowing from major has an ironic character: the singer knows (as do his listeners) that his beloved is no longer his "Schatz." The real inner feelings of the narrator are poignantly articulated in the ♮$\hat{3}$–$\hat{2}$–$\hat{1}$ descent which occurs in the piano accompaniment.

The continuity of voice leading across different registers

One of the most frequent situations in which a note of the top voice appears to be transferred into the bass is the voice exchange in which two different parts articulate notes previously stated by the other. This usually results from the repositioning of a single chord; the transference from one part into another is

---

6. For other examples, see Carl Schachter, "The Prelude from Bach's Suite No. 4 for Violoncello Solo: The Submerged Urlinie," *Current Musicology* 56 (1994), pp. 54–71; and "The Prelude in E Minor Op. 28 No. 4: Autograph Sources and Interpretation," in *Chopin Studies 2*, ed. John Rink and Jim Samson (Cambridge: Cambridge University Press, 1994), p. 167, where Example 9.3 shows how the top voice of the Prelude descends into the inner voice.

Example 6 Schubert, "Du bist die Ruh"

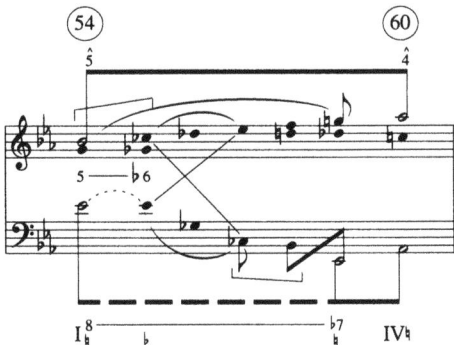

a conceptual rather than a literal exchange. Often the effect is an exchange of notes rather than the motion of a voice (i.e., a linear continuity). Sometimes, however, motivic connections can occur across two separate parts through a voice exchange, and the integrity of the motive creates a linear connection.[7] In Schubert's "Du bist die Ruh," for example, the melodic neighbor-note figure B♭–C–B♭, which appears throughout the song as an important motivic idea, is expanded into the bass through a voice exchange. In the third strophe (bars 54ff.) the vocal line rises up a seventh from b♭¹ to a♭². The neighbor-note motive is embedded within this ascent, appearing in its minor form as b♭¹ rising to c♭². As a result of the voice exchange between the outer voices in bars 55–57, c♭ reappears in the bass before descending to b♭ in bar 58 (Example 6).

In voice exchanges with chromatic inflections of one (or both) of the parts, melodic motion can also be implied across different voices. In the second movement of Mozart's Piano Concerto in F major, K.459, the motivic idea of an ascending chromatic third is stated across two voices through a voice exchange. The chromatic inflection of f² in the top voice to f♯ in the bass on the second beat of bar 4 allows for an expanded repetition of this chromatic motive (Example 7). Although the respective identities of the outer parts remain distinct, they articulate the rising chromatic motive together. Furthermore, the chromatic inflection of F to F♯ in the voice exchange transforms the relatively stable IV⁶ into a diminished triad (♯IV) intensifying the motion from I to V.

As these examples have shown, continuity of voice leading can be maintained across different registers. This also applies to dissonances, which, as long as they are ultimately resolved properly, can also be transferred into other voices in different registers.[8] Sevenths are frequently articulated over different registers.

---

7. Motivic associations across different voices are not exclusive to voice exchanges. In Schubert's Ländler in D major, Op. 171, No. 3, the chromatically varied neighbor figure in the inner voice of bar 7 (b♭–a–b♮–a) is echoed in bars 9–12; the figure passes from the bass (a♯–a♮) to the top voice (b–a). Thus the succession of notes in the outer voices enharmonically recalls a detail of figuration in the inner voice.

8. The transferred resolution to a different voice in the same register occurs frequently in free composition. For example, in the second movement of Brahms's Clarinet Trio Op. 114 the bass voice C, the seventh of the V⁴₂ articulated in the cello in bars 2–3, resolves to the B in the piano part in the following bar.

Example 7 Mozart, Piano Concerto in F major, K.459, Allegretto

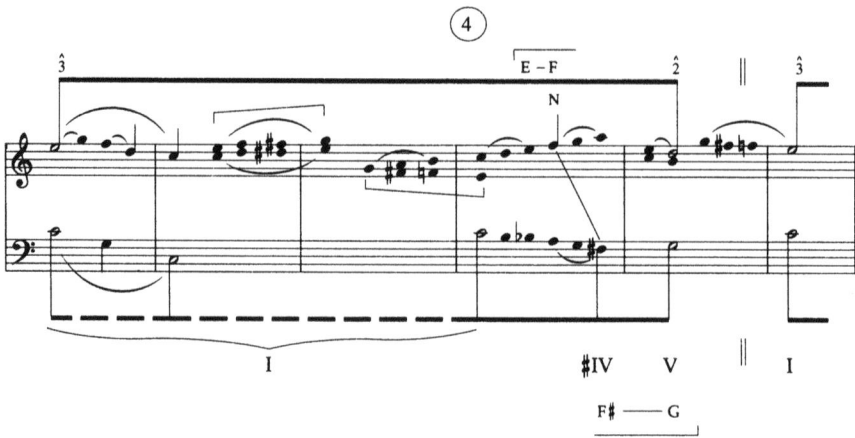

Because of the natural tendency of these sevenths to resolve downwards, they are usually transferred from a higher to a lower voice.[9] The transferred resolution of sevenths, especially scale degree 4 as the seventh of V^7, has been an acknowledged voice-leading technique since the late seventeenth century, and is described in numerous figured bass manuals. A reference to this specific procedure appears in Schenker's commentary to Beethoven's Piano Sonata in A major, Op. 101, which contains his earliest published voice-leading graphs. He remarks that the seventh of V^7, the d^2 in bar 2 of the opening theme, resolves into the c♯ in the bass in bar 4. (He reads the a in the bass in the second half of bar 3 as an inner voice.)[10]

In Figure 109/e2 of *Free Composition*, Schenker shows a more elaborate transferred resolution: it appears in the opening theme of Beethoven's Cello Sonata in A major, Op. 69. Schenker reads 5̂ as the main structural melodic note, and shows a prolongation of this scale degree by a motion down a third and back up again. Despite its appearance in the lowest register, the C♯ in bar 5 is the culmination of a descending third-progression in the top voice. Scale degree 4̂ in bar 3 is essentially the seventh of an implied V^7 chord; its resolution to 3̂ appears in the bass in bar 5. As well as regaining the top voice tone 5̂, the ascending third at the end of the phrase has the harmonic implication of a motion from I^6 through ♯IV to V.[11]

---

9. The reverse procedure of resolving a seventh from the bass into a higher voice does sometimes occur. In the Sarabande from Bach's French Suite in E♭ major (bars 17–20) the sevenths are transferred from the melody to the bass line before resolving in the top voice.
10. Schenker, *Erläuterungsausgabe, Op. 101*, p. 27; rev. edn, p. 16.
11. The descent to 3̂ in the bass represents a motion into an inner voice beneath a retained 5̂. (Exactly the same voice-leading motion appears in the first movement of Haydn's String Quartet in G major, Op. 76, No. 1.) This kind of motion quite frequently connects the two phrases of a parallel period construction, with 5̂ retained as the main tone over the antecedent phrase. See Schachter, "The Prelude in E Minor Op. 28 No. 4," Example 9.3, pp. 167–68; see also Cadwallader, "Foreground Motivic Ambiguity," pp. 61–63, where Ernst Oster's reading of Brahms's Intermezzo in B♭ minor, Op. 117, No. 2, is discussed.

Example 8 Mozart, Divertimento in E♭ major, K.563, Allegro (last movement)

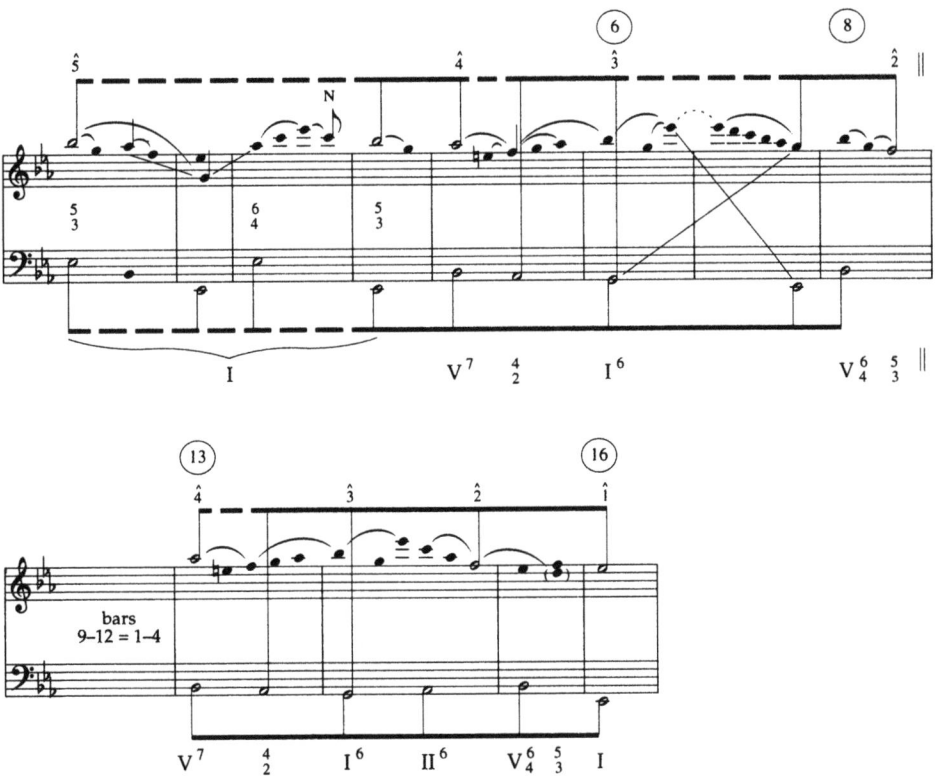

The *Urlinie* descent of $\hat{4}$–$\hat{3}$

The opening theme of a piece or movement will often foreshadow in miniature the structure of an entire work; in Schenkerian terms, these themes project a form of the fundamental structure transferred to a later level. In the final movement of Mozart's Divertimento in E♭ major, K.563 (Example 8), the $\hat{4}$ of the opening theme's structural line (a♭²) moves into the bass, where it resolves to $\hat{3}$ (g). Despite the simultaneous appearance of scale degree 4 in the outer voices on the last eighth note of bar 5, the bass articulates the principal dissonance; the top voice a♭² appears incidentally as a passing note in the fourth-motion from f² to b♭².¹² Through a voice exchange in bars 6–7, the g in the bass is brought back into the top voice before completing the descent to $\hat{2}$ (f²) at the end of the antecedent phrase in bar 8. In the consequent phrase (bars 9–16), the fundamental melodic line completes the melodic descent from $\hat{5}$ to $\hat{1}$ with a similar articulation of $\hat{4}$ and $\hat{3}$ in the bass in bars 13–14.

Though different in character and style from the Mozart example, the opening theme of Brahms's Clarinet Sonata, Op. 120, No. 2, also in E♭, displays a similar structural melodic descent. Here a♭² ($\hat{4}$), the climax of the melody in bar 5, does not move directly into the bass but reappears two bars later where it

---

12. Similar examples can be found in the second movement of Beethoven's "Pastorale" Symphony (bar 4), and in the Brahms song, "Wie bist du, meine Königin," Op. 32, No. 9 (bar 9).

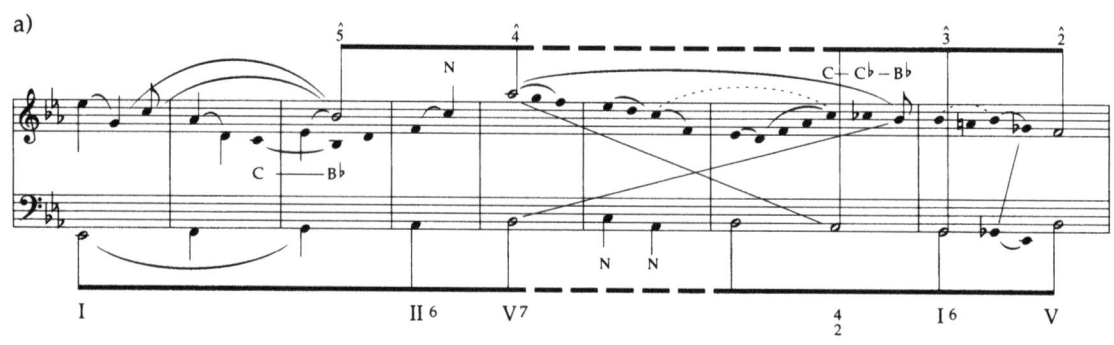

Example 9 Brahms, Clarinet Sonata in E♭ major, Op. 120, No. 2, Allegro amabile

b) Bars 1–4

N.B. reaching-over in inner voice

supports a V$^4_2$ chord which resolves to G ($\hat{3}$) in the bass at the beginning of bar 8. There is a voice exchange between A♭ and B♭ in bars 5–7, and G ($\hat{3}$) is chromatically inflected to G♭ before it resurfaces in the melodic line (Example 9).

The transference of $\hat{4}$ from the top voice into the bass can occur in the *Urlinie* proper – the structural line of an entire piece.[13] In the recapitulation of the first movement of Beethoven's Piano Sonata in F minor, Op. 2, No. 1, for example, part of the fundamental melodic line is articulated in the bass. Example 10 pre-

---

13. Although the articulation of the fundamental melodic line in the bass voice is not discussed in any of Schenker's published writings, there is an unpublished analysis of Brahms's Intermezzo Op. 76, No. 4, in which the *Urlinie* descends into the bass. A detailed *Urlinie-Tafel* of this piece, found in the "Brahms folder" of the Oster Collection at the New York Public Library (see file 34, items 45–52), was made by Schenker in conjunction with his student Angi Elias. (Concerning the Brahms folder, see Allen Cadwallader and William Pastille's essay in this volume.) Also included in the folder is a graphic analysis of this work by Ernst Oster. I am grateful to John Rothgeb for providing me with a photocopy of this graph, and to William Rothstein, who called attention to these unpublished analyses in his article "On Implied Tones," *Music Analysis* 10/3 (1991), p. 307 and p. 325, n. 39.

While it is beyond the scope of this paper to examine the many fascinating details in Schenker's analysis, it is worth examining his interpretation of the final section of the piece. In Schenker's reading, $\hat{4}$ prevails as the top voice throughout the A and B sections until the return of the A' section in bar 32. In bar 42, $\hat{4}$, supporting a V$^4_2$ chord, is transferred into the bass where it resolves to $\hat{3}$ in the following bar. What is particularly interesting about Schenker's reading is that the fundamental line continues its descent in the bass. In a comment accompanying his sketch of the piece, Schenker writes that "the necessity of creating a parallelism with bars 10–13 prevented Brahms from bringing $\hat{3}\,\hat{2}\,\hat{1}$ in the top voice" ("Die Notwendigkeit, den Takten 10–13 einen Parallelismus beizugeben hat Br[ahms] gehindert, die $\hat{3}\,\hat{2}\,\hat{1}$ in der Oberst[imme] zu bringen"). Thus the rhythmic profile of the top voice in the cadence in G minor at the end of the first A section is echoed.

Several published Schenkerian analyses show $\hat{4}$–$\hat{3}$ descents in the bass. Among these are the analysis of the Prelude in A minor from the *Well-Tempered Clavier*, Book I, in David Beach, "The Fundamental Line from Scale Degree 8: Criteria for Evaluation," *Journal of Music Theory* 32/2 (1988), pp. 283–88 and Figure 5 (see especially p. 288, where Beach gives an explanation of his "interpreta-

Example 10 Beethoven, Sonata in F minor, Op. 2, No. 1, Allegro

sents a voice-leading reduction of the recapitulation of this movement.[14] The movement's initial top-voice tone, c^3 ($\hat{5}$), is regained seven bars into the recapitulation (bar 107), and prolonged until bar 132. This c^3 is brought down two octaves through a rapid descending scale to c^1 in bar 134. In the following bar, $\hat{4}$ (B♭) appears in the bass before resolving to $\hat{3}$ (A♭) at the beginning of bar 136. Bars 136–38 are an exact repetition of bars 132–34, but the fundamental top voice over these bars is to be read differently. Although c^3 reappears in the top voice, it is the A♭ in the bass at the beginning of bar 136 which articulates the *Urlinie*. This A♭ ($\hat{3}$) in the bass continues in the top voice with g ($\hat{2}$), the last eighth note in bar 139, descending to f ($\hat{1}$) at the beginning of bar 140.[15]

So far, we have examined situations in which $\hat{4}$ in the *Urlinie* is transferred from the top voice into the bass before resolving to $\hat{3}$. However, $\hat{4}$ need not always go into the bass in such progressions. The foreground procedure of transferring a resolution into another voice (see Schenker's discussion of Beethoven's Op. 101 and Op. 69 Sonatas, cited above) can occur at deeper structural levels. Bach's Prelude in E♭ minor from Book I of the *Well-Tempered Clavier* provides an example of a transferred resolution in the *Urlinie* in which $\hat{4}$ skips directly from the top voice to $\hat{3}$ in the bass (Example 11). The primary structural tone of the piece, $\hat{5}$, descends to $\hat{4}$ supported by IV in bar 20. The applied dominant seventh chord preceding IV relates back to the opening tonic, and I $^{8-7}$ is the basic progression in bars 1–19.[16] After the arrival on $\hat{4}$ at

tion, borrowed from Ernst Oster . . ., particularly in regard to the transfer of the fundamental line to the bass"); the analysis of the duet "Bei Männern" from *Die Zauberflöte* in Larry Laskowski, "Voice Leading and Meter: An Unusual Mozart Autograph," in *Trends in Schenkerian Research*, ed. Allen Cadwallader (New York: Schirmer Books, 1990), pp. 41–49; and the analysis of the Prelude from Bach's D minor English Suite in Channan Willner, "Bach's Periodicities Re-Examined," *Irish Musical Studies 4: The Maynooth International Musicological Conference, 1995, part 1*, ed. Patrick Devine and Harry White (Dublin: Four Courts Press, 1996), pp. 93–102.

14. A descent from $\hat{5}$ to $\hat{1}$ that remains in the top voice appears in the coda, bars 146–51.
15. Cf. Schenker's analysis of this Sonata in *Tonwille* 2 (1922), pp. 25–48, where the *Urlinie* descent from $\hat{4}$ to $\hat{2}$ occurs in bar 139.
16. Tovey regards this passage, with its alteration of the minor tonic into an applied dominant of IV, as one of "highest pathos." He notes that the altered tonic "means the tragic irony of a momentary major tonic chord, implying a hope which is frustrated at the very moment by the flattened seventh." See Donald Francis Tovey, *Beethoven* (London: Oxford University Press, 1944), p. 26.

Example 11 Bach, Prelude in E♭ minor, *Well-Tempered Clavier*, Book I

b) Middleground graph

the beginning of bar 20, a♭² in the top voice becomes the seventh of V⁷. The dominant harmony is outlined by the outer parts articulated in canon over bars 20–21, and the dissonant a♭² ($\hat{4}$) in the top voice resolves to G♭ ($\hat{3}$) in the bass at the beginning of bar 22.[17] Following this "leap into the abyss," the *Urlinie* moves back into the top part, arriving on the Phrygian $\hat{2}$ (♭$\hat{2}$) in bar 26.[18] The ♭II⁶ of this bar leads through an apparent "V$^4_2$" chord (resulting from a passing note F♮ and neighbor D♮) in bar 27 to a cadential $^6_4$ in the following bar. Upon the arrival on the dominant at the last beat of bar 28, F♭, the natural form of scale degree 2, is restored in the inner voice. The fundamental melodic line completes its descent on $\hat{1}$ in bar 29, where a deceptive cadence on IV⁶ initiates a twelve-bar coda.[19]

The possibility of articulating $\hat{4}$ and $\hat{3}$ in the bass naturally presupposes $\hat{5}$ as the *Urlinie*'s primary melodic tone. But the most significant consequence of a $\hat{4}$–$\hat{3}$ descent in the bass is that it allows a fully consonant support for $\hat{5}$ and $\hat{3}$ without the articulation of a double harmonic progression in which $\hat{3}$ is supported by I. Usually when *Urlinie* descents are articulated as a single harmonic progression, $\hat{3}$ will occur either as a dissonant passing tone or as a sixth over a cadential $^6_4$, which, of course, is a dissonant sonority.[20]

Other instances of $\hat{3}$ in the bass: the relationship between the cadential $^6_4$ and "I⁶"

The descent from $\hat{4}$ to $\hat{3}$ in the progression V$^4_2$ (or V⁷) to I⁶ is not the only situation in which part of the *Urlinie* can occur in the bass. Occasionally the cadential $^6_4$ chord can be elaborated by transferring the $\hat{3}$ in the top voice into the bass. The resultant "I⁶" chord is not a return to the tonic, but an elaboration within the dominant. Such an instance appears in the first movement of Beethoven's Piano Sonata in A major, Op. 101 (Example 12). At the final cadence (bars 71ff.)

17. Schenker's graph of this Prelude in *Tonwille* 1 (1921), p. 38, shows the transferred resolution.
18. The lowered second step, F♭, is an important motivic element which becomes emphasized gradually during the course of the Prelude. It appears initially in bar 5, where it tonicizes a C♭ chord, and is expanded in bars 17–19 before reaching its ultimate realization as ♭II in bar 26. The tragic veil it casts over the piece may have a programmatic significance, with F♭ representing a premonition of death.
19. In his essay on this Prelude, Schenker refers to the version in the Forkel MS, where four alternative bars exist in place of bars 29–40 (see *Tonwille* 1, p. 41). These four bars are similar to bars 37–40 of the final version, suggesting that bars 29–36 were inserted later. Schenker dismisses the Forkel version on the grounds of the principle of obligatory register. He reads the primary register of the *Urlinie* as that of b♭¹ ($\hat{5}$), and notes that the "shorter" Forkel version, which ends on e♭² ($\hat{1}$), conflicts with this. In my reading the primary melodic register is an octave higher (with the b♭² in bar 7 as the initial $\hat{5}$, reached by an arpeggiation), and the *Urlinie* closes on e♭² ($\hat{1}$) in bar 29. The octave descent in the coda thus balances the register of the opening statement of $\hat{5}$ on b♭¹. Thus, although the "extra bars" in this Prelude are similar to those added by Bach in the final version of the Prelude in C major from Book I of the *Well-Tempered Clavier*, I believe they are made to achieve registral balance rather than for the sake of preserving the obligatory register as in the C major Prelude.

    The Forkel MS to which Schenker refers is the earliest known source for the *Well-Tempered Clavier*; it served as the basis for the edition published by Hoffmeister in 1802. The manuscript is in an anonymous hand, with a title page by Forkel, and is known today as the Konwitschny MS. The manuscript is no longer extant, but a microfilm is preserved in the Bach-Archiv in Leipzig.
20. An extended discussion of the second possibility can be found in David Beach's "The Cadential Six-Four as Support for Scale-Degree Three of the Fundamental Line," *Journal of Music Theory* 34/1 (1990), pp. 81–99, and its sequel, "More on the Six-Four," *Journal of Music Theory* 34/2 (1990), pp. 281–90.

Example 12 Beethoven, Sonata in A major, Op. 101, Allegretto ma non troppo

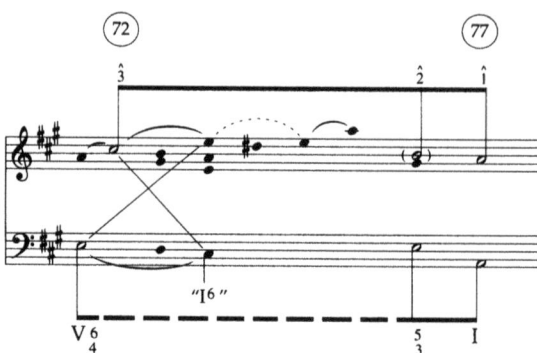

$\hat{3}$ in the top voice of the cadential $^6_4$ goes into the bass supporting "I⁶" before finally resolving in bar 77. Similarly, at the end of Schumann's song "Wehmut," Op. 39, No. 9, a I⁶ chord grows out of the cadential $^6_4$ in bar 24 (Example 13). What is unusual here is that the *Urlinie* continues to descend in the bass, creating a voice-leading analogy to the text's "tiefe Leid im Lied" (the hidden sorrow in [the nightingale's] song).

Example 13 Schumann, "Wehmut," Op. 39, No. 9

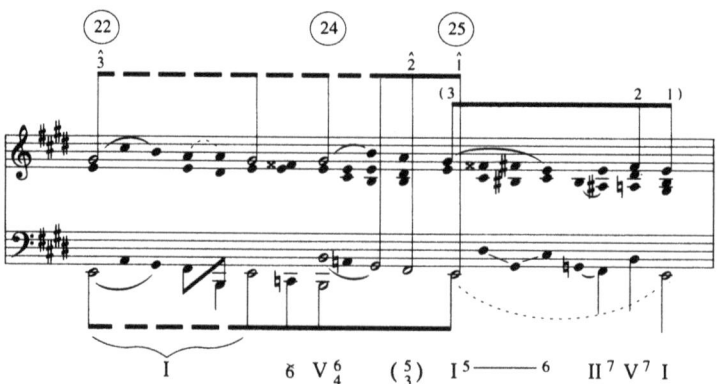

Sometimes "I⁶" occurs not merely as part of a contrapuntal elaboration of the cadential $^6_4$ but rather as a replacement for it.[21] Brahms's Intermezzo in A minor, Op. 76, No. 7, presents a striking example of this possibility (Example 14). In bar 31 the bass voice of the augmented sixth chord does not resolve properly: instead of descending by step from f to e, it jumps down to c, highlighting the *Urlinie*'s descent to $\hat{3}$.[22] This c in the bass is anticipated by the inner voice c² of

---

21. The substitution of "I⁶" for a cadential $^6_4$ can sometimes occur as a voice-leading corrective. In Brahms's Waltz in A♭ major, Op. 39, No. 15, the melodic line of bar 3, with its grace note figure, is expanded in bars 5–8. In bar 7, where the bass note G is expected as the dominant of C minor, Brahms instead writes E♭, supporting a "I⁶" chord, in order to avoid parallel octaves with the top voice.
22. This interpretation is similar to that of Allen Cadwallader in "More on Scale Degree Three and the Cadential Six-Four," *Journal of Music Theory* 36/1 (1992), pp. 193–94.

Example 14 Brahms, Intermezzo in A minor, Op. 76, No. 7

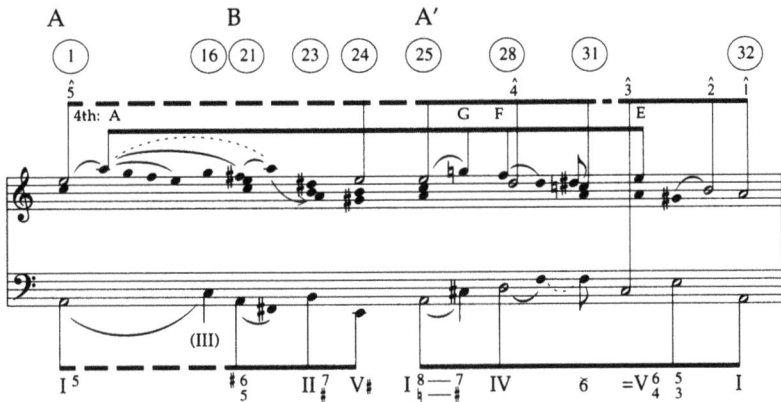

the augmented sixth chord, and the prominence of e^2 in the top voice at this point completes the large-scale motivic expansion of the opening theme's descending fourth in a subsidiary line above the *Urlinie*.

$\hat{2}$ in the bass

While we have a number of situations whereby $\hat{3}$ of the *Urlinie* can be articulated in the bass, instances involving $\hat{2}$ are significantly less frequent. One of the principal reasons for this is the fact that when scale degree 5, the root of the dominant, appears above $\hat{2}$, a vertical interval of a fourth occurs. Although the contrapuntal dissonance of a fourth is not possible as a background structure, it can appear in foreground situations. In Bach's Sarabande from the Partita in D major, for example, such a "consonant" fourth ushers in the recapitulation of the opening theme in bar 29 (Example 15).

In deeper levels of structure, when $\hat{2}$ appears in the bass it will usually be unfolded horizontally. The second movement of Mozart's Piano Concerto in F major (K.459) provides an example. We have already looked at part of the A section (bars 1–10), organized in the antecedent–consequent construction of a

Example 15 Bach, Partita No. 4 in D major, Sarabande

Example 16 Mozart, Piano Concerto in F major, K.459, Allegretto

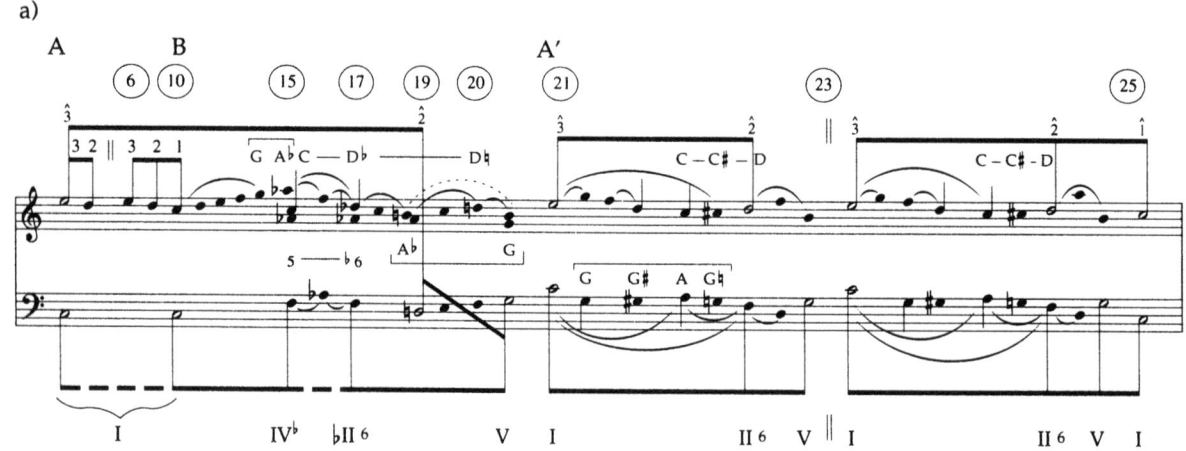

b) Bars 17–19

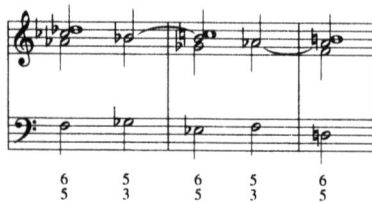

parallel period (see Example 7). The B section (bars 10–20) elaborates the motion from the expanded tonic of the A section to the structural dominant which leads to the return of the A' section (bars 21–25). The B section is not only cast in the minor mode, but also invokes the Phrygian II chord (D♭ major) in bar 17. This tonally distant harmony, as well as the sequence which follows it, creates a dark and ominous effect in stark contrast to the "white" diatonic world of the A section's C major. As shown in Example 16, the ♭II grows out of a 5–6 motion from the minor form of IV expanded in bars 15–16. Usually in a progression leading from the Phrygian II to the dominant, the lowered scale degree 2 is "corrected" to its natural form in an inner voice of the dominant chord. Here, however, the ♭II leads to V through a poignant sequence that brings in the natural form of $\hat{2}$ in the bass. The diminished seventh chord at the beginning of bar 19 represents the structural dominant with $a\flat^1$ as an inner-voice suspension descending to g^1. The d in the bass represents the *Urlinie*'s $\hat{2}$ which unfolds up a fourth to V (g) on the second beat of bar 20. The first violins (and flute) moving in parallel sixths above the bass bring $\hat{2}$ (d^2) back in the "correct" top voice placement on the first beat of bar 20.

The progression from I to V that takes place in the A and B sections supports the interrupted melodic descent from $\hat{3}$ to $\hat{2}$. The chromatic line C–D♭–D♮ expanded in the B section, is later incorporated into the A' section where it is enharmonically reinterpreted as C–C♯–D. The descending motion A♭–G which

Example 17 Brahms, Symphony No. 2 in D major, Allegro non troppo

occurred within the prolongation of the structural dominant at the end of the B section is also echoed in the A' section, where it becomes inverted and enharmonically rewritten as G–G♯–A in the bass.

A more expanded statement of the *Urlinie*'s $\hat{2}$ in the bass occurs just before the coda of the first movement in Brahms's Second Symphony (Example 17). The final *Urlinie* descent from $\hat{2}$ to $\hat{1}$ occurs in the magnificent horn solo beginning in bar 454. Example 17 shows how e^2 ($\hat{2}$) is transferred from the top voice into the bass and back again through voice exchanges. At the climactic diminished seventh chord in bar 469, $\hat{2}$ (E) appears in the bass. The bass ascends chromatically to the dominant scale degree again in bars 470–75, unfolding a fourth from E to A. Within this entire passage the neighbor-note figure E–F♯–E, stated by the horn at the start of its solo, is expanded between the outer voices.

Besides horizontalizing the dominant chord in the bass, the melodic presentation of $\hat{2}$ and $\hat{5}$ can also represent the scale step succession of II–V. The bass-line theme that opens Schubert's "Unfinished" Symphony presents such a dual function, as Schenker indicates in his graph of the theme (*Free Composition*, Figure 109/e4). The lowest note, C♯, represents the arrival of $\hat{2}$; at the same time it functions as the root of II. Thus it is possible (though surely unusual) for one and the same note in an unsupported polyphonic melody to represent both a top voice and the bass.

Example 18 Chopin, Polonaise in C minor, Op. 40, No. 2

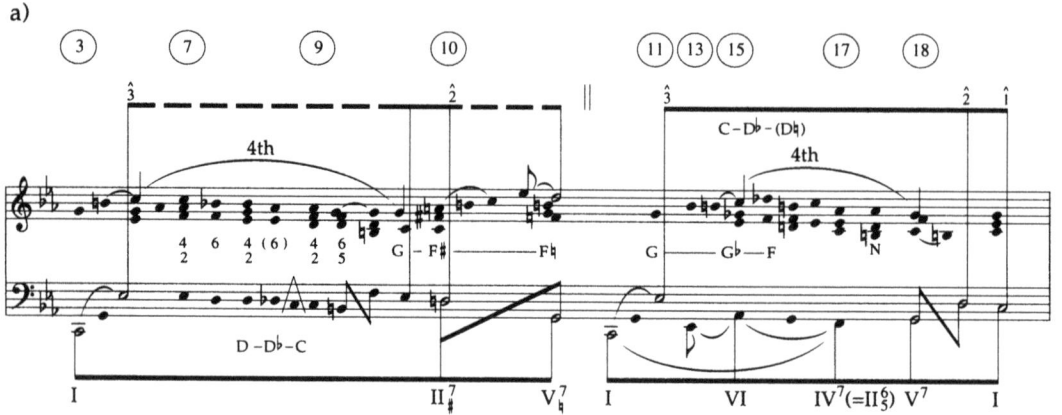

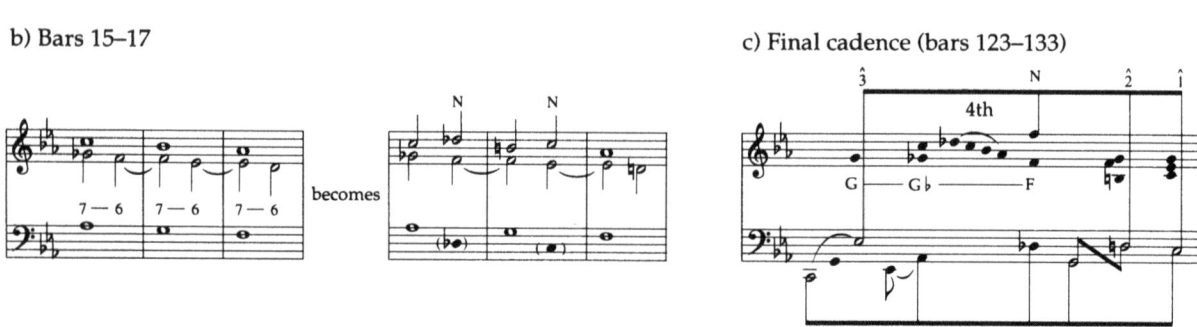

A similar example can be found in Chopin's Polonaise in C minor, Op. 40, No. 2 (Example 18). Here the principal theme, cast in the antecedent–consequent construction of a parallel period, is stated almost entirely in the bass as a polyphonic melody.[23] The initial tone of the *Urlinie* ($\hat{3}$) appears in the bass in bar 3, and the antecedent phrase closes on $\hat{2}$. This $\hat{2}$ first appears in the left-hand part at the beginning of bar 10, where it supports the II^7 chord. When V enters at the end of the bar, the $\hat{2}$ is heard in retrospect as its top-voice tone. Almost simultaneously, the $\hat{2}$ is transferred up two octaves into the right-hand part, forming a link between the two phrases. (Bar 10 is the one place in this opening section where, for a brief moment, the right hand takes center stage.) In the consequent phrase, the overall progression leads from I to V through VI and IV^7. Again the $\hat{2}$ appears as an arpeggiation above V, but this time following rather than preceding the dominant scale step.

In its dual function as both part of the *Urlinie* and the root of II (or II^7), $\hat{2}$ need not always form part of a melodic line which is stated in the bass. In the

---

23. There are frequent instances of placing the melody in the bass in Chopin's works, e.g., the Preludes in B minor and G minor, Op. 28, Nos. 6 and 22. In the Etude in C♯ minor, Op. 25, No. 7, the bass line expresses a melody which states both top voice and bass.

Example 19 Brahms, Clarinet Sonata in E♭ major, Op. 120, No. 2, Allegro amabile

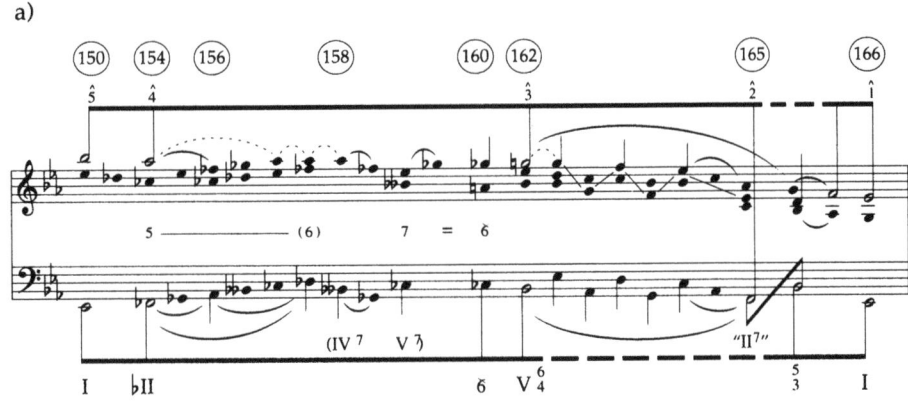

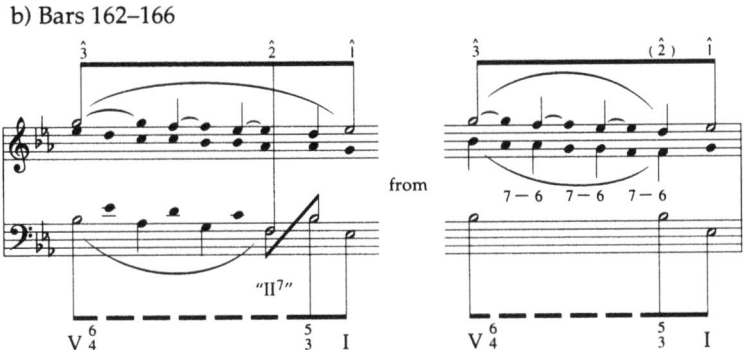

b) Bars 162–166

coda of the first movement of the Brahms Clarinet Sonata in E♭ major, Op. 120, No. 2, despite the presence of a distinct melodic line in the top voice, the bass note of the II⁷ at the final cadence in bars 165–66 serves as $\hat{2}$ in the *Urlinie*. Example 19 presents a voice-leading reduction of the entire coda which descends from $\hat{5}$ (bars 150–66). Paralleling the beginning of the development section, the lowered seventh, D♭, is brought in above the E♭ tonic chord in bar 153. However, instead of tonicizing IV, this altered tonic chord cadences on an F♭ chord (the Phrygian II in the key of E♭) supporting $\hat{4}$. Brahms writes F♭ as E♮ for the sake of notational convenience, but this enharmonic change also recalls the chromatic motive E♭–E♮–F which prevails throughout the movement.

The key of F♭ is expanded by a motion to its own V⁷ (with C♭, notated as B♮, as its root) in bar 160. At this point Brahms effects a marvelous enharmonic modulation by transforming this C♭ seventh chord into an augmented sixth chord which resolves on the dominant of E♭ major. With the arrival on the dominant in bar 162, $\hat{3}$ in the top voice, supported by a cadential $^6_4$, resolves to $\hat{2}$ in the bass of the "II⁷" in bar 165. As shown in the successive reductions, the sequence in descending fifths in bars 162–65 derives from a 7–6 suspension series over the dominant scale step.

The recasting of upper-voice themes into the bass

In this last section of the essay we shall explore how the recasting of top-voice themes into the bass can alter our perception of the *Urlinie*.[24] Although the notes of the *Urlinie* may still retain their identity in the bass, they may be subject to other factors. In the last movement of Beethoven's Piano Sonata in A major, Op. 101, for example, when the opening theme appears in the bass in bars 25ff. the primary melodic note C♯ ($\hat{3}$) serves to resolve a prominent top-voice seventh (d^2) preceding it (bars 21–24).[25]

In the next example (Example 20), the tonal structure of a whole section is directly influenced by the reappearance of a theme in the bass voice. In the F minor section (bars 95–116) of the Rondo movement from Mozart's Piano Sonata in F major, K.533/494, the outer voices appear in contrapuntal inversion at the return of the principal theme in bar 109: the original melody is now in the bass, and the characteristic descending fifths of the original bass appear in the top voice. In order to avoid beginning the return with a fourth between the outer parts (the inversion of the fifth with which the section begins), the "new" top voice is delayed by half a bar. Most unusually, dominant harmony underlies the entire inverted statement, although the original A section, consisting of essentially the same material, expresses the tonic. The *Urlinie* descent (of the F minor section, not of the entire Rondo) begins together with the prolonged dominant of the reprise. The descent of $\hat{5}$ to $\hat{4}$ unfolds in the bass (bars 109–12), and tonic harmony is only reestablished at the arrival on $\hat{3}$ in the bass (a♭) in the second half of bar 112. This $\hat{3}$ is prolonged in the next two bars and brought up into the top voice, where the *Urlinie* completes its descent. It is worth noting the augmented sixth chord in bar 113, which resolves irregularly up through V^6_5 to I, allowing for an echo of the bass line of bars 106–107.[26]

Finally, let us return to the Brahms Intermezzo in A major, Op. 118, No. 2, cited at the outset of this essay. We have already observed that the opening upbeat figure in the melody returns in the bass voice in bar 30. As in the beginning of the piece, the first note of this upbeat, C♯, articulates $\hat{3}$ in the *Urlinie* (see Examples 21a and 21b). This low C♯ is not, however, the initial statement of $\hat{3}$ in the return of the A′ section. The C♯ in the bass of bar 30 relates back to the $c\sharp^2$ in bar 28 which initiates the disguised repetition of the opening theme. The $A^4_{\flat 3}$ chord represents the return to the tonic expected at the beginning of the A′

---

24. The consideration of fugues is a special matter, as there will often be a permutation of voices in which the main theme (i.e., the subject) appears in the lowest voice. Sometimes the subject's appearance as a bass voice will articulate part of the *Urlinie* descent. In Bach's Fugue in C minor from the *Well-Tempered Clavier*, Book I, for example, the final note of the last statement of the subject in the bass (E♭ in bar 28) represents the structural $\hat{3}$ of the entire piece. See Carl Schachter's analysis of this passage in his article, "Schoenberg's Hat and Lewis Carroll's Trousers," in *Aflame with Music: 100 Years of Music at the University of Melbourne*, ed. Brenton Broadstock et al. (Melbourne: Centre for Studies in Australian Music, 1996), p. 336, Example 6d.
25. Schenker discusses this passage in the *Erläuterungsausgabe, Op. 101*, p. 50; rev. edn, p. 66. The upbeat E that precedes the C♯ functions as an incomplete upper neighbor. This incomplete upper neighbor is recalled yet again in the coda by the sixteenth-note upbeat figures (bars 318–19, 322–23, and 324–25).
26. Cf. the opening theme of Mozart's Piano Concerto in C minor, K.491, where the bass of an augmented sixth chord (bar 10) moves upwards.

Bass-line articulations of the Urlinie   295

Example 20 Mozart, Sonata in F major, K. 533/494, Rondo (F minor section)

[musical example]

section.²⁷ The dissonant g♮ is the lowered seventh scale degree in A major and transforms the tonic into an applied dominant leading to IV.²⁸ (This same altered tonic bridges the first and second phrases of the opening theme in bar 5.) By bringing back the return of the opening theme at the beginning of the A' section in such a tentative way Brahms simulates the fleeting manner in which the opening upbeat of the piece states the initial 3̂ of the *Urlinie*. Although the upbeat figure is reiterated in the bass in bars 30–34, the opening theme remains incomplete. Only in bar 34 does it return fully, coming back triumphantly in the top voice, where it is playfully articulated in inversion.

A beautiful detail of registral displacement appears in the final bars of the A' section (and again at the very end of the piece) where the opening theme is

27. Although he does not discuss the formal design of the piece, David Epstein also views bar 28 as representing tonic harmony. His main point, however, is that the A major chords in this piece appear "generally inverted and unstable," and that the tonic "is never heard as a point of rest until the closing measures." See *Beyond Orpheus: Studies in Musical Structure* (Cambridge, Mass.: MIT Press, 1979), pp. 175–76.
28. Cf. bar 59 of Schubert's "Du bist die Ruh" (see Example 6 above) and bar 19 of Bach's E♭ minor Prelude from the *Well-Tempered Clavier*, Book I (see Example 11 above).

296 Eric Wen

Example 21 Brahms, Intermezzo in A major, Op. 118, No. 2

a)

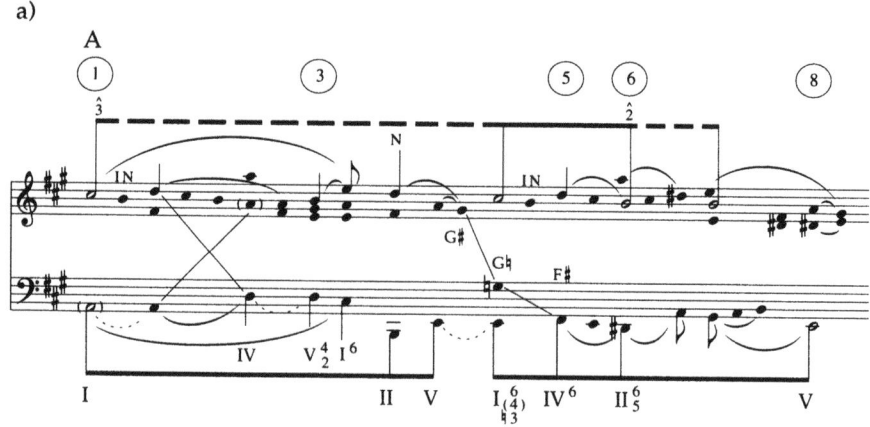
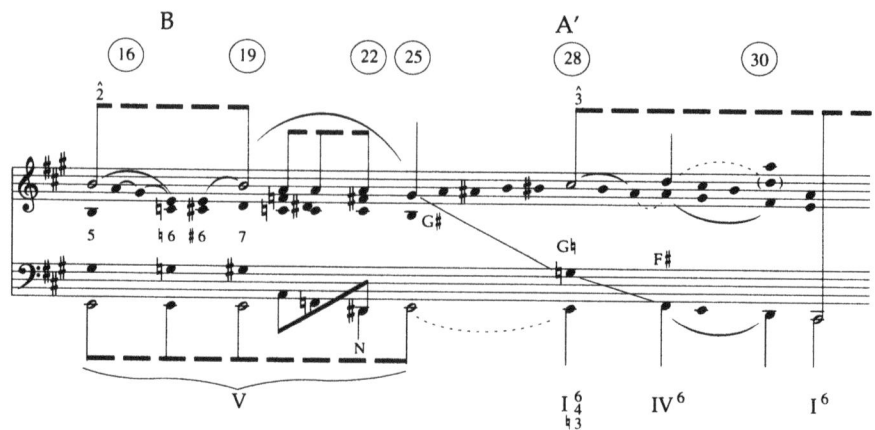

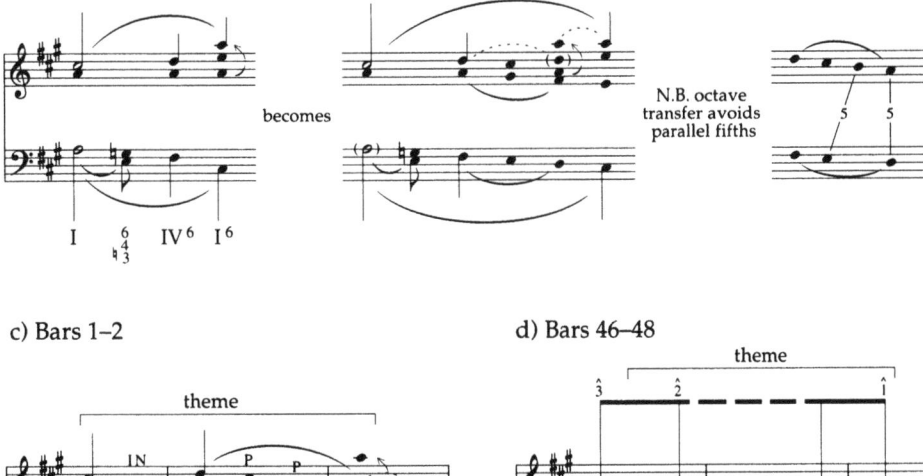

b) Bars 28–30

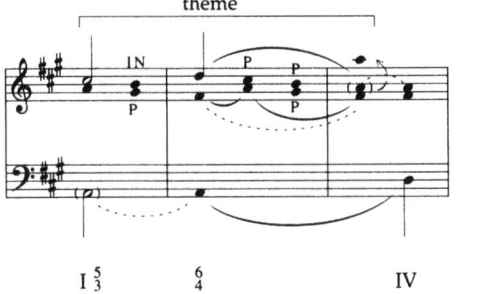

c) Bars 1–2

d) Bars 46–48

stated in the inner voice. As shown in Example 21c, the ascending seventh from b¹ to a² in the original statement of the theme represents the inversion of a descending second, b¹–a¹. At the end of the section (bars 46–48), with the arpeggiation of the final tonic chord (see Example 21d), we hear the melody in the inner voice descend a second from b to a within the motion of a third c♯¹–b–a. The last note of the broken chord (a¹) is heard as an echo of the final a, 1̂ in the alto, and the tension of the leap up a seventh is relieved.

As we have seen in this essay, the voice-leading technique of continuing the melodic top voice into the bass can be extended deep into a composition's structure to embrace the *Urlinie* itself. This does not obscure the distinction between the *Urlinie* and the bass arpeggiation, but demonstrates the flexibility of the *Ursatz*'s framework in maintaining coherent voice leading throughout the different structural levels. Although unusual, bass-line articulations of the *Urlinie* do not contradict Schenker's notion of the *Ursatz*, but evolve from the very principles of tonal organization which create the *Ursatz* itself.

Structure as foreground: "das Drama des Ursatzes"

Carl Schachter

Charles Rosen has cited a well-known but probably apocryphal story about Schoenberg's reaction to the "Eroica" analysis of Heinrich Schenker: "Schoenberg once looked at Schenker's graph of the *Eroica*, and said, 'But where are my favorite passages? Ah, there they are, in those tiny notes.'"[1] Rosen uses this story to point up what he regards as weaknesses in Schenker's approach: a disregard of proportions and a tendency to minimize the salient and explicit features of a work by putting them into "tiny notes." But Schenker's followers often make a similar point from an opposite perspective; it is almost a truism among them that interest and individuality reside precisely in those "tiny notes" of the middleground and foreground, the fundamental structure acting as guarantor of coherence. Thus Victor Zuckerkandl writes, "The main interest is not in the background itself but in *how* background and foreground are connected, i.e., the middle ground."[2] According to Allen Forte and Steven E. Gilbert, "The closer we get to the background, the more similar any two pieces are likely to appear."[3] And here is Felix Salzer explaining melodic analysis: "The structural tones are the spine of a melody; they establish its basic direction. What makes a structural line live, however, are the many different types of prolongation, since they provide the character, rhythmic interest, and color of a melody."[4]

Without in the least disputing these statements, I should like to suggest a slightly different way of viewing background structure. It seems self-evident that any awareness of a background depends on its being embodied somehow in a foreground. And that "somehow" is extremely variable. At times, the elements that represent the background – far from constituting a mere framework – participate in the most striking events of the foreground and are integral to its tonal conflicts, its unexpected twists, and its climaxes. In other words elements of the background are "foregrounded," to use the term more or less as

---

1. Charles Rosen, "Art has its Reasons," *The New York Review of Books* 16/11 (17 June 1971), p. 34. Milton Babbitt reports that he checked a version of the story with people who were in a position to know; they assured him that it was untrue. See Milton Babbitt, *Words about Music*, ed. Stephen Dembski and Joseph N. Straus (Madison: The University of Wisconsin Press, 1987), pp. 139–40.
2. Victor Zuckerkandl, "Schenker System," in Willi Apel, *The Harvard Dictionary of Music*, 2nd edn (Cambridge, Mass.: Harvard University Press, 1969), pp. 754–55.
3. Allen Forte and Steven E. Gilbert, *Introduction to Schenkerian Analysis* (New York: Norton, 1982), p. 131.
4. Felix Salzer, *Structural Hearing: Tonal Coherence in Music*, 2nd edn (New York: Dover, 1962), Vol. 1, p. 41.

literary critics do. This need not occur through simple and obvious emphasis. Often the foreground's ellipses, transformations, and multiple meanings can complicate the inference of an underlying structure so that the relation between perceived surface and inferred structure becomes problematic; and it is the problematic character that brings the background up to the front of the stage.

The suppression of structural notes: "das Drama des Ursatzes"

In this paper I shall explore a few of the varied ways in which the projection of an implicit background forms part of the explicit compositional discourse; under "background" I am including the resumed initial tonic and dominant following an interruption (as in a sonata recapitulation). Design and structure relate in a particularly intense manner in the Finale of Beethoven's "Moonlight" Sonata, Op. 27, No. 2. In a splendid article, and in a footnote to his English edition of *Free Composition*, Ernst Oster has pointed out that a single basic motive pervades all three movements of this "Sonata quasi una Fantasia."[5] It is the broken chord G#–C#–E, heard in the first three right-hand notes of the first movement and the Finale, and spread out to form middleground arpeggiations in both movements. In the Finale, the opening thematic statement encompasses only the G# and C# of the big arpeggio; the goal note E, $\hat{3}$ of the fundamental line, arrives only in the brief bridge passage (bars 16–18). The $\hat{2}$ follows immediately, over the tonicized V of the second theme. (The appearance of $\hat{2}$ at the second theme is typical for sonata movements that modulate to V, but the modulation itself rarely occurs in minor-key sonatas.) In his recapitulation, Beethoven omits any bridge passage, proceeding directly from the elaborated fermata at the end of the first theme to the second theme, now transposed to the tonic. This omission entails a most ominous consequence for the structure of the recapitulation: the E, goal of the primary motive and initial note of the fundamental line, does not reappear. As a result, both motive and fundamental line fail to achieve fulfillment in the recapitulation, doing so only in the coda's tragic climax. In the "Moonlight" Finale, the fundamental line interacts closely with the sequence of events in the foreground, including – indeed especially including – its discontinuities and surprises. The $\hat{3}$, in particular, with its delayed first appearance, its suppression in the recapitulation, and its reappearance at the catastrophe, almost takes on the role of a character in a story or play. Here, if ever, Schenker's phrase "das Drama des Ursatzes" is justified.[6]

A dramatic projection of structure can result from a large-scale juxtaposition of major and minor, such as we often find in the music of Schubert. In his lied

---

5. The article is "The *Fantasie-Impromptu:* A Tribute to Beethoven," *Musicology* 1/4 (1947), pp. 407–29, repr. in *Aspects of Schenkerian Theory*, ed. David Beach (New Haven: Yale University Press, 1983), pp. 189–207. The footnote is in §26 of *Free Composition*, p. 16, n. 8, and refers to Fig. 7.
6. *Der freie Satz*, p. 210. In Oster's English version the phrase is translated as "the drama of the fundamental structure." See *Free Composition*, p. 137. Schenker is countering Wagner's opinion that the recapitulation in Beethoven's *Leonore* Overture No. 3 is untrue to the drama. Note that Schenker speaks of the *Ursatz* even though he is referring to the recapitulation, whose initial tonic belongs to the first level of middleground according to Schenker's own formulation of his theory. But this tonic replicates and represents the first tonic of the *Ursatz*; Schenker's wording is truer to musical experience than would be a more theoretically rigorous formulation.

Example 1 Schubert, "Ihr Bild": modal mixture

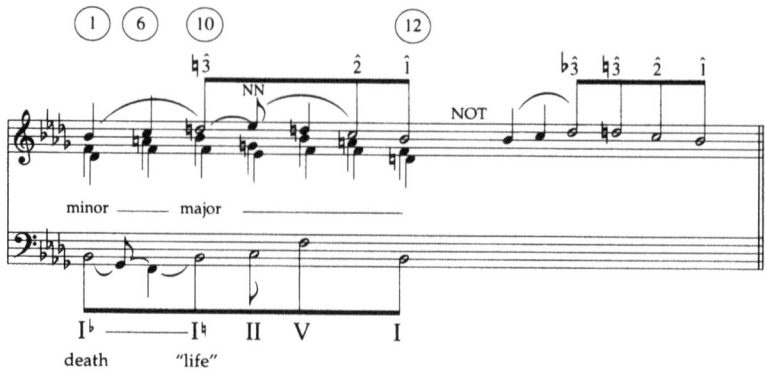

"Ihr Bild" the life that seems to stir in the woman's portrait is depicted by D♮, the major form of 3̂. Since this B♭ song is basically in minor – see the key signature, the postlude, the G♭ key area of the middle section – the D♮ would normally come from a prior D♭, already established as a structural tone in the vocal line. Such a juxtaposition of minor and major 3̂ would create an effective melodic contrast, and it would seem to be an appropriate way to depict death transformed into life. What Schubert does, however, is to start the vocal line on 1̂ and lead up to 3̂ by a stepwise motion, an *Anstieg* or initial ascent, as we can see in Example 1. The B♭ and C are in the domain of minor; one would expect them to lead to D♭ as the culminating note before any change to major might take place. But no structural D♭ occurs, and 3̂ arrives *only* in its major form.

Example 2 shows how the ♮3̂ arrives, entering in the bass, as though in the shadowy parts of the picture, and only gradually making its way into the vocal line, as the woman's face begins to appear alive. Although this ♮3̂ is anchored to the background by the surrounding tonic prolongation, it is supported locally only by a ⁶₄ chord, so that the major seems hesitant and insubstantial, a kind of tonal mirage. Because the major is heard as a modal inflection of the opening minor, the ♮3̂ must count as an alteration of D♭, the minor third. And because of the priority of minor in the song, the fundamental line must logically comprise the notes D♭–C–B♭. Yet the D♭ *never* appears as a structural note in the vocal line: 3̂ is literally represented only by the implicit D♭'s transformation into major.[7]

Heine's poem begins by suggesting immobility. The first verb is *stand*, and the second is *anstarrt*, a word associated with the ideas of rigidity, numbness, and paralysis. (The English cognate "stared at" also involves the notion of fixity, but not as powerfully as the German word.) Because *stand* and *starrt* sound so much alike, the two verbs strengthen each other through a kind of mutual resonance; and they suggest not only motionlessness but also a lack of felt life (*eine*

---

7. As I hear it, the D♭ of bar 3 is clearly a foreground embellishment and cannot serve to represent the 3̂. I do not, therefore, agree with Forte and Gilbert, who maintain that bars 1–8 should be read as 3̂–2̂ over I–V; see *Introduction to Schenkerian Analysis*, p. 218. Nonetheless the D♭ is an important note, our first indication that the song is in minor.

Example 2 Schubert, "Ihr Bild": how major emerges

Erstarrung) in the narrator.[8] The tonic note – the fixed center of the tonal system – is the only appropriate pitch to convey this immobility. The vocal line rising from this static pitch, the texture gradually fleshing out the bare octaves of the opening, the minor giving way to major: what a wonderful musical expression of revitalization, both of the face in the picture and of the viewer's feelings.

Schubert's beginning on 1 and reaching the active, "living," scale degree 3̂ only in its major form can therefore be understood as a response to the poem he was setting: the rise to D♮ represents the appearance of life in the portrait. A contrasting motive – the descending fourth B♭–F – symbolizes the reality of death. We can view the "history" of this figure in Example 3. At the opening of the vocal line (bars 3–6), before the portrait takes on life, the fourth is expressed as a partly disjunct motion, B♭–G♭–F (Example 3a); the 6–5 semitone, especially in connection with the 8–5 descending fourth, is a venerable musical symbol of death and lamentation. When the portrait begins to live, chromatic steps fill in the gap between 8 and 6; now that we are in major, however, 6 is expressed as G♮ (bars 10–13, Example 3b). Note that the one missing chromatic step is the ominous G♭; only the major form of 6 appears. This absence of G♭ is as strong a signal of life as the rise to D♮.

The missing G♭, expanded into the key area of G♭ major, forms the basis of the song's middle section (Example 3c). As long as the G♭ trance continues, the major mode sustains the illusion of life. Even the descending fourth B♭–A♭–G♭–F holds no terrors: in a G♭ context, the F is a leading tone, and the functional interval is not the fourth but rather the third B♭–G♭. But the G♭ major forms part of a larger B♭ minor; the two bars of interlude (bars 23–24) restore the main key, and in so doing, carry the G♭ down to its delayed but inevitable goal. The temporary major has crystallized on the very note of the minor scale whose resolution to 5 evokes the idea of death. The reprise of the

---

8. Schenker suggests that the slow repeated B♭s of the piano introduction make us "stare" at the note, the rearticulation bringing the sound's immobility to our ears much more powerfully than would a single sustained pitch. See "Franz Schubert: Ihr Bild," *Tonwille* 1 (1921), p. 46. This is one of the earliest "graphic analyses" that Schenker published. The graph itself gives an inadequate picture of the large structure and of some details, but it points out important motivic connections; the accompanying essay contains wonderful remarks about prosody and other aspects of text setting.

Example 3 Schubert, "Ihr Bild": the descending fourth B♭–F

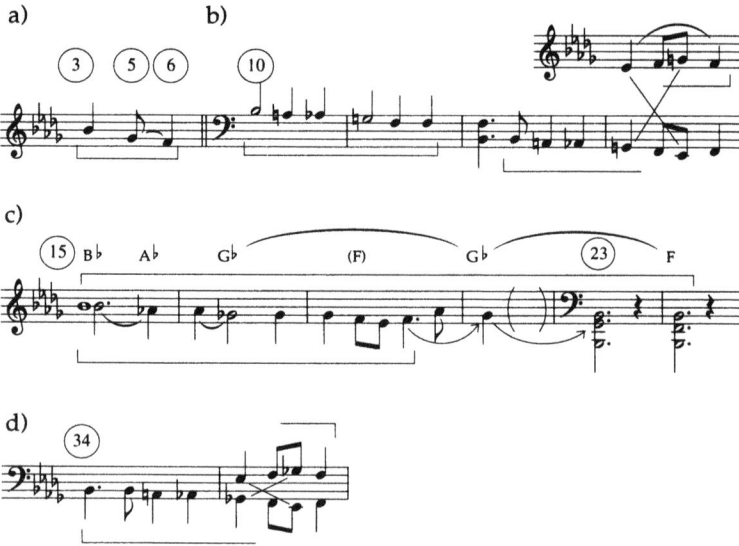

opening section fits the new words differently from the old ones, but equally convincingly. When the narrator tells us that he can't believe he has lost the woman (bars 31–34), we are again in the domain of major, and G♭ is absent. But the devastating postlude restores both the minor mode and the tragic, minor form of the descending tetrachord (Example 3d).

"Ihr Bild," with its suppressed $\hat{3}$, calls into question the widespread belief (even among many Schenkerians) that Schenker's approach is based on reduction. According to Forte and Gilbert, for example, "Analysis involves the progressive reduction of a finished work to its fundamental outline. Foreground events are taken directly from the piece itself, one or more levels of middleground are derived from the foreground, while the final stage of reduction represents the background."[9] Although "progressive reduction" is indeed often a valuable analytic strategy, it is not the only one. Many pieces and passages need a very different approach, as "Ihr Bild" demonstrates. There is no D♭ to be "taken directly from the piece itself" and placed into a foreground "reduction"; and with that crucial first step unavailable, the road to the background through reduction becomes blocked. What the analyst must do is to arrive at the intuition of some higher level – middleground or background – and to test that intuition against the totality of impressions made by the piece. Each higher level – from piece to foreground to the various layers of middleground and to background – represents a horizon that clarifies and gives meaning to the level beneath it; but not every element of the higher level need be literally present in the lower one.

In the Schubert song, the $\hat{3}$ of the fundamental line is suppressed in the foreground, represented only by its transformation into major. This strategy results

---

9. *Introduction to Schenkerian Analysis*, p. 131.

Example 4 Chopin, Mazurka in A♭ major, Op. 41, No. 3 (4): with two added bars

for the listener in a possible (though temporary) sense of uncertainty as to the primary mode: will major (life) or minor (death) prevail? But the musical discourse is in no way fragmentary or discontinuous; there is a clear beginning, middle, and end. In Chopin's Mazurka in A♭ (Op. 41, No. 3 or No. 4, depending on the edition),[10] the final structural phase is omitted: the $\hat{2}$–$\hat{1}$ of the fundamental line. And here the discourse *does* break off; not only is there no resolution to $\hat{1}$, but also the last phrase, which would contain that resolution, sounds incomplete, with only two bars instead of the four that prevail everywhere else in the Mazurka. It would be very easy to supply a final cadence for this piece, filling in the missing bars, and I have done so in Example 4; I imagine that most knowledgeable listeners would expect something more or less like it.[11]

As is well known, many Chopin mazurkas reflect the folk origins of the genre through their lack of a strong sense of closure at the end. Mostly these open-ended pieces have in fact achieved a structural cadence and open up only after having done so. The unresolved F at the end of the A minor Mazurka, Op. 17, No. 4, for example, occurs in the coda following a strong cadence (bar 108) that forms the structural close. And even the amusingly folk-like and fragmentary C major Mazurka, Op. 7, No. 5, marked "Dal segno senza Fine," has a normal cadence in bar 12 that would sound more or less like an ending even if the pianist decided to stop somewhere else. Op. 41, No. 3, is really a piece "senza Fine," and it is highly unusual in its genuine lack of a structural cadence. To be sure the last two bars contain a harmonic resolution to I, but the melodic line remains up in the air, closing on $\hat{3}$. By truncating the expected four-bar group at the end, Chopin reinforces the subversion of normal closure, but paradoxically this very reinforcement subverts the subversion. That is because the experienced listener senses that two bars are missing and has a fairly good idea of what the last two bars of such a piece might contain. It's a bit like trying not to think of something: the attempted denial turns into an affirmation.

In view of the "foregrounded" incompleteness of the Mazurka's melodic structure, it would be wrong to summarize that structure as simply $\hat{5}$–$\hat{4}$–$\hat{3}$. The

---

10. The German first edition (Breitkopf) prints the C♯ minor Mazurka as No. 1 instead of No. 4, as in the French and English editions. Our A♭ Mazurka, then, becomes No. 4 in the Breitkopf edition and some later ones.
11. In the French first edition, the first eight bars of the reprise are repeated, as they are at the beginning. Thus the last two measures are bars 81 and 82 (rather than bars 73 and 74) in that edition and in modern ones that follow it. My examples follow the German edition.

Example 5 Chopin, Mazurka Op. 41, No. 3 (4): first strain

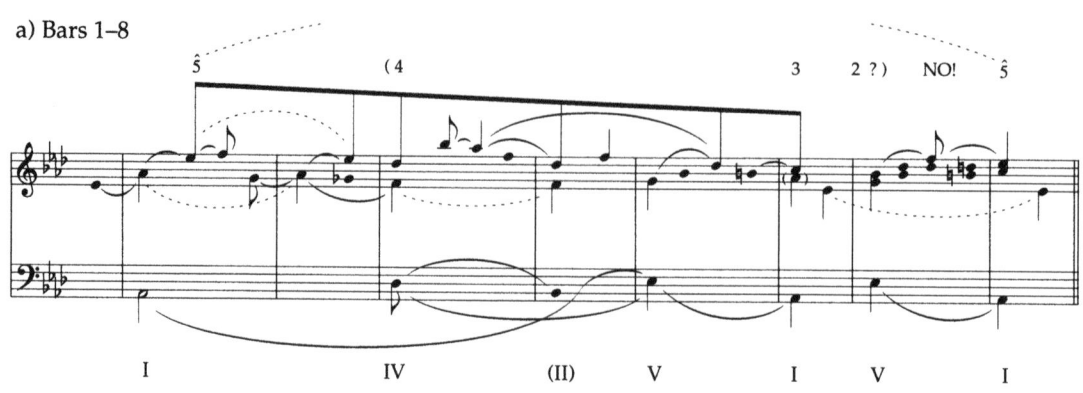

ghostly presence of the missing $\hat{2}$ and $\hat{1}$ is so clearly evident that the analysis should suggest something like the following: $\hat{5}$–$\hat{4}$–$\hat{3}$ – but where are $\hat{2}$ and $\hat{1}$? Often, as here, Schenker's theory is able to accommodate structural anomalies without the need for extending it by postulating, for example, new *Ursatz*-forms. The Mazurka, then, would count as a transformed $\hat{5}$-line piece, and not one that simply traverses a third from $\hat{5}$ to $\hat{3}$. The Mazurka and, less obviously, "Ihr Bild" also teach us something about the relation of structure to perception. The hearing of structure cannot be confined to the mental representation of "what is there" in the music, but must also encompass the active searching out of what is implied by what is there.

What characteristics of this piece might help to explain its peculiar ending? One factor is a tendency, manifested throughout, to avoid cadential closure on A♭. Already in bars 7–8 – the first possible location for a cadence on A♭ – Chopin deflects the line back up to $\hat{5}$, and underscores this procedure by adding a second voice to the right-hand part. As Example 5a shows, the upper line has proceeded in an orderly fashion, from E♭ to D♭ to C. Nothing would be easier than to go on to B♭ and A♭ in more or less similar fashion to the D♭–C of bars 5–6 (Example 5b). The repetition of the opening eight bars gives the line another chance to resolve to A♭, as a kind of *seconda volta* in bars 15–16, but these measures simply repeat bars 7–8 with their ascent back to $\hat{5}$. The suppressed final cadence at the end is the last and strongest expression of this tendency to avoid melodic closure.[12]

12. A word on phrase rhythm. It is no coincidence that the missing cadence would be two bars long rather than some other length. Two-bar groupings are clearly articulated by the design of the first eight-bar phrase, and the fourth of these groupings (bars 7–8) is where the upper line might have

Example 6 Chopin, Mazurka Op. 41, No. 3 (4): form

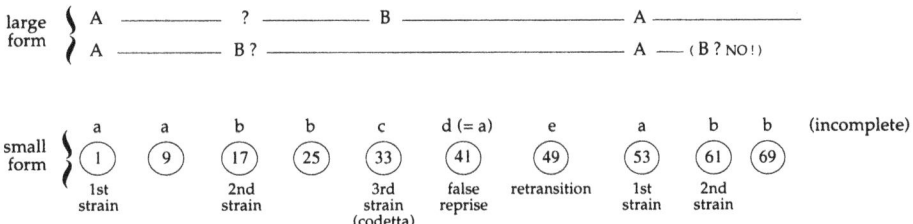

A second cause of the truncated ending is an idiosyncrasy of the Mazurka's form, which makes it fatally easy for the A section to slip, almost by accident, into the B. A new strain begins in bar 17, but its formal status is quite ambiguous, for prospective and retrospective hearing suggest two different interpretations. Prospective hearing registers the lack of melodic closure in the first sixteen bars, the continued tonic harmony, and the close harmonic and contrapuntal connection between the end of one strain and the beginning of the next. All of these conspire to make us hear the new material as a second strain within the A section rather than as a contrasting B section. And in a way the reprise, which includes a restatement of this new material, tends to support this interpretation. On the other hand, the cadence tonicizing III (C minor) continues without a break into the new material of bars 33ff., and by this time we seem definitely to have moved into the B section. Bar 33, however, hardly sounds like the beginning of that section; if anything it sounds like a codetta. But a codetta to what? To the previous strain, of course, and that strain begins in bar 17. Retrospective hearing, therefore, would make us date the beginning of the B section from bar 17. Example 6, a chart of the form, attempts to depict this ambiguity. The lower-case letters represent the smaller formal components, and the upper-case ones the ambiguous groupings into larger sections. Note that strain d quotes the Mazurka's opening figure, and that strain e, the retransition to the reprise, has only four bars – all of the other strains have eight apiece.

The tonal structure underlying bars 17–53 is included in Example 7, a middleground graph of the entire Mazurka. Up to the reprise, the big upper line forms a descending fifth from E♭ to A♭, but the way Chopin composes this line reveals that it is not structural for the Mazurka as a whole. Its goal, A♭, like the first note of bar 1, represents an inner-voice note of the arpeggiated tonic chord, so the line functions as a large-scale motion into the inner voice. And though a V may be inferred from the right-hand part of bar 52, the lack of explicit harmonic support cancels any cadential effect. In any case the beginning of the reprise would be a most improbable location for the last note of a fundamental line. As I mentioned earlier, the reprise encompasses the second strain that we heard first in bar 17, and it even slips into the first tonicization

moved down to 1̂. That "missed opportunity" at the beginning of the Mazurka is the ground on which the suppressed cadence at the end is prepared. A more direct connection occurs at bars 23–24 (= bars 67–68), where the C minor cadence, also two bars long, closes the antecedent of which the missing tonic cadence would close the consequent.

Example 7 Chopin, Mazurka Op. 41, No. 3 (4): middleground graph

of C minor (bar 68). This suggests that the Mazurka will be trapped in infinity, reaching the reprise a second time, proceeding to yet another C minor and perhaps a third reprise, thus going over the same ground again and again, in the manner of a real folk dance. The last bar, however, concludes with a pure A♭ triad, rather than a ⁴₃ chord leading to C minor. This opens up the possibility for a structural tonic cadence like the one I sketched in Example 4. That this possibility remains unrealized, except as supplied mentally by the listener, keeps alive the notion of the dance as a pattern that never really ends, even though any particular manifestation of it will have to stop at some point. In a very general way, therefore, the Mazurka's suppressed cadence is programmatic.

The transformation of structural notes

Brahms suppresses or transforms structural cadences in a surprisingly large number of his songs.[13] The early song "An eine Äolsharfe," Op. 19, No. 5, provides a remarkable example of a text-determined musical transformation.[14] Mörike's poem is autobiographical. The beloved dead boy he speaks of is his younger brother, who had died at seventeen, many years before the poem was written. Much of the poem is taken up with an invocation to the winds, who come to the poet from the direction of his brother's grave. They blow gently at first, perfumed by springtime blossoms and awakening soft music from the aeolian harp. But at the end of the poem a sudden gust draws a cry from the harp and scatters rose petals at the poet's feet.

The music for the rose petals includes the final cadence of the song, and it is notable for its lack of a V–I progression (bars 91–99, Example 8a). At first

13. This topic is treated in Heather Anne Platt, "Text–Music Relationships in the Lieder of Johannes Brahms" (Ph.D. diss., The City University of New York, 1992). See especially Chapter 8, pp. 298–357.
14. Platt discusses this song at several points in her study. The discussion on pp. 340–48 is particularly pertinent to my argument here.

Structure as foreground

Example 8 Brahms, "An eine Äolsharfe," Op. 19, No. 5

a) Final cadence (voice-leading sketch, bars 91–99)

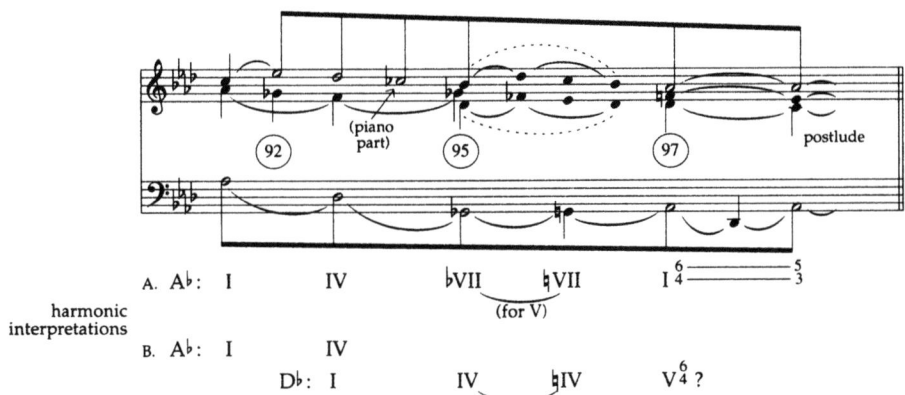

b) Bars 97–99 recomposed

glance this passage might seem to be the typical plagal close of a coda, but it is in fact something far more unusual. The passage does not at all sound like a coda, especially since the $\hat{2}$–$\hat{1}$ melodic closure occurs in these bars, $\hat{2}$ (over a G♭ harmony in bars 95–96) moving to $\hat{1}$ (over a D♭ $^6_4$ and then an A♭ tonic in bars 97–99). Furthermore, the passage creates a puzzling tonal ambiguity that goes far beyond what one might expect to encounter in a plagal cadence, even one that tonicizes the IV. We might characterize this ambiguity as follows. Interpretation A: in the key of A♭, the G♭ chord counts as ♭VII, moving through ♮VII (=V$^6_5$) to I ornamented by a plagal inflection. Interpretation B: the G♭ chord represents a IV of D♭ in what might be construed as a modulation to the sub-dominant. The $^6_4$ that follows sounds at first like a cadential elaboration of the V of D♭ major, and one might well expect a continuation more or less like the one I provide in Example 8b. How a cadence in D♭ would fit into a larger context is another question, but from a moment-by-moment perspective this interpretation is more plausible at first than the other. But the $^6_4$ never resolves to a V, the cadence never materializes, and the D♭ chord soon makes its way to the

Example 9 Brahms, "An eine Äolsharfe": middleground graph

Aḅ tonic pedal that persists through the remaining six bars of music, so Aḅ wins out after all. This means that our first, initially less plausible, interpretation gives the primary sense of the passage. The two forms of VII, which occur under the $\hat{2}$, substitute for V; VII often represents the upper third of dominant harmony, though, to be sure, it seldom stands in for V at a final, structural cadence.

Example 9 presents a middleground sketch of the whole song together with an indication of the form. The relation of harmony to form and design results in a series of antecedents to which only the final, ambiguous phrase forms a consequent. The introductory recitative ends with a half cadence, as do both components of the first A section and the first phrase of the final A section. The V chord that ends the first A section becomes structural for the song as a whole, for it is prolonged through all of the B section. Thus the song does not at all lack a normal structural V. This prolonged V represents the first (or dividing) dominant of the interrupted structural progression. It is the final, cadential dominant (belonging to the second segment of the interrupted progression) that is replaced by ♭VII as its upper third. The sketch also shows the beautiful preparation throughout the song for the G♭–G♮ of bars 95–96.

I am certain that this strange and perhaps unique close is Brahms's response to the implications of the poem's imagery. The fragrance carried by the wind and the music of the aeolian harp might certainly count as intimations of immortality – messages of comfort and hope from beyond the grave. The shower of rose petals sends a more questionable and disturbing signal. On the one hand it is a rich and beautiful image, feeding the sense of sight as the perfume does smell and the music hearing. But unlike the other two, the shower of petals almost inevitably invokes thoughts of death and decay, for it results from the disintegration of the rose. The ambivalence inherent in this image is perfectly matched by Brahms's ambivalent cadence, which threatens the stabil-

Structure as foreground

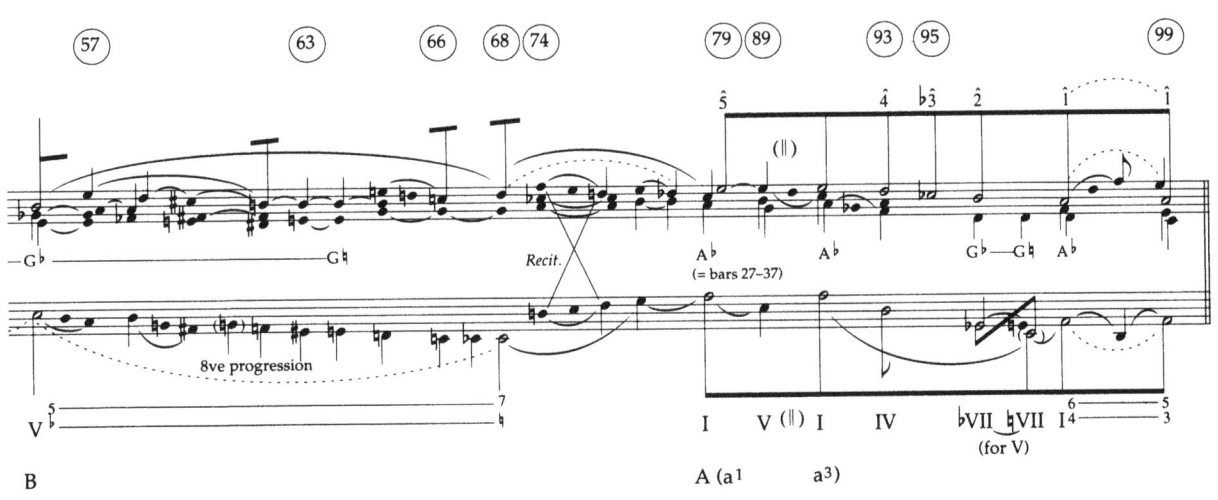

ity of the song's tonal foundations at the very moment where we should expect a strong affirmation of that stability.[15]

The apparent redundancy of structural elements

In the pieces I have cited so far, elements of the fundamental structure have become charged with dramatic tension through their suppression or their transformation, almost beyond recognition, in the foreground. An equally conflicted relation between levels can result from what seems to be a kind of redundancy. By this I mean that the music might contain two (or even more) passages that suggest competing locations for some structural event – the return of the tonic after interruption, for example. This situation can create difficulties not only for the inference of a tonal structure but also for the hearing of form.

Such is the case in my final example, the Quartet "Non ti fidar" from the first act of *Don Giovanni*, one of the many pieces in which interruption leads to some kind of tripartite form. The Quartet begins with a broadly prolonged initial tonic that moves to a prolonged dividing dominant, the two together forming the first segment of the interrupted structural progression; a final tonic section represents the closing segment of the interrupted progression. My

---

15. The ambivalence of the poem's final image is perhaps prefigured by the frequent use of oxymoron, especially in the later parts of the poem: "wie süss bedrängt ihr dies Herz," "wohllautender Wehmut," "zu süssem Erschrecken," etc. But these obvious paradoxes are far less powerful than the unacknowledged contradiction implied by the scattered rose petals. That Brahms had ambivalence on his mind when writing this song is suggested by a curious reminiscence: bars 50–53 are almost a transposition of bars 59–61 of Cherubino's second-act aria from *The Marriage of Figaro*. The words in the aria are, "Ma pur mi piace languir così," and in the song, "Wie süss bedrängt ihr dies Herz."

description so far would apply to thousands of other pieces, including our Brahms song, but the realization of this underlying pattern results in a unique form, more unusual even than the Brahms. The first tonic section consists of three antecedent–consequent pairs, sung in turn by Elvira, by Anna and Ottavio as a duet, and by Giovanni. Each of the three antecedents is different, but all the consequents are essentially the same. The final section repeats the consequent phrase a number of times, but does not quote any of the antecedents, so it is far from a normal reprise, and the Quartet as a whole is not at all a *da capo* piece.

In his excellent book on *Don Giovanni*, Julian Rushton has called attention to the Quartet's sonata-like qualities, and these are undeniable, though they don't entirely add up to a sonata movement.[16] The opening tonic section is closed off by very strong cadences – much more sharply than any normal "first theme" – but it then moves to the dominant (F major) through a modulatory bridge, quite like a sonata exposition. The resemblance to a sonata movement continues, for a developmental section follows, carrying forward the prolongation of V while briefly tonicizing other degrees (II and VI) of the B♭ tonic. The one essential part of a sonata movement to which nothing in the Quartet corresponds is a recapitulation (Rushton acknowledges this). There is, however, a final section in B♭. It does not provide the typical thematic resolution of a recapitulation, for it balances only the tonic area of the "exposition"; the V area is never recast in I. But the tonic prolongation does fulfill the tonal function of a recapitulation, and the "exposition's" consequent phrase (bars 6–9) permeates the end of the piece. This consequent phrase seems to represent Elvira – the dominating character of the Quartet – almost in the manner of a local *Leitmotif*; not only does she sing it, but also the other characters echo it when singing about her, and disguised references to it pervade the "development." Its cadential tag, with the characteristic descent of a diminished fifth (slurred when played by instruments), is a sighing figure, a most appropriate musical signature for Elvira. Mozart, who usually ends things quickly – sometimes even abruptly – repeats the cadential tag over and over, both at the end of the first tonic prolongation and at the end of the Quartet. It is this consequent phrase, rather than the antecedent, that forms the leading thematic idea of the opening section, so its return at the end, with all its repeated cadences, closes the circle quite effectively. As Example 10 indicates, the E♭–A diminished fifth substitutes for C; the cadential tag, therefore, represents the transformation of a $\hat{3}$–$\hat{2}$–$\hat{1}$ descent.

The consequent phrase comes back in B♭ at bar 79, preceded by four and a half bars of elaborate dominant preparation, forming the closest thing to a reprise that the Quartet can show. Not long before, however (in bar 70), an almost equally powerful B♭ had already appeared, following an even longer dominant preparation (bars 62–69). And earlier yet, a fleeting V–I of B♭ had found its way into the "development" section (bar 61). One of the strangest features of the Quartet is the presence of three V–I progressions in B♭ in close proximity to each other and in an area of the piece where a reprise, or at least a

---

16. Julian Rushton, *W. A. Mozart: Don Giovanni* (Cambridge: Cambridge University Press, 1981), pp. 92–94.

Example 10 Mozart, *Don Giovanni*, Act I, "Non ti fidar": cadential tag

Example 11 Mozart, "Non ti fidar": bars 68–70 recomposed

definitive tonic return, is expected. The earliest B♭, in the midst of the "development," is hardly a serious contender for the location of such a return, but the next one (in bar 70) is a serious contender indeed; Rushton dates the final section from here, and with very good reason.[17] The passage leading into the B♭ is the typical dominant preparation before a tonic return; I have recomposed the music in Example 11 to show how naturally a reprise of the beginning would fit in.

The way Mozart actually composes this B♭, however, sounds nothing like a reprise, not only because it doesn't repeat earlier material, but also because Elvira's desperate and furious outbursts negate any sense of arrival or stability. On the other hand, the B♭ of bar 79 projects just such a sense of arrival through its return to the primary (though not the initial) thematic component of the opening tonic section. Tovey makes the important observation that "Classical composers do not expect even the tonic to be recognized without the collateral evidence of a return to themes heard or expected to be heard in the tonic."[18] As a general rule Tovey's statement is certainly correct (though less characteristic of operatic than of instrumental forms), and the "intentional fallacy" it contains is a perfectly reasonable inference from the observation and analysis of the literature. The almost palpable sense of arrival, the structural downbeat, if you will, that the thematic return of bar 79 creates is testimony to the validity of Tovey's idea. But what then is one to make of the B♭ of bar 70? Given the extremely narrow modulatory range of the Quartet – one structural modulation to V and a few fleeting tonicizations to regions close to the main tonic – it would seem that B♭ major is never far beyond the immediate horizon of tonal perception. Therefore recognizing bar 70 as a return to the initial tonic hardly poses a problem for experienced listeners. The elaborate preparatory domi-

---

17. *Ibid.*, pp. 93–94.
18. See Donald Francis Tovey, *A Companion to Beethoven's Pianoforte Sonatas* (London: Associated Board, 1931), p. 7.

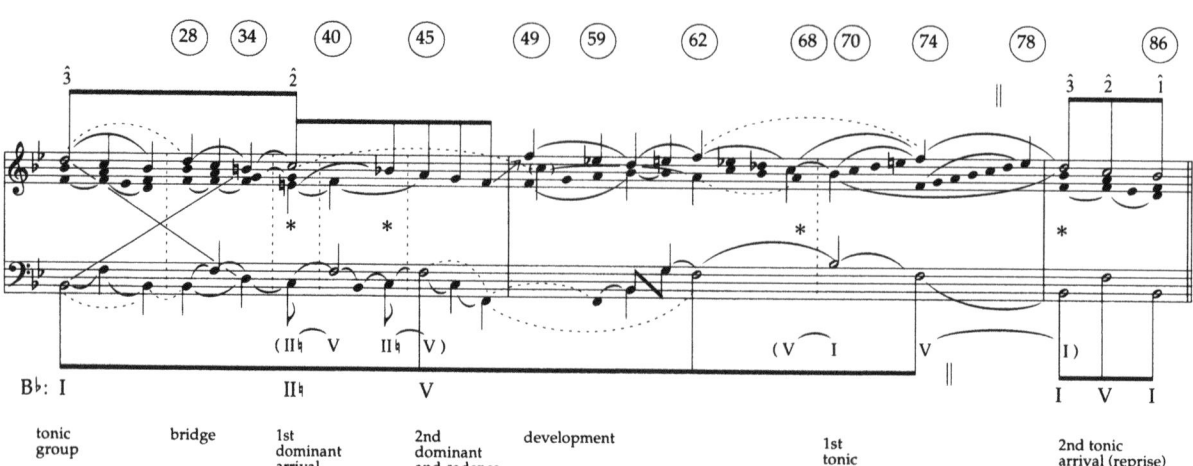

Example 12 Mozart, "Non ti fidar": middleground graph

nant, consequently, would lead such listeners to hear a structural return at the B♭'s first impact, though the subsequent course of the music, with its agitated transition into yet another dominant pedal, might well cause them to revise, or at least to question, that inference. Example 12 is a synoptic middleground graph of the entire Quartet. It shows that I regard the B♭ of bar 70 as a tonic, though not yet as "the" tonic.

In a way, this "premature" tonic is a kind of large-scale anticipation of the later tonic, whose greater structural weight is confirmed by the thematic design. But a more precise way of relating the anticipatory B♭ to the later one is to invoke the notion of "unfolding" or polyphonic melody. The first resolution into the B♭ chord (bar 70) takes place under a melodic progression C to B♭. This certainly does not represent a motion into the 1̂ of the fundamental line. In relation to the big melodic progression of the fundamental line and the highest-level middleground prolongations, it represents an inner-voice line, even though locally it functions as the highest part.[19] The second, and primary, resolution has as its melodic line F and E♭ forming an 8–7 over V moving into D as the resumed 3̂ of the fundamental line. Thus the thematic return coincides with and emphasizes a return to the fundamental line after a detour into the inner voice; design reinforces and confirms structure. The B♭ harmony of bar 70, which supports the lower-level segment of the unfolded melodic complex, would naturally count as a lower-level harmonic arrival. Example 12 shows that the modulation to V also involves a double arrival supporting a melodic unfolding (bars 40 and 45). This sets up a middleground parallelism between dominant area and reprise, though not the foreground parallelism of a true recapitulation, which involves both structure and thematic design. (The asterisks between the staves of Example 12 point out this parallelism.)

19. The move to "1̂" is not unlike the descent at the beginning of the reprise of the Chopin Mazurka, which is also non-structural.

Anticipating a tonic return before a thematic reprise is a highly unusual procedure. It creates a problem for large-scale rhythm different in scale though not in kind from what happens when a beginning harmony student repeats a chord or bass note over the bar line. The anticipated chord or bass note contradicts the meter and weakens the next local downbeat. The anticipated tonic return conflicts with and presumably weakens the structural downbeat that normally results from a thematic reprise. Sometimes, of course, a weak/strong chord repetition produces an excellent effect, in a composition or even in a student's exercise. And the greatest composers will sometimes anticipate a tonic return. In the Quartet, the combination of thematic and structural emphases makes clear the priority of the later return; and the conflict between the two returns gives stunning musical expression to the conflict between Don Giovanni and Donna Elvira.

During the dominant pedal before the first tonic return, Anna and Ottavio say that they are beginning to suspect something. They are beginning, in fact, to believe Elvira's accusations against Giovanni; his efforts to persuade them that she is crazy have failed. Giovanni, therefore, turns his attention away from them and toward Elvira. He urges her to keep quiet and to behave more prudently lest people think ill of her. His attempts to silence her take the musical form of a V–I progression in the Quartet's main key. He wants to call an end to this embarrassing scene; and what better way to end it musically than by a resolution into the tonic, and with a 2–1 melodic line to boot. Elvira, however, will have none of it. She sees no point in being prudent; what she wants is to proclaim Giovanni's guilt and her own sufferings to the world. Elvira's music, therefore, cancels any sense of closure Giovanni's had created. Her melodic line moves up, away from Giovanni's last note, B♭; and the accompanying harmony eventually leaves the B♭ chord and moves to another F pedal. This time the V–I of B♭ is on Elvira's terms, leading musically to the reprise of "her" phrase (which carries the fundamental line's $\hat{3}$) and dramatically to her winning over Anna and Ottavio.

Charles Rosen concludes the article I cited at the beginning of this paper by suggesting that Schenker's method, for all its undeniable value, ultimately leads down from the music's surface into a kind of secret inner chamber from which it is impossible to climb back out. "He turns his principles of organization into a hidden, esoteric form. This is so because his method takes the form of a gradual reduction of the surface of the music to his basic phrase, and the analysis moves in one direction, away from what is actually heard and toward a form which is more or less the same for every work. It is a method which, for all it reveals, concentrates on a single aspect of the music and, above all, makes it impossible to bring the other aspects into play. The work appears to drain away into the secret form hidden within itself."[20]

My disagreements with Rosen's statement are probably obvious to anyone who is reading this paper, and I don't want to belabor them here. In any case I am not quoting these words to argue but – in part – to agree. In doing analysis,

---

20. Rosen, "Art has its Reasons," p. 38.

in teaching it, in trying to learn it, even in reading Schenker's graphs, it can become all too easy to fall into the heresy of valuing the work's deep structure more highly than the work itself. Of course concentrating on the background and on deep levels of the middleground is sometimes necessary – especially in some phases of teaching. But ultimately the analysis must lead back to the work and must illuminate its sensuous surface. In this paper I have tried to show that the most striking and individual aspects of the surface can be precisely elements of Schenker's *Ursatz* or "basic phrase" – that "form which is more or less the same for every work."

INDEX

Abbott, Bud 76
Alegant, Brian 200
Aristophanes 68

Babbitt, Milton 165, 298
Bach, Carl Philipp Emanuel
    Sonatas: H.70, W.63/1 (A minor *Probestück*) 51; H.71, W.63/2 (G minor *Probestück*) 51–55, 66; H.72, W.63/3 (A major *Probestück*) 60–66; H.173, W.57/6 (F minor) 56–60, 66; H.208, W.57/4 (D minor) 54
    Versuch 23, 31, 51, 57
Bach, Johann Sebastian 6, 8, 107, 199, 213
    English Suites: No. 3 (G minor), Gavotte 200; No. 5 (E minor), Sarabande 213; No. 6 (D minor), Prelude 285
    French Suites: No. 4 (E♭ major), Sarabande 282; No. 5 (G major), Gavotte 199
    Partitas, keyboard: No. 4 (D major), Sarabande 289; No. 5 (G major), Corrente 199; No. 1 (B♭ major), Sarabande 278–79
    Partita, unaccompanied violin, No. 3 (E major), Preludio 9
    Passacaglia, organ (C minor) 278
    Sonata, unaccompanied violin, No. 3 (C major): Largo 31; Adagio 277–78
    Suites, unaccompanied cello: No. 4 (E♭ major), Prelude 280; No. 5 (C minor), Sarabande 278
    Well-Tempered Clavier 51; Book I: Prelude I (C major) 287; Prelude II (C minor) 131–32, 294; Prelude VIII (E♭ minor) 285–87, 295; Prelude XX (A minor) 284
Bacon, Francis 222, 225–26, 238
Badura-Skoda, Paul 83
Baillot, Pierre Marie François de Sales 90
Baker, Nancy Kovaleff 85, 98
Baltrusaitis, Jurgis 240
Beach, David 198, 231–32, 254, 284, 287
Beethoven, Ludwig van 8, 40, 77, 112–13, 117, 212
    Leonore Overture No. 3 299
    Sonatas, cello: Op. 5, No. 2 (G minor) 78; Op. 69 (A major) 282, 285
    Sonatas, piano: Op. 2, No. 1 (F minor) 56, 136–37, 284–85; Op. 26 (A♭ major) 227; Op. 27, No. 2 (C♯ minor) "Moonlight" 223–31, 233, 279, 299; Op. 31, No. 2 (D minor), "Tempest" 132–34; Op. 101 (A major) 282, 285, 287–88, 294; Op. 109 (E major) 129–30; Op. 110 (A♭ major) 231–38
    Symphonies: No. 3 (E♭ major), "Eroica" 110, 298; No. 6 (F major), "Pastorale" 283; No. 9 (D minor), *Ode to Joy* 249
Berg, Alban
    Quartet, strings, Op. 3 162
    Sonata, piano (D minor), uncompleted 172–73
    Wozzeck 160–91
Berg, Darrell 50
Berger, Arthur Asa 68
Berkeley, Lennox 109
Bonds, Mark Evan 72
Botelho, Mauro 208
Brahms, Johannes 6, 8, 212
    "An eine Äolsharfe" 306–10
    Ballade, Op. 118, No. 3 (G minor), 128–29, 134
    Intermezzi: Op. 76, No. 4 (B♭ major) 284; Op. 76, No. 7 (A minor) 35, 288–89; Op. 117, No. 1 (E♭ major) 27; Op. 117, No. 2 (B♭ minor) 35, 247, 249, 282; Op. 118, No. 2 (A major) 35, 276–77, 294–97; Op. 119, No. 1 (B minor) 28, 31–36; Op. 119, No. 2 (E minor) 28–31, 36–40, 43–46
    Sonata, clarinet, Op. 120, No. 2 (E♭ major) 283–84, 293
    Symphony No. 2 (D major) 291
    Trio, clarinet, Op. 114 (A minor) 281
    Variations on a Theme of Handel, Op. 24 (B♭ major) 26
    Variations on a Theme of Haydn, Op. 56a and 56b (B♭ major) 240–75

Brahms, Johannes (*cont.*)
   Variations (Studies) on a Theme of Paganini, Op. 35 (A minor) 31
   Waltzes, Op. 39 31: No. 14 (C♯ minor) 129; No. 15 (A♭ major) 288
   "Wie bist du, meine Königin" 283
Branson, David 121
Brown, Matthew 12
Broyles, Michael 50, 95
Bruckner, Anton 8
Büchner, Georg 162, 184
Bülow, Hans von 26
Burkhart, Charles 16
Burkholder, J. Peter 162, 189
Burney, Charles 49
Busoni, Ferruccio 5

Cadwallader, Allen 247, 249, 276, 282, 285, 288
Caplin, William E. 56, 207, 215
Carse, Adam 97
Cavett-Dunsby, Esther 112–13
Chaplin, Charles 68, 77
Chmara, Barbara 121
Chopin, Frédéric 8
   Barcarolle, Op. 60 (F♯ minor) 113
   Concertos, piano 113
   Etudes: Op. 10 120; Op. 25, No. 7 (C♯ minor), 292
   Fantasy, Op. 13 (A major) 113
   Mazurkas: Op. 6 119; Op. 7 119; Op. 7, No. 5 (C major) 303; Op. 17, No. 4 (A minor) 303; Op. 41, No. 3 [4] (A♭ major) 303–306, 312
   Nocturnes: Op. 9, No. 1 (B♭ major) 119; Op. 9, No. 2 (E♭ minor) 109–26; Op. 9, No. 3 (B major) 116; Op. 15, No. 2 (F♯ major) 8, 113, 119; Op. 32, No. 1 (B major) 117
   Polonaise, Op. 40, No. 2 (C minor) 292
   Polonaise brillante, Op. 3 (C major) 113
   Preludes, Op. 28: No. 4 (E minor) 137–38, 280, 282; No. 6 (B minor) 292; No. 22 (G minor) 292
   Rondo, Op. 73 (C major) 113
   Rondo à la mazur, Op. 5 (F major) 113
   Sonata, Op. 35 (B♭ minor) 153
   Waltz (E minor) 113
Churgin, Bathia 82–84, 91
Cohn, Richard 222, 234
Cone, Edward T. 28, 226
Coren, Daniel 247
Costello, Lou 76
Couperin, François 213
Cube, Felix-Eberhard von 14
Culler, Jonathan 239

Daschner, Hubert 72, 76
Dempster, Douglas 222
Drabkin, William 14, 231
Dubiel, Joseph 23
Dunsby, Jonathan 33

Eigeldinger, Jean-Jacques 115, 121–22, 124–25
Einstein, Albert 5
Elias, Angi 31–32, 34–36, 41, 284
Epstein, David 295
Esser, Heribert 8
Eybl, Martin 6

Federhofer, Hellmut 12, 14, 16, 26, 30
Feibleman, James K. 68
Feil, Arnold 213
Fétis, François-Joseph 107
Field, John 121–22, 124–26
   Nocturnes: No. 1 (E♭ major) 109, 120–22; No. 9 (E♭ major) 109, 121–23
Fischer, Wilhelm 207
Fliess, Wilhelm 184
Forkel, Johann Nikolaus 56, 287
Forte, Allen 163–64, 166, 177, 187–89, 298, 300, 302
Fortescue, Virginia 125
Foucault, Michel 10
Fox, Pamela 50
Frisch, Walter 33, 274
Furtwängler, Wilhelm 4–5, 7, 10

Gabrieli, Giovanni, *Sacrae symphoniae* 84
Gilbert, Henry F. 76
Gilbert, Steven E. 298, 300, 302
Gould, Murray 251
Grave, Floyd K. 207, 213, 216
Gray, Cecil 141
Green, Douglass 187
Gruner, Charles 69
Gutwirth, Marcel 68

Hadow, William Henry 241, 274
Halm, August 5, 7, 12, 14, 16
Handel, George Frideric
   Concerti Grossi: Op. 3, No. 2 (B♭ major) 197; Op. 3, No. 4 (F major) 197, 202–205; Op. 6, No. 2 (F major) 196, 204–11, 215; Op. 6, No. 3 (E minor), Allegro 196, 201; Op. 6, No. 4 (A minor) 208; Op. 6, No. 6 (G minor) 197; Op. 6, No. 8 (C minor) 201; Op. 6, No. 10 (D minor) 216
   Concertos, organ, Op. 7 212
   Messiah, "Hallelujah" Chorus 209
   Music for the Royal Fireworks 211–12, 216–21
   Suite, keyboard (1720, F minor): Allemande 194–96, 207; Courante 197
Harden, Maximilian 26
Hauer, Josef Matthias 162
Haydn, Franz Joseph 212, 241

"Chorale St. Antoni" *see* Brahms, Variations on a Theme of Haydn
Quartets, strings: Op. 33, No. 5 (G major) 78; Op. 76, No. 1 (G major) 282
Symphonies 86, 88: No. 45 (F♯ minor), "The Farewell" 71; No. 46 (B major) 71; No. 55 (E♭ major), "Der Schulmeister" 77–78; No. 58 (F major) 75–76; No. 60 (C major), "Der Zerstreute" 71; No. 64 (A major) 76–77; No. 72 (D major) 76; No. 78 (C minor) 72; No. 83 (G minor) "La Poule" 73–74; No. 88 (G major) 76; No. 90 (C major) 78–81; No. 92 (G major) 80; No. 93 (D major) 67, 73–76; No. 94 (G major), "The Surprise" 71, 76, 80
Headlam, Dave 162–63, 187, 189
Heine, Heinrich 300
Helm, Eugene 51
Hertzka, Emil 7, 14
Hilmar, Ernst 241
Hinterberger, Heinrich 4, 6
Hoboken, Anthony van 27
Hoffmeister, Franz Anton 287
Hopkins, Robert G. 113–14, 117
Horstmann, Angelika 241, 250
Hoyt, Peter A. 78
Hutcheson, Francis 67
Hyde, Martha 166

Irving, Howard 71

Jarman, Douglas 163–68, 170, 172, 180, 184, 187, 190
Jenner, Gustav 6
Jonas, Oswald 4, 12, 24, 56

Kalbeck, Max 46
Kallberg, Jeffrey 109, 112, 118–19
Kalmus, Alfred 7
Karpath, Ludwig 7
Kerman, Joseph 112, 117, 160, 162, 184, 188
Kidd, James C. 71, 76
Kirkpatrick, Ralph 53
Kirnberger, Johann Philipp 198, 208–209
Koch, Heinrich Christoph 85, 95, 97–98, 100, 112
Kollman, Augustus 82–83, 86
Komma, Karl Michael 233, 236
Kosovsky, Robert 21, 27, 242
Kostka, Stefan 187
Krebs, Harald 221
Krenek, Ernst 6
Kretzschmar, Hermann 250
Kunselman, JoAn 5

Lang, Robert 5
LaRue, Jan 213

Laskowski, Larry 285
Laufer, Edward 51, 228
Leacock, Stephen 69
Leeman, Fred 240
Leichtentritt, Hugo 110–11, 114–15
Lenz, Wilhelm von 109, 111, 125
Lerdahl, Fred 177, 188–89, 209
Lester, Joel 207, 212
Levas, Santeri 137, 141, 159
Levy, Janet M. 72
Lewin, David 165, 226
Lewis, Christopher 177
Lewis, Clive Staples 69
Liebstöckl, Hans 6
Liszt, Franz 109, 122
Locke, John 10
Lockwood, Lewis 227
Loeb, David 127
London, Justin 198
Lubben, Joseph 23

Maignan, Emmanuel 240
Marx, Groucho 70
Maus, Fred 234
McCorkle, Donald 241, 249, 267, 269
McLean, Don 200
Mead, Andrew 166
Meeùs, Nicolas 12
Mitchell, William J. 23, 31, 51
Molière, Jean-Baptiste 76
Montaigne, Michel de 222
Mörike, Eduard 306
Morreall, John 69
Morris, Robert 166
Mozart, Constanze 4
Mozart, Wolfgang Amadeus 112–13, 189, 212
Concertos, piano: K.459 (F major) 281–82, 289–91; K.491 (C minor) 294; K.503 (C major) 105–106
Divertimento, K.563 (E♭ major) 283
Don Giovanni, "Non ti fidar" 309–13
Ein musikalischer Spass 71
Le nozze di Figaro 309
Quartet, strings, K.387 (G major) 83, 87–90
Sonatas, piano: K.330 (C major) 214–16, 219; K.533/494 (F major) 294–95
Suite, K.399, "Suite in the Style of Handel," Allemande 192–94, 196, 198
Symphonies: No. 34, K.338 (C major) 83–93, 96–97, 106; No. 35, K.385 (D major), "Haffner" 83, 87, 91–99, 106; No. 38, K.504 (D major), "Prague" 83, 100–107; No. 40, K.550 (G minor) 84, 198; No. 41, K.551 (C major), "Jupiter" 101, 107
Die Zauberflöte, "Bei Männern" 285
Murtomäki, Veijo 127, 149

Narmour, Eugene 113
Newman, William S. 49

Olson, Elder 68
Orel, Alfred 241
Oster, Ernst 4, 12, 14, 51, 223, 228, 282, 284–85, 299

Parmet, Simon 149
Pastille, William 12, 19, 23, 284
Patrick, J. Max 226
Paul, Steven E. 71
Perle, George 161–64, 167–69, 171–72, 175, 183, 185, 187–90
Perry-Camp, Jane 71
Petty, Wayne 21, 24
Piddington, Ralph 70
Pien, Diana 69
Plantinga, Leon 274
Platt, Heather Anne 306
Pople, Anthony 187
Porter, Charles 162

Raffman, Diana 189
Ratner, Leonard 69, 86
Ratz, Erwin 4
Redlich, Hans Ferdinand 168
Réti, Rudolf 5, 7
Riemann, Hugo 211, 232
Riepel, Joseph 198, 200
Rosen, Charles 77, 298, 313
Rothbart, Mary K. 69
Rothgeb, John 16, 23–24, 31, 51, 110, 279
Rothstein, William 6, 53, 56, 109–10, 198–99, 201, 207–10, 222–23, 225, 228, 232, 284
Rushton, Julian 310–11

Salzer, Felix 4–5, 33, 35, 110, 114, 117, 241, 298
Salzer, Hedwig 5, 27
Samarotto, Frank 199
Samson, Jim 121–22
Saussure, Ferdinand de 239
Scarlatti, Domenico 53
  Sonata, K.78 (F major) 209, 223
Schachter, Carl 194, 199, 209, 222–23, 236, 238, 280, 282, 294
Schenker, Heinrich
  Beethoven, Sonate Op. 27, Nr. 2 (facsimile edition) 227
  Beethovens neunte Sinfonie (Beethoven's Ninth Symphony) 28
  "Erinnerungen an Brahms" 6, 26
  Erläuterungsausgabe 27–28: *Op. 101* 16, 19, 24, 282, 285, 294; *Op. 110* 232, 235–36
  Der freie Satz (Free Composition) 4, 6, 8, 10, 12–25, 36, 81, 91, 110, 112, 117, 119–20, 135, 198, 222–23, 228, 242–43, 245–48, 251, 278–79, 282, 291, 299
  Fünf Urlinie-Tafeln (Five Graphic Music Analyses) 27, 242–43
  Harmonielehre (Harmony) 7, 17, 20, 30
  Kontrapunkt (Counterpoint) 12–25, 30, 199
  "Eine Lehre vom Vortrag" 8
  Meisterwerk (Masterwork) 23, 27, 31, 110, 198, 231, 279
  "Niedergang der Kompositionskunst" 8
  "Das Tonsystem" 7
  Tonwille 7, 23–24, 27, 36, 285, 287, 301
  "Urlinientafel zu Haydns 'Chorale St. Antoni'" 241–47
Schenker, Jeanette 3–8, 14, 28, 31
Schlegel, August Wilhelm von 43
Schmalfeldt, Janet 56, 163–64, 166–67, 180, 182–83, 187–88
Schoenberg, Arnold 5, 162, 215, 298
Schopenhauer, Arthur 10
Schreier, Irene 8
Schubert, Franz 213, 299
  "Du bist die Ruh" 281, 295
  "Gretchen am Spinnrade" 130–31, 134
  "Ihr Bild" 300–304
  Ländler, Op. 171, No. 3, D.790 (D major) 281
  "Die liebe Farbe" 280
  Sonata, piano, Op. 143, D.784 (A minor) 132, 134–35
  Symphony No. 7 [8] (B minor), "Unfinished" 291
Schulenberg, David 50, 54, 56
Schumann, Eugenie 254
Schumann, Robert
  "Ich grolle nicht" 127–28
  "Wehmut" 288
Schulz, Johann Abraham Peter 82–84, 90–91
Schütz, Heinrich, *Symphoniae sacrae* 84
Shakespeare, William 43, 70
Sheridan, Richard Brinsley 68
Sibelius, Jean
  Symphony No. 4 (A minor) 135–59
Sincero, Dino 56
Sisman, Elaine R. 198
Smith, A. M. Sheridan 10
Snarrenberg, Robert 276
Solie, Ruth A. 113
Stowell, Robin 90
Straus, Joseph N. 177, 188
Strauss, Richard 8
Suls, Jerry M. 69
Sulzer, Johann Georg 82

Taruskin, Richard 188
Thym, Jürgen 198

Tosi, Pier Francesco 115
Tovey, Donald Francis 106, 235, 285, 311
Treitler, Leo 171

Violin, Moriz 14
Vrieslander, Otto 14

Wagner, Richard 8, 160–61
Waldbauer, Ivan 211
Wason, Robert 12
Webster, James 82
Wheelock, Gretchen 71, 76–77
Whittingham, Alfred 107

Willner, Channan 285
Wintle, Christopher 198
Wolf, Hans 21
Wolf, Hugo 8
Wollenberg, Susan 76
Woolf, Virginia 238
Wotquenne, Alfred 51

Young, Percy M. 137

Zaleska-Rosengardt, Zofia 125
Zaslaw, Neal 90
Zuckerkandl, Victor 298

For EU product safety concerns, contact us at Calle de José Abascal, 56–1°,
28003 Madrid, Spain or eugpsr@cambridge.org.

www.ingramcontent.com/pod-product-compliance
Ingram Content Group UK Ltd.
Pitfield, Milton Keynes, MK11 3LW, UK
UKHW050109230326
469255UK00020B/467